# THE
# 100 BEST
# ANNUITIES
# YOU CAN BUY

# THE
# 100 BEST
# ANNUITIES
# YOU CAN BUY

Gordon K. Williamson

New York • Chichester • Brisbane • Toronto • Singapore

This text is printed on acid-free paper.

Copyright © 1995 by Gordon K. Williamson
Published by John Wiley & Sons, Inc.

This publication is designed to provide accurate and authoritative
information in regard to the subject matter covered. It is sold
with the understanding that the publisher is not engaged in
rendering legal, accounting, or other professional services. If
legal advice or other expert assistance is required, the services
of a competent professional person should be sought.

*Library of Congress Cataloging-in-Publication Data:*

Williamson, Gordon K.
    The 100 best annuities you can buy / Gordon K. Williamson.
       p.  cm.
    ISBN 0-471-01025-1
    1. Annuities—Unitied States.   2. Variable annuities—United
States.  I. Title.  II. Title: One hundred best annuities you
can buy.  III. Title: One hundred best annuities you can
buy.
HG8790.W549   1995
368.3'7'00973—dc20            94-38102

Printed in the United States of America

10  9  8  7  6  5  4  3  2  1

# ACKNOWLEDGMENT

I would like to acknowledge and thank several people who contributed ample time and energy to this book. Sven Haynie assisted in development of the screening process, scoring (check mark) system, and the 100 subaccount presentations. For each subaccount, he compiled the performance, risk, expense, management, insurance company, investment options, and family performance data and merged all of the data into the book. He also compiled the market index statistics and produced many of the charts and tables. Karen Morris and Cynthia Robertson logged many hours accumulating information on each annuity contract, including addresses, phone numbers, and the information in each of the profile tables. Amie Folse helped with the data entry. Their attention to details was very helpful. Helen Nicoll completed the grueling task of proofreading. Her assistance and friendship are greatly appreciated. I would also like to thank Ursel Jones for her never-ending patience and behind-the-scenes efforts in managing my office. I would not have the time to write without all of their help.

# CONTENTS

# Introduction

Variable annuities are one of the two *best* investment vehicles developed in the 20th century; mutual funds are the other best vehicle. As you will see throughout this book, there is tremendous similarity between variable annuities and mutual funds. Some aspects of variable annuity investing make it more appealing than investing in mutual funds, and vice versa. These differences will be explored.

When properly selected, variable annuities combine professional management, ease of purchase and redemption, simple record keeping, risk reduction, and superb performance—all in one type of investment. There are dozens of other types of investments, but only a couple of them (e.g., variable life insurance and mutual funds) match the overall versatility of variable annuities.

When you invest in a variable annuity or mutual fund, your money is pooled with that of thousands of other investors. This large pool of money is overseen by portfolio managers who invest it in one or more types of investments. The universe of investments includes the following: common stocks, preferred stocks, foreign securities, corporate bonds, U.S. Government obligations, zero coupon bonds, convertible securities, money market instruments, gold, silver, and real estate. The amount of money invested in one or more of these categories depends on the variable annuity's objectives and restrictions, and on management's perception of the economy. As the investor, you decide which of these portfolios your money will be invested in and what dollar figure goes into each fund. (The words *portfolio* and *subaccount* are used interchangeably throughout this book; both refer to variable annuity investment choices. *Fund* refers either to mutual funds or an investment selection [subaccount] within a variable annuity, such as a growth fund or corporate bond fund.)

Once an investor decides on the *type* of investment desired, variable annuities offer several portfolios, known as subaccounts, that fulfill the criteria. The track record of these subaccounts can be easily obtained—as contrasted with the track records of stockbrokers, who are not ranked at all. A few variable annuity sources even look at a subaccount's *risk-adjusted* return, a standard of measurement that has not been emphasized enough in the past.

This book was written to fill a void. This first and only book that ranks variable annuities is, in fact, only the second book ever written about annuities; I wrote the first one a little less than two years ago (*All About Annuities,* Wiley, 0-471-57425-2).

There are now over 6,500 different mutual funds and close to 1,500 different variable annuity subaccounts. The word *subaccount* used to describe a specific portfolio within the variable annuity family; is similar to the term *XYZ growth fund,* which represents a specific fund within the XYZ mutual fund family.

There are approximately 1,500 existing subaccounts. This book will save you a great deal of time because it has narrowed them down to the best 100, ranked by specific category, performance, and risk level.

Investors and financial advisors are not concerned with mediocre or poor performers; they simply want the best variable annuity subaccount(s), *given certain parameters.* Personal investment considerations should include one's time horizon, existing portfolio, tax bracket, financial goals, and risk tolerance. Parameters within a given subaccount category (e.g., growth, corporate bond, international stock, and so on) include performance, risk, and consistency.

Newspapers and periodicals that cover variable annuities focus on how a subaccount or variable annuity family has performed in the past. Studies clearly point out that when a subaccount's performance is in the top half one year, it has a 50-50 chance of being in the bottom half the next year, or the year after that. Because there is little correlation between the past and the future when it comes to market returns, this book concentrates on consistency in management and the amount of risk being taken.

According to a 1994 article in *Barron's,* "Academics and other researchers have scoured their data banks repeatedly, searching for even a hint of evidence to support the notion that choosing funds based on historic results makes sense. And almost every time, they reach the same conclusion: Past performance helps not a whit in predicting future returns." Such studies have not been done with variable annuities, but because these products share a great number of similarities and are often entrusted to the same portfolio managers or management team, there is no reason to think that any such studies would result in a different conclusion.

At the beginning of 1994, Dalbar, a mutual fund consulting firm, conducted a study that sought to determine the value of buying funds with the best 10-year performance records. According to the Dalbar study, people who at the beginning of 1993 had been invested in the 100 best-performing stock funds (over the preceding 10 years) would have *underperformed* a portfolio of the 100 funds that previously had been with the *worst* 10-year performers. The 10-year stock leaders (1984–1993) returned an average 15.8% in 1993; the worst performing funds returned a 22.2% average.

Dalbar repeated the study for each of the past six years, again using 10-year time frames (e.g., 1983–1992, 1982–1991, 1981–1990, and so on). The results were similar, but much narrower. The buy-the-best strategy ended up producing an average annual return of 14.2%; the buy-the-worst-100-funds strategy averaged 14.5% annually. Other studies bear out similar conclusions.

SEI, a well-known research firm, sought to determine whether investors were better off buying funds that had 5-year track records among the top quarter of the fund universe or those that ranked in the bottom quarter. SEI's findings, published in the January/February 1994 issue of *Personal Financial Planning,* matched Dalbar's: "It's clear that historical performance rankings should not be the primary criterion for selecting mutual funds." If this is the case, how should one select a mutual fund or variable annuity subaccount?

First, find someone who has a clearly defined investment style. Experience is an important consideration. Keep in mind that performance with many categories of investments is dependent on management's investment style. Look for a seasoned person or team, someone who has weathered bad times. Second, seek out portfolio managers who do not attempt to time the market. According to SEI, "Switching strategies to time the market is a major reason for underperformance." Third, and most important, stick with investment categories (e.g., growth, high-yield bonds, international stocks, and so on) that have performed well over the long haul, not just the most recent 1-, 3-, 5-, or 10-year period.

The selection process used to determine the 100 best was completely "blind." As an active investment advisor, I favor certain variable annuities, mutual funds, and other investments more than others. To make sure that none of this bias found its way into this book, I used a screening process that left out the names of all sub-accounts until the final 100 were determined. The selection process was blind because every step (or screen) was based on statistical information only; no names were included.

The selection process for the subaccounts that appear in this book incorporated the philosophy I have just described. The selection process was a completely objective, logical, commonsense approach that cut through the statistical jargon and is easy to understand. The model used to rank the 100 best is fully described in Chapter 5.

Performance figures for the last one, three, and five years are *dramatically* lower with the inclusion of 1994. Figures for all 100 subaccounts would have been radically higher if the periods included ended with the 1993 calendar year. This is important to note since a number of readers may look at these figures and think to themselves that they could have done better over the past year (in some cases *much* better) by investing in Treasury bills, bank CDs, or money market accounts. Such thinking, although correct, would be very short-sighted.

If your investment time horizon is only a couple of years, investments such as T-bills and bank CDs are the right choice. However, once one's time horizon is extended to five years (and most of the time as little as 3 years), stocks and bonds are the answer. Moreover, the longer you are willing to keep your money invested, the better equities (stocks) look. The introductory pages at the beginning of each investment category provide statistical figures that support this view. These figures also show that bonds, particulary high-yield bonds, are better than "cash equivalents" (T-bills, money market accounts, CDs, etc.).

The fact that virtually all stock and bond accounts posted losses for 1994 means that 1995 is almost guaranteed to be a better year. It is rare that stocks and bonds lose ground the same year. It is even less likely to see either category suffer losses two years in a row.

GORDON K. WILLIAMSON

Chapter

# 1

# What Is a Variable Annuity?

A variable annuity is a hybrid instrument that is almost exclusively an investment, but a small part of it deals with insurance. The insurance feature, referred to as a "guaranteed death benefit," is described in detail in Chapter 2. For now, let us expand on our definition of a variable annuity.

A variable annuity is an investment company, an entity that makes investments on behalf of individuals and institutions that share common financial goals. The subaccounts, or portfolios (very similar to funds within a mutual fund *family*), pool the money of many people, each of whom invests a different amount. Some variable annuities allow initial investments of as little as $10; others require at least $10,000.

Professional money managers for each subaccount use the pool of money to buy a variety of stocks, bonds, or money market instruments that, in their judgment, will help the subaccount's shareholders achieve their financial objectives. Usually, the objective of the manager is easy to discern; if the subaccount is called the "ABC Growth Portfolio," it is safe to assume that most, if not all, of the portfolio is comprised of common stocks. Similarly, if the name of the subaccount is the "ABC High-Yield Portfolio," it is safe to assume that management is concentrating on high-yield corporate bonds. Whether the amount invested is $100 or $1 million, each investor gets the same *percentage* yield, or return, as everyone else in the subaccount.

Each subaccount's investment objective, described in the prospectus, is important to both the portfolio's manager and the potential investor. The manager uses it as a guide when choosing investments for the subaccount. Prospective investors use it to determine which subaccounts are suitable for their needs. By law, each investor must receive a prospectus prior to or at the time of the investment. The prospectus details investment objectives and restrictions as well as all of the costs and expenses associated with the investment. Variable annuity investment objectives cover a wide range. Those in search of higher returns follow aggressive investment policies that involve greater risk; others seek current income from more conservative investments.

Figure 1.1 shows how investors divided up their monies as of the beginning of 1994. Fixed-rate subaccounts (which are somewhat similar to bank CDs) attracted the most money, followed by growth subaccounts. Later in the book, we will see why what the majority of people have done is wrong—fixed-rate (also known as fixed-interest) and money market subaccounts are not good choices most of the time.

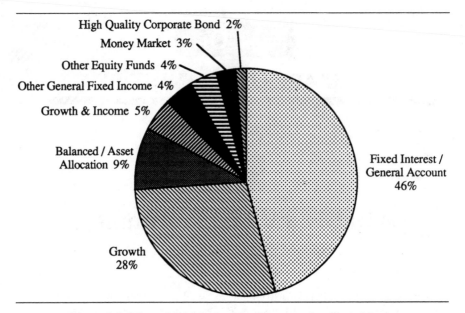

High Quality Corporate Bond 2%
Money Market 3%
Other Equity Funds 4%
Other General Fixed Income 4%
Growth & Income 5%
Balanced / Asset Allocation 9%
Growth 28%
Fixed Interest / General Account 46%

**Figure 1.1** Where Variable Annuity Investors Put Their Money

When a subaccount earns money (e.g., dividends, interest, and/or capital gains), it does not automatically distribute them to the investors. Unless an investor, known as the contract owner, makes a request for the money, it is reinvested. The automatic reinvestment is reflected in an increase in the price per unit of the variable annuity subaccount (in a mutual fund, the investor ends up with more shares). Phrased another way, all variable annuity profits are reflected in an increased value (price) per unit. Mutual fund investors may see an increase in the price per share or in the number of shares (the effect of having dividends, interest, and/or capital gains reinvested).

Variable annuities are popular because they are convenient and efficient investment vehicles that give all individuals—even those with small sums to invest—access to a splendid array of opportunities. Variable annuities are uniquely democratic institutions. They can take a portfolio of giant blue-chip companies like IBM, General Electric, and General Motors, and slice it into small enough pieces that almost anyone can buy.

Variable annuities allow an opportunity to participate in foreign stock and bond markets, which would normally be inaccessible because of time, expertise, or expense. International subaccounts make investing across sovereign borders no more difficult than investing across state lines. Over the next decade, as securities markets develop in the former Iron Curtain countries, variable annuities no doubt will give investors many opportunities to participate in those markets, too.

Mutual funds and variable annuities have opened up a world of fixed-income investing to people who, not too many years ago, had few choices other than passbook accounts and savings bonds. Through bond funds (in the case of mutual funds) and subaccounts (in the case of variable annuities), individuals can tap into interest payments from any kind of fixed-income security imaginable and many they had never heard of before. The range goes from U.S. Treasury Bonds (T-Bonds) to collateralized mortgage obligations (CMOs), adjustable rate preferred stocks, floating-rate notes, and even to other countries' debts—denominated in U.S. dollars and in other currencies.

What is heavily marketed is not necessarily what is appropriate for you to invest in. A global biotech subaccount may be a great investment, but it may not be the right portfolio for you. Buying what is hot rather than what is appropriate is one of the most common mistakes made by investors. This issue is addressed throughout the book.

## HISTORICAL BACKGROUND

Variable annuities came into being in 1952, through the work of economist William Greenough, an economist with the Teachers Insurance and Annuity Association. Greenough wanted a retirement vehicle comprised of equities, to counterbalance post-World War II inflation.

As income tax rates increase and company retirement benefits decrease, individuals must take on a larger and larger role in their own retirement planning. Annuities have become one of the primary tools for warding off taxes and building a larger nest egg. Annuity sales have easily doubled since 1987; sales were estimated at $80 billion in 1993 alone. A recent study showed that about one in seven of all U.S. households owned at least one annuity at the beginning of 1994. Although that figure is impressive, about twice as many households own mutual funds, leaving substantial room for annuity sales growth. More than 11 million U.S. households own mutual funds but do not own annuities.

# Chapter

## 2

# How an Annuity Works

A variable annuity subaccount is owned by all of its contract owners (shareholders), the people who purchased units of the subaccount. The day-to-day operation of a subaccount is delegated to a management company. The management company, often an outside mutual fund group, but sometimes the organization that created the variable annuity, may offer other financial products and services as well as different kinds of insurance.

The investment advisor manages the subaccount's portfolio of securities. The advisor is paid for its services; the fee is based on the total value of the fund's assets. Fees average 0.75% (vs. 1.11% for the typical mutual fund). The advisor employs professional portfolio managers who invest the subaccount's money by purchasing a number of stocks, bonds, or money market instruments, depending on the portfolio's investment objective (as described in the prospectus).

These professionals decide where to invest the subaccount's assets. The money managers make their investment decisions based on extensive, ongoing research into the financial performance of individual companies, taking into account general economic and market trends. In addition, they are backed up by economic and statistical resources. On the basis of their research, money managers decide what and when to buy, sell, or hold for the portfolio, in light of the subaccount's specific investment objective.

In addition to the investment advisor, the variable annuity company may contract with an underwriter, who arranges for the distribution of the subaccount's units to the investing public. The underwriter may act as a wholesaler, selling units to security dealers, or it may retail directly to the public. A mutual fund group operates in a very similar manner.

An annuity is an investment between you and an insurance company. It represents a contractual relationship between you and the company. And, although *offered* only by the insurance industry, annuities do not have anything to do with life or any other type of insurance coverage. Annuities are *marketed and sold through* brokerage firms, insurance agencies, banks, savings and loan institutions, financial planners, and investment advisors.

When you purchase or invest in an annuity, you are given certain assurances by the insurance company. These promises depend on the company issuing the contract (the investment) and the type of annuity chosen. There are two different types of annuities: (1) fixed (a set rate of return) and (2) variable (the investor chooses from a series of portfolios that range from conservative to aggressive—very similar to the choices available within a family of mutual funds). *This book deals only with variable annuities.* For most people, variable annuities are the better alternative.

There are always four parties to each annuity: (1) the insurer, (2) the contract owner, (3) the annuitant, and (4) the beneficiary. A description of each of these four parties follows.

## THE INSURER

Whether you invest in an annuity through your local bank, financial planner, brokerage firm, or anyone else who is licensed to sell this product, the agreement is always between you and an insurance company. There are over 2,000 insurance companies in the United States; several hundred of these insurers deal in annuities.

The insurance company you choose, also known as the *insurer,* invests your money according to how you fill out the application (e.g., "50% in growth, 20% in high-yield bonds, 30% in global stocks"). The insurer is always an insurance company. In addition to placing the money, the company makes certain promises. These assurances and the terms of the agreement are contained within the annuity contract. The contract spells out what can and cannot be done. Items such as adding more money, making withdrawals, cancellation penalties, and guarantees are all stated in detail.

Perhaps the best way to explain how the insurer operates is by analogy. When you invest in a bank certificate of deposit (CD), you sign an agreement. If you purchase a mutual fund, you fill out an application. These agreements and contracts are between you and the financial institutions. They tell you what your rights and privileges are; they also point out what will happen if you decide not to abide by the terms. When you invest in an annuity, you enter into a similar arrangement; the terms may be different and the other party is an insurance company, but other than that, it is very similar.

## THE CONTRACT OWNER

Those who invest in annuities are known as contract owners. It is their money; they decide among the different options being offered. A contract owner has the right and ability to add more money, make investment decisions or changes (within the family of subaccounts), terminate the agreement, withdraw part or all of the money, or change the parties named in the contract. Only the contract owner has these rights. (Throughout the book, the term *owner* or *contract owner* is intended to refer to *one or more persons.*)

A contract owner is similar to the purchaser of a mutual fund. When you buy a mutual fund, you are the owner. You have the right to invest more money, liquidate the entire account, take some or all of the money out, and change the title of the account (its ownership).

The contract owner can be an individual, a couple, a trust, a corporation, or a partnership. The only requirement is that the owner must be an adult. A minor can be the owner as long as the policy lists the minor's custodian (e.g., "Gina Tracey, custodian for the benefit of John Tracey").

Because the contract owner controls this investment, he or she can gift or will part or all of the contract to anyone or any entity at any time.

# THE ANNUITANT

If there is one party to the annuity that it is difficult to understand, it is the annuitant. The best way to understand the purpose of the annuitant is also by analogy. When you purchase life insurance, the insured party is named. The life insurance policy continues in force until the owner terminates the contract or fails to make any required premium payments, or until the insured party dies. An annuity remains in force until the contract owner makes a change or the annuitant dies. Thus, the annuitant is like the insured party in a life insurance policy.

Looked at another way, the annuitant is *the measuring life*. The annuitant, like an insured, has no voice in or control of the contract. The annuitant does not have the power to make withdrawals or deposits, to change the names of the parties to the agreement, or to terminate the contract. And just as is the case when you purchase life insurance on someone else (the insured), the annuitant must sign the annuity contract.

The person you name as the annuitant (the insured party) can be anyone: yourself or your spouse; a parent, child, or other relative; a friend or neighbor. The only requirement is that the named annuitant must be an actual person (*not* a living trust, corporation, partnership, or similar entity) who is currently living and is under a certain age. The maximum age of the proposed annuitant depends on the insurance company. Most companies require that the annuitant be under the age of 75 when the contract is initially signed. Other companies set a maximum age of 70 or 80. It is important to note that the contract (the investment) usually stays in force after the annuitant reaches the maximum age. A few companies allow the use of co-annuitants; this means that there would be two measuring lives.

Most annuities allow the contract owner to change the annuitant at any time. The only stipulation is that the new annuitant must have been alive when the contract was originally set up.

# THE BENEFICIARY

The beneficiary of an annuity is of little consequence until the death of a certain individual. The beneficiary has a role only after the death of the annuitant. And, like the beneficiary of a life insurance policy, the beneficiary of an annuity has no voice in the control or management of the policy. The only way in which the beneficiary can prosper from an annuity is to still be alive upon the death of the annuitant. (Throughout the book, the term *beneficiary* is to be understood as referring to *one or more persons*.)

The named beneficiary can be children, spouses, friends, relatives, neighbors, trusts, corporations, or partnerships. The annuity application allows for multiple beneficiary designations of varying or similar proportions (e.g., "25% to Mary Jones, 15% to Jack Jones, 10% to Edward Smith, and 50% to the Nelson Family Trust").

For a married couple, it is quite common for the contract owner to be one spouse and for the annuitant to be the other spouse. (A few companies allow co-ownership, in which case both spouses could be owners.) This type of multiple titling protects the assets of the couple in case the annuitant dies an untimely death. After all, if the annuitant-spouse were to die before the other spouse, most couples would not want the annuity proceeds to go to a charity or child while one of the spouses was still alive.

A single person, widow, or widower will usually name himself or herself as the contract owner and annuitant, and a loved one or entity (e.g., a living trust, charity, corporation, and so on) as the beneficiary. By making such an election, the individual retains complete control and dominion over the investment during his or her lifetime. Upon the death of the owner (assuming he or she is also the annuitant), the money will automatically pass to the intended heir (the beneficiary named in the contract).

If the contract owner dies before the annuitant, neither the annuitant nor the named beneficiary has any rights to the investment (the contract). Instead, heirs named in the owner's will or trust become the new owners. If the contract owner dies without a valid will or trust, the new contract owner is determined by *intestate succession:* the decedent's spouse and/or children would be first in line, followed by the parent(s) of the owner (if there is no living spouse or children) and then the decedent's brothers and/or sisters (if there is no living spouse, child, or parent).

The contract owner can change the beneficiary at any time; consent by the existing beneficiary is not necessary. You do not need to notify someone that he or she has been listed as a beneficiary of your annuity; similarly, you do not have to tell anyone that he or she has been removed as an intended beneficiary.

## ONE PERSON CAN HAVE MULTIPLE TITLES

At the time you invest in an annuity, the insurance company needs to know the name of the owner, annuitant, and beneficiary. As previously mentioned, the owner and beneficiary do not have to be people—they can be entities. Only the annuitant, the measuring life, has to be a natural person.

As pointed out earlier, the same person can hold multiple titles. Thus, you could be the contract owner and beneficiary of your own contract. Or, you could be the owner, annuitant, and/or beneficiary; any combination you can think of is acceptable. Keep in mind that if you choose an entity (a living trust, corporation, and so on), the entity can only be the contract owner and/or beneficiary; a living individual under a certain age must be named as the annuitant. (A few contracts allow you to list co-annuitants.) The insurer is *always* an insurance company; for you to change insurers, you must change insurance companies.

## AN EXAMPLE

Suppose you have $20,000 to invest in a variable annuity. The variable annuity that you are considering offers eight investment options: (1) aggressive growth, (2) growth, (3) growth and income, (4) balanced, (5) high-yield bonds, (6) government securities, (7) foreign stocks, and (8) money market. You decide to invest your money as follows: $5,000 in the growth portfolio, $7,000 in balanced, and $8,000 in foreign stocks. The only other decision you need to make is who the parties will be.

You are married and have two children, ages 12 and 23; you are 57 and your wife is 52. You and your spouse decide that both of you will be the joint owners and that your wife will be the beneficiary and you will be the annuitant.

Several years pass, and your $20,000 variable annuity investment is now worth $50,000. You die. Because your wife is the beneficiary, she has a choice: She can either terminate the investment and request a check for $50,000 (she will have to send the insurance company a certified copy of your death certificate and a written request for the distribution), or she can continue on with the investment indefinitely. Let us suppose she decides to keep the investment intact.

As the sole owner of this investment, your wife (the surviving spouse) must now decide who will be the new annuitant and beneficiary. She decides to name herself as the annuitant and your two children as beneficiaries (each to receive 50% of the contract's value upon her death). The investment (contract) then continues until your wife makes a change or dies. If no changes are made between now and her death, your children will automatically inherit the annuity upon their mother's death. Prior to her death, their mother could drop one or both children as the beneficiary or change the percentage that one or both will later receive—all without the children's knowledge.

# Chapter

# 3

# How to Invest in a Variable Annuity

Investing in a variable annuity means buying units (shares) of one or more subaccounts. An investor becomes an owner of a set number of units in a subaccount, just as he or she might be an owner of a designated number of shares of stock in a large corporation. The difference is that a variable annuity's only business is investing in securities; the price of the units in any given subaccount is directly related to the value of the securities held by that specific subaccount.

Variable annuity subaccounts continually issue new shares for purchase by the public. Existing investors' (contract owners') price per unit does not decrease because of the ongoing issuance of new units (shares); each unit created is offset by the amount of new money coming in. A subaccount's unit price can change from day to day, depending on the daily value of the securities held in the portfolio. The unit price is calculated as follows: the total value of the subaccount's investments at the end of the day, after expenses, is divided by the number of units outstanding.

Unlike mutual funds, variable annuity subaccounts are not reported by newspapers on a regular basis. The only publication that reports the values of subaccounts, on a weekly basis, is *Barron's,* where variable annuity information is found toward the back of each issue. The example shown below, from the February 28, 1994, issue of *Barron's,* warrants a line-by-line explanation.

The first line, "Allianz . . . ," indicates the name of the insurance company offering this particular variable annuity product.

The second line, "Franklin Valuemark II," is the name of the variable annuity. As is often the case, the title tells which company is managing the subaccounts. In

### Allianz Life Insurance Co.
### Franklin Valuemark II

| Fund Name | Unit Price | 4-Week Total Return | 52-Week Total Return |
|---|---|---|---|
| Equity Growth | 14.283 | 1.07 | 15.01 |
| Global Income | 14.696 | −1.07 | 12.76 |
| Int'l Equity | 12.923 | 1.273 | 34.04 |
| Zero Coupon 2000 | 16.391 | −2.98 | 5.48 |

this case, Franklin, a well-known mutual fund company, is overseeing the various portfolios (subaccounts).

The third line is similar to a legend on a map. The different headings describe what information is to be gained. "Fund Name" is the name of the subaccount. In this example, it is the name of the Franklin Valuemark II subaccount. The "Unit Price" shows existing investors the current price per share (unit) of their investment. Thus, if someone in Valuemark II's Equity Growth portfolio had originally bought in at $13 per unit, a profit of $1.28 per unit has been realized so far ($14.283 minus $13.00). The "4-Week Total Return" shows how much the subaccount has appreciated or declined in value over the past month (ending February 28, 1994, in this example). The Equity Growth portfolio has appreciated 1.07% (annualized, this 4-week rate would amount to approximately 13%). The actual return for this investment (subaccount) during the past year has been 15.01%; as shown in the final column, "52-Week Total Return." Equity Growth, a stock-type portfolio, has appreciated 15.01% during the past 52 weeks.

The remaining lines give performance figures for three other subaccounts (funds) within the Valuemark II family. Global Income, a portfolio of U.S. and foreign bonds, has also done well, increasing by almost 13% during the year ending February 28, 1994. Int'l Equity, a subaccount of foreign stocks, is selling at $12.92 per unit and went up 34.04% during the previous year. Zero Coupon 2000, a subaccount comprised of zero coupon bonds that mature in the year 2000, is down almost 3% for the previous 4 weeks, but up 5.48% for the past 52 weeks.

# Chapter

# Reading a Variable
# Annuity Prospectus

The purpose of any annuity's prospectus is to provide the reader—often, the potential owner—with full and complete disclosure. For easy reference, the prospectus includes a table of contents that typically has the following sections, in the order indicated:

1. **Special Terms**—similar to a glossary (describes terms such as *death benefit*).
2. **Expense Table**—all costs incurred by the contract owner, including any contingent deferred sales charge (or up-front commission), plus the annual contract fee (typically in the $30 range), the mortality risk and expense fees (normally in the 1.2% range), and management fee (approximately 0.5%).
3. **Synopsis**—answers to commonly asked questions (e.g., "Who invests my money?" and "Do I get a 'free look' at this contract?")
4. **Condensed Financial Information**—how each subaccount within the contract (e.g., growth portfolio, high-yield bond portfolio, and so on) has performed over each of the past several years.
5. **Investment Results**—a policy statement indicating how sales-literature figures are determined or evaluated.
6. **Financial Statements**—where detailed financial information about the insurer can be obtained (usually, this is part of the SAI; see item 21 in this listing).
7. **The Insurance Company**—the full name, address, and brief description of the insurance company that issues the annuity contract.
8. **Variable Account**—how the investment vehicles were orginally set up, and what regulations and securities laws apply to them.
9. **Investments of the Variable Account**—a description of the investment advisor (portfolio manager) and the different subaccounts (portfolios) that are available to the investor.
10. **Charges and Other Deductions**—the annual maintenance and administrative charge, the contingent deferred sales charge (if any), and the declining penalty period (if any), as well as mortality and expense risk charges (this pays for the death benefit) and deductions for state premium taxes and other necessary expenditures.

11. The Contracts—how to go about making an investment and how valuations, transfers, reinvestment, ownership, and the death benefit are determined.
12. Annuity Payments—annuitization options (income to the owner over a specific period of time or over the life of the annuitant; a specified dollar amount each period; or regular payments that last as long as one of two people is alive).
13. Federal Tax Status—a statement that annuity contracts do not pay current income taxes (deferred growth) but there are Internal Revenue Service (IRS) penalties and costs if money is taken prior to age 59½ unless: (1) death or disability occurs, (2) distributions are made in substantially equal installments as a life annuity, (3) there is a structured settlement, (4) the annuity is immediately annuitized, (5) the investment was part of a certain type of retirement plan, or (6) the owner reaches age 59½.
14. Voting Rights—a statement that the owner is given one vote per share (unit) purchased; voting takes place when the issuer or management company wants to change a policy or other item previously described in the prospectus.
15. Distribution of Contracts—how the contract (investment) is sold and distributed.
16. Return Privilege—a description of the free-look period (at least 10 days, but longer in some states); the contract may be returned within this period of time, for a complete no-questions-asked refund. Normally, the investor is subject to any market risk during the free-look period.
17. State Regulation—what state the insurance company is licensed in and how it is governed.
18. Records and Reports—how the issuer is required to mail reports to each investor at least semi-annually.
19. Legal Proceedings—a statement of any legal proceedings against the insurance company (usually there are none).
20. Other Information—where additional information can be obtained (rarely needed or requested by any investor).
21. Table of Contents of the Statement of Additional Information (SAI)—a summary description of the information contained in the statement of additional information (SAI). This document must be requested; few investors ask for or need it.

The remainder of the prospectus covers, in detail, the different investment options (subaccounts), including what the portfolios invest in and all of the risks associated with such securities.

Chapter

## 5

# How the 100 Best Subaccounts Were Determined

With an entry field that numbers close to 1,500, it is no easy task to determine the 100 best subaccounts. Magazines and newspapers report on the "best" by relying on performance figures over a specific period, usually 1, 3, 5, or 10 years. Investors often rely on these sources and invest accordingly, only to be disappointed later.

Studies from around the world bear out what investors typically experience: *There is no correlation between how a stock or bond performs in one year and how it performs in the next.* The same can be said for individual money managers—and, sadly, for most variable annuities.

The criteria used to determine the 100 best variable annuity subaccounts were unique and far-reaching. For a subaccount to be considered for this book, it had to pass four tests.

1. All money market and fixed-rate subaccounts were excluded from consideration. Once inflation and income taxes (which are eventually paid by contract owners or their heirs) are factored in, these types of subaccounts lose money (purchasing power) in about 3 out of every 4 years. More importantly, variable annuities are not really appropriate for such investments unless one's holding period in a money market or fixed-rate account is less than 18 months.

The very conservative investor, who would normally be attracted to a money market or guaranteed rate of return (fixed-rate subaccount), would fare better by going into a mutual fund money market account, taxable or tax-free, depending on the investor's bracket. An even better approach would be to look at short or intermediate-term bond funds, again either taxable or tax-free. These types of alternatives have little, if any, volatility, and can be managed more efficiently by a mutual fund company.

2. All subaccounts that have had managers for less than 5 years were excluded, except where the managers have been overseeing their "clones" (the mutual fund portfolios the annuity accounts are modeled after) for 5 years or more.

This second step alone eliminated well over half the contenders. The reasoning for this cutoff is simple: a subaccount is only as good as its manager (unless the subaccount is a money market or is indexed). An outstanding 10- or 15-year track record may end up in a periodical, but how relevant is this performance if the manager who oversaw the subaccount left a year or two ago?

3. The remaining contenders were sorted out to find those subaccounts that had the same manager, investment style, and objective, and were offered by more than one variable annuity company. Where such duplication existed, all but one of the subaccounts was eliminated. For this third step only, the selected subaccount was determined strictly on the basis of its net rate of return. Thus, if the XYZ and ABC variable annuity companies both offered an aggressive growth subaccount managed by Mary Smith, but the XYZ investment netted better results (because of lower expenses), the XYZ aggressive growth subaccount was included and the ABC aggressive growth subaccount was dropped. In a few cases, the "duplicate" subaccount was eliminated because of an extra-ordinary penalty period (longer than 7 years) or an up-front commission charge (few annuities charge any such fee, but a handful nick the investor for up to 10%).

4. Subaccounts that demonstrated either abnormally high risk or low returns, based on their investment objective, were eliminated. All growth and income subaccounts were looked at as a single universe; growth subaccounts were looked at as a different universe, and so on.

Three other points are worth mentioning. First, the information available about variable annuities is not nearly as complete as the information on mutual funds. Consequently, the task of screening and analyzing subaccounts is not as precise as it will be next year and the year after that. As this investment vehicle becomes even more popular, the number of studies and resources devoted to this area will greatly increase. This means that any analysis or any rating system will become that much more accurate and, in a few cases, more fair with each subsequent annual edition of this book.

Second, as mentioned earlier, the selection process used to determine the 100 best was completely blind. I admit to favoring certain variable annuities, mutual funds, and other investments more than others, and was intent on keeping this bias out of the book. I left out the names of all subaccounts until the final 100 were determined. Every step of my screening was based on statistical information only.

Third, this is the first book ever written about what are supposed to be the very best variable annuities. Each subsequent edition will include refinements and improvements. Subaccounts that appear in this edition may get bumped in the next edition either because of a change in management or because a competing subaccount will then have consecutive management for 5 or more years.

## Chapter

# 6

# About the 100 Best Subaccounts

As discussed previously, the methodology used to narrow down the universe of subaccounts has been based on performance, risk, and management. *Every one of these 100 subaccounts is a superlative choice.* However, there must still be a means whereby these subaccounts are compared and ranked within their peer group.

Each of the 100 subaccounts is first categorized by its investment objective. The category breakdown used is as follows:

| Category of Subaccount | Number |
|---|---|
| Aggressive growth | 5 |
| Balanced | 18 |
| Corporate bonds | 8 |
| Global equities (stocks) | 5 |
| Government bonds | 6 |
| Growth | 24 |
| Growth & income | 16 |
| High-yield bonds | 10 |
| Specialty/Sector | 3 |
| World bonds | 5 |
| Total | 100 subaccounts |

Each of the variable annuities reviewed in this book is ranked as excellent, very good, fair, or poor for each of the following characteristics: performance, risk control, expense minimization, management, investment options, and family rating. A subaccount's rating for each of these characteristics ranges from 0 to 5 points. Each point is represented by a check mark (✓). The check marks, or points, can be transcribed as follows:

none = poor
✓ = fair
✓✓ = good
✓✓✓ = very good
✓✓✓✓ = superior
✓✓✓✓✓ = excellent

All of the rankings for each subaccount are based on how the subaccount fared when matched against its peer group. Thus, even though a given rating may only be fair or even poor, it is still within a category that includes only the very best. There is a strong likelihood that a subaccount given a low score in one category here would still rate highly when compared to the entire universe of subaccounts or to other subaccounts within the same category but not included in the book because they did not meet the selection criteria.

Do not be fooled by a low rating for any subaccount on any of the characteristics listed above. All 100 of these subaccounts are true winners. The purpose of the ratings is to list the best in the order of their superiority.

The remainder of this chapter provides a description of each of the characteristics reviewed and ranked for the 100 subaccounts that appear in this book.

## PERFORMANCE

Return figures and the subsequent ratings are based on the three calendar years ending December 31, 1994. In the event that two or more subaccounts were competing for the same category or slot, a five-year period ending December 31, 1994, was used. Performance figures represent total return figures: unit appreciation (similar to a stock's price per share) plus any dividends or interest payments were included.

A three-year period was used because a number of subaccounts that appear in the book have less than a three-year record but are based on, or modeled after, a similar mutual fund managed by the same person or team for at least five years. Because these "clone" funds are not identical to their annuity counterparts, the most inclusive time period was used, to give a greater likelihood that the overwhelming majority of the ratings were based on actual subaccount performance and not on "clone mutual fund" numbers.

A 10-year time horizon was not used because only a handful of variable accounts have been in existence that long. Performance over one year was not used because such figures could be the result of either luck or a one-time event.

All performance figures include a tabulation that shows how the subaccount has performed against a specific index. For the equity subaccounts (aggressive growth, growth, growth and income, and international stock), one of three indexes was used: Russell 2000 (a domestic small company index), the S&P 500 (the major corporations in the United States), or Europe, Australia, Far East (EAFE) (measures stock market returns outside of the United States). For the debt subaccounts (corporate bond, government bond, high-yield, and world bond), one of the following indexes was used: Lehman Brothers Government/Corporate Bond Index, First Boston High-Yield Bond Index, or the Salomon Brothers Non-U.S. Dollar World Government Bond Index. Finally, for the balanced subaccounts, the Lehman Brothers Government/Corporate Bond Index was used along with the S&P 500. This comparison will show how a particular subaccount, or the "clone" that it is modeled after, has performed against its appropriate benchmark over each of the past several years.

## RISK CONTROL

The system used for determining risk in this book is not widely used, but is a fair and meaningful measurement: For how many months, over the past three years, did a subaccount underperform what is popularly referred to as a "risk-free" vehicle, something like a bank CD or U.S. Treasury Bill (T-Bill)? The more months a subaccount fell below this safe return, the more the subaccount was punished in its risk ranking.

*Risk-adjusted return* looks at how well an account performed, based on the amount of risk it took. We would all like to get a great return on an investment without taking much risk, but this is not usually possible. More often than not, risk is commensurate with return. Earning a 100% return on principal sounds very appealing, but if I said that we would have to go to Las Vegas and bet on red or black on the roulette table to have a chance for 100% return, I doubt that very many people would sign up for the trip.

If an account receives high marks for risk control, this means that the fund took X amount of risk but received an X plus Y rate of return. A portfolio that is rated poorly in this area may still have good results but took higher-than-normal risks, compared to its peer group (e.g., X amount of risk taken resulted in an X minus Y rate of return). You should not necessarily avoid variable annuities that are rated either fair or poor for risk control; a higher-than-normal risk can be counterbalanced by the addition of a low-risk investment to your portfolio.

Although not generally used for rating purposes in this book, standard deviation and beta figures were included to give you a sense of the subaccounts' volatility and market-related risk. Both of these figures are valuable because they represent alternate ways of measuring risk.

## EXPENSE MINIMIZATION

The impact of expense minimization is often exaggerated by the press and by investors and advisors who focus on statistics. True, over time, a 0.25% added expense will have a minor impact on total return, but this is not nearly as important as whether you are in the right category to begin with, or whether your subaccount has a good portfolio manager who is conscious of risk-adjusted returns.

Nevertheless, total expenses, including the annual contract charge, are rated. This is the most straightforward and objective of the rated categories. It is also, almost always, the least important.

## MANAGEMENT

The subaccount must either possess an excellent risk-adjusted return *or* have had superior returns with very low levels of risk. It is assumed that most readers are equally concerned with risk and reward. Thus, the foundation of the text is based on which variable annuity subaccounts have the best *risk-adjusted* returns.

The rating for this characteristic was based on the subaccount's performance and risk control, both of which are usually heavily influenced by management. In a few cases, other considerations such as standard deviation and beta were also factored in to determine the rating.

## INVESTMENT OPTIONS

This was the most complex area to measure. Subaccounts and contracts were rewarded (up to a total of two check marks) if they allowed dollar-cost averaging and/or allowed a high number of transfers per year. Most of the rating for this characteristic was based on the number of subaccounts available within the variable annuity "family" and the diversification of such choices or options. Thus, a contract that included a single global stock or world bond subaccount was looked at more favorably than a contract that had no overseas exposure but had two, three, or four growth subaccounts.

## FAMILY RATING

This characteristic points out how many subaccounts are available within the variable annuity contract and the caliber of these investment options, based on their respective *risk-adjusted* returns. A family (the number of choices offered to you) could be quite small (e.g., four subaccounts), but still get the highest rating (excellent) if most, or all, of the subaccounts performed superbly, when viewed on a risk-adjusted return basis.

What may appear to be confusing here is the number of subaccounts mentioned versus the number of check marks shown by the different investment options (e.g., aggressive growth, growth, growth and income, and so on). A family rating may indicate that the contract includes 10 subaccounts, but the number of check marks for investment options may be 7. This simply means that the contract includes a couple of growth subaccounts or a couple of balanced subaccounts, or multiple representation in another category.

## TOTAL POINT SCORE

A total score is given for rough comparison purposes. The total is determined by adding up the number of check marks (0 through 5) for each of the characteristics described (performance, risk control, expense minimization, management, investment options, and family rating). Conceptually, total point scores could range from 0 to 30 check marks (points).

# Chapter

**7**

# Aggressive Growth Subaccounts

These subaccounts focus strictly on appreciation, with no concern about generating income. Aggressive growth subaccounts strive for maximum capital growth, frequently using such trading strategies as leveraging, purchasing restricted securities, or buying stocks of "emerging growth" companies. Portfolio composition is almost always completely comprised of U.S. stocks.

Aggressive growth subaccounts can go up in value quite rapidly during favorable market conditions. These subaccounts will often outperform other categories of U.S. stocks during bull markets, but suffer greater percentage losses during bear markets. Another category, small company stocks, has been combined with aggressive growth for purposes of this book. "Small company" refers to stocks whose market capitalization is less than $1 billion. Usually, small company stocks are less volatile than the better known aggressive growth stocks.

Over the 15 years ending December 31, 1994, small stocks outperformed common stocks by 18%, as measured by the Standard & Poor's 500 Stock Index. From 1980 to 1994, small stocks averaged 17.0% (compounded per year) versus 15.7% for common stocks. A $10,000 investment in small stocks grew to $105,600 over the 15-year period; a similar initial investment in the S&P 500 grew to $89,300.

During the 30 years ending December 31, 1994, there were eleven 20-year periods (e.g., 1964–1983, 1965–1984, and so on). The Small Stock Index, made up from the smallest 20% of companies listed on the New York Stock Exchange (NYSE), as measured by market capitalization, *outperformed* the S&P 500 in all of those 20-year periods.

During the 20 years ending December 31, 1994, there were eleven 10-year periods (e.g., 1974–1983, 1975–1984, and so on). The Small Stock Index *outperformed* the S&P 500 in six of those eleven 10-year periods.

Over the 50 years ending December 31, 1994, there were forty-one 10-year periods (e.g., 1944–1953, 1945–1954, and so on). The Small Stock Index *outperformed* the S&P 500 in twenty-seven of those forty-one 10-year periods.

A dollar invested in small stocks in 1945 grew to over $1,230 by the beginning of 1995. This translates into an average compound return of 15.3% per year. Over the 50-year period, the worst year for small stocks was 1973, when a loss of 31% was suffered. Two years later, these same stocks posted a gain of almost 53% in one year. The best year was 1967, when small stocks posted a gain of 84%.

To obtain the types of returns described above, investors would have needed quite a bit of patience and understanding. Small company stocks have had a standard deviation (variation of return) of 27%, versus 16% for common stocks and 9% for

### Aggressive Growth Category Statistics: Subaccounts vs. Mutual Funds

| Description | Subaccounts | Funds |
| --- | --- | --- |
| **Composition of portfolio** | | |
| U.S. stocks | 78% | 79% |
| Cash | 14% | 10% |
| Foreign stocks | 7% | 6% |
| Bonds | 0% | 1% |
| Other | 1% | 4% |
| **Fees and expenses** | | |
| Underlying fund expense | 0.85% | 1.70% |
| Insurance expense | 1.25% | — |
| Total expenses | 2.10% | 1.70%/4.2%* |
| **Operations** | | |
| Net assets (in millions) | $78 | $270 |
| Manager tenure | 3 years | 5 years |
| **Portfolio statistics** | | |
| Beta | 1.2% | 1.1% |
| Standard deviation | 4.9% | 5.7% |
| Price/earnings ratio | 30 | 28 |
| Turnover ratio (annual) | 126% | 129% |
| Median market capitalization | $2.5 billion | $1.7 billion |
| Number of subaccounts/funds | 70 | 60 |

*Total expenses for this mutual fund category increase to this figure if the average mutual fund commission is added to the 1.70% figure.

long-term government bonds. This means that an investor's return over the 50-year period would have ranged from −8% to +45% two-thirds of the time.

The table below shows year-by-year, as well as 3-, 5-, and 10-year averages for this investment category. The variable annuity subaccount category is compared against the similar mutual fund category. These performance figures are average figures, representing all funds and subaccounts that fall within this investment objective.

The variable annuity subaccounts outperformed their mutual fund counterparts for 1994, 1992, 1991, 1989, 1987, and for the 3-, 5-, and 10-year periods ending December 31, 1994.

Aggressive growth subaccounts are not for the faint of heart. They should probably be avoided by traditional investors, perhaps comprising no more than 10% in a *diversified,* conservative portfolio. I recommend a 10% commitment to this category for the moderate investor and 30% for the aggressive portfolio. As is true with any category of variable annuities, whenever larger dollar amounts are involved, more than one subaccount per category should be used.

### Average Annual Returns: Aggressive Growth Subaccounts vs. Aggressive Growth Mutual Funds

| Year | Subaccount | Mutual Fund |
|---|---|---|
| 1994 | −1.0% | −1.3% |
| 1993 | 17.0% | 17.9% |
| 1992 | 11.2% | 8.6% |
| 1991 | 55.6% | 50.4% |
| 1990 | −8.4% | −7.9% |
| 1989 | 31.3% | 27.2% |
| 1988 | 11.5% | 15.7% |
| 1987 | −2.5% | −2.9% |
| 3-yr. average | 13.1% | 8.3% |
| 5-yr. average | 12.1% | 11.5% |
| 10-yr. average | 14.5% | 13.3% |

The table above shows statistics you might find useful when comparing variable annuity subaccounts versus their mutual fund counterparts or "clones." The category averages are based on information available at the beginning of 1995.

Figure 7.1 shows the year-by-year returns for this category of variable annuities for the period 1987 through 1994. These are composite figures and therefore include all of the subaccounts that comprise the aggressive growth category.

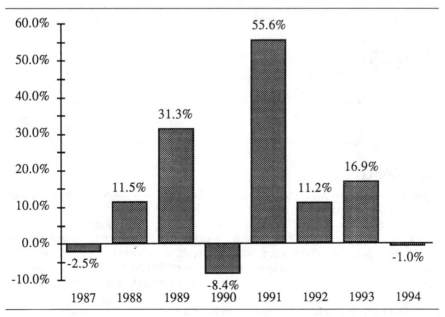

**Figure 7.1** Aggressive Growth Subaccounts

---

**American Skandia Advisors Plan (ASAP)**
**Alger Small Capitalization**
P.O. Box 883
Shelton, CT  06484
(800) 752-6342

---

| | |
|---|---|
| Performance | ✓✓ |
| Risk control | ✓ |
| Expense minimization | ✓✓ |
| Management | ✓✓✓ |
| Investment options | ✓✓✓✓✓ |
| Family rating | ✓ |
| Total point score | 14 points |

## Performance  ✓✓

During the 3-year and 5-year periods ending December 31, 1994, Alger Small Capitalization had an average annual compound return of 2.5% and 12.4%, respectively. A $10,000 investment made into this subaccount 5 years before that date grew to $17,900 ($10,800, if only the last 3 years of that period are used).

Compared to other aggressive growth variable annuity subaccounts, this one ranks in the bottom half for the 3-year period but in the top 10% for the 5-year period. The inception month of this subaccount was May 1992. The performance figures (shown below) for periods before the subaccount's inception in May 1992 are hypothetical, based on the underlying clone fund's returns. This subaccount is modeled (cloned) after the Alger Small Capitalization Portfolio, which had an inception date of November 1986, and has an asset base of $300 million.

The year-by-year returns for this subaccount and the mutual fund it is modeled after are:

| Year | Annual Return | Russell 2000 |
|---|---|---|
| 1994 | −5.7% | −1.8% |
| 1993 | 11.7% | 18.9% |
| 1992 | 2.1% | 18.4% |
| 1991 | 55.3% | 46.1% |
| 1990 | 7.2% | −19.5% |
| 1989 | 62.2% | 16.2% |
| 1988 | 17.5% | 24.9% |
| 1987 | −1.5% | −8.8% |

## Risk Control

Over the 3-year and 5-year periods studied, this fund was much riskier than the average equity subaccount.

The typical standard deviation for aggressive growth subaccounts was 4.9% during the 3-year period. The standard deviation for this subaccount was 6.0% over this same period, which means it was 23% more volatile than its peer group. The price/earnings (p/e) ratio averages 38 for this portfolio compared to the typical aggressive growth subaccount's p/e ratio of 30. In general, the higher the p/e ratio, the riskier the portfolio.

The beta (market-related risk) of this subaccount was 1.4 over the 3-year period. Beta for this entire category was 1.2 over this same period. The market index

(the S&P 500 Index for equity subaccounts) always has a beta of 1.0. The *risk-adjusted* return for this variable annuity subaccount can be described as very good.

## Expense Minimization                                          ✓✓

The typical expenses incurred by aggressive growth subaccounts are 2.1% per year. The total expenses for American Skandia Advisors Plan Alger Small Capitalization, 2.4%, are higher than its peer group average. Total expenses include all charges to the investor (except the annual contract charge, which is always expressed as a dollar figure), including management fees, overhead, administration, and mortality expenses. The free annual withdrawals percentage is based on the original principal.

| | | | |
|---|---|---|---|
| Maximum surrender charge | 8% | Total expenses | 2.4% |
| Duration of surrender charge | 7 years | Annual contract charge | $30 |
| Declining surrender charge | yes | Free annual withdrawals | 10% |

## Management                                                   ✓✓✓

American Skandia Advisors Plan is offered by American Skandia Life Assurance Corporation. The company has a Duff & Phelps rating of AA−. The portfolio (and/or the mutual fund it is modeled after) was managed by David Alger for the 7 years ending December 31, 1994. The portfolio's size is $110 million. The typical security in the portfolio has a market capitalization of $500 million. Alger also manages the Alger Small Capitalization mutual fund.

## Investment Options                                           ✓✓✓✓✓

Investors may make additional contributions into this portfolio at any time. This is known as a flexible premium annuity. Investors in this variable annuity can choose from all of the subaccount categories below that have a check mark:

| | | |
|---|---|---|
| ✓ Aggressive growth | ___ Government bonds | ✓ Money market |
| ✓ Balanced | ✓ Growth | ✓ Specialty/Sector |
| ✓ Corporate bonds | ✓ Growth & income | ✓ World bonds |
| ✓ Global equities (stocks) | ✓ High-yield bonds | |

## Family Rating                                                ✓

There are 31 subaccounts within the ASAP family.

   The subaccounts within this variable annuity all have an *increasing* guaranteed death benefit. This means that the beneficiary is guaranteed to receive *the greater of* the contract's value on the date of the annuitant's death or the value of the original investment(s) compounded by 5% each year (less any withdrawals made).

## Summary

American Skandia Advisors Plan (ASAP) Alger Small Capitalization is the subaccount choice for the patient investor who understands the market's ups and downs. With this type of portfolio, you can make a killing by following one of two strategies: (1) staying in for the long haul, or (2) buying in after one or two particularly bad quarters.

   Alger is known to have some of the very best money managers in the financial community. Management's approach to security selection is quite different from the herd instinct often followed by others. The small-stock arena is such that a portfolio manager can look like a genius during one period and a bum during the next quarter or year. Investors who have stayed with David Alger and the firm's other decision makers have done very well. It is difficult to find fault with performance figures that beat out 90% of the competition. If 5-year figures were used, instead of 3-year numbers, to rate the portfolio's returns, this Alger offering would have easily earned a rating of "excellent."

The annuity issuer, American Skandia, continues to add to its already impressive array of money managers from a wide range of money management companies, including: Alliance, Neuberger & Berman, Janus, INVESCO, Federated, Phoenix, T. Rowe Price, Scudder, J. P. Morgan, Henderson International, and PIMCO. As some of these new portfolios begin to mature, contract owners will see the wisdom in Skandia's selection of investment advisors. Few annuities can boast of the diversity that ASAP has when it comes to category selection and breadth of management.

A few years ago, American Skandia began to implement a policy wherein the company would seek out only the best specialists within each investment category. This strategy has almost been completely implemented, and the future looks very promising for this entire group.

## Profile

| | | | |
|---|---|---|---|
| Minimum investment | $1,000 | Telephone exchanges | yes |
| Retirement account minimum | $1,000 | Transfers allowed per year | 12 |
| Co-annuitant allowed | yes | Maximum issuance age | none |
| Co-owner allowed | yes | Maximum annuitization age | none |
| Dollar-cost averaging | yes | Number of subaccounts | 34 |
| Systematic withdrawal plans | yes | Available in all 50 states | no* |

*Not available in NY.

---

### First Investors Variable Annuity C
### Discovery
95 Wall Street
New York, NY  10005
(800) 832-7783

| | |
|---|---|
| Performance | ✓✓✓✓ |
| Risk control | ✓✓✓ |
| Expense minimization | ✓✓✓✓ |
| Management | ✓✓✓✓✓ |
| Investment options | ✓✓✓ |
| Family rating | ✓✓✓ |
| Total point score | 22 points |

## Performance                                           ✓✓✓✓

During the 3-year and 5-year periods ending December 31, 1994, Discovery had an average annual compound return of 10.1% and 13.5%, respectively. This means that a $10,000 investment made into this subaccount 5 years before that date grew to $18,800 ($13,300, if only the last 3 years of that period are used).

Compared to other aggressive growth variable annuity subaccounts, this one ranks in the top third for the 3- and 5-year periods. The inception month of this subaccount was October 1990. The performance figures (shown below) for periods before the subaccount's inception in October 1990 are hypothetical, based on the underlying clone fund's returns. This subaccount is modeled (cloned) after the First

Investors Life Discovery Series, which had an inception date of December 1987, and has an asset base of $20 million.

The year-by-year returns for this subaccount and the portfolio it is modeled after are:

| Year | Annual Return | Russell 2000 |
|------|--------|------|
| 1994 | -3.6% | -1.8% |
| 1993 | 21.0% | 18.9% |
| 1992 | 14.5% | 18.4% |
| 1991 | 51.5% | 46.1% |
| 1990 | -6.7% | -19.5% |
| 1989 | 22.3% | 16.2% |
| 1988 | 2.6% | 24.9% |

## Risk Control ✓✓✓

Over the 3-year and 5-year periods studied, this fund was slightly riskier than the average equity subaccount.

The typical standard deviation for aggressive growth subaccounts was 4.9% during the 3-year period. The standard deviation for this subaccount was 4.7% over this same period, which means that it was 4% less volatile than its peer group. The price/earnings (p/e) ratio averages 32 for this portfolio compared to the typical aggressive growth subaccount's p/e ratio of 30. In general, the higher the p/e ratio, the riskier the portfolio.

The beta (market-related risk) of this subaccount was 1.2 over the 3-year period. Beta for this entire category was also 1.2 over this same period. The market index (the S&P 500 Index for equity subaccounts) always has a beta of 1.0. The *risk-adjusted* return for this variable annuity subaccount can be described as very good.

## Expense Minimization ✓✓✓✓

The typical expenses incurred by aggressive growth subaccounts are 2.1% per year. The total expenses for First Investors Variable Annuity C Discovery, 1.9%, are lower than its peer group average. Total expenses include all charges to the investor (except the annual contract charge, which is always expressed as a dollar figure), including management fees, overhead, administration, and mortality expenses.

| | | | |
|---|---|---|---|
| Maximum surrender charge | 0% | Total expenses | 1.9% |
| Duration of surrender charge | n/a | Annual contract charge | $0 |
| Declining surrender charge | n/a | Free annual withdrawals | 100% |

## Management ✓✓✓✓✓

First Investors Variable Annuity C is offered by First Investors Life Insurance Company. The company has an A.M. Best rating of B+. The portfolio (and/or the mutual fund it is modeled after) was managed by Patricia D. Poitra for the 7 years ending December 31, 1994. The portfolio's size is a mere $15 million. The typical security in the portfolio has a market capitalization of $560 million. Poitra also manages the First Investors Special Situations Series mutual fund.

## Investment Options                                          ✓✓✓

Investors may make additional contributions into this portfolio at any time. This is known as a flexible premium annuity. Investors in this variable annuity can choose from all of the subaccount categories below that have a check mark:

| | | |
|---|---|---|
| ✓ Aggressive growth | ✓ Government bonds | ✓ Money market |
| ___ Balanced | ✓ Growth | ___ Specialty/Sector |
| ✓ Corporate bonds | ✓ Growth & income | ___ World bonds |
| ✓ Global equities (stocks) | ✓ High-yield bonds | |

## Family Rating                                              ✓✓✓

There are 9 subaccounts within the First Investors Variable Annuity C family. Overall, this family of subaccounts can be described as good on a *risk-adjusted* return basis.

## Summary

First Investors Variable Annuity C Discovery is one of the few variable annuity subaccounts to receive top honors in management. The total point score of this investment vehicle is very impressive. The combination of impressive performance and sound risk control makes this subaccount a great choice for any investor who wants the diversity and performance small cap stocks provide without getting badly burned during turbulent times.

There is still strong belief in academic circles and among those who market index funds that the market is so efficient that one cannot beat the averages. Discovery gives such thinking a black eye. The ability of this subaccount to distance itself from its peer group and from the Russell 2000 Index in both good and bad times is uncanny.

It is surprising that this First Investors' portfolio has not attracted more money. However, the general public's loss can work to your advantage. First Investors includes the all-important global or foreign equity category among the choices offered by the variable annuity. Overseas securities, which add enhanced returns and lower overall risk, are a critical step toward proper diversification.

## Profile

| | | | |
|---|---|---|---|
| Minimum investment | $2,000 | Telephone exchanges | no |
| Retirement account minimum | $2,000 | Transfers allowed per year | unlimited |
| Co-annuitant allowed | no | Maximum issuance age | 80 |
| Co-owner allowed | yes | Maximum annuitization age | 85 |
| Dollar-cost averaging | yes | Number of subaccounts | 9 |
| Systematic withdrawal plans | yes | Available in all 50 states | no* |

*Not available in the following states: AK, AR, DE, HI, ID, KS, ME, MT, NV, NH, NM, ND, SC, SD, and VT.

---

**John Hancock Independence Annuity**
**Aggressive Stock**
John Hancock Place
Boston, MA 02117
(800) 422-0237

---

| | |
|---|---|
| Performance | ✓ |
| Risk control | ✓✓✓✓ |
| Expense minimization | ✓✓✓ |
| Management | ✓✓✓ |
| Investment options | ✓✓ |
| Family rating | ✓✓✓ |
| Total point score | 19 points |

## Performance                                                    ✓

During the 3-year and 5-year periods ending December 31, 1994, Aggressive Stock had an average annual compound return of 5.7% and 9.3%, respectively. This means that a $10,000 investment made into this subaccount 5 years before that date grew to $15,600 ($11,800, if only the last 3 years of that period are used).

Compared to other aggressive growth variable annuity subaccounts, this one ranks in the bottom quartile for the 3-year period. The inception month of this subaccount was July 1990. The performance figures (shown below) for periods before the subaccount's inception in July 1990 are hypothetical, based on the underlying clone fund's returns. This subaccount is modeled (cloned) after the John Hancock Special Equities mutual fund, which had an inception date of March 1986, and has an asset base of $300 million.

The year-by-year returns for this subaccount and the mutual fund it is modeled after are:

| Year | Annual Return | Russell 2000 |
|---|---|---|
| 1994 | −2.9% | −1.8% |
| 1993 | 12.2% | 18.9% |
| 1992 | 8.4% | 18.4% |
| 1991 | 23.7% | 46.1% |
| 1990 | −8.7% | −19.5% |
| 1989 | 27.9% | 16.2% |
| 1988 | 20.6% | 24.9% |
| 1987 | −17.3% | −8.8% |

## Risk Control                                              ✓✓✓✓

Over the 3-year period studied, this fund was 25% safer than the average equity subaccount.

The typical standard deviation for aggressive growth subaccounts was 4.9% during the 3-year period. The standard deviation for this subaccount was 2.9% over this same period, which means that it was 41% less volatile than its peer group. The price/earnings (p/e) ratio averages 21 for this portfolio, compared to the typical aggressive growth subaccount's p/e ratio of 30. In general, the higher the p/e ratio, the riskier the portfolio.

The beta (market-related risk) of this subaccount was 0.9 over the 3-year period. Beta for this entire category was 1.2 over this same period. The market index (the S&P 500 Index for equity subaccounts) always has a beta of 1.0. The *risk-adjusted* return for this variable annuity subaccount can be described as good.

## Expense Minimization ✓✓✓✓

The typical expenses incurred by aggressive growth subaccounts are 2.1% per year. The total expenses for John Hancock Independence Annuity Aggressive Stock, 1.9%, are lower than its peer group average. Total expenses include all charges to the investor (except the annual contract charge, which is always expressed as a dollar figure), including management fees, overhead, administration, and mortality expenses. The free annual withdrawals percentage is based on the account value.

| | | | |
|---|---|---|---|
| Maximum surrender charge | 8% | Total expenses | 1.9% |
| Duration of surrender charge | 7 years | Annual contract charge | $30 |
| Declining surrender charge | yes | Free annual withdrawals | 10% |

## Management ✓✓✓✓

John Hancock Independence Annuity is offered by John Hancock Mutual Life Insurance Company. The company has a Duff & Phelps rating of AAA and an A.M. Best rating of A++. The portfolio (and/or the mutual fund it is modeled after) was managed by Samuel A. Otis for the 8 years ending December 31, 1994. The portfolio's size is $65 million. The typical security in the portfolio has a market capitalization of $12 billion.

## Investment Options ✓✓

Investors may make additional contributions into this portfolio at any time. This is known as a flexible premium annuity. Investors in this variable annuity can choose from all of the subaccount categories below that have a check mark:

| | | |
|---|---|---|
| ✓ Aggressive growth | ___ Government bonds | ✓ Money market |
| ✓ Balanced | ✓ Growth | ✓ Specialty/Sector |
| ✓ Corporate bonds | ___ Growth & income | ___ World bonds |
| ✓ Global equities (stocks) | ___ High-yield bonds | |

## Family Rating ✓✓✓

There are 7 subaccounts within the John Hancock Independence Annuity family. Overall, this family of subaccounts can be described as good on a *risk-adjusted* return basis.

## Summary

John Hancock Independence Annuity Aggressive Stock portfolio understands the importance of keeping risk to its barest minimum. John Hancock has long understood the many facets of risk and has incorporated this thinking in the advisor's management of this variable annuity subaccount.

The John Hancock Independence Annuity also deserves praise. The company is able to keep expenses low (something of particular importance when it comes to fixed-rate and bond subaccount performance) while still offering a number of investment category selections and features.

## Profile

| | | | |
|---|---|---|---|
| Minimum investment | $1,000 | Telephone exchanges | yes |
| Retirement account minimum | $1,000 | Transfers allowed per year | 12 |
| Co-annuitant allowed | no | Maximum issuance age | 84 |
| Co-owner allowed | yes | Maximum annuitization age | none |
| Dollar-cost averaging | no | Number of subaccounts | 7 |
| Systematic withdrawal plans | no | Available in all 50 states | no* |

*Not available in WA.

---

**Manulife Financial Variable Annuity**
**Separate Account 2**
**Emerging Growth Equity**
200 Bloor Street East
Toronto, Ontario, Canada M4W-IE5
(800) 387-2728

---

| | |
|---|---|
| Performance | ✓✓✓✓ |
| Risk control | ✓ |
| Expense minimization | ✓✓✓✓ |
| Management | ✓✓✓ |
| Investment options | ✓ |
| Family rating | ✓✓✓✓ |
| Total point score | 21 points |

---

## Performance                                           ✓✓✓✓

During the 3-year and 5-year periods ending December 31, 1994, Emerging Growth Equity had an average annual compound return of 3.8% and 6.5%, respectively. This means that a $10,000 investment made into this subaccount 5 years before that date grew to $13,700 ($11,200, if only the last 3 years of that period are used).

Compared to other aggressive growth variable annuity subaccounts, this one ranks in the top 5% for the 3-year period and in the top quartile for the 5-year period. The inception month of this subaccount was November 1987. This subaccount is modeled (cloned) after the Manulife Series Emerging Growth Equity Fund, which had an inception date of June 1984, and has an asset base of $50 million.

The year-by-year returns for this subaccount are:

| Year | Annual Return | Russell 2000 |
|---|---|---|
| 1994 | −5.2% | −1.8% |
| 1993 | 22.7% | 18.9% |
| 1992 | 20.6% | 18.4% |
| 1991 | 69.7% | 46.1% |
| 1990 | −15.8% | −19.5% |
| 1989 | 40.8% | 16.2% |
| 1988 | 15.8% | 24.9% |

## Risk Control                                                    ✓

Over the 3-year and 5-year periods studied, this fund was much riskier than the average equity subaccount.

The typical standard deviation for aggressive growth subaccounts was 4.9% during the 3-year period. The standard deviation for this subaccount was 6.6% over this same period, which means that it was 36% more volatile than its peer group. The price/earnings (p/e) ratio averages 23 for this portfolio, compared to the typical aggressive growth subaccount's p/e ratio of 30. In general, the higher the p/e ratio, the riskier the portfolio.

The beta (market-related risk) of this subaccount was 1.5 over the 3-year period. Beta for this entire category was 1.2 over this same period. The market index (the S&P 500 Index for equity subaccounts) always has a beta of 1.0. The *risk-adjusted* return for this variable annuity subaccount can be described as excellent.

## Expense Minimization    ✓✓✓✓

The typical expenses incurred by aggressive growth subaccounts are 2.1% per year. The total expenses for Manulife Financial Variable Annuity Separate Account 2 Emerging Growth Equity, 1.5%, are lower than its peer group average. Total expenses include all charges to the investor (except the annual contract charge, which is always expressed as a dollar figure), including management fees, overhead, administration, and mortality expenses. The free annual withdrawals percentage is based on the account value.

| | | | |
|---|---|---|---|
| Maximum surrender charge | 8% | Total expenses | 1.5% |
| Duration of surrender charge | 8 years | Annual contract charge | $30 |
| Declining surrender charge | yes | Free annual withdrawals | 10% |

## Management    ✓✓✓✓

Manulife Financial Variable Annuity Separate Account 2 is offered by Manufacturers Life Insurance Company of America. The company has a Duff & Phelps rating of AAA and an A.M. Best rating of A++. The portfolio was managed by Veronica Onyskiw, Angela Eaton, Diane Haflidson, and Steven Kahn for the 7 years ending December 31, 1994. The portfolio's size is $25 million. The typical security in the portfolio has a market capitalization of $205 million.

## Investment Options    ✓

Investors may make additional contributions into this portfolio at any time. This is known as a flexible premium annuity. Investors in this variable annuity can choose from all of the subaccount categories below that have a check mark:

| | | |
|---|---|---|
| ✓ Aggressive growth | ___ Government bonds | ✓ Money market |
| ✓ Balanced | ✓ Growth | ✓ Specialty/Sector |
| ✓ Corporate bonds | ___ Growth & income | ___ World bonds |
| ___ Global equities (stocks) | ___ High-yield bonds | |

## Family Rating    ✓✓✓✓

There are 6 subaccounts within the Manulife Financial Variable Annuity Separate Account 2 family. Overall, this family of subaccounts can be described as excellent on a *risk-adjusted* return basis.

The subaccounts within this variable annuity all have a death benefit based on the value at the date of death (what is referred to in the industry as "accumulated value"). Unlike the death benefit found with most variable annuities, the accumulated value death benefit does not protect the beneficiary from possible market loss.

## Summary

Manulife Financial Variable Annuity Separate Account 2 Emerging Growth Equity outperforms all other small-company and aggressive subaccounts in this book. It is easy to see how its 3-year record puts it in the very top tier of *all* subaccounts.

What cannot be fully appreciated within the confines of this review is the exceptional quality of other investment choices offered by Manulife Financial Variable Annuity Separate Account 2. Only a very small percentage of the variable annuity family universe has this type of performance across the board.

The parent company and this particular subaccount are to be commended for performance, management, and family rating. It is hoped that the contract will soon offer investors more investment selections. Although not the type of vehicle in which you would want to put all of your money, this would certainly be a wise choice for the aggressive growth, growth, and corporate bond portions of your total holdings.

## Profile

| | | | |
|---|---|---|---|
| Minimum investment | $1,000 | Telephone exchanges | yes |
| Retirement account minimum | $1,000 | Transfers allowed per year | 6 |
| Co-annuitant allowed | yes | Maximum issuance age | 70 |
| Co-owner allowed | yes | Maximum annuitization age | none |
| Dollar-cost averaging | yes | Number of subaccounts | 6 |
| Systematic withdrawal plans | no | Available in all 50 states | no* |

*Not available in ME, NJ, NY, and PR.

---

**Metropolitan Life Preference Plus Annuity**
**Aggressive Growth**
1 Madison Avenue
New York, NY  10010
(800) 553-4459

| | |
|---|---|
| Performance | ✓✓✓✓ |
| Risk control | ✓✓ |
| Expense minimization | ✓✓✓ |
| Management | ✓✓✓✓ |
| Investment options | ✓✓ |
| Family rating | ✓✓✓ |
| Total point score | 18 points |

---

## Performance                                                         ✓✓✓✓

During the 3-year period ending December 31, 1994, Aggressive Growth had an average annual compound return of 8.6%. This means that a $10,000 investment made into this subaccount 3 years before that date grew to $12,800.

Compared to other aggressive growth variable annuity subaccounts, this one ranks in the top quintile for the 3-year period. The inception month of this subaccount was July 1990. The performance figures (shown below) for periods before the subaccount's inception in July 1990 are hypothetical, based on the underlying clone fund's returns. This subaccount is modeled (cloned) after the Metropolitan Series Fund Aggressive Growth Portfolio, which had an inception date of April 1988, and has an asset base of $400 million.

The year-by-year returns for this subaccount and the portfolio it is modeled after are:

| Year | Annual Return | Russell 2000 |
|---|---|---|
| 1994 | −3.1% | −1.8% |
| 1993 | 21.1% | 18.9% |
| 1992 | 9.0% | 18.4% |
| 1991 | 64.4% | 46.1% |
| 1990 | −13.7% | −19.5% |
| 1989 | 31.6% | 16.2% |
| 1988 | 21.6% | 24.9% |

## Risk Control ✓✓

Over the 3-year period studied, this fund was somewhat riskier than the average equity subaccount.

The typical standard deviation for aggressive growth subaccounts was 4.9% during the 3-year period. The standard deviation for this subaccount was 5.6% over this same period, which means that it was 15% more volatile than its peer group. The price/earnings (p/e) ratio averages 33.3 for this portfolio, compared to the typical aggressive growth subaccount's p/e ratio of 30. In general, the higher the p/e ratio, the riskier the portfolio.

The beta (market-related risk) of this subaccount was 1.5 over the 3-year period. Beta for this entire category was 1.2 over this same period. The market index (the S&P 500 Index for equity subaccounts) always has a beta of 1.0. The *risk-adjusted* return for this variable annuity subaccount can be described as very good.

## Expense Minimization ✓✓✓

The typical expenses incurred by aggressive growth subaccounts are 2.1% per year. The total expenses for Metropolitan Life Preference Plus Annuity Aggressive Growth, 2.0%, are lower than its peer group average. Total expenses include all charges to the investor (except the annual contract charge, which is always expressed as a dollar figure), including management fees, overhead, administration, and mortality expenses. The free annual withdrawals percentage is based on the account value.

| | | | |
|---|---|---|---|
| Maximum surrender charge | 7% | Total expenses | 2.0% |
| Duration of surrender charge | 7 years | Annual contract charge | $0 |
| Declining surrender charge | yes | Free annual withdrawals | 10% |

## Management ✓✓✓✓

Metropolitan Life Preference Plus Annuity is offered by Metropolitan Life Insurance Company. The company has a Duff & Phelps rating of AAA and an A.M. Best rating of A+. The portfolio has been managed by Frederick R. Kobrick for the 6 years ending December 31, 1994. The portfolio's size is $250 million. The typical security in the portfolio has a market capitalization of $1.3 billion. Kobrick also manages the Met Life-State Street Capital Appreciation mutual fund.

## Investment Options ✓✓

Investors may make additional contributions into this portfolio at any time. This is known as a flexible premium annuity. Investors in this variable annuity can choose from all of the subaccount categories below that have a check mark:

| | | |
|---|---|---|
| ✓ Aggressive growth | ___ Government bonds | ___ Money market |
| ✓ Balanced | ✓ Growth | ___ Specialty/Sector |
| ✓ Corporate bonds | ✓ Growth & income | ___ World bonds |
| ✓ Global equities (stocks) | ___ High-yield bonds | |

## Family Rating ✓✓✓

There are 7 subaccounts within the Metropolitan Life Preference Plus Annuity family. Overall, this family of subaccounts can be described as good on a *risk-adjusted* return basis.

The subaccounts within this variable annuity all have an *increasing* guaranteed death benefit. This means that the beneficiary is guaranteed to receive *the greater of* the contract's value on the date of the annuitant's death or the value of the original investment(s) compounded by 5% each year (less any withdrawals made).

## Summary

Metropolitan Life Preference Plus Annuity Aggressive Growth's performance and management are impressive enough that one might think they would be a little more exclusive, yet this annuity has no minimum investment requirements. Other features of this fine contract are also quite liberal. This is one of the few contracts that does not impose an annual contract charge.

The Aggressive Growth portfolio is a smart choice for anyone who wants to beat the market most of the time. The fact that this Metropolitan Life annuity also offers a wide range of other equity subaccounts should not go unnoticed. Metropolitan has concentrated its desire for category diversification within equities, and this is a wise decision. Study after study shows that the ideal candidate or investor for a variable annuity is the stock investor.

## Profile

| | | | |
|---|---|---|---|
| Minimum investment | none | Telephone exchanges | yes |
| Retirement account minimum | none | Transfers allowed per year | unlimited |
| Co-annuitant allowed | no | Maximum issuance age | 99 |
| Co-owner allowed | yes | Maximum annuitization age | none |
| Dollar-cost averaging | yes | Number of subaccounts | 7 |
| Systematic withdrawal plans | no | Available in all 50 states | no* |

*Not available in NJ or WA.

# Chapter

**8**

# Balanced Subaccounts

The objective of balanced subaccounts, also referred to as *total return subaccounts,* is to provide both growth and income. Subaccount management purchases common stocks, bonds, and convertible securities. Portfolio composition is almost always completely comprised of U.S. securities. Weighting of stocks versus bonds depends on the portfolio manager's perception of the stock market, interest rates, and risk levels. Rarely is less than 30% of the subaccount's holdings in stocks or bonds.

Balanced subaccounts offer neither the best nor the worst of both worlds. These subaccounts will often outperform the different categories of bond subaccounts during bull markets, but suffer greater percentage losses during stock market declines. Conversely, when interest rates are on the rise, balanced subaccounts will typically decline less on a total return basis (current yield plus or minus principal appreciation) than a bond subaccount. When rates are falling, balanced subaccounts can also outperform bond subaccounts if stocks are also doing well.

Balanced subaccounts are the perfect choice for the investor who cannot decide between stocks and bonds. This hybrid security is a middle-of-the-road approach, ideal for someone who wants a subaccount manager to determine the portfolio's weighting of stocks, bonds, and convertibles.

The table at the top of page 39 shows year-by-year, as well as 3-, 5-, and 10-year averages for this investment category. The variable annuity subaccount category is compared against the similar mutual fund category. These performance figures are average figures, representing all funds and subaccounts that fall within this investment objective.

As you can see, the variable annuity subaccounts outperformed their mutual fund counterparts for 1990 and 1987.

Conservative investors should have no more than 40% of their portfolios committed to this category. Moderate investors could place up to 80% of their holdings in balanced subaccounts. These high levels assume that a portfolio's diversification is largely dependent on using only a few categories of variable annuity subaccounts. I recommend a 20% commitment to this category for the conservative investor and only 10% for the moderate portfolio. As is true with any category of

### Average Annual Returns:
### Balanced Subaccounts vs. Balanced Mutual Funds

| Year | Subaccount | Mutual Fund |
|---|---|---|
| 1994 | −3.9% | −2.8% |
| 1993 | 11.3% | 11.2% |
| 1992 | 6.8% | 7.1% |
| 1991 | 22.8% | 26.4% |
| 1990 | 0.1% | −0.6% |
| 1989 | 18.5% | 19.6% |
| 1988 | 11.0% | 12.2% |
| 1987 | 2.1% | 1.8% |
| 3-yr. average | 4.3% | 5.1% |
| 5-yr. average | 7.0% | 7.8% |
| 10-yr. average | 10.4% | 11.5% |

variable annuities, whenever larger dollar amounts are involved, more than one subaccount per category should be used.

The table below shows statistics you might find useful when comparing variable annuity subaccounts versus their mutual fund counterparts or "clones." The category averages are based on information available at the beginning of 1995.

### Balanced Category Statistics:
### Subaccounts vs. Mutual Funds

| Description | Subaccounts | Funds |
|---|---|---|
| **Composition of portfolio** | | |
| U.S. stocks | 40% | 47% |
| Cash | 15% | 9% |
| Foreign stocks | 11% | 7% |
| Bonds | 29% | 34% |
| Other | 5% | 3% |
| **Fees and expenses** | | |
| Underlying fund expense | 0.75% | 1.20% |
| Insurance expense | 1.25% | — |
| Total expenses | 2.0% | 1.20%/3.3%* |
| **Operations** | | |
| Net assets (in millions) | $151 | $530 |
| Manager tenure | 5 years | 5 years |
| **Portfolio statistics** | | |
| Beta | 0.6% | 0.7% |
| Standard deviation | 2.0% | 2.5% |
| Price/earnings ratio | 23 | 22 |
| Turnover ratio (annual) | 82% | 77% |
| Median market capitalization | $6.6 billion | $7.3 billion |
| Number of subaccounts/funds | 175 | 110 |

*Total expenses for this mutual fund category increase to this figure if the average mutual fund commission is added to the 1.20% figure.

Figure 8.1 shows the year-by-year returns for this category of variable annuities for the period 1987 through 1994. These are composite figures and therefore include all of the subaccounts that comprise the balanced category.

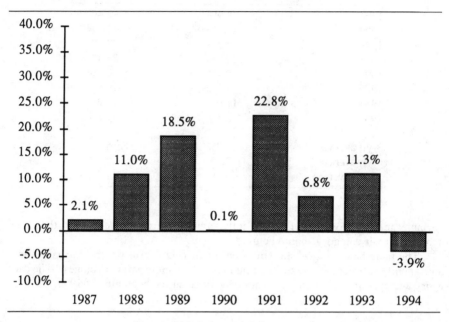

**Figure 8.1** Balanced Subaccounts

**American United Life Variable Annuity**
**Fidelity Asset Manager**
P.O. Box 368
Indianapolis, IN 46206-0368
(800) 634-1629

| | |
|---|---|
| Performance | ✓✓✓✓ |
| Risk control | ✓✓✓✓ |
| Expense minimization | ✓✓✓ |
| Management | ✓✓✓✓ |
| Investment options | ✓✓✓ |
| Family rating | ✓ |
| Total point score | 22 points |

## Performance                                    ✓✓✓✓

During the 3-year and 5-year periods ending December 31, 1994, Fidelity Asset Manager had an average annual compound return of 7.0% and 8.8%, respectively. This means that a $10,000 investment made into this subaccount 5 years before that date grew to $15,200 ($12,300, if only the last 3 years of that period are used).

Compared to other balanced variable annuity subaccounts, this one ranks in the top 5% for the 3-year period. The inception month of this subaccount was May 1993. The performance figures (shown below) for periods before the subaccount's inception in May 1993 are hypothetical, based on the underlying clone fund's returns. This subaccount is modeled (cloned) after the Fidelity VIP II Fund Asset Manager Portfolio, which had an inception date of September 1989, and has an asset base of $1.8 billion.

The year-by-year returns for this subaccount and the portfolio it is modeled after are:

| Year | Annual Return | S&P 500 | Lehman Bros. Gov't/Corp. Bond Index |
|---|---|---|---|
| 1994 | −7.3% | 1.3% | −3.5% |
| 1993 | 22.4% | 10.1% | 11.1% |
| 1992 | 13.1% | 7.6% | 7.6% |
| 1991 | 21.0% | 30.5% | 16.1% |
| 1990 | 5.4% | −3.1% | 8.3% |
| 1989 | 15.3% | 31.7% | 14.2% |

## Risk Control                                    ✓✓✓✓

Over the 3-year period studied, this fund was substantially safer than the average hybrid subaccount.

The typical standard deviation for balanced subaccounts was 2.0% during the 3-year period. The standard deviation for this subaccount was 1.6% over this same period, which means that it was 21% less volatile than its peer group. The price/earnings (p/e) ratio averages 25 for this portfolio, compared to the typical balanced subaccount's p/e ratio of 23. In general, the higher the p/e ratio, the riskier the portfolio.

The beta (market-related risk) of this subaccount was 0.4 over the 3-year period. Beta for this entire category was 0.6 over this same period. The market index (the S&P 500 Index for "hybrid" subaccounts such as balanced subaccounts) always has a beta of 1.0. The *risk-adjusted* return for this variable annuity subaccount can be described as very good.

## Expense Minimization ✓✓✓

The typical expenses incurred by balanced subaccounts are 2.0% per year. The total expenses for American United Life Variable Annuity Fidelity Asset Manager, 2.2%, are higher than its peer group average. Total expenses include all charges to the investor (except the annual contract charge, which is always expressed as a dollar figure), including management fees, overhead, administration, and mortality expenses. The free annual withdrawals percentage is based on the account value.

| | | | |
|---|---|---|---|
| Maximum surrender charge | 8% | Total expenses | 2.2% |
| Duration of surrender charge | 10 years | Annual contract charge | $30 |
| Declining surrender charge | no | Free annual withdrawals | 10% |

## Management ✓✓✓✓✓

American United Life Variable Annuity is offered by American United Life Insurance Company. The company has a Duff & Phelps rating of AA+ and an A.M. Best rating of A+. The portfolio (and/or the mutual fund it is modeled after) was managed by Robert A. Beckwitt for the 5 years ending December 31, 1994. The portfolio's size is a mere $1 million. The typical security in the portfolio has a market capitalization of $3.8 billion. Beckwitt also manages the Fidelity Asset Manager mutual fund.

## Investment Options ✓✓✓

Investors may make additional contributions into this portfolio at any time. This is known as a flexible premium annuity. Investors in this variable annuity can choose from all of the subaccount categories below that have a check mark:

| | | |
|---|---|---|
| ___ Aggressive growth | ___ Government bonds | ✓ Money market |
| ✓ Balanced | ✓ Growth | ___ Specialty/Sector |
| ✓ Corporate bonds | ✓ Growth & income | ___ World bonds |
| ✓ Global equities (stocks) | ✓ High-yield bonds | |

## Family Rating ✓

There are 9 subaccounts within the American United Life Variable Annuity family. The subaccounts within this variable annuity all have a death benefit based on the value at the date of death (what is referred to in the industry as "accumulated value"). Unlike the death benefit found with most variable annuities, the accumulated value death benefit does not protect the beneficiary from possible market loss.

## Summary

American United Life Variable Annuity Fidelity Asset Manager gets a perfect score in the most important categories: performance, risk control, and management. Very few variable annuity subaccounts can boast of this type of score.

The contract itself offers some important features: a low initial investment, a systematic withdrawal plan for the income-oriented investor, an unlimited number of telephone exchanges, no age restrictions, and availability in every state. The contract has few other star performers, but investors need not be overly concerned. The diverse nature of this particular subaccount is such that it offers something for everyone. However, the contract is available only for qualified accounts (i.e., IRAs, pension plans, Keoghs, and so on).

Fidelity Asset Manager is one of the very best balanced or "asset allocation" portfolios to appear in this book. This offering by American United Life Variable Annuity is an ideal choice for investors who want the best of all worlds.

## Profile

| | | | |
|---|---|---|---|
| Minimum investment | $300 | Telephone exchanges | yes |
| Retirement account minimum | n/a | Transfers allowed per year | unlimited |
| Co-annuitant allowed | no | Maximum issuance age | none |
| Co-owner allowed | no | Maximum annuitization age | none |
| Dollar-cost averaging | no | Number of subaccounts | 9 |
| Systematic withdrawal plans | yes | Available in all 50 states | yes |

---

**Dean Witter Variable Annuity II**
**Managed Assets**
Two World Trade Center
74th Floor
New York, NY 10048
(800) 869-3863

---

| | |
|---|---|
| Performance | ✓✓✓ |
| Risk control | ✓✓ |
| Expense minimization | ✓✓✓✓ |
| Management | ✓✓✓ |
| Investment options | ✓✓✓✓ |
| Family rating | ✓✓✓✓ |
| Total point score | 20 points |

---

## Performance                                                        ✓✓✓

During the 3-year and 5-year periods ending December 31, 1994, Managed Assets had an average annual compound return of 5.7% and 8.4%, respectively. This means that a $10,000 investment made into this subaccount 5 years before that date grew to $15,000 ($11,800, if only the last 3 years of that period are used).

Compared to other balanced variable annuity subaccounts, this one ranks in the top half for the 3-year period. The inception month of this subaccount was October 1990. The performance figures (shown below) for periods before the subaccount's inception in October 1990 are hypothetical, based on the underlying clone fund's returns. This subaccount is modeled (cloned) after the Dean Witter VIS Managed Assets Portfolio, which had an inception date of March 1987, and has an asset base of $220 million.

The year-by-year returns for this subaccount and the portfolio it is modeled after are:

| Year | Annual Return | S&P 500 | Lehman Bros. Gov't/Corp. Bond Index |
|---|---|---|---|
| 1994 | 2.6% | 1.3% | −3.5% |
| 1993 | 8.9% | 10.1% | 11.1% |
| 1992 | 5.8% | 7.6% | 7.6% |
| 1991 | 26.5% | 30.5% | 16.1% |
| 1990 | −1.0% | −3.1% | 8.3% |
| 1989 | 9.5% | 31.7% | 14.2% |

## Risk Control ✓✓

Over the 3-year period studied, this fund was a little safer than the average hybrid subaccount.

The typical standard deviation for balanced subaccounts was 2.0% during the 3-year period. The standard deviation for this subaccount was 2.8% over this same period, which means that it was 37% more volatile than its peer group. The price/earnings (p/e) ratio averages 24 for this portfolio, compared to the typical balanced subaccount's p/e ratio of 23. In general, the higher the p/e ratio, the riskier the portfolio.

The beta (market-related risk) of this subaccount was 0.8 over the 3-year period. Beta for this entire category was 0.6 over this same period. The market index (the S&P 500 Index for "hybrid" subaccounts such as balanced subaccounts) always has a beta of 1.0. The *risk-adjusted* return for this variable annuity subaccount can be described as fair.

## Expense Minimization ✓✓✓

The typical expenses incurred by balanced subaccounts are 2.0% per year. The total expenses for Dean Witter Variable Annuity II Managed Assets, 1.9%, are lower than its peer group average. Total expenses include all charges to the investor (except the annual contract charge, which is always expressed as a dollar figure), including management fees, overhead, administration, and mortality expenses. The free annual withdrawals percentage is based on the original principal.

| | | | |
|---|---|---|---|
| Maximum surrender charge | 6% | Total expenses | 1.9% |
| Duration of surrender charge | 6 years | Annual contract charge | $30 |
| Declining surrender charge | yes | Free annual withdrawals | 15% |

## Management ✓✓✓

Dean Witter Variable Annuity II is offered by Northbrook Life Insurance Company. The company has an A.M. Best rating of A+. The portfolio (and/or the mutual fund it is modeled after) was managed by Kenton Hinchliffe for the 7 years ending December 31, 1994. The portfolio's size is $170 million. The typical security in the portfolio has a market capitalization of $9.3 billion. Hinchliffe also manages the Dean Witter Managed Assets mutual fund.

## Investment Options ✓✓✓

Investors may make additional contributions into this portfolio at any time. This is known as a flexible premium annuity. Investors in this variable annuity can choose from all of the subaccount categories below that have a check mark:

| | | |
|---|---|---|
| ___ Aggressive growth | ___ Government bonds | ✓ Money market |
| ✓ Balanced | ✓ Growth | ✓ Specialty/Sector |
| ✓ Corporate bonds | ✓ Growth & income | ___ World bonds |
| ✓ Global equities (stocks) | ✓ High-yield bonds | |

## Family Rating ✓✓✓

There are 11 subaccounts within the Dean Witter Variable Annuity II family. Overall, this family of subaccounts can be described as *very good* on a *risk-adjusted* return basis.

The subaccounts within this variable annuity all have an *increasing* guaranteed death benefit. This means that the beneficiary is guaranteed to receive *the greater of* the contract's value on the date of the annuitant's death or the value of the original investment(s) compounded by 5% each year (less any withdrawals made).

## Summary

Dean Witter Variable Annuity II Managed Assets turns in a solid and consistent score across the board; it is a good example of what you can expect from a well-managed balanced portfolio.

Managed Assets is just one of the great subaccounts offered by Dean Witter Variable Annuity II. This annuity includes a wide range of excellent investment choices and features, such as its free 15% annual withdrawal privilege and liberal issuance age.

## Profile

| | | | |
|---|---|---|---|
| Minimum investment | $1,000 | Telephone exchanges | yes |
| Retirement account minimum | $4,000 | Transfers allowed per year | 12 |
| Co-annuitant allowed | no | Maximum issuance age | 90 |
| Co-owner allowed | yes | Maximum annuitization age | 85 |
| Dollar-cost averaging | yes | Number of subaccounts | 11 |
| Systematic withdrawal plans | yes | Available in all 50 states | yes |

---

**Equitable Momentum Plus**
**Balanced**
787 Seventh Avenue
New York, NY 10019
(800) 528-0204

---

| | |
|---|---|
| Performance | ✓✓✓✓ |
| Risk control | ✓✓✓ |
| Expense minimization | ✓✓✓✓ |
| Management | ✓✓ |
| Investment options | ✓✓✓ |
| Family rating | ✓✓✓ |
| Total point score | 19 points |

## Performance ✓✓✓✓

During the 3-year and 5-year periods ending December 31, 1994, Balanced had an average annual compound return of −1.2% and 5.9%, respectively. This means that a $10,000 investment made into this subaccount 5 years before that date grew to $13,300 ($9,600, if only the last 3 years of that period are used).

The inception month of this subaccount was September 1993. The performance figures (shown below) for periods before the subaccount's inception in September 1993 are hypothetical, based on the underlying clone fund's returns. This subaccount is modeled (cloned) after the Hudson River Trust Balanced Portfolio, which had an inception date of January 1986, and has an asset base of $1.3 billion.

The year-by-year returns for this subaccount and the portfolio it is modeled after are:

| Year | Annual Return | S&P 500 | Lehman Bros. Gov't/Corp. Bond Index |
|------|------|------|------|
| 1994 | −9.3% | 1.3% | −3.5% |
| 1993 | 12.6% | 10.1% | 11.1% |
| 1992 | −4.0% | 7.6% | 7.6% |
| 1991 | 41.4% | 30.5% | 16.1% |
| 1990 | 0.6% | −3.1% | 8.3% |
| 1989 | 25.1% | 31.7% | 14.2% |
| 1988 | 13.6% | 16.6% | 7.6% |

## Risk Control                                                    ✓✓✓

Over the 3-year period studied, this fund was about as safe as the average hybrid subaccount.

The price/earnings (p/e) ratio averages 24 for this portfolio, compared to the typical balanced subaccount's p/e ratio of 23. In general, the higher the p/e ratio, the riskier the portfolio.

## Expense Minimization                                            ✓✓✓✓

The typical expenses incurred by balanced subaccounts are 2.0% per year. The total expenses for Equitable Momentum Plus Balanced, 1.8%, are lower than its peer group average. Total expenses include all charges to the investor (except the annual contract charge, which is always expressed as a dollar figure), including management fees, overhead, administration, and mortality expenses. The free annual withdrawals percentage is based on the account value.

| | | | |
|------|------|------|------|
| Maximum surrender charge | 6% | Total expenses | 1.8% |
| Duration of surrender charge | 5 years | Annual contract charge | $25 |
| Declining surrender charge | no | Free annual withdrawals | 10% |

## Management                                                      ✓✓

Equitable Momentum Plus is offered by Equitable Life Assurance Society of the United States. The company has a Duff & Phelps rating of A+. The portfolio (and/or the mutual fund it is modeled after) was managed by Judith A. Taylor for the 6 years ending December 31, 1994. The portfolio's size is a whopping $1.4 billion. The typical security in the portfolio has a market capitalization of $2.0 billion. Taylor also manages the Alliance Balanced mutual fund.

## Investment Options                                              ✓✓✓

Investors may make additional contributions into this portfolio at any time. This is known as a flexible premium annuity. Investors in this variable annuity can choose from all of the subaccount categories below that have a check mark:

| | | |
|------|------|------|
| ✓ Aggressive growth | ✓ Government bonds | ✓ Money market |
| ✓ Balanced | ✓ Growth | ___ Specialty/Sector |
| ___ Corporate bonds | ___ Growth & income | ___ World bonds |
| ✓ Global equities (stocks) | ✓ High-yield bonds | |

## Family Rating ✓✓✓

There are 10 subaccounts within the Equitable Momentum Plus family. Overall, this family of subaccounts can be described as good on a *risk-adjusted* return basis. The subaccounts within this variable annuity all have a death benefit based on the value at the date of death (what is referred to in the industry as "accumulated value"). Unlike the death benefit found with most variable annuities, the accumulated value death benefit does not protect the beneficiary from possible market loss.

## Summary

Equitable Momentum Plus Balanced is a fine example of very good performance and expense minimization. Equitable Life Assurance Society of the United States dominates the balanced category; three of its subaccounts appear in this book. It is easy to see why this subaccount is so popular with investors. It has attracted more money than the vast majority of other subaccounts in *any* category. However, the contract is available only for qualified accounts (i.e., IRAs, pension plans, Keoghs, and so on).

Equitable Momentum Plus provides one of the more appealing variable annuity contracts. The levels of its surrender charge and duration are both on the low end of the scale, making this more palatable to investors. The contract also has a dollar-cost averaging program, to reduce market risk; allows a co-annuitant, which helps reduce the likelihood of triggering an unwanted tax event; and accepts investments of all sizes.

## Profile

| | | | |
|---|---|---|---|
| Minimum investment | n/a | Telephone exchanges | yes |
| Retirement account minimum | n/a | Transfers allowed per year | n/a |
| Co-annuitant allowed | yes | Maximum issuance age | none |
| Co-owner allowed | no | Maximum annuitization age | none |
| Dollar-cost averaging | yes | Number of subaccounts | 10 |
| Systematic withdrawal plans | no | Available in all 50 states | no* |

*Not available in CA, PA, or WA.

---

**Fortis Benefits Opportunity Annuity**
**Asset Allocation**
P.O. Box 64272
St. Paul, MN 55164
(800) 800-2638

| | |
|---|---|
| Performance | ✓✓ |
| Risk control | ✓✓✓✓ |
| Expense minimization | ✓✓✓✓ |
| Management | ✓✓✓ |
| Investment options | ✓✓✓ |
| Family rating | ✓✓✓ |
| Total point score | 19 points |

## Performance ✓✓

During the 3-year and 5-year periods ending December 31, 1994, Asset Allocation had an average annual compound return of 4.0% and 7.3%, respectively. This means that a $10,000 investment made into this subaccount 5 years before that date grew to $14,200 ($11,200, if only the last 3 years of that period are used).

Compared to other balanced variable annuity subaccounts, this one ranks as average for the 3-year period but in the top quartile for the 5-year period. The inception month of this subaccount was May 1988. This subaccount is modeled (cloned) after the Fortis Series Fund Asset Allocation Series, which had an inception date of April 1987, and has an asset base of $180 million.

The year-by-year returns for this subaccount are:

| Year | Annual Return | S&P 500 | Lehman Bros. Gov't/Corp. Bond Index |
|------|------|------|------|
| 1994 | −1.7% | 1.3% | −3.5% |
| 1993 | 8.0% | 10.1% | 11.1% |
| 1992 | 5.4% | 7.6% | 7.6% |
| 1991 | 25.9% | 30.5% | 16.1% |
| 1990 | 0.6% | −3.1% | 8.3% |
| 1989 | 22.1% | 31.7% | 14.2% |
| 1988 | 2.2% | 16.6% | 7.6% |

## Risk Control                                               ✓✓✓✓

Over the 3-year period studied, this fund was 36% safer than the average hybrid subaccount. During the 5-year period, it was 35% safer.

The typical standard deviation for balanced subaccounts was 2.0% during the 3-year period. The standard deviation for Fortis Benefits Opportunity Annuity Asset Allocation was 1.8% over this same period, which means that this subaccount was 12% less volatile than its peer group. The price/earnings (p/e) ratio averages 32 for this portfolio. The typical balanced subaccount has a p/e ratio of 23. In general, the higher the p/e ratio, the riskier the portfolio.

The beta (market-related risk) of this subaccount was 0.5 over the 3-year period. Beta for this entire category was 0.6 over this same period. The market index (the S&P 500 Index for "hybrid" subaccounts such as balanced subaccounts) always has a beta of 1.0. The *risk-adjusted* return for this variable annuity subaccount can be described as very good.

## Expense Minimization                                       ✓✓✓✓

The typical expenses incurred by balanced subaccounts are 2.0% per year. The total expenses for Fortis Benefits Opportunity Annuity Asset Allocation, 2.0%, are lower than its peer group average. Total expenses include all charges to the investor (except the annual contract charge, which is always expressed as a dollar figure), including management fees, overhead, administration, and mortality expenses. The free annual withdrawals percentage is based on the original principal.

| | | | |
|------|------|------|------|
| Maximum surrender charge | 5% | Total expenses | 2.0% |
| Duration of surrender charge | 5 years | Annual contract charge | $35 |
| Declining surrender charge | yes | Free annual withdrawals | 10% |

## Management ✓✓✓

Fortis Benefits Opportunity Annuity is offered by Fortis Benefits Insurance Company. The company has an A.M. Best rating of A+. The portfolio (and/or the mutual fund it is modeled after) was managed by Dennis Ott and Stephen Poling for the 7 years ending December 31, 1994. The portfolio's size is $115 million. The typical security in the portfolio has a market capitalization of $3.7 billion. Ott and Poling also manage the Fortis Advantage Portfolios Asset Allocation Portfolio.

## Investment Options ✓✓✓

Investors may make additional contributions into this portfolio at any time. This is known as a flexible premium annuity. Investors in this variable annuity can choose from all of the subaccount categories below that have a check mark:

|  |  |  |
|---|---|---|
| ___ Aggressive growth | ✓ Government bonds | ✓ Money market |
| ✓ Balanced | ✓ Growth | ___ Specialty/Sector |
| ✓ Corporate bonds | ___ Growth & income | ___ World bonds |
| ✓ Global equities (stocks) | ___ High-yield bonds | |

## Family Rating ✓✓✓

There are 6 subaccounts within the Fortis Benefits Opportunity Annuity family. Overall, this family of subaccounts can be described as good on a *risk-adjusted* return basis.

## Summary

Fortis Benefits Opportunity Annuity Asset Allocation represents a breed of management that is all too often missing in the financial marketplace: respectable returns coupled with low risk. Since its inception, this subaccount has never had a negative year. This portfolio is a good choice for the nervous or uncertain investor.

The Fortis Benefits Opportunity Annuity contract provides some very appealing features: a low minimum investment requirement, the ability to name a co-owner, dollar-cost averaging for those who want to slowly percolate into stocks and bonds, a systematic withdrawal plan for investors interested in receiving a monthly or quarterly check, unlimited telephone exchanges, and a liberal issuance age. The surrender charges and their duration are also some of the best in the entire annuity industry.

## Profile

| | | | |
|---|---|---|---|
| Minimum investment | $50 | Telephone exchanges | yes |
| Retirement account minimum | $50 | Transfers allowed per year | unlimited |
| Co-annuitant allowed | no | Maximum issuance age | 90 |
| Co-owner allowed | yes | Maximum annuitization age | 70.5 |
| Dollar-cost averaging | yes | Number of subaccounts | 6 |
| Systematic withdrawal plans | yes | Available in all 50 states | no* |

*Not available in NJ or NY.

---

**Franklin Valuemark II**
**Income Securities**
10 Valley Stream Parkway
Malvern, PA 19355
(800) 342-3863

---

| | |
|---|---|
| Performance | ✓✓✓✓✓ |
| Risk control | ✓✓✓✓✓ |
| Expense minimization | ✓✓✓ |
| Management | ✓✓✓✓✓ |
| Investment options | ✓✓✓✓✓ |
| Family rating | ✓✓ |
| Total point score | 25 points |

## Performance ✓✓✓✓✓

During the 3-year and 5-year periods ending December 31, 1994, Income Securities had an average annual compound return of 6.5% and 8.7%, respectively. This means that a $10,000 investment made into this subaccount 5 years before that date grew to $15,200 ($12,100, if only the last 3 years of that period are used).

Compared to other balanced variable annuity subaccounts, this one ranks in the top 2% for the 3-year period. The inception month of this subaccount was June 1989. The performance figures (shown below) for periods before the subaccount's inception in June 1989 are hypothetical, based on the underlying clone fund's returns. This subaccount is modeled (cloned) after the Franklin Income Series, a mutual fund that had an inception date of August 1948, and has an asset base of $4.5 billion.

The year-by-year returns for this subaccount and the mutual fund it is modeled after are:

| Year | Annual Return | S&P 500 | Lehman Bros. Gov't/Corp. Bond Index |
|---|---|---|---|
| 1994 | −7.6% | 1.3% | −3.5% |
| 1993 | 17.0% | 10.1% | 11.1% |
| 1992 | 11.6% | 7.6% | 7.6% |
| 1991 | 38.0% | 30.5% | 16.1% |
| 1990 | −8.7% | −3.1% | 8.3% |
| 1989 | 12.7% | 31.7% | 14.2% |
| 1988 | 8.8% | 16.6% | 7.6% |
| 1987 | 4.9% | 5.3% | 2.3% |

## Risk Control ✓✓✓✓✓

Over the 3-year period studied, this fund was dramatically safer than the average hybrid subaccount.

The typical standard deviation for balanced subaccounts was 2.0% during the 3-year period. The standard deviation for Franklin Valuemark II Income Securities was 1.8% over this same period, which means that this subaccount was 11% less volatile than its peer group. The price/earnings (p/e) ratio averages 17 for this portfolio. The typical balanced subaccount has a p/e ratio of 23. In general, the higher the p/e ratio, the riskier the portfolio.

The beta (market-related risk) of this subaccount was 0.3 over the 3-year period. Beta for this entire category was 0.6 over this same period. The market index

(the S&P 500 Index for "hybrid" subaccounts such as balanced subaccounts) always has a beta of 1.0. The *risk-adjusted* return for this variable annuity subaccount can be described as excellent.

## Expense Minimization ✓✓✓

The typical expenses incurred by balanced subaccounts are 2.0% per year. The total expenses for Franklin Valuemark II Income Securities, 2.1%, are higher than its peer group average. Total expenses include all charges to the investor (except the annual contract charge, which is always expressed as a dollar figure), including management fees, overhead, administration, and mortality expenses. The free annual withdrawals percentage is based on the original principal.

| | | | |
|---|---|---|---|
| Maximum surrender charge | 5% | Total expenses | 2.1% |
| Duration of surrender charge | 5 years | Annual contract charge | $30 |
| Declining surrender charge | yes | Free annual withdrawals | 15% |

## Management ✓✓✓✓✓

Franklin Valuemark II is offered by Allianz Life Insurance Company of North America. The company has an A.M. Best rating of A+. The portfolio was managed by Matthew Avery and Charles Johnson for the 5 years ending December 31, 1994. The portfolio's size is $550 million. The typical security in the portfolio has a market capitalization of $7.4 billion. Avery and Johnson also manage the Franklin Income Series mutual fund.

## Investment Options ✓✓✓✓✓

Investors may make additional contributions into this portfolio at any time. This is known as a flexible premium annuity. Investors in this variable annuity can choose from all of the subaccount categories below that have a check mark:

| | | |
|---|---|---|
| ___ Aggressive growth | ✓ Government bonds | ✓ Money market |
| ✓ Balanced | ✓ Growth | ✓ Specialty/Sector |
| ✓ Corporate bonds | ___ Growth & income | ✓ World bonds |
| ✓ Global equities (stocks) | ✓ High-yield bonds | |

## Family Rating ✓✓

There are 18 subaccounts within the Franklin Valuemark II family. Overall, this family of subaccounts can be described as fair on a *risk-adjusted* return basis.

The subaccounts within this variable annuity all have an *increasing* guaranteed death benefit. This means that the beneficiary is guaranteed to receive *the greater of* the contract's value on the date of the annuitant's death or the value of the original investment(s) compounded by 5% each year (less any withdrawals made).

## Summary

Franklin Valuemark II Income Securities has an exceptional track record. Over the 3 years studied, this balanced portfolio managed to outperform both the stock market and the bond market. This is nothing short of amazing, considering how well this subaccount does at managing risk. In fact, this account scores a perfect score in all of the important categories: performance, risk control, management, and investment options. This balanced portfolio is highly recommended.

The Franklin Valuemark II is one of the best annuity contracts in the industry. Valuemark II has some of the very best contract provisions: 15% free withdrawals per year (vs. an industry average of 10%), a 5-year penalty schedule (vs. a 7-year average), allowing co-annuitants and co-ownership between spouses, and availability in all 50 states. It is no surprise to see that this variable annuity has become the industry's number-one seller. The number of investment choices is immense. Several other members of this family appear elsewhere in this book.

## Profile

| | | | |
|---|---|---|---|
| Minimum investment | $2,000 | Telephone exchanges | yes |
| Retirement account minimum | $5,000 | Transfers allowed per year | 12 |
| Co-annuitant allowed | yes | Maximum issuance age | none |
| Co-owner allowed | spouses only | Maximum annuitization age | 80 |
| Dollar-cost averaging | yes | Number of subaccounts | 18 |
| Systematic withdrawal plans | yes | Available in all 50 states | yes |

---

**Golden American GoldenSelect**
**Fully Managed**
1001 Jefferson Street
Suite 400
Wilmington, DE  19801
(800) 243-3706

---

| | |
|---|---|
| Performance | ✓✓ |
| Risk control | ✓ |
| Expense minimization | ✓✓✓ |
| Management | ✓ |
| Investment options | ✓✓✓ |
| Family rating | ✓ |
| Total point score | 11 points |

## Performance                                                    ✓✓

During the 3-year and 5-year periods ending December 31, 1994, Fully Managed had an average annual compound return of 0.9% and 4.7%, respectively. This means that a $10,000 investment made into this subaccount 5 years before that date grew to $12,600 ($10,300 for the last 3 years).

Compared to other balanced variable annuity subaccounts, this one ranks a little below average for the 3-year period. The inception month of this subaccount was January 1989. This subaccount is modeled (cloned) after the GCG Trust Fully Managed Series, which had an inception date of January 1989, and has an asset base of $100 million.

The year-by-year returns for this subaccount are:

| Year | Annual Return | S&P 500 | Lehman Bros. Gov't/Corp. Bond Index |
|---|---|---|---|
| 1994 | −8.2% | 1.3% | −3.5% |
| 1993 | 6.5% | 10.1% | 11.1% |
| 1992 | 5.2% | 7.6% | 7.6% |
| 1991 | 27.6% | 30.5% | 16.1% |
| 1990 | −4.2% | −3.1% | 8.3% |

# Risk Control ✓

Over the 3-year period studied, this fund was somewhat riskier than the average hybrid subaccount.

The typical standard deviation for balanced subaccounts was 2.0% during the 3-year period. The standard deviation for Golden American GoldenSelect Fully Managed was 2.9% over this same period, which means that this subaccount was 45% more volatile than its peer group. The price/earnings (p/e) ratio averages 25 for this portfolio. The typical balanced subaccount has a p/e ratio of 23. In general, the higher the p/e ratio, the riskier the portfolio.

The beta (market-related risk) of this subaccount was 0.8 over the 3-year period. Beta for this entire category was 0.6 over this same period. The market index (the S&P 500 Index for "hybrid" subaccounts such as balanced subaccounts) always has a beta of 1.0. The *risk-adjusted* return for this variable annuity subaccount can be described as poor.

# Expense Minimization ✓✓✓

The typical expenses incurred by balanced subaccounts are 2.0% per year. The total expenses for Golden American GoldenSelect Fully Managed are also 2%. Total expenses include all charges to the investor (except the annual contract charge, which is always expressed as a dollar figure), including management fees, overhead, administration, and mortality expenses. The free annual withdrawals percentage is based on the account value.

| | | | |
|---|---|---|---|
| Maximum surrender charge | 6% | Total expenses | 2.0% |
| Duration of surrender charge | 6 years | Annual contract charge | $40 |
| Declining surrender charge | no | Free annual withdrawals | 15% |

# Management ✓

Golden American GoldenSelect is offered by Golden American Life Insurance Company. The portfolio (and/or the mutual fund it is modeled after) was managed by A. Roy Knutsen and Stephen Weiss for the 5 years ending December 31, 1994. The portfolio's size is $100 million. The typical security in the portfolio has a market capitalization of $4.3 billion. Knutsen also manages the WPG Growth & Income mutual fund.

# Investment Options ✓✓✓

Investors may make additional contributions into this portfolio at any time. This is known as a flexible premium annuity. Investors in this variable annuity can choose from all of the subaccount categories below that have a check mark:

| | | |
|---|---|---|
| ✓ Aggressive growth | ___ Government bonds | ✓ Money market |
| ✓ Balanced | ✓ Growth | ✓ Specialty/Sector |
| ✓ Corporate bonds | ✓ Growth & income | ___ World bonds |
| ✓ Global equities (stocks) | ___ High-yield bonds | |

# Family Rating ✓

There are 11 subaccounts within the Golden American GoldenSelect family. Overall, this family of subaccounts can be described as poor on a *risk-adjusted* return basis.

The subaccounts within this variable annuity all have an *increasing* guaranteed death benefit. This means that the beneficiary is guaranteed to receive *the greater of* the contract's value on the date of the annuitant's death or the value of the original investment(s) compounded by 5% each year (less any withdrawals made).

## Summary

Golden American GoldenSelect Fully Managed may not seem like a worthy contender at first, but when viewed on its own, it becomes much more attractive. A return of over 12% per year over the 3 years studied is something a lot of other balanced portfolios cannot lay claim to; for the expense-conscious investor, the contract offers a very liberal withdrawal privilege and a declining surrender charge.

Golden American GoldenSelect variable annuity offers some investment choices not found with the majority of other contracts: an international equities subaccount for diversification, and a specialty subaccount for the more adventuresome. The enhanced death benefit will certainly appeal to an older individual or couple who is looking out for a loved one.

## Profile

| | | | |
|---|---|---|---|
| Minimum investment | $1,500 | Telephone exchanges | yes |
| Retirement account minimum | $10,000 | Transfers allowed per year | unlimited |
| Co-annuitant allowed | yes | Maximum issuance age | 85 |
| Co-owner allowed | yes | Maximum annuitization age | 90 |
| Dollar-cost averaging | yes | Number of subaccounts | 11 |
| Systematic withdrawal plans | yes | Available in all 50 states | no* |

*Not available in CT, ME, or NY.

---

### Kemper Passport
### Total Return
120 South LaSalle Street
Chicago, IL 60603
(800) 554-5426

| | |
|---|---|
| Performance | ✓✓✓✓ |
| Risk control | ✓✓✓ |
| Expense minimization | ✓✓✓✓ |
| Management | ✓✓ |
| Investment options | ✓✓✓ |
| Family rating | ✓✓✓ |
| Total point score | 19 points |

## Performance ✓✓✓✓

During the 3-year and 5-year periods ending December 31, 1994, Total Return had an average annual compound return of −0.3% and 7.1%, respectively. This means that a $10,000 investment made into this subaccount 5 years before that date grew to $14,100 ($9,900, if only the last 3 years before that date are used).

The inception month of this subaccount was January 1992. The performance figures (shown below) for periods before the subaccount's inception in January 1992 are hypothetical, based on the underlying clone fund's returns. This subaccount is modeled (cloned) after the Kemper Total Return Fund, which had an inception date of March 1964, and has an asset base of $1.6 billion.

The year-by-year returns for this subaccount and the mutual fund it is modeled after are:

| Year | Annual Return | S&P 500 | Lehman Bros. Gov't/Corp. Bond Index |
|---|---|---|---|
| 1994 | −10.6% | 1.3% | −3.5% |
| 1993 | 10.8% | 10.1% | 11.1% |
| 1992 | 0.2% | 7.6% | 7.6% |
| 1991 | 40.2% | 30.5% | 16.1% |
| 1990 | 4.1% | −3.1% | 8.3% |
| 1989 | 19.8% | 31.7% | 14.2% |
| 1988 | 8.8% | 16.6% | 7.6% |
| 1987 | −2.4% | 5.3% | 2.3% |

## Risk Control                                                      ✓✓✓

Over the 3-year period studied, this fund was as safe as the average hybrid subaccount.

The price/earnings (p/e) ratio averages 28 for this portfolio. The typical balanced subaccount has a p/e ratio of 23. In general, the higher the p/e ratio, the riskier the portfolio.

## Expense Minimization                                              ✓✓✓✓

The typical expenses incurred by balanced subaccounts are 2.0% per year. The total expenses for Kemper Passport Total Return, 1.9%, are lower than its peer group average. Total expenses include all charges to the investor (except the annual contract charge, which is always expressed as a dollar figure), including management fees, overhead, administration, and mortality expenses. The free annual withdrawals percentage is based on the account value.

| | | | |
|---|---|---|---|
| Maximum surrender charge | 6% | Total expenses | 1.9% |
| Duration of surrender charge | 6 years | Annual contract charge | $30 |
| Declining surrender charge | no | Free annual withdrawals | 10% |

## Management                                                        ✓✓

Kemper Passport is offered by Kemper Investors Life Insurance Company. The company has a Duff & Phelps rating of A+ and an A.M. Best rating of A−. The portfolio (and/or the mutual fund it is modeled after) was managed by Gordon P. Wilson for the 12 years ending December 31, 1994. The portfolio's size is only $55 million. The typical security in the portfolio has a market capitalization of $4.5 billion. Wilson also manages the Kemper Total Return mutual fund.

## Investment Options                                                ✓✓✓

Investors may not add to their initial investment in this portfolio. This is known as a single premium annuity. Investors in this variable annuity can choose from all of the subaccount categories below that have a check mark:

| | | |
|---|---|---|
| ___ Aggressive growth | ✓ Government bonds | ✓ Money market |
| ✓ Balanced | ✓ Growth | ___ Specialty/Sector |
| ___ Corporate bonds | ___ Growth & income | ___ World bonds |
| ✓ Global equities (stocks) | ✓ High-yield bonds | |

## Family Rating                                              ✓✓✓

There are 7 subaccounts within the Kemper Passport family. Overall, this family of subaccounts can be described as good on a *risk-adjusted* return basis.

The subaccounts within this variable annuity all have an *increasing* guaranteed death benefit. This means that the beneficiary is guaranteed to receive *the greater of* the contract's value on the date of the annuitant's death or the value of the original investment(s) compounded by 5% each year (less any withdrawals made).

## Summary

Kemper Passport Total Return brings home the bacon. The track record of this balanced portfolio is very good. Management has also been successful at keeping risk down to acceptable levels and keeping operating expenses down. Most years, this balancing act has been able to outperform the S&P 500 or Lehman Brothers Bond Index (or both).

Kemper has long been a household word when it comes to insurance and mutual funds. By providing some of the best features of both products (i.e., an enhanced death benefit and a good number of investment options), Kemper continues to make a name for itself. Besides this total return (balanced) subaccount, look into their high-yield bond portfolio.

## Profile

| | | | |
|---|---|---|---|
| Minimum investment | $5,000 | Telephone exchanges | yes |
| Retirement account minimum | $5,000 | Transfers allowed per year | approx. 24 |
| Co-annuitant allowed | yes | Maximum issuance age | 85 |
| Co-owner allowed | yes | Maximum annuitization age | none |
| Dollar-cost averaging | yes | Number of subaccounts | 7 |
| Systematic withdrawal plans | yes | Available in all 50 states | no* |

*Not available in NY.

---

**Keyport Preferred Advisor**
**SteinRoe Managed Assets**
125 High Street
Boston, MA  02110-2712
(800) 367-3653

---

| | |
|---|---|
| Performance | ✓✓ |
| Risk control | ✓✓✓ |
| Expense minimization | ✓✓✓ |
| Management | ✓✓✓ |
| Investment options | ✓✓✓ |
| Family rating | ✓✓✓ |
| Total point score | 17 points |

## Performance                                              ✓✓

During the 3-year and 5-year periods ending December 31, 1994, SteinRoe Managed Assets had an average annual compound return of 3.0% and 6.2%, respectively. This means that a $10,000 investment made into this subaccount 5 years before that date grew to $13,500 ($10,900, if only the last 3 years before that date are used).

Compared to other balanced variable annuity subaccounts, this one ranks in the top half for the 3-year period. The inception month of this subaccount was May 1989. The performance figures (shown below) for periods before the subaccount's inception in May 1989 are hypothetical, based on the underlying clone fund's returns. This subaccount is modeled (cloned) after the SteinRoe Total Return Fund, which had an inception date of August 1949, and has an asset base of $250 million.

The year-by-year returns for this subaccount and the mutual fund it is modeled after are:

| Year | Annual Return | S&P 500 | Lehman Bros. Gov't/Corp. Bond Index |
|------|------|------|------|
| 1994 | −4.5% | 1.3% | −3.5% |
| 1993 | 7.8% | 10.1% | 11.1% |
| 1992 | 6.0% | 7.6% | 7.6% |
| 1991 | 26.2% | 30.5% | 16.1% |
| 1990 | −2.1% | −3.1% | 8.3% |
| 1989 | 20.3% | 31.7% | 14.2% |
| 1988 | 7.9% | 16.6% | 7.6% |
| 1987 | 0.7% | 5.3% | 2.3% |

# Risk Control     ✓✓✓

Over the 3-year period, this fund was 25% safer than the average hybrid subaccount.

The typical standard deviation for balanced subaccounts was 2.0% during the 3-year period. The standard deviation for Keyport Preferred Advisor SteinRoe Managed Assets was 2.2% over this same period, which means that this subaccount was 9% more volatile than its peer group. The price/earnings (p/e) ratio averages 21 for this portfolio. The typical balanced subaccount has a p/e ratio of 23. In general, the higher the p/e ratio, the riskier the portfolio.

The beta (market-related risk) of this subaccount was 0.7 over the 3-year period. Beta for this entire category was 0.6 over this same period. The market index (the S&P 500 Index for "hybrid" subaccounts such as balanced subaccounts) always has a beta of 1.0. The *risk-adjusted* return for this variable annuity subaccount can be described as good.

# Expense Minimization     ✓✓✓

The typical expenses incurred by balanced subaccounts are 2.0% per year. The total expenses for Keyport Preferred Advisor SteinRoe Managed Assets, 2.1%, are higher than its peer group average. Total expenses include all charges to the investor (except the annual contract charge, which is always expressed as a dollar figure), including management fees, overhead, administration, and mortality expenses. The free annual withdrawals percentage is based on the value of the account at its anniversary amount.

| | | | |
|------|------|------|------|
| Maximum surrender charge | 7% | Total expenses | 2.1% |
| Duration of surrender charge | 7 years | Annual contract charge | $30 |
| Declining surrender charge | yes | Free annual withdrawals | 10% |

## Management                                          ✓✓✓

Keyport Preferred Advisor is offered by Keyport Life Insurance Company. The company has a Duff & Phelps rating of AA− and an A.M. Best rating of A+. The portfolio was managed by Robert A. Christensen for the 5 years ending December 31, 1994. The portfolio's size is $160 million. The typical security in the portfolio has a market capitalization of $3.4 billion. Christensen also manages the SteinRoe Total Return Fund.

## Investment Options                                   ✓✓✓

Investors may make additional contributions into this portfolio at any time. This is known as a flexible premium annuity. Investors in this variable annuity can choose from all of the subaccount categories below that have a check mark:

| | | |
|---|---|---|
| ✓ Aggressive growth | ✓ Government bonds | ✓ Money market |
| ✓ Balanced | ✓ Growth | ✓ Specialty/Sector |
| ✓ Corporate bonds | ✓ Growth & income | ___ World bonds |
| ___ Global equities (stocks) | ___ High-yield bonds | |

## Family Rating                                        ✓✓✓

There are 10 subaccounts within the Keyport Preferred Advisor family. Overall, this family of subaccounts can be described as good on a *risk-adjusted* return basis.

   The subaccounts within this variable annuity all have an *increasing* guaranteed death benefit. This means that the beneficiary is guaranteed to receive *the greater of* the contract's value on the date of the annuitant's death or the value of the original investment(s) compounded by 5% each year (less any withdrawals made).

## Summary

Keyport Preferred Advisor SteinRoe Managed Assets is a balanced portfolio that is well rounded not only in its investment mix, but also in all of the categories of interest to any investor. In a word, this offering is good. The investment is not a disappointment at any level. This is one of two total return offerings by Keyport in this book.

   The Keyport Preferred Advisor is a variable annuity contract that has a declining surrender charge and, more importantly, a free annual withdrawals provision based on the current value of the investment, not the original principal. Because it allows co-ownership (a feature not found with most contracts), this variable annuity will be particularly appealing to married couples.

## Profile

| | | | |
|---|---|---|---|
| Minimum investment | $5,000 | Telephone exchanges | yes |
| Retirement account minimum | $5,000 | Transfers allowed per year | 12 |
| Co-annuitant allowed | no | Maximum issuance age | 80 |
| Co-owner allowed | yes | Maximum annuitization age | 90 |
| Dollar-cost averaging | yes | Number of subaccounts | 10 |
| Systematic withdrawal plans | yes | Available in all 50 states | no* |

*Not available in NY.

**Keyport Preferred Advisor**
**SteinRoe Strategic Managed Assets**
125 High Street
Boston, MA 02110-2712
(800) 367-3653

| | |
|---|---|
| Performance | ✓✓✓✓ |
| Risk control | ✓✓✓ |
| Expense minimization | ✓ |
| Management | ✓✓✓✓ |
| Investment options | ✓✓✓ |
| Family rating | ✓✓✓ |
| Total point score | 18 points |

## Performance                              ✓✓✓✓

During the 3-year and 5-year periods ending December 31, 1994, SteinRoe Strategic Managed Assets had an average annual compound return of 3.4% and 6.4%, respectively. This means that a $10,000 investment made into this subaccount 5 years before that date grew to $13,600 ($11,100 for the last 3 years).

Compared to other balanced variable annuity subaccounts, this one ranks in the top third for the 3-year period. The inception month of this subaccount was May 1989. This subaccount is modeled (cloned) after the SteinRoe Total Return Fund, which had an inception date of August 1949, and has an asset base of $250 million.

The year-by-year returns for this subaccount are:

| Year | Annual Return | S&P 500 | Lehman Bros. Gov't/Corp. Bond Index |
|---|---|---|---|
| 1994 | −1.4% | 1.3% | −3.5% |
| 1993 | 0.5% | 10.1% | 11.1% |
| 1992 | 11.5% | 7.6% | 7.6% |
| 1991 | 36.6% | 30.5% | 16.1% |
| 1990 | −9.8% | −3.1% | 8.3% |

## Risk Control                              ✓✓✓

Over the 3-year period, this fund was 20% safer than the average hybrid subaccount.

The typical standard deviation for balanced subaccounts was 2.0% during the past 3-year period. The standard deviation for Keyport Preferred Advisor SteinRoe Strategic Managed Assets was 2.9% over this same period, which means that this subaccount was 42% more volatile than its peer group. The price/earnings (p/e) ratio averages 23 for this portfolio. The typical balanced subaccount has a p/e ratio of 23. In general, the higher the p/e ratio, the riskier the portfolio.

The beta (market-related risk) of this subaccount was 0.8 over the 3-year period. Beta for this entire category was 0.6 over this same period. The market index (the S&P 500 Index for "hybrid" subaccounts such as balanced subaccounts) always has a beta of 1.0. The *risk-adjusted* return for this variable annuity subaccount can be described as good.

## Expense Minimization ✓

The typical expenses incurred by balanced subaccounts are 2.0% per year. The total expenses for Keyport Preferred Advisor SteinRoe Strategic Managed Assets, 2.6%, are higher than its peer group average. Total expenses include all charges to the investor (except the annual contract charge, which is always expressed as a dollar figure), including management fees, overhead, administration, and mortality expenses. The free annual withdrawals percentage is based on the value of the account at its anniversary amount.

| | | | |
|---|---|---|---|
| Maximum surrender charge | 7% | Total expenses | 2.6% |
| Duration of surrender charge | 7 years | Annual contract charge | $30 |
| Declining surrender charge | yes | Free annual withdrawals | 10% |

## Management ✓✓✓✓

Keyport Preferred Advisor is offered by Keyport Life Insurance Company. The company has a Duff & Phelps rating of AA− and an A.M. Best rating of A+. The portfolio was managed by Jay Vawter for the 5 years ending December 31, 1994. The portfolio's size is only $70 million. The typical security in the portfolio has a market capitalization of $8.9 billion.

## Investment Options ✓✓✓

Investors may make additional contributions into this portfolio at any time. This is known as a flexible premium annuity. Investors in this variable annuity can choose from all of the subaccount categories below that have a check mark:

✓ Aggressive growth     ✓ Government bonds     ✓ Money market
✓ Balanced              ✓ Growth               ✓ Specialty/Sector
✓ Corporate bonds       ✓ Growth & income      ___ World bonds
___ Global equities (stocks)   ___ High-yield bonds

## Family Rating ✓✓✓

There are 10 subaccounts within the Keyport Preferred Advisor family. Overall, this family of subaccounts can be described as good on a *risk-adjusted* return basis.

The subaccounts within this variable annuity all have an *increasing* guaranteed death benefit. This means that the beneficiary is guaranteed to receive *the greater of* the contract's value on the date of the annuitant's death or the value of the original investment(s) compounded by 5% each year (less any withdrawals made).

## Summary

Preferred Advisor SteinRoe Strategic Managed Assets is the second of two Keyport balanced subaccounts in this book. This particular portfolio offers superior performance and very good management. The increasing death benefit will attract investors who are getting into equities late in life or have been suffering from bad bond markets.

The Keyport Preferred Advisor is a variable annuity contract that has a declining surrender charge and, more importantly, a free annual withdrawal provision based on the current value of the investment, not the original principal. Because it allows co-ownership (a feature not found with most contracts), this variable annuity will be particularly appealing to married couples.

## Profile

| | | | | |
|---|---|---|---|---|
| Minimum investment | $5,000 | | Telephone exchanges | yes |
| Retirement account minimum | $5,000 | | Transfers allowed per year | 12 |
| Co-annuitant allowed | no | | Maximum issuance age | 80 |
| Co-owner allowed | yes | | Maximum annuitization age | 90 |
| Dollar-cost averaging | yes | | Number of subaccounts | 10 |
| Systematic withdrawal plans | yes | | Available in all 50 states | no* |

*Not available in NY.

---

### Life of Virginia Commonwealth
### Life of Virginia Total Return
6610 West Broad Street
Richmond, VA 23230
(800) 521-8884

| | |
|---|---|
| Performance | ✓✓✓ |
| Risk control | ✓✓✓ |
| Expense minimization | ✓✓ |
| Management | ✓✓✓✓ |
| Investment options | ✓✓✓ |
| Family rating | ✓✓ |
| Total point score | 23 points |

## Performance                              ✓✓✓

During the 3-year and 5-year periods ending December 31, 1994, Life of Virginia Total Return had an average annual compound return of 6.6% and 7.7%, respectively. This means that a $10,000 investment made into this subaccount 5 years before that date grew to $14,500 ($12,100, if only the last 3 years of that period are used).

Compared to other balanced variable annuity subaccounts, this one ranks in the top third for the 3-year period and in the top half for the 5-year period. The inception month of this subaccount was May 1988. This subaccount is modeled (cloned) after the Life of Virginia Series Fund Total Return Portfolio, which had an inception date of July 1985, and has an asset base of $10 million.

The year-by-year returns for this subaccount are:

| Year | Annual Return | S&P 500 | Lehman Bros. Gov't/Corp. Bond Index |
|---|---|---|---|
| 1994 | 1.4% | 1.3% | −3.5% |
| 1993 | 12.3% | 10.1% | 11.1% |
| 1992 | 6.3% | 7.6% | 7.6% |
| 1991 | 26.0% | 30.5% | 16.1% |
| 1990 | −5.0% | −3.1% | 8.3% |
| 1989 | 18.1% | 31.7% | 14.2% |

## Risk Control                              ✓✓✓

Over the 3-year period, this fund was 40% safer than the average hybrid subaccount. During the 5-year period, it was 20% safer.

The typical standard deviation for balanced subaccounts was 2.0% during the 3-year period. The standard deviation for Life of Virginia Commonwealth Life of Virginia Total Return was 1.91% over this same period, which means that this subaccount was 5% less volatile than its peer group. The price/earnings (p/e) ratio averages 21 for this portfolio. The typical balanced subaccount has a p/e ratio of 23. In general, the higher the p/e ratio, the riskier the portfolio.

The beta (market-related risk) of this subaccount was 0.6 over the 3-year period. Beta for this entire category was 0.6 over this same period. The market index (the S&P 500 Index for "hybrid" subaccounts such as balanced subaccounts) always has a beta of 1.0. The *risk-adjusted* return for this variable annuity subaccount can be described as good.

## Expense Minimization                              ✓✓✓

The typical expenses incurred by balanced subaccounts are 2.0% per year. The total expenses for Life of Virginia Commonwealth Life of Virginia Total Return, 2.1%, are higher than its peer group average. Total expenses include all charges to the investor (except the annual contract charge, which is always expressed as a dollar figure), including management fees, overhead, administration, and mortality expenses. The free annual withdrawals percentage is based on the account value.

| | | | |
|---|---|---|---|
| Maximum surrender charge | 6% | Total expenses | 2.1% |
| Duration of surrender charge | 6 years | Annual contract charge | $30 |
| Declining surrender charge | yes | Free annual withdrawals | 10% |

## Management                              ✓✓✓✓✓

Life of Virginia Commonwealth is offered by Life Insurance Company of Virginia. The company has a Duff & Phelps rating of AA+ and an A.M. Best rating of A+. The portfolio was managed by Mark Burka and Paul Van Kampen for the 7 years ending December 31, 1994. The portfolio's size is a mere $8 million. The typical security in the portfolio has a market capitalization of $6.2 billion.

## Investment Options                              ✓✓✓

Investors may make additional contributions into this portfolio at any time. This is known as a flexible premium annuity. Investors in this variable annuity can choose from all of the subaccount categories below that have a check mark:

| | | |
|---|---|---|
| ✓ Aggressive growth | ✓ Government bonds | ✓ Money market |
| ✓ Balanced | ✓ Growth | ___ Specialty/Sector |
| ✓ Corporate bonds | ✓ Growth & income | ___ World bonds |
| ✓ Global equities (stocks) | ✓ High-yield bonds | |

## Family Rating                              ✓✓✓

There are 22 subaccounts within the Life of Virginia Commonwealth family. Overall, this family of subaccounts can be described as good on a *risk-adjusted* return basis.

The subaccounts within this variable annuity all have an *increasing* guaranteed death benefit. This means that the beneficiary is guaranteed to receive *the greater of* the contract's value on the date of the annuitant's death or the value of the original investment(s) compounded by 5% each year (less any withdrawals made).

## Summary

Life of Virginia Commonwealth Total Return's exceptional management has provided its investors with a very high level of returns and low risk—a combination not easily achieved. Managers Burka and Van Kampen have somehow been able to subject contract owners to less volatile securities while still turning in impressive results. This is a very small subaccount—perhaps a reason why the portfolio's decision makers have been so agile. Most investors have never heard of this account; don't make the same mistake.

Life of Virginia has a variable annuity that offers more investment choices than almost any other company. With close to two dozen choices, contract owners have the ability to switch around among a number of investment styles and philosophies. A stepped-up death benefit and declining surrender charge are icing-on-the-cake features.

## Profile

| | | | |
|---|---|---|---|
| Minimum investment | $5,000 | Telephone exchanges | yes |
| Retirement account minimum | $5,000 | Transfers allowed per year | 12 |
| Co-annuitant allowed | no | Maximum issuance age | 75 |
| Co-owner allowed | yes | Maximum annuitization age | none |
| Dollar-cost averaging | yes | Number of subaccounts | 22 |
| Systematic withdrawal plans | yes | Available in all 50 states | no* |

*Not available in ME, NY, or WA.

---

**Lincoln National American Legacy II**
**Asset Allocation**
P.O. Box 2340
Fort Wayne, IN 46801
(800) 421-9900

---

| | |
|---|---|
| Performance | ✓✓ |
| Risk control | ✓✓✓✓ |
| Expense minimization | ✓✓✓✓ |
| Management | ✓✓✓ |
| Investment options | ✓✓✓ |
| Family rating | ✓✓✓✓ |
| Total point score | 20 points |

## Performance                                    ✓✓

During the 3-year and 5-year periods ending December 31, 1994, Asset Allocation had an average annual compound return of 4.7% and 6.1%, respectively. This means that a $10,000 investment made into this subaccount 5 years before that date grew to $13,400 ($11,500, if only the last 3 years of that period are used).

Compared to other balanced variable annuity subaccounts, this one ranks in the bottom third for the 3-year period. The inception month of this subaccount was August 1989. The performance figures (shown below) for periods before the subaccount's inception in August 1989 are hypothetical, based on the underlying clone fund's returns. This subaccount is modeled (cloned) after the American Balanced fund, which had an inception date of January 1933, and has an asset base of $1.8 billion.

The year-by-year returns for this subaccount and the mutual fund it is modeled after are:

| Year | Annual Return | S&P 500 | Lehman Bros. Gov't/Corp. Bond Index |
|------|---------------|---------|-------------------------------------|
| 1994 | −1.6% | 1.3% | −3.5% |
| 1993 | 9.0% | 10.1% | 11.1% |
| 1992 | 7.1% | 7.6% | 7.6% |
| 1991 | 20.2% | 30.5% | 16.1% |
| 1990 | −2.4% | −3.1% | 8.3% |
| 1989 | 21.5% | 31.7% | 14.2% |
| 1988 | 12.9% | 16.6% | 7.6% |
| 1987 | 4.0% | 5.3% | 2.3% |

## Risk Control                                          ✓✓✓✓

Over the 3-year period, this fund was 40% safer than the average hybrid subaccount.

The typical standard deviation for balanced subaccounts was 2.0% during the 3-year period. The standard deviation for Lincoln National American Legacy II Asset Allocation was 1.7% over this same period, which means that this subaccount was 18% less volatile than its peer group. The price/earnings (p/e) ratio averages 19 for this portfolio. The typical balanced subaccount has a p/e ratio of 23. In general, the higher the p/e ratio, the riskier the portfolio.

The beta (market-related risk) of this subaccount was 0.5 over the 3-year period. Beta for this entire category was 0.6 over this same period. The market index (the S&P 500 Index for "hybrid" subaccounts such as balanced subaccounts) always has a beta of 1.0. The *risk-adjusted* return for this variable annuity subaccount can be described as good.

## Expense Minimization                                   ✓✓✓✓

The typical expenses incurred by balanced subaccounts are 2.0% per year. The total expenses for Lincoln National American Legacy II Asset Allocation, 1.9%, are lower than its peer group average. Total expenses include all charges to the investor (except the annual contract charge, which is always expressed as a dollar figure), including management fees, overhead, administration, and mortality expenses. The free annual withdrawals percentage is based on the original principal.

| | | | |
|---|---|---|---|
| Maximum surrender charge | 6% | Total expenses | 1.9% |
| Duration of surrender charge | 7 years | Annual contract charge | $35 |
| Declining surrender charge | yes | Free annual withdrawals | 10% |

## Management                                             ✓✓✓

Lincoln National American Legacy II is offered by Lincoln National Life Insurance Company. The company has a Duff & Phelps rating of AAA and an A.M. Best rating of A+. The portfolio (and the mutual fund it is modeled after) has been managed by Capital Guardian (American Funds) since inception. The portfolio's size is $625 million. The typical security in the portfolio has a market capitalization of $13.4 billion.

## Investment Options  ✓✓✓

Investors may make additional contributions into this portfolio at any time. This is known as a flexible premium annuity. Investors in this variable annuity can choose from all of the subaccount categories below that have a check mark:

| | | |
|---|---|---|
| ___ Aggressive growth | ✓ Government bonds | ✓ Money market |
| ✓ Balanced | ✓ Growth | ___ Specialty/Sector |
| ___ Corporate bonds | ✓ Growth & income | ___ World bonds |
| ✓ Global equities (stocks) | ✓ High-yield bonds | |

## Family Rating  ✓✓✓✓

There are 7 subaccounts within the Lincoln National American Legacy II family. Overall, this family of subaccounts can be described as very good on a *risk-adjusted* return basis.

## Summary

Lincoln National American Legacy II Asset Allocation is managed by the same group that oversees American Funds, perhaps the best large mutual fund family in the country. A shortcoming of financial articles and books (including this one) is that the caliber of management and the *long-term* performance are not emphasized enough. We all share some of the blame. The press is guilty of getting caught up in the moment (e.g., how the mutual fund or variable annuity performed during last week's crisis or during the most recent 1-, 3-, or 5-year period). The public takes its cue from what it reads and pretty much has a philosophy of: What have you done for me lately?

When you are looking at the best management around, it is often difficult to compare the short term against a long-term investment style that has proven highly efficient for over half a century. In short, the longer the period of time studied, the greater the likelihood that you will see the portfolio managers at American in the winner's circle. I recommend that they be part of most people's money management team. Asset Allocation represents one of several subaccounts directed by Capital Guardian (the division that oversees all of American's mutual funds and variable annuity subaccounts) that should not be missed.

## Profile

| | | | |
|---|---|---|---|
| Minimum investment | $300 | Telephone exchanges | yes |
| Retirement account minimum | $1,500 | Transfers allowed per year | 12 |
| Co-annuitant allowed | no | Maximum issuance age | 75 |
| Co-owner allowed | yes | Maximum annuitization age | 85 |
| Dollar-cost averaging | yes | Number of subaccounts | 7 |
| Systematic withdrawal plans | yes | Available in all 50 states | no* |

*Not available in NY.

---

**Mass Mutual Separate Account 2 Flex V Annuity**
**Blend Fund**
1295 State Street
Springfield, MA  01111
(800) 272-2216

---

| | |
|---|---|
| Performance | ✓✓ |
| Risk control | ✓✓✓ |
| Expense minimization | ✓✓✓✓ |
| Management | ✓✓✓ |
| Investment options | ✓ |
| Family rating | ✓✓✓ |
| Total point score | 16 points |

---

## Performance                                                        ✓✓

During the 3-year and 5-year periods ending December 31, 1994, Blend Fund had an average annual compound return of 5.8% and 7.9%, respectively. This means that a $10,000 investment made into this subaccount 5 years before that date grew to $14,600 ($11,800, if only the last 3 years of that period are used).

Compared to other balanced variable annuity subaccounts, this one ranks in the top half for the 3-year period and in the top 40% for the 5-year period. The inception month of this subaccount was April 1987. This subaccount is modeled (cloned) after the MML Series Investment Fund Blend Fund, which had an inception date of February 1984, and has an asset base of only $1 million.

The year-by-year returns for this subaccount are:

| Year | Annual Return | S&P 500 | Lehman Bros. Gov't/Corp. Bond Index |
|---|---|---|---|
| 1994 | 1.2% | 1.3% | −3.5% |
| 1993 | 8.3% | 10.1% | 11.1% |
| 1992 | 8.0% | 7.6% | 7.6% |
| 1991 | 22.5% | 30.5% | 16.1% |
| 1990 | 1.1% | −3.1% | 8.3% |
| 1989 | 18.5% | 31.7% | 14.2% |
| 1988 | 11.9% | 16.6% | 7.6% |
| 1987 | 2.1% | 5.3% | 2.3% |

## Risk Control                                                       ✓✓✓

Over the 3-year period, this fund was 30% safer than the average hybrid subaccount. During the 5-year period, it was 25% safer.

The typical standard deviation for balanced subaccounts was 2.0% during the 3-year period. The standard deviation for Mass Mutual Separate Account 2 Flex V Annuity Blend Fund was 2.1% over this same period, which means that this subaccount was 1% more volatile than its peer group. The price/earnings (p/e) ratio averages 21 for this portfolio. The typical balanced subaccount has a p/e ratio of 23. In general, the higher the p/e ratio, the riskier the portfolio.

The beta (market-related risk) of this subaccount was 0.6 over the 3-year period. Beta for this entire category was 0.6 over this same period. The market index (the S&P 500 Index for "hybrid" subaccounts such as balanced subaccounts) always has a beta of 1.0. The *risk-adjusted* return for this variable annuity subaccount can be described as very good.

## Expense Minimization ✓✓✓✓

The typical expenses incurred by balanced subaccounts are 2.0% per year. The total expenses for Mass Mutual Separate Account 2 Flex V Annuity Blend Fund, 1.7%, are lower than its peer group average. Total expenses include all charges to the investor (except the annual contract charge, which is always expressed as a dollar figure), including management fees, overhead, administration, and mortality expenses. The free annual withdrawals percentage is based on the account value.

| | | | |
|---|---|---|---|
| Maximum surrender charge | 5% | Total expenses | 1.7% |
| Duration of surrender charge | 5 years | Annual contract charge | $30 |
| Declining surrender charge | no | Free annual withdrawals | 10% |

## Management ✓✓✓

Mass Mutual Separate Account 2 Flex V Annuity is offered by Massachusetts Mutual Life Insurance Company. The company has a Duff & Phelps rating of AAA. The portfolio was managed by Hamline C. Wilson, Jr., for the 8 years ending December 31, 1994. The portfolio's size is a whopping $1.0 billion. The typical security in the portfolio has a market capitalization of $6.5 billion.

## Investment Options ✓

Investors may not add to their initial investment in this portfolio. This is known as a single premium annuity. Investors in this variable annuity can choose from all of the subaccount categories below that have a check mark:

| | | |
|---|---|---|
| ___ Aggressive growth | ___ Government bonds | ✓ Money market |
| ✓ Balanced | ___ Growth | ___ Specialty/Sector |
| ✓ Corporate bonds | ✓ Growth & income | ___ World bonds |
| ___ Global equities (stocks) | ___ High-yield bonds | |

## Family Rating ✓✓✓

There are 5 subaccounts within the Mass Mutual Separate Account 2 Flex V Annuity family. Overall, this family of subaccounts can be descried as good on a *risk-adjusted* return basis.

## Summary

Mass Mutual Separate Account 2 Flex V Annuity Blend Fund is one of only a handful of balanced subaccounts that has never had a negative year. Equally impressive, this portfolio has turned in respective returns while displaying about 25% less risk than its peer group.

Mass Mutual Separate Account 2 Flex V Annuity can boast of an expense minimization record that is about 20% less than its competitors'. This type of control is particularly important for a conservative portfolio that contains a moderate weighting in bonds and cash. The actual contract is also pleasing: the low surrender charge and the schedule make it a delight to uncertain investors. Finally, withdrawal privileges during the penalty period are based on account value, not original principal, and are some of the most liberal in the industry. It is hoped that Mass Mutual will add more investment options to the present fine stable of offerings.

## Profile

| | | | | |
|---|---|---|---|---|
| Minimum investment | $25,000 | Telephone exchanges | yes |
| Retirement account minimum | $25,000 | Transfers allowed per year | 4 |
| Co-annuitant allowed | no | Maximum issuance age | 75 |
| Co-owner allowed | yes | Maximum annuitization age | none |
| Dollar-cost averaging | yes | Number of subaccounts | 5 |
| Systematic withdrawal plans | yes | Available in all 50 states | yes |

---

**MFS/Sun Life (US) Regatta Gold**
**Total Return Series**
P.O. Box 1024
Boston, MA  02103
(800) 752-7218

| | |
|---|---|
| Performance | ✓✓✓ |
| Risk control | ✓✓✓✓ |
| Expense minimization | ✓✓ |
| Management | ✓ |
| Investment options | ✓✓✓✓ |
| Family rating | ✓✓✓ |
| Total point score | 17 points |

## Performance                                                    ✓✓✓

During the 3-year and 5-year periods ending December 31, 1994, Total Return Series had an average annual compound return of 4.8% and 7.9%, respectively. This means that a $10,000 investment made into this subaccount 5 years before that date grew to $14,600 ($11,500, if only the last 3 years of that period are used).

The inception month of this subaccount was November 1991. The performance figures (shown below) for periods before the subaccount's inception in November 1991 are hypothetical, based on the underlying clone fund's returns. This subaccount is modeled (cloned) after the MFS Total Return Fund—Class A, which had an inception date of October 1970, and has an asset base of $1.9 billion.

The year-by-year returns for this subaccount and the mutual fund it is modeled after are:

| Year | Annual Return | S&P 500 | Lehman Bros. Gov't/Corp. Bond Index |
|---|---|---|---|
| 1994 | −3.6% | 1.3% | −3.5% |
| 1993 | 11.8% | 10.1% | 11.1% |
| 1992 | 6.9% | 7.6% | 7.6% |
| 1991 | 21.6% | 30.5% | 16.1% |
| 1990 | −2.3% | −3.1% | 8.3% |
| 1989 | 23.1% | 31.7% | 14.2% |
| 1988 | 14.9% | 16.6% | 7.6% |
| 1987 | 3.4% | 5.3% | 2.3% |

## Risk Control                                            ✓✓✓✓

Over the 3-year period, this fund was safer than the average hybrid subaccount.

The price/earnings (p/e) ratio averages 22 for this portfolio. The typical balanced subaccount has a p/e ratio of 23. In general, the higher the p/e ratio, the riskier the portfolio.

## Expense Minimization                                     ✓✓

The typical expenses incurred by balanced subaccounts are 2.0% per year. The total expenses for MFS/Sun Life (US) Regatta Gold Total Return Series, 2.3%, are higher than its peer group average. Total expenses include all charges to the investor (except the annual contract charge, which is always expressed as a dollar figure), including management fees, overhead, administration, and mortality expenses. The free annual withdrawals percentage is based on the original principal.

| | | | |
|---|---|---|---|
| Maximum surrender charge | 6% | Total expenses | 2.3% |
| Duration of surrender charge | 7 years | Annual contract charge | $30 |
| Declining surrender charge | yes | Free annual withdrawals | 10% |

## Management                                               ✓

MFS/Sun Life Regatta Gold is offered by Sun Life Assurance Company of Canada (US). The portfolio (and/or the mutual fund it is modeled after) was managed by Richard E. Dahlberg for the 6 years ending December 31, 1994. The portfolio's size is $330 million. The typical security in the portfolio has a market capitalization of $6.3 billion. Dahlberg also manages the MFS Total Return Fund.

## Investment Options                                       ✓✓✓✓

Investors may make additional contributions into this portfolio at any time. This is known as a flexible premium annuity. Investors in this variable annuity can choose from all of the subaccount categories below that have a check mark:

| | | |
|---|---|---|
| ✓ Aggressive growth | ✓ Government bonds | ✓ Money market |
| ✓ Balanced | ✓ Growth | ___ Specialty/Sector |
| ___ Corporate bonds | ✓ Growth & income | ✓ World bonds |
| ✓ Global equities (stocks) | ✓ High-yield bonds | |

## Family Rating                                            ✓✓✓

There are 10 subaccounts within the MFS/Sun Life (US) Regatta Gold family. Overall, this family of subaccounts can be described as good on a *risk-adjusted* return basis.

The subaccounts within this variable annuity all have an *increasing* guaranteed death benefit. This means that the beneficiary is guaranteed to receive *the greater of* the contract's value on the date of the annuitant's death or the value of the original investment(s) compounded by 5% each year (less any withdrawals made).

## Summary

MFS/Sun Life (US) Regatta Gold Total Return Series has been able to turn in good numbers while keeping investment risk quite low. This winning combination is not new to MFS: they introduced the first mutual fund in the country in the early 1920s (a fund that is still around and has an exceptional track record since inception).

MFS/Sun Life (US) Regatta Gold is the newest variable annuity offering by MFS. Each of the MFS products represents an improvement or enhancement from previous contracts. For this reason, prospective investors may have shied away from an investment vehicle they believe has only a short-term track record. In reality, a number of the MFS money managers have been around for a long time, managing virtually identical variable annuities no longer offered to new investors.

The Regatta Gold contract provides investors with a wide range of investment selections, including global equities and world bonds, which are missing from well over 90% of all other annuities. This variable annuity provides the flexibility needed for a properly diversified investment.

## Profile

| | | | |
|---|---|---|---|
| Minimum investment | $5,000 | Telephone exchanges | yes |
| Retirement account minimum | $5,000 | Transfers allowed per year | 12 |
| Co-annuitant allowed | yes | Maximum issuance age | 85 |
| Co-owner allowed | yes | Maximum annuitization age | 90 |
| Dollar-cost averaging | yes | Number of subaccounts | 10 |
| Systematic withdrawal plans | yes | Available in all 50 states | no* |

*Not available in NY or VT.

---

**Penn Mutual Diversifier II**
**Flexibly Managed**
Independence Square
Philadelphia, PA  19172
(800) 548-1119

---

| | |
|---|---|
| Performance | ✓✓✓✓ |
| Risk control | ✓✓✓✓✓ |
| Expense minimization | ✓✓✓ |
| Management | ✓✓✓✓✓ |
| Investment options | ✓✓✓✓ |
| Family rating | ✓✓✓ |
| Total point score | 24 points |

## Performance                                               ✓✓✓✓

During the 3-year and 5-year periods ending December 31, 1994, Flexibly Managed had an average annual compound return of 8.4% and 8.4%, respectively. This means that a $10,000 investment made into this subaccount 5 years before that date grew to $15,000 ($12,700, if only the last 3 years of that period are used).

Compared to other balanced variable annuity subaccounts, this one ranks in the top third for the 3-year and 5-year periods studied. The inception month of this subaccount was August 1984. This subaccount is modeled (cloned) after the Penn Series Fund Flexibly Managed Fund, which had an inception date of July 1984, and has an asset base of $75 million.

The year-by-year returns for this subaccount are:

| Year | Annual Return | S&P 500 | Lehman Bros. Gov't/Corp. Bond Index |
|------|--------------|---------|-------------------------------------|
| 1994 | 2.9% | 1.3% | −3.5% |
| 1993 | 14.4% | 10.1% | 11.1% |
| 1992 | 8.2% | 7.6% | 7.6% |
| 1991 | 20.1% | 30.5% | 16.1% |
| 1990 | −2.1% | −3.1% | 8.3% |
| 1989 | 19.6% | 31.7% | 14.2% |
| 1988 | 17.4% | 16.6% | 7.6% |
| 1987 | 22.0% | 5.3% | 2.3% |

## Risk Control                    ✓✓✓✓

Over the 3-year period, this fund was 50% safer than the average hybrid subaccount. During the 5-year period, it was 25% safer.

The typical standard deviation for balanced subaccounts was 2.0% during the 3-year period. The standard deviation for Penn Mutual Diversifier II Flexibly Managed was 1.7% over this same period, which means that this subaccount was 15% less volatile than its peer group. The price/earnings (p/e) ratio averages 26 for this portfolio. The typical balanced subaccount has a p/e ratio of 23. In general, the higher the p/e ratio, the riskier the portfolio.

The beta (market-related risk) of this subaccount was 0.5 over the 3-year period. Beta for this entire category was 0.6 over this same period. The market index (the S&P 500 Index for "hybrid" subaccounts such as balanced subaccounts) always has a beta of 1.0. The *risk-adjusted* return for this variable annuity subaccount can be described as very good.

## Expense Minimization               ✓✓✓

The typical expenses incurred by balanced subaccounts are 2.0% per year. The total expenses for Penn Mutual Diversifier II Flexibly Managed, 2.1%, are higher than its peer group average. Total expenses include all charges to the investor (except the annual contract charge, which is always expressed as a dollar figure), including management fees, overhead, administration, and mortality expenses. The free annual withdrawals percentage is based on the account value.

| | | | |
|---|---|---|---|
| Maximum surrender charge | 7% | Total expenses | 2.1% |
| Duration of surrender charge | 10 years | Annual contract charge | $30 |
| Declining surrender charge | no | Free annual withdrawals | 10% |

## Management                     ✓✓✓✓

Penn Mutual Diversifier II is offered by Penn Mutual Life Insurance Company. The company has a Duff & Phelps rating of AA− and an A.M. Best rating of A+. The portfolio was managed by Richard P. Howard for the 5 years ending December 31, 1994. The portfolio's size is $100 million. The typical security in the portfolio has a market capitalization of $2.6 billion.

## Investment Options                                        ✓✓✓✓

Investors may make additional contributions into this portfolio at any time. This is known as a flexible premium annuity. Investors in this variable annuity can choose from all of the subaccount categories below that have a check mark:

|   | | | | | |
|---|---|---|---|---|---|
| ___ | Aggressive growth | ___ | Government bonds | ✓ | Money market |
| ✓ | Balanced | ✓ | Growth | ___ | Specialty/Sector |
| ✓ | Corporate bonds | ✓ | Growth & income | ___ | World bonds |
| ✓ | Global equities (stocks) | ✓ | High-yield bonds | | |

## Family Rating                                             ✓✓✓

There are 10 subaccounts within the Penn Mutual Diversifier II family. Overall, this family of subaccounts can be described as good on a *risk-adjusted* return basis.

   The subaccounts within this variable annuity all have an *increasing* guaranteed death benefit. This means that the beneficiary is guaranteed to receive *the greater of* the contract's value on the date of the annuitant's death or the value of the original investment(s) compounded by 5% each year (less any withdrawals made).

## Summary

Penn Mutual Diversifier II Flexibly Managed is not only a top-performing balanced account, it is also a star when it comes to risk reduction. This subaccount achieves an almost perfect score for performance, risk control, and management. This investment is a great choice for any investor who desires high returns with about half the risk normally associated with such a portfolio.

   The 10-year penalty schedule is one of the most onerous in the industry, but the contract is able to counter this concern by providing a healthy number of investment options that can be easily moved into as conditions or personal outlooks change. Fortunately, free annual withdrawals are based on the account value.

## Profile

| | | | | |
|---|---|---|---|---|
| Minimum investment | $250 | | Telephone exchanges | yes |
| Retirement account minimum | $2,500 | | Transfers allowed per year | 12 |
| Co-annuitant allowed | yes | | Maximum issuance age | 80 |
| Co-owner allowed | yes | | Maximum annuitization age | 85 |
| Dollar-cost averaging | yes | | Number of subaccounts | 10 |
| Systematic withdrawal plans | yes | | Available in all 50 states | yes |

---

**Phoenix Home Life Big Edge Plus**
**Total Return**
100 Bright Meadow Boulevard
Enfield, CT  06083-1900
(800) 447-4312

---

| | |
|---|---|
| Performance | ✓✓✓✓ |
| Risk control | ✓✓✓ |
| Expense minimization | ✓✓✓✓ |
| Management | ✓✓✓✓ |
| Investment options | ✓✓ |
| Family rating | ✓✓✓✓✓ |
| Total point score | 22 points |

# Performance  ✓✓✓✓

During the 3-year and 5-year periods ending December 31, 1994, Total Return had an average annual compound return of 5.3% and 9.2%, respectively. This means that a $10,000 investment made into this subaccount 5 years before that date grew to $15,500 ($11,700, if only the last 3 years of that period are used).

Compared to other balanced variable annuity subaccounts, this one ranks in the top third for the 3-year period and in the top 15% for the 5-year period. The inception month of this subaccount was January 1987. This subaccount is modeled (cloned) after the Phoenix Balanced Fund Series, a mutual fund that had an inception date of January 1981, and has an asset base of $3.2 billion.

The year-by-year returns for this subaccount are:

| Year | Annual Return | S&P 500 | Lehman Bros. Gov't/Corp. Bond Index |
|------|--------------|---------|-------------------------------------|
| 1994 | −2.7% | 1.3% | −3.5% |
| 1993 | 9.6% | 10.1% | 11.1% |
| 1992 | 9.3% | 7.6% | 7.6% |
| 1991 | 27.7% | 30.5% | 16.1% |
| 1990 | 4.4% | −3.1% | 8.3% |
| 1989 | 18.4% | 31.7% | 14.2% |
| 1988 | 1.1% | 16.6% | 7.6% |

# Risk Control  ✓✓✓

Over the 3-year period, this fund was 30% safer than the average hybrid subaccount. During the 5-year period, it was 35% safer.

The typical standard deviation for balanced subaccounts was 2.0% during the 3-year period. The standard deviation for Phoenix Home Life Big Edge Plus Total Return was 2.3% over this same period, which means that this subaccount was 12% more volatile than its peer group. The price/earnings (p/e) ratio averages 24 for this portfolio. The typical balanced subaccount has a p/e ratio of 23. In general, the higher the p/e ratio, the riskier the portfolio.

The beta (market-related risk) of this subaccount was 0.7 over the 3-year period. Beta for this entire category was 0.6 over this same period. The market index (the S&P 500 Index for "hybrid" subaccounts such as balanced subaccounts) always has a beta of 1.0. The *risk-adjusted* return for this variable annuity subaccount can be described as excellent.

# Expense Minimization  ✓✓✓✓

The typical expenses incurred by balanced subaccounts are 2.0% per year. The total expenses for Phoenix Home Life Big Edge Plus Total Return, 1.8%, are lower than its peer group average. Total expenses include all charges to the investor (except the annual contract charge, which is always expressed as a dollar figure), including management fees, overhead, administration, and mortality expenses. The free annual withdrawals percentage is based on the value of the account on its anniversary date.

| | | | |
|---|---|---|---|
| Maximum surrender charge | 6% | Total expenses | 1.8% |
| Duration of surrender charge | 6 years | Annual contract charge | $35 |
| Declining surrender charge | yes | Free annual withdrawals | 10% |

## Management                                                         ✓✓✓

Phoenix Home Life Big Edge Plus is offered by Phoenix Home Life Mutual Insurance Company. The company has a Duff & Phelps rating of AA and an A.M. Best rating of A. The portfolio (and/or the mutual fund it is modeled after) was managed by Robert Milnamow for the 5 years ending December 31, 1994. The portfolio's size is $150 million. The typical security in the annuity has a market capitalization of $7.6 billion. Milnamow also manages the Phoenix Total Return mutual fund.

## Investment Options                                                 ✓✓

Investors may make additional contributions into this portfolio at any time. This is known as a flexible premium annuity. Investors in this variable annuity can choose from all of the subaccount categories below that have a check mark:

| | | |
|---|---|---|
| ___ Aggressive growth | ___ Government bonds | ✓ Money market |
| ✓ Balanced | ✓ Growth | ___ Specialty/Sector |
| ✓ Corporate bonds | ___ Growth & income | ___ World bonds |
| ✓ Global equities (stocks) | ___ High-yield bonds | |

## Family Rating                                                      ✓✓✓✓

There are 6 subaccounts within the Phoenix Home Life Big Edge Plus family. Overall, this family of subaccounts can be described as excellent on a *risk-adjusted* return basis.

   The subaccounts within this variable annuity all have an *increasing* guaranteed death benefit. This means that the beneficiary is guaranteed to receive *the greater of* the contract's value on the date of the annuitant's death or the value of the original investment(s) compounded by 5% each year (less any withdrawals made).

## Summary

Phoenix Home Life Big Edge Plus Total Return is strong on performance, expense minimization, and management. It is one of the few subaccounts that are part of an overall family that is rated as excellent. This particular subaccount has never had a negative year. Portfolio manager Milnamow has been able to attain this feat while exposing his investors to 25–33% less risk than with the typical balanced subaccount.

   All of the Phoenix Home Life subaccounts are overseen by the same people who manage Phoenix mutual funds, one of the best *medium-size* mutual fund family in the country. This company is not well known. It spends little money on advertising, preferring instead to appeal to more sophisticated investment advisors and investors. This is a fine company across the board. Not enough good things can be said about the money managers or this particular balanced subaccount.

## Profile

| | | | |
|---|---|---|---|
| Minimum investment | $25 | Telephone exchanges | yes |
| Retirement account minimum | $1,000 | Transfers allowed per year | unlimited |
| Co-annuitant allowed | no | Maximum issuance age | 85 |
| Co-owner allowed | spouses only | Maximum annuitization age | 85 |
| Dollar-cost averaging | yes | Number of subaccounts | 6 |
| Systematic withdrawal plans | yes | Available in all 50 states | yes |

---

**Prudential Discovery Plus
Aggressively Managed Flexible**
Prudential Plaza
Newark, NJ 07102-3777
(201) 802-6000

---

| | |
|---|---|
| Performance | ✓✓✓✓ |
| Risk control | ✓✓✓ |
| Expense minimization | ✓✓✓✓ |
| Management | ✓✓✓✓ |
| Investment options | ✓✓✓ |
| Family rating | ✓✓✓ |
| Total point score | 21 points |

---

# Performance                                              ✓✓✓✓

During the 3-year and 5-year periods ending December 31, 1994, Aggressively Managed Flexible had an average annual compound return of 5.1% and 7.7%, respectively (11.6% for 10 years). This means that a $10,000 investment made into this subaccount 5 years before that date grew to $14,500 ($11,600, if only the last 3 years of that period are used).

Compared to other balanced variable annuity subaccounts, this one ranks in the top third for the 3-year period and in the top quartile for the 5-year period. (It ranks in the top 35% for the 10 years ending December 31, 1994.) The inception month of this subaccount was February 1989. The performance figures (shown below) for periods before the subaccount's inception in February 1989 are hypothetical, based on the underlying clone fund's returns. This subaccount is modeled (cloned) after the Prudential Series Fund Aggressively Managed Flexible Portfolio, which had an inception date of May 1983, and has an asset base of $3.1 billion.

The year-by-year returns for this subaccount and the portfolio it is modeled after are:

| Year | Annual Return | S&P 500 | Lehman Bros. Gov't/Corp. Bond Index |
|---|---|---|---|
| 1994 | −4.3% | 1.3% | −3.5% |
| 1993 | 14.2% | 10.1% | 11.1% |
| 1992 | 6.3% | 7.6% | 7.6% |
| 1991 | 23.9% | 30.5% | 16.1% |
| 1990 | 0.7% | −3.1% | 8.3% |
| 1989 | 20.3% | 31.7% | 14.2% |
| 1988 | 11.5% | 16.6% | 7.6% |
| 1987 | −3.0% | 5.3% | 2.3% |

# Risk Control                                              ✓✓✓

Over the 3-year and 5-year periods studied, this fund was 25% safer than the average hybrid subaccount.

The typical standard deviation for balanced subaccounts was 2.0% during the 3-year period. The standard deviation for Prudential Discovery Plus Aggressively Managed Flexible was 2.2% over this same period, which means that this subaccount was 10% more volatile than its peer group. The price/earnings (p/e) ratio averages 23 for this portfolio. The typical balanced subaccount also has a p/e ratio of 23. In general, the higher the p/e ratio, the riskier the portfolio.

The beta (market-related risk) of this subaccount was 0.7 over the 3-year period. Beta for this entire category was 0.6 over this same period. The market index (the S&P 500 Index for "hybrid" subaccounts such as balanced subaccounts) always has a beta of 1.0. The *risk-adjusted* return for this variable annuity subaccount can be described as good.

## Expense Minimization                                              ✓✓✓✓

The typical expenses incurred by balanced subaccounts are 2.0% per year. The total expenses for Prudential Discovery Plus Aggressively Managed Flexible, 1.9%, are lower than its peer group average. Total expenses include all charges to the investor (except the annual contract charge, which is always expressed as a dollar figure), including management fees, overhead, administration, and mortality expenses. The free annual withdrawals percentage is based on the account value.

| | | | |
|---|---|---|---|
| Maximum surrender charge | 7% | Total expenses | 1.9% |
| Duration of surrender charge | 6 years | Annual contract charge | $0 |
| Declining surrender charge | yes | Free annual withdrawals | 10% |

## Management                                                        ✓✓✓✓

Prudential Discovery Plus is offered by Prudential Insurance Company of America. The company has a Duff & Phelps rating of AA+. The portfolio was managed by James McHugh, Anthony M. Gleason, and Kay Willcox for the 8 years ending December 31, 1994. The portfolio's size is an impressive $350 million. The typical security in the portfolio has a market capitalization of $6 billion.

## Investment Options                                                ✓✓✓

Investors may make additional contributions into this portfolio at any time. This is known as a flexible premium annuity. Investors in this variable annuity can choose from all of the subaccount categories below that have a check mark:

| | | |
|---|---|---|
| ___ Aggressive growth | ✓ Government bonds | ✓ Money market |
| ✓ Balanced | ✓ Growth | ✓ Specialty/Sector |
| ✓ Corporate bonds | ✓ Growth & income | ___ World bonds |
| ✓ Global equities (stocks) | ✓ High-yield bonds | |

## Family Rating                                                     ✓✓✓

There are 12 subaccounts within the Prudential Discovery Plus family. Overall, this family of subaccounts can be described as good on a *risk-adjusted* return basis.

## Summary

Prudential Discovery Plus Aggressively Managed Flexible is rated quite highly in the areas of total return, expense minimization, and overall management. This balanced subaccount also receives good marks when it comes to risk control, investment options, and family rating. Over the past half-dozen years, the portfolio has shown only positive returns, often beating the stock and bond indexes with 25% less risk.

The Aggressively Managed Flexible subaccount is one of the larger portfolios in the industry. Size is an important advantage at this level: It allows management greater purchasing power for the bond portion of the portfolio, and greater diversification on the equity side.

Prudential Discovery Plus is a variable annuity that offers some neat extras, including global equities, high-yield bonds, and a specialty subaccount. The contract includes some favorable investor provisions not widely found within the annuity industry.

## Profile

| | | | |
|---|---|---|---|
| Minimum investment | $10,000 | Telephone exchanges | yes |
| Retirement account minimum | $10,000 | Transfers allowed per year | 4 |
| Co-annuitant allowed | yes | Maximum issuance age | 85 |
| Co-owner allowed | yes | Maximum annuitization age | 90 |
| Dollar-cost averaging | yes | Number of subaccounts | 12 |
| Systematic withdrawal plans | no | Available in all 50 states | yes |

---

**Scudder Horizon Plan**
**Balanced**
8301 Maryland Avenue
St. Louis, MO 63105
(800) 225-2470

| | |
|---|---|
| Performance | ✓✓ |
| Risk control | ✓✓ |
| Expense minimization | ✓✓✓✓✓ |
| Management | ✓✓ |
| Investment options | ✓✓ |
| Family rating | ✓✓✓ |
| Total point score | 16 points |

## Performance ✓✓

During the 3-year and 5-year periods ending December 31, 1994, Balanced had an average annual compound return of 3.3% and 6.2%, respectively. This means that a $10,000 investment made into this subaccount 5 years before that date grew to $13,500 ($11,000, if only the last 3 years of that period are used).

Compared to other balanced variable annuity subaccounts, this one ranks in the bottom half for the 3-year and 5-year periods. The inception month of this subaccount was October 1988.

The year-by-year returns for this subaccount are:

| Year | Annual Return | S&P 500 | Lehman Bros. Gov't/Corp. Bond Index |
|---|---|---|---|
| 1994 | −2.7% | 1.3% | −3.5% |
| 1993 | 6.7% | 10.1% | 11.1% |
| 1992 | 6.2% | 7.6% | 7.6% |
| 1991 | 26.0% | 30.5% | 16.1% |
| 1990 | −2.9% | −3.1% | 8.3% |
| 1989 | 18.3% | 31.7% | 14.2% |

## Risk Control ✓✓

Over the 3-year period, this fund was slightly riskier than the average hybrid subaccount. During the 5-year period, it was slightly safer.

The typical standard deviation for balanced subaccounts was 2.0% during the 3-year period. The standard deviation for Scudder Horizon Plan Balanced was 2.6%

over this same period, which means that this subaccount was 29% more volatile than its peer group. The price/earnings (p/e) ratio averages 22 for this portfolio. The typical balanced subaccount has a p/e ratio of 23. In general, the higher the p/e ratio, the riskier the portfolio.

The beta (market-related risk) of this subaccount was 0.7 over the 3-year period. Beta for this entire category was 0.6 over this same period. The market index (the S&P 500 Index for "hybrid" subaccounts such as balanced subaccounts) always has a beta of 1.0. The *risk-adjusted* return for this variable annuity subaccount can be described as fair.

## Expense Minimization                                    ✓✓✓✓

The typical expenses incurred by balanced subaccounts are 2.0% per year. The total expenses for Scudder Horizon Plan Balanced, 1.5%, are lower than its peer group average. Total expenses include all charges to the investor (except the annual contract charge, which is always expressed as a dollar figure), including management fees, overhead, administration, and mortality expenses. The free annual withdrawals percentage is based on the account value.

| | | | |
|---|---|---|---|
| Maximum surrender charge | 0% | Total expenses | 1.5% |
| Duration of surrender charge | n/a | Annual contract charge | $0 |
| Declining surrender charge | n/a | Free annual withdrawals | 10% |

## Management                                              ✓✓

Scudder Horizon Plan is offered by Charter National Life Insurance Company. The company has an A.M. Best rating of A. The portfolio was managed by Ruth Heisler, William M. Hutchinson, Howard F. Ward, and Bruce F. Beaty for the 9 years ending December 31, 1994. The portfolio's size is $35 million. The typical security in the portfolio has a market capitalization of $11.4 billion.

## Investment Options                                      ✓✓

Investors may make additional contributions into this portfolio at any time. This is known as a flexible premium annuity. Investors in this variable annuity can choose from all of the subaccount categories below that have a check mark:

| | | |
|---|---|---|
| ___ Aggressive growth | ___ Government bonds | ✓ Money market |
| ✓ Balanced | ✓ Growth | ___ Specialty/Sector |
| ✓ Corporate bonds | ___ Growth & income | ___ World bonds |
| ✓ Global equities (stocks) | ___ High-yield bonds | |

## Family Rating                                           ✓✓✓

There are 5 subaccounts within the Scudder Horizon Plan family. Overall, this family of subaccounts can be described as good on a *risk-adjusted* return basis.

## Summary

Scudder Horizon Plan Balanced is one of the few subaccounts that has no strings attached. Investors can add or take money out at any time without any insurance company penalties or costs. This variable annuity contract also has some of the lowest overhead in the entire industry.

Total point score for this portfolio is decent; however, other offerings within the family may be more to your liking. Nevertheless, this investment is a great way for someone unfamiliar with annuities to get their feet wet.

# Profile

| | | | |
|---|---|---|---|
| Minimum investment | $2,500 | Telephone exchanges | yes |
| Retirement account minimum | $2,500 | Transfers allowed per year | unlimited |
| Co-annuitant allowed | no | Maximum issuance age | none |
| Co-owner allowed | yes | Maximum annuitization age | none |
| Dollar-cost averaging | yes | Number of subaccounts | 5 |
| Systematic withdrawal plans | yes | Available in all 50 states | no* |

*Not available in the following states: HI, KY, LA, NM, and WY.

---

**Security Benefit Variflex
Income-Growth**
700 Southwest Harrison Street
Topeka, KS 66636
(800) 888-2461

| | |
|---|---|
| Performance | ✓✓✓✓ |
| Risk control | ✓ |
| Expense minimization | ✓✓✓ |
| Management | ✓✓✓ |
| Investment options | ✓✓✓ |
| Family rating | ✓ |
| Total point score | 15 points |

# Performance ✓✓✓✓

During the 3-year and 5-year periods ending December 31, 1994, Income-Growth had an average annual compound return of 2.9% and 7.0%, respectively (11.9% for 10 years). This means that a $10,000 investment made into this subaccount 5 years before that date grew to $14,000 ($10,900, if only the last 3 years of that period are used).

Compared to other balanced variable annuity subaccounts, this one ranks in the top quartile for the 3-year period and in the top quintile for the 5-year period. (It ranks in the top 20% for the 10 years ending December 31, 1994.) The inception month of this subaccount was June 1984.

The year-by-year returns for this subaccount are:

| Year | Annual Return | S&P 500 | Lehman Bros. Gov't/Corp. Bond Index |
|---|---|---|---|
| 1994 | −4.1% | 1.3% | −3.5% |
| 1993 | 8.3% | 10.1% | 11.1% |
| 1992 | 5.0% | 7.6% | 7.6% |
| 1991 | 36.2% | 30.5% | 16.1% |
| 1990 | −5.6% | −3.1% | 8.3% |
| 1989 | 26.9% | 31.7% | 14.2% |
| 1988 | 17.9% | 16.6% | 7.6% |
| 1987 | 2.4% | 5.3% | 2.3% |

## Risk Control                                                    ✓

Over the 3-year and 5-year periods, this fund was somewhat riskier than the average hybrid subaccount.

The typical standard deviation for balanced subaccounts was 2.0% during the 3-year period. The standard deviation for Security Benefit Variflex Income-Growth was 3.0% over this same period, which means that this subaccount was 50% more volatile than its peer group. The price/earnings (p/e) ratio averages 22 for this portfolio. The typical balanced subaccount has a p/e ratio of 23. In general, the higher the p/e ratio, the riskier the portfolio.

The beta (market-related risk) of this subaccount was 0.8 over the 3-year period. Beta for this entire category was 0.6 over this same period. The market index (the S&P 500 Index for "hybrid" subaccounts such as balanced subaccounts) always has a beta of 1.0. The *risk-adjusted* return for this variable annuity subaccount can be described as fair.

## Expense Minimization                                           ✓✓✓

The typical expenses incurred by balanced subaccounts are 2.0% per year. The total expenses for Security Benefit Variflex Income-Growth, 2.1%, are higher than its peer group average. Total expenses include all charges to the investor (except the annual contract charge, which is always expressed as a dollar figure), including management fees, overhead, administration, and mortality expenses. The free annual withdrawals percentage is based on the account value.

| | | | |
|---|---|---|---|
| Maximum surrender charge | 8% | Total expenses | 2.1% |
| Duration of surrender charge | 8 years | Annual contract charge | $30 |
| Declining surrender charge | no | Free annual withdrawals | 10% |

## Management                                                     ✓✓✓

Security Benefit Variflex is offered by Security Benefit Life Insurance Company. The company has an A.M. Best rating of A+. The portfolio has been managed by John D. Cleland since its inception. The portfolio's size is an impressive $550 million. The typical security in the portfolio has a market capitalization of $6.2 billion. Cleland also manages the Security Growth & Income mutual fund.

## Investment Options                                             ✓✓✓

Investors may make additional contributions into this portfolio at any time. This is known as a flexible premium annuity. Investors in this variable annuity can choose from all of the subaccount categories below that have a check mark:

| | | |
|---|---|---|
| ✓ Aggressive growth | ___ Government bonds | ✓ Money market |
| ✓ Balanced | ✓ Growth | ___ Specialty/Sector |
| ✓ Corporate bonds | ___ Growth & income | ___ World bonds |
| ✓ Global equities (stocks) | ___ High-yield bonds | |

## Family Rating                                                    ✓

There are 7 subaccounts within the Security Benefit Variflex family. Overall, this family of subaccounts can be described as poor on a *risk-adjusted* return basis.

The subaccounts within this variable annuity all have an *increasing* guaranteed death benefit. This means that the beneficiary is guaranteed to receive *the greater of* the contract's value on the date of the annuitant's death or the value of the original investment(s) compounded by 5% each year (less any withdrawals made).

## Summary

Security Benefit Variflex Income-Growth scores high where it counts the most—in performance. The subaccount has had to be slightly riskier than its peer group, but the strategy has paid off. This subaccount has attracted quite a bit of money.

The Security Benefit Variflex annuity contract offers a stepped-up death benefit, unlimited telephone exchanges, co-ownership, and a low minimum investment. Few other contracts in the industry include all of these useful features.

## Profile

| | | | |
|---|---|---|---|
| Minimum investment | $25 | Telephone exchanges | yes |
| Retirement account minimum | $500 | Transfers allowed per year | unlimited |
| Co-annuitant allowed | no | Maximum issuance age | 80 |
| Co-owner allowed | yes | Maximum annuitization age | none |
| Dollar-cost averaging | yes | Number of subaccounts | 7 |
| Systematic withdrawal plans | yes | Available in all 50 states | no* |

*Not available in NY.

**9**

# Corporate Bond Subaccounts

Traditionally, bond subaccounts are held by investors who require stability and low risk. Corporate bond subaccounts are primarily comprised of bonds issued by corporations. Portfolio composition is almost always completely comprised of U.S. issues.

Normally purchased because of its reinvested income stream, one's principal in a bond subaccount can fluctuate. The major influence on bond prices, and therefore the value of the underlying subaccount, is interest rates. There is an *inverse* relationship between interest rates and bond values; whatever one does, the other does the opposite. If interest rates rise, the price of a bond subaccount will fall, and vice versa. Gains (or losses) are increased (or offset) by the yield from the bonds.

The amount of appreciation or loss of a corporate bond subaccount primarily depends on the average maturity of the bonds in the portfolio and the yield of the bonds in the subaccount's portfolio. *Short-term* bond subaccounts, comprised of debt instruments with an average maturity of 5 years or less, are subject to very little interest rate risk or reward. *Medium-term* bond subaccounts, with maturities averaging between 6 and 15 years, are subject to one-third to one-half the risk level of long-term subaccounts. A long-term corporate bond (maturity ranging from 16 to 30 years) subaccount will average an 8% increase or decrease in share price for every cumulative 1% change in interest rates.

Often, investors can determine the type of corporate bond subaccount they are purchasing by its name. Unless the subaccount includes the term *short* in its title, chances are that it is a medium- or long-term bond subaccount. Investors would be wise to contact the subaccount, or counsel with an investment advisor, to learn more about the portfolio's average maturity; most bond subaccounts will dramatically reduce their portfolio's maturity during periods of interest rate uncertainty.

Over the 15-year period from 1979 to 1993, individual corporate bonds underperformed common stocks by more than 40%. Long-term corporate bonds averaged 11.6% compounded per year, versus 15.7% for common stocks and 17.0% for small stocks. A $10,000 investment in corporate bonds grew to $51,700 over that same 15-year period; a similar initial investment in common stocks grew to $89,300. For small stocks, the investment grew to $105,600.

Within a longer time frame, corporate bonds have only outpaced inflation on a pretax basis. A dollar invested in corporate bonds in 1945 grew to $15.01 by the beginning of 1995. This translates into an average compound return of 5.6% per year. During this same period, $1 inflated to $8.37, which translates into an average annual inflation rate of 4.3%. Over the 50 years ending December 31, 1994, the worst year for long-term corporate bonds, on a *total return* basis (yield plus or minus principal appreciation or loss), was 1969, when a loss of 8% was suffered. The best year was 1982, when corporate bonds posted a gain of 44%.

The table below shows year-by-year, as well as 3-, 5-, and 10-year averages for this investment category. The variable annuity subaccount category is compared against the similar mutual fund category. These performance figures are average figures, representing all funds and subaccounts that fall within this investment objective.

As you can see, the variable annuity subaccounts outperformed their mutual fund counterparts for 1993, 1991, and the 3-year period ending December 31, 1994.

Corporate bond subaccounts are not for speculative investors. They should comprise no more than 40% of a *diversified,* conservative portfolio. A moderate portfolio should have less than 30% of its assets devoted to long-term corporate bonds. I recommend a 20% commitment to this category for the conservative investor and 5% for the moderate portfolio. As is true with any category of variable annuities, whenever larger dollar amounts are involved, more than one subaccount per category should be used.

The table on page 84 shows statistics you might find useful when comparing variable annuity subaccounts versus their mutual fund counterparts or "clones." The category averages are based on information available at the beginning of 1995.

Figure 9.1 on page 84 shows the year-by-year returns for this category of variable annuities for the period 1987 through 1994. These are composite figures and therefore include all of the subaccounts that comprise the corporate bond category.

### Average Annual Returns: Corporate Bond Subaccounts vs. Corporate Bond Mutual Funds

| Year | Subaccount | Mutual Fund |
|------|-----------|-------------|
| 1994 | −5.0% | −3.6% |
| 1993 | 9.8% | 8.6% |
| 1992 | 6.1% | 6.4% |
| 1991 | 15.2% | 14.3% |
| 1990 | 5.7% | 7.7% |
| 1989 | 10.7% | 11.7% |
| 1988 | 6.6% | 7.3% |
| 1987 | 0.5% | 2.5% |
| | | |
| 3-yr. average | 3.4% | 4.6% |
| 5-yr. average | 6.0% | 7.3% |
| 10-yr. average | 8.1% | 9.5% |

### Corporate Bond Category Statistics: Subaccounts vs. Mutual Funds

| Description | Subaccounts | Funds |
| --- | --- | --- |
| **Composition of portfolio** | | |
| U.S. stocks | 1% | 0% |
| Cash | 7% | 10% |
| Foreign stocks | 0% | 0% |
| Bonds | 92% | 87% |
| Other | 0% | 3% |
| **Fees and expenses** | | |
| Underlying fund expense | 0.64% | 0.83% |
| Insurance expense | 1.24% | — |
| Total expenses | 1.88% | 0.83%/2.3%* |
| **Operations** | | |
| Net assets (in millions) | $68 | $290 |
| Manager tenure | 5 years | 4 years |
| **Portfolio statistics** | | |
| Average maturity | 11 years | 8 years |
| Standard deviation | 1.1% | 1.1% |
| Average weighted coupon | 7.5% | 7.5% |
| Turnover ratio (annual) | 95% | 159% |
| Number of subaccounts/funds | 150 | 290 |

*Total expenses for this mutual fund category increase to this figure if the average mutual fund commission is added to the 0.83% figure.

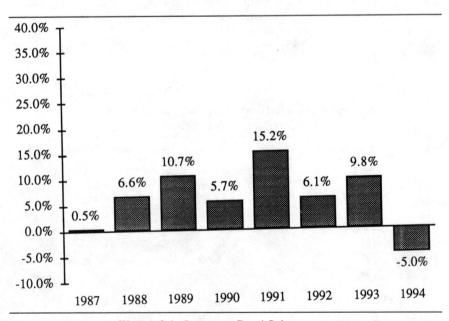

**Figure 9.1** Corporate Bond Subaccounts

---

**Connecticut Mutual Panorama**
**Income**
P.O. Box 13217
Kansas City, MO  64199
(800) 234-5606 ext. 5232

---

| | |
|---|---|
| Performance | ✓✓✓✓ |
| Risk control | ✓✓✓ |
| Expense minimization | ✓✓✓✓✓ |
| Management | ✓✓✓ |
| Investment options | ✓ |
| Family rating | ✓✓✓✓✓ |
| Total point score | 21 points |

---

# Performance                                                  ✓✓✓✓

During the 3-year and 5-year periods ending December 31, 1994, Income had an average annual compound return of 4.1% and 6.9%, respectively (10.7% for 10 years). This means that a $10,000 investment made into this subaccount 5 years before that date grew to $14,000 ($11,300, if only the last 3 years of that period are used).

Compared to other corporate bond variable annuity subaccounts, this one ranks in the top quintile for the 3-year and 5-year periods. (It ranks in the top quartile for the 10 years ending December 31, 1994.) The inception month of this subaccount was February 1982.

The year-by-year returns for this subaccount are:

| Year | Annual Return | Lehman Bros. Corporate Bond Index |
|---|---|---|
| 1994 | −4.7% | −3.9% |
| 1993 | 11.3% | 12.2% |
| 1992 | 6.3% | 8.7% |
| 1991 | 17.5% | 18.5% |
| 1990 | 5.1% | 7.2% |
| 1989 | 13.1% | 14.0% |
| 1988 | 7.1% | 9.2% |
| 1987 | 1.0% | 2.6% |

# Risk Control                                                  ✓✓✓

Over the 3-year period, this fund was slightly safer than the average fixed-income subaccount. During the 5-year period, it was slightly riskier.

The typical standard deviation for corporate bond subaccounts was 1.1% during the 3-year period. The standard deviation for Connecticut Mutual Panorama Income was 1.25% over this same period, which means that this subaccount was 15% more volatile than its peer group. The average maturity of the bonds in this account is 9 years; the weighted coupon rate averages 8.1%. The typical corporate bond subaccount has an average maturity of just under 11 years and a weighted coupon rate of 7.5%.

The beta (market-related risk) of this subaccount was 1.2 over the 3-year period. Beta for this entire category was 1.1 over this same period. The market index (the Lehman Brothers Aggregate Bond Index for debt subaccounts) always has a beta of 1.0. The *risk-adjusted* return for this variable annuity subaccount can be described as good.

## Expense Minimization                    ✓✓✓✓

The typical expenses incurred by corporate bond subaccounts are 1.9% per year. The total expenses for Connecticut Mutual Panorama Income, 1.5%, are lower than its peer group average. Total expenses include all charges to the investor (except the annual contract charge, which is always expressed as a dollar figure), including management fees, overhead, administration, and mortality expenses. The free annual withdrawals percentage is based on the account value.

| | | | |
|---|---|---|---|
| Maximum surrender charge | 5% | Total expenses | 1.5% |
| Duration of surrender charge | 10 years | Annual contract charge | $40 |
| Declining surrender charge | no | Free annual withdrawals | 10% |

## Management                    ✓✓✓

Connecticut Mutual Panorama is offered by Connecticut Mutual Life Insurance Company. The company has a Duff & Phelps rating of AA and an A.M. Best rating of A+. The portfolio was managed by Stephen F. Libera for the 12 years ending December 31, 1994. The portfolio's size is $65 million. Libera also manages the Connecticut Mutual Income Fund.

## Investment Options                    ✓

Investors may make additional contributions into this portfolio at any time. This is known as a flexible premium annuity. Investors in this variable annuity can choose from all of the subaccount categories below that have a check mark:

| | | |
|---|---|---|
| ___ Aggressive growth | ___ Government bonds | ✓ Money market |
| ✓ Balanced | ✓ Growth | ___ Specialty/Sector |
| ✓ Corporate bonds | ___ Growth & income | ___ World bonds |
| ___ Global equities (stocks) | ___ High-yield bonds | |

## Family Rating                    ✓✓✓✓

There are 4 subaccounts within the Connecticut Mutual Panorama family. Overall, this family of subaccounts can be described as excellent on a *risk-adjusted* return basis.

## Summary

Connecticut Mutual Panorama Income scores high in two of the most important categories: performance and overall family rating. Few variable annuity subaccounts belong to a family whose overall description is excellent.

This particular subaccount has shown only positive results over the past several years, including 1987, the year of the crash. It is hoped that the company will add even more subaccounts, making Panorama Income that much more appealing.

The contract includes one feature to watch out for: a 10-year penalty period. On a more positive note, the maximum surrender charge is one of the lowest in the industry, operating expenses are quite a bit lower than other variable annuity accounts, and withdrawals are based on the value of the account, not original principal.

## Profile

| | | | |
|---|---|---|---|
| Minimum investment | n/a | Telephone exchanges | yes |
| Retirement account minimum | $5,000 | Transfers allowed per year | unlimited |
| Co-annuitant allowed | no | Maximum issuance age | 75 |
| Co-owner allowed | no | Maximum annuitization age | none |
| Dollar-cost averaging | yes | Number of subaccounts | 4 |
| Systematic withdrawal plans | yes | Available in all 50 states | yes |

---

**Dean Witter Variable Annuity II
Quality Income Plus**
Two World Trade Center
74th Floor
New York, NY 10048
(800) 869-3863

| | |
|---|---|
| Performance | ✓✓✓✓ |
| Risk control | ✓✓ |
| Expense minimization | ✓✓✓ |
| Management | ✓✓ |
| Investment options | ✓✓✓✓ |
| Family rating | ✓✓✓✓ |
| Total point score | 19 points |

## Performance ✓✓✓✓

During the 3-year and 5-year periods ending December 31, 1994, Quality Income Plus had an average annual compound return of 3.1% and 6.2%, respectively. This means that a $10,000 investment made into this subaccount 5 years before that date grew to $13,500 ($11,000, if only the last 3 years of that period are used).

Compared to other corporate bond variable annuity subaccounts, this one ranks in the top quintile for the 3-year period. The inception month of this subaccount was October 1990. The performance figures (shown below) for periods before the subaccount's inception in October 1990 are based on the subaccount's predecessor, the Dean Witter VIS Quality Income Plus Portfolio, which had an inception date of March 1987.

The year-by-year returns for this subaccount and its predecessor are:

| Year | Annual Return | Lehman Bros. Corporate Bond Index |
|---|---|---|
| 1994 | −7.9% | −3.9% |
| 1993 | 11.5% | 12.2% |
| 1992 | 6.8% | 8.7% |
| 1991 | 16.9% | 18.5% |
| 1990 | 8.5% | 7.2% |
| 1989 | 11.1% | 14.0% |
| 1988 | 6.7% | 9.2% |
| 1987 | 3.7% | 2.6% |

## Risk Control                                                    ✓✓

Over the 3-year period, this fund was slightly riskier than the average fixed-income subaccount.

The typical standard deviation for corporate bond subaccounts was 1.1% during the 3-year period. The standard deviation for Dean Witter Variable Annuity II Quality Income Plus was 1.3% over this same period, which means that this subaccount was 23% more volatile than its peer group. The average maturity of the bonds in this account is 16 years; the weighted coupon rate averages 7.7%. The typical corporate bond subaccount has an average maturity of just under 11 years and a weighted coupon rate of 7.5%.

The beta (market-related risk) of this subaccount was 1.3 over the 3-year period. Beta for this entire category was 1.1 over this same period. The market index (the Lehman Brothers Aggregate Bond Index for debt subaccounts) always has a beta of 1.0. The *risk-adjusted* return for this variable annuity subaccount can be described as very good.

## Expense Minimization                                            ✓✓✓

The typical expenses incurred by corporate bond subaccounts are 1.9% per year. The total expenses for Dean Witter Variable Annuity II Quality Income Plus, 1.9%, are equivalent to its peer group average. Total expenses include all charges to the investor (except the annual contract charge, which is always expressed as a dollar figure), including management fees, overhead, administration, and mortality expenses. The free annual withdrawals percentage is based on the original principal.

| | | | |
|---|---|---|---|
| Maximum surrender charge | 6% | Total expenses | 1.9% |
| Duration of surrender charge | 6 years | Annual contract charge | $30 |
| Declining surrender charge | yes | Free annual withdrawals | 15% |

## Management                                                      ✓✓

Dean Witter Variable Annuity II is offered by Northbrook Life Insurance Company. The company has an A.M. Best rating of A+. The portfolio's size is $345 million. The portfolio and its predecessor were managed by Paula LaCosta for the 7 years ending December 31, 1994.

## Investment Options                                              ✓✓✓✓

Investors may make additional contributions into this portfolio at any time. This is known as a flexible premium annuity. Investors in this variable annuity can choose from all of the subaccount categories below that have a check mark:

| | | |
|---|---|---|
| ___ Aggressive growth | ___ Government bonds | ✓ Money market |
| ✓ Balanced | ✓ Growth | ✓ Specialty/Sector |
| ✓ Corporate bonds | ✓ Growth & income | ___ World bonds |
| ✓ Global equities (stocks) | ✓ High-yield bonds | |

## Family Rating                                                   ✓✓✓✓

There are 11 subaccounts within the Dean Witter Variable Annuity II family. Overall, this family of subaccounts can be described as very good on a *risk-adjusted* return basis.

The subaccounts within this variable annuity all have an *increasing* guaranteed death benefit. This means that the beneficiary is guaranteed to receive *the greater of* the contract's value on the date of the annuitant's death or the value of the original investment(s) compounded by 5% each year (less any withdrawals made).

## Summary

Dean Witter Variable Annuity II Quality Income Plus is a winner. The subaccount has had only one negative year; its performance figures are considered to be very good. One of the appeals of this subaccount is that it is part of a Dean Witter family of portfolios whose risk-adjusted return ratings are also quite good.

Like the other Dean Witter subaccount that appears in this book (see Chapter 8), this one is part of a contract that includes several beneficial features: a low initial investment requirement, the ability to have co-ownership, dollar-cost averaging, a systematic withdrawal plan, and availability in all 50 states. This last point is of particular interest. A large number of variable annuity contracts are not available in all states because they do not fulfill some of the more stringent requirements, particularly those found in New York and California.

## Profile

| | | | |
|---|---|---|---|
| Minimum investment | $1,000 | Telephone exchanges | yes |
| Retirement account minimum | $4,000 | Transfers allowed per year | 12 |
| Co-annuitant allowed | no | Maximum issuance age | 90 |
| Co-owner allowed | yes | Maximum annuitization age | 85 |
| Dollar-cost averaging | yes | Number of subaccounts | 11 |
| Systematic withdrawal plans | yes | Available in all 50 states | yes |

---

**Lutheran Brotherhood Variable Annuity Income**
625 Fourth Avenue South
Minneapolis, MN 55415
(800) 423-7056

| | |
|---|---|
| Performance | ✓✓✓✓ |
| Risk control | ✓✓✓✓ |
| Expense minimization | ✓✓✓✓ |
| Management | ✓✓✓✓ |
| Investment options | ✓ |
| Family rating | ✓✓✓✓ |
| Total point score | 26 points |

## Performance ✓✓✓✓

During the 3-year and 5-year periods ending December 31, 1994, Income had an average annual compound return of 4.0% and 7.1%, respectively. This means that a $10,000 investment made into this subaccount 5 years before that date grew to $14,100 ($11,200, if only the last 3 years of that period are used).

Compared to other corporate bond variable annuity subaccounts, this one ranks in the top 10% for the 3-year period and in the top 15% for the 5-year period. The inception month of this subaccount was March 1988. The performance figures (shown below) for periods before the subaccount's inception in March 1988 are based on the Lutheran Brotherhood Variable Insurance Products Series Fund Income Portfolio, which had an inception date of January 1987.

The year-by-year returns for this subaccount and the portfolio it is modeled after are:

| Year | Annual Return | Lehman Bros. Corporate Bond Index |
|------|------|------|
| 1994 | −5.7% | −3.9% |
| 1993 | 10.5% | 12.2% |
| 1992 | 8.0% | 8.7% |
| 1991 | 18.4% | 18.5% |
| 1990 | 5.8% | 7.2% |
| 1989 | 10.9% | 14.0% |
| 1988 | 10.9% | 9.2% |
| 1987 | 2.7% | 2.6% |

## Risk Control                                               ✓✓✓✓

Over the 3-year period, this fund was 45% safer than the average fixed-income subaccount. During the 5-year period, it was a little safer.

The typical standard deviation for corporate bond subaccounts was 1.1% during the 3-year period. The standard deviation for Lutheran Brotherhood Variable Annuity Income was 1.0% over this same period, which means that this subaccount was 11% less volatile than its peer group. The average maturity of the bonds in this account is 13 years; the weighted coupon rate averages 7.5%. The typical corporate bond subaccount has an average maturity of just under 11 years and a weighted coupon rate of 7.5%.

The beta (market-related risk) of this subaccount was 0.9 over the 3-year period. Beta for this entire category was 1.1 over this same period. The market index (the Lehman Brothers Aggregate Bond Index for debt subaccounts) always has a beta of 1.0. The *risk-adjusted* return for this variable annuity subaccount can be described as very good.

## Expense Minimization                                       ✓✓✓✓

The typical expenses incurred by corporate bond subaccounts are 1.9% per year. The total expenses for Lutheran Brotherhood Variable Annuity Income, 1.5%, are lower than its peer group average. Total expenses include all charges to the investor (except the annual contract charge, which is always expressed as a dollar figure), including management fees, overhead, administration, and mortality expenses. The free annual withdrawals percentage is based on the account value.

| | | | | |
|---|---|---|---|---|
| Maximum surrender charge | 6% | | Total expenses | 1.5% |
| Duration of surrender charge | 6 years | | Annual contract charge | $30 |
| Declining surrender charge | no | | Free annual withdrawals | 10% |

## Management                                                 ✓✓✓✓

Lutheran Brotherhood Variable Annuity is offered by Lutheran Brotherhood Variable Insurance Products Company. The company has a Duff & Phelps rating of AAA and an A.M. Best rating of A++. The portfolio and the portfolio it is modeled after were managed by Charles E. Heeren for the 7 years ending December 31, 1994. The portfolio's size is $560 million. Heeren also manages the Lutheran Brotherhood Income Fund.

## Investment Options ✓

Investors may make additional contributions into this portfolio at any time. This is known as a flexible premium annuity. Investors in this variable annuity can choose from all of the subaccount categories below that have a check mark:

| | | |
|---|---|---|
| ___ Aggressive growth | ___ Government bonds | ✓ Money market |
| ___ Balanced | ✓ Growth | ___ Specialty/Sector |
| ✓ Corporate bonds | ___ Growth & income | ___ World bonds |
| ___ Global equities (stocks) | ✓ High-yield bonds | |

## Family Rating ✓✓✓✓

There are 4 subaccounts within the Lutheran Brotherhood Variable Annuity family. Overall, this family of subaccounts can be described as excellent on a *risk-adjusted* return basis.

The subaccounts within this variable annuity all have an *increasing* guaranteed death benefit. This means that the beneficiary is guaranteed to receive *the greater of* the contract's value on the date of the annuitant's death or the value of the original investment(s) compounded by 5% each year (less any withdrawals made).

## Summary

Lutheran Brotherhood Variable Annuity Income is a subaccount that has no peers. This portfolio rates a perfect score in virtually every category: performance, risk control, expense minimization, management, and family rating. The only thing negative that can be said about this portfolio is that the parent company does not offer more investment options.

This subaccount is truly great. The Lutheran Brotherhood Income account has turned in positive returns every year, with close to 50% less risk than other corporate bond portfolios. Even the contract has a large number of impressive features. One can only hope that Lutheran Brotherhood will bless us with more selections in the near future.

## Profile

| | | | |
|---|---|---|---|
| Minimum investment | $600 | Telephone exchanges | yes |
| Retirement account minimum | $600 | Transfers allowed per year | unlimited |
| Co-annuitant allowed | yes | Maximum issuance age | 96 |
| Co-owner allowed | yes | Maximum annuitization age | 99 |
| Dollar-cost averaging | yes | Number of subaccounts | 4 |
| Systematic withdrawal plans | yes | Available in all 50 states | no* |

*Not available in the following states: CT, GA, MA, ME, NH, NY, RI, VT, and WY.

---

**New England Zenith Accumulator
Bond Income Series**
501 Boylston Street
Boston, MA  02116
(800) 346-0399

---

| | |
|---|---|
| Performance | ✓✓✓✓ |
| Risk control | ✓✓✓ |
| Expense minimization | ✓✓✓✓ |
| Management | ✓✓✓ |
| Investment options | ✓✓ |
| Family rating | ✓✓✓✓ |
| Total point score | 20 points |

---

## Performance                                                    ✓✓✓✓

During the 3-year and 5-year periods ending December 31, 1994, Bond Income Series had an average annual compound return of 4.2% and 7.0%, respectively (10.0% for 10 years). This means that a $10,000 investment made into this subaccount 5 years before that date grew to $14,000 ($11,300, if only the last 3 years of that period are used).

Compared to other corporate bond variable annuity subaccounts, this one ranks in the top third for the 3-year and 5-year periods. The inception month of this subaccount was August 1983.

The year-by-year returns for this subaccount are:

| Year | Annual Return | Lehman Bros. Corporate Bond Index |
|---|---|---|
| 1994 | −4.7% | −3.9% |
| 1993 | 11.1% | 12.2% |
| 1992 | 6.7% | 8.7% |
| 1991 | 16.4% | 18.5% |
| 1990 | 6.7% | 7.2% |
| 1989 | 10.9% | 14.0% |
| 1988 | 6.8% | 9.2% |
| 1987 | 0.9% | 2.6% |

## Risk Control                                                    ✓✓✓

Over the 3-year and 5-year periods, this fund was slightly safer than the average fixed-income subaccount.

The typical standard deviation for corporate bond subaccounts was 1.1% during the 3-year period. The standard deviation for New England Zenith Accumulator Bond Income Series was 1.3% over this same period, which means that this subaccount was 17% more volatile than its peer group. The average maturity of the bonds in this account is 10 years; the weighted coupon rate averages 8.1%. The typical corporate bond subaccount has an average maturity of just under 11 years and a weighted coupon rate of 7.5%.

The beta (market-related risk) of this subaccount was 1.3 over the 3-year period. Beta for this entire category was 1.06 over this same period. The market index (the Lehman Brothers Aggregate Bond Index for debt subaccounts) always has a beta of 1.0. The *risk-adjusted* return for this variable annuity subaccount can be described as very good.

## Expense Minimization ✓✓✓✓

The typical expenses incurred by corporate bond subaccounts are 1.9% per year. The total expenses for New England Zenith Accumulator Bond Income Series, 1.8%, are lower than its peer group average. Total expenses include all charges to the investor (except the annual contract charge, which is always expressed as a dollar figure), including management fees, overhead, administration, and mortality expenses. The free annual withdrawals percentage is based on the account value.

| | | | |
|---|---|---|---|
| Maximum surrender charge | 7% | Total expenses | 1.8% |
| Duration of surrender charge | 10 years | Annual contract charge | $30 |
| Declining surrender charge | no | Free annual withdrawals | 10% |

## Management ✓✓✓

New England Zenith Accumulator is offered by New England Mutual Life Insurance Company. The company has a Duff & Phelps rating of AA. The portfolio was managed by Catherine L. Bunting for the 5 years ending December 31, 1994. The portfolio's size is $120 million. Bunting also manages the TNE Bond Income mutual fund.

## Investment Options ✓✓

Investors may make additional contributions into this portfolio at any time. This is known as a flexible premium annuity. Investors in this variable annuity can choose from all of the subaccount categories below that have a check mark:

| | | |
|---|---|---|
| ___ Aggressive growth | ___ Government bonds | ✓ Money market |
| ✓ Balanced | ✓ Growth | ___ Specialty/Sector |
| ✓ Corporate bonds | ✓ Growth & income | ___ World bonds |
| ___ Global equities (stocks) | ___ High-yield bonds | |

## Family Rating ✓✓✓✓

There are 10 subaccounts within the New England Zenith Accumulator family. Overall, this family of subaccounts can be described as very good on a *risk-adjusted* return basis.

## Summary

New England Zenith Accumulator Bond Income Series has an overall rating somewhere between good and very good. This corporate bond subaccount takes a middle-of-the-road approach, getting investors the best yield possible with a modest interest-rate risk exposure.

The New England family of variable annuity subaccounts is one of the few groups whose overall profile is quite positive. The Bond Income Series represents a fine choice for investors interested in having corporate bonds as part of their holdings.

## Profile

| | | | |
|---|---|---|---|
| Minimum investment | $300 | Telephone exchanges | yes |
| Retirement account minimum | $300 | Transfers allowed per year | 4 |
| Co-annuitant allowed | no | Maximum issuance age | 75 |
| Co-owner allowed | no | Maximum annuitization age | 95 |
| Dollar-cost averaging | yes | Number of subaccounts | 10 |
| Systematic withdrawal plans | yes | Available in all 50 states | yes |

---

**Pacific Mutual Select Variable Annuity**
**Managed Bond**
700 Newport Center Drive
P.O. Box 7500
Newport Beach, CA 92658-7500
(800) 800-7681

---

| | |
|---|---|
| Performance | ✓✓✓✓ |
| Risk control | ✓✓✓✓ |
| Expense minimization | ✓✓ |
| Management | ✓✓✓✓ |
| Investment options | ✓✓✓✓ |
| Family rating | ✓✓ |
| Total point score | 20 points |

---

## Performance                                            ✓✓✓✓

During the 3-year and 5-year periods ending December 31, 1994, Managed Bond had an average annual compound return of 3.8% and 6.7%, respectively. This means that a $10,000 investment made into this subaccount 5 years before that date grew to $13,800 ($11,200, if only the last 3 years of that period are used).

Compared to other corporate bond variable annuity subaccounts, this one ranks in the top third for the 3-year and 5-year periods. The inception month of this subaccount was September 1990. The performance figures (shown below) for periods before the subaccount's inception in September 1990 are based on the subaccount's predecessor, the Pacific Select Fund Managed Bond Series.

The year-by-year returns for this subaccount and its predecessor are:

| Year | Annual Return | Lehman Bros. Corporate Bond Index |
|---|---|---|
| 1994 | −5.6% | −3.9% |
| 1993 | 10.3% | 12.2% |
| 1992 | 7.3% | 8.7% |
| 1991 | 16.0% | 18.5% |
| 1990 | 6.9% | 7.2% |
| 1989 | 10.1% | 14.0% |

## Risk Control                                            ✓✓✓✓

Over the 3-year period, this fund was 25% safer than the average fixed-income subaccount. During the 5-year period, it was slightly riskier.

The typical standard deviation for corporate bond subaccounts was 1.1% during the 3-year period. The standard deviation for Pacific Mutual Select Variable Annuity Managed Bond was 1.1% over this same period, which means that this subaccount was 4% more volatile than its peer group. The average maturity of the bonds in this account is 15 years; the weighted coupon rate averages 9.2%. The typical corporate bond subaccount has an average maturity of just under 11 years and a weighted coupon rate of 7.5%.

The beta (market-related risk) of this subaccount was 1.1 over the 3-year period. Beta for this entire category was also 1.1 over this same period. The market index (the Lehman Brothers Aggregate Bond Index for debt subaccounts) always has a beta of 1.0. The *risk-adjusted* return for this variable annuity subaccount can be described as good.

## Expense Minimization ✓✓

The typical expenses incurred by corporate bond subaccounts are 1.9% per year. The total expenses for Pacific Mutual Select Variable Annuity Managed Bond, 2.1%, are higher than its peer group average. Total expenses include all charges to the investor (except the annual contract charge, which is always expressed as a dollar figure), including management fees, overhead, administration, and mortality expenses. The free annual withdrawals percentage is based on the original principal.

| | | | |
|---|---|---|---|
| Maximum surrender charge | 6% | Total expenses | 2.1% |
| Duration of surrender charge | 6 years | Annual contract charge | $30 |
| Declining surrender charge | yes | Free annual withdrawals | 10% |

## Management ✓✓✓

Pacific Mutual Select Variable Annuity is offered by Pacific Mutual Life Insurance Company. The company has a Duff & Phelps rating of AA+ and an A.M. Best rating of A+. The portfolio (and/or the mutual fund it is modeled after) was managed by William H. Gross for the 6 years ending December 31, 1994. The portfolio's size is $19 million. Gross also manages the PFAMCo Managed Bond & Income Fund.

## Investment Options ✓✓✓

Investors may make additional contributions into this portfolio at any time. This is known as a flexible premium annuity. Investors in this variable annuity can choose from all of the subaccount categories below that have a check mark:

| | | |
|---|---|---|
| ___ Aggressive growth | ✓ Government bonds | ✓ Money market |
| ✓ Balanced | ✓ Growth | ___ Specialty/Sector |
| ✓ Corporate bonds | ✓ Growth & income | ___ World bonds |
| ✓ Global equities (stocks) | ✓ High-yield bonds | |

## Family Rating ✓✓

There are 9 subaccounts within the Pacific Mutual Select Variable Annuity family. Overall, this family of subaccounts can be described as fair on a *risk-adjusted* return basis.

## Summary

Pacific Mutual Select Variable Annuity Managed Bond is a very impressive corporate bond subaccount. This investment is very good in all of the important categories: performance, risk control, management, and investment options.

The expenses for this contract are a little on the high side, but this will change once the portfolios become bigger. This is a fine investment that offers contract owners the ability to move into a global stock or high-yield bond portfolio. The contract includes some very nice features. This variable annuity is recommended.

## Profile

| | | | |
|---|---|---|---|
| Minimum investment | $2,000 | Telephone exchanges | yes |
| Retirement account minimum | $5,000 | Transfers allowed per year | unlimited |
| Co-annuitant allowed | yes | Maximum issuance age | 85 |
| Co-owner allowed | yes | Maximum annuitization age | 95 |
| Dollar-cost averaging | yes | Number of subaccounts | 9 |
| Systematic withdrawal plans | yes | Available in all 50 states | no* |

*Not available in NY.

---

**Scudder Horizon Plan**
**Bond**
8301 Maryland Avenue
St. Louis, MO 63105
(800) 225-2470

---

| | |
|---|---|
| Performance | ✓✓✓✓ |
| Risk control | ✓✓✓ |
| Expense minimization | ✓✓✓✓✓ |
| Management | ✓✓✓ |
| Investment options | ✓✓ |
| Family rating | ✓✓✓ |
| Total point score | 20 points |

---

## Performance                                              ✓✓✓✓

During the 3-year and 5-year periods ending December 31, 1994, Bond had an average annual compound return of 3.9% and 7.0%, respectively. This means that a $10,000 investment made into this subaccount 5 years before that date grew to $14,000 ($11,200, if only the last 3 years of that period are used).

Compared to other corporate bond variable annuity subaccounts, this one ranks in the top quartile for the 3-year and 5-year periods. The inception month of this subaccount was October 1988. This subaccount is modeled (cloned) after the Scudder Income Fund Corporate Bond Series Class A, which had an inception date of July 1985, and has an asset base of $130 million.

The year-by-year returns for this subaccount are:

| Year | Annual Return | Lehman Bros. Corporate Bond Index |
|---|---|---|
| 1994 | −5.5% | −3.9% |
| 1993 | 11.6% | 12.2% |
| 1992 | 6.3% | 8.7% |
| 1991 | 16.8% | 18.5% |
| 1990 | 7.0% | 7.2% |
| 1989 | 10.5% | 14.0% |

## Risk Control                                              ✓✓✓

Over the 3-year and 5-year periods, this fund was a little safer than the average fixed-income subaccount.

The typical standard deviation for corporate bond subaccounts was 1.1% during the 3-year period. The standard deviation for Scudder Horizon Plan Bond was 1.3% over this same period, which means that this subaccount was 17% more volatile than its peer group. The average maturity of the bonds in this account is slightly less than 11 years; the weighted coupon rate averages 6.7%. The typical corporate bond subaccount has an average maturity of just under 11 years and a weighted coupon rate of 7.5%.

The beta (market-related risk) of this subaccount was 1.3 over the 3-year period. Beta for this entire category was 1.1 over this same period. The market index (the Lehman Brothers Aggregate Bond Index for debt subaccounts) always has a beta of 1.0. The *risk-adjusted* return for this variable annuity subaccount can be described as very good.

# Expense Minimization                                    ✓✓✓✓

The typical expenses incurred by corporate bond subaccounts are 1.9% per year. The total expenses for Scudder Horizon Plan Bond, 1.3%, are lower than its peer group average. Total expenses include all charges to the investor (except the annual contract charge, which is always expressed as a dollar figure), including management fees, overhead, administration, and mortality expenses. The free annual withdrawals percentage is based on the account value.

| | | | |
|---|---|---|---|
| Maximum surrender charge | 0% | Total expenses | 1.3% |
| Duration of surrender charge | n/a | Annual contract charge | $0 |
| Declining surrender charge | n/a | Free annual withdrawals | 10% |

# Management                                              ✓✓✓

Scudder Horizon Plan is offered by Charter National Life Insurance Company. The company has an A.M. Best rating of A. The portfolio has been managed by Ruth Heisler and William M. Hutchinson since its inception. The portfolio's size is $18 million. Hutchinson also manages the Scudder Income Fund Corporate Bond Series Class A.

# Investment Options                                      ✓✓

Investors may make additional contributions into this portfolio at any time. This is known as a flexible premium annuity. Investors in this variable annuity can choose from all of the subaccount categories below that have a check mark:

| | | |
|---|---|---|
| ___ Aggressive growth | ___ Government bonds | ✓ Money market |
| ✓ Balanced | ✓ Growth | ___ Specialty/Sector |
| ✓ Corporate bonds | ___ Growth & income | ___ World bonds |
| ✓ Global equities (stocks) | ___ High-yield bonds | |

# Family Rating                                           ✓✓✓

There are 5 subaccounts within the Scudder Horizon Plan family. Overall, this family of subaccounts can be described as good on a *risk-adjusted* return basis.

# Summary

Scudder Horizon Plan Bond is not the only Scudder offering included in this book, but this particular corporate bond subaccount is one of their best. It is one of the few subaccounts that has no strings attached. Investors can add or take money out at any time without any insurance company penalties or costs. And, speaking of costs, this variable annuity contract has some of the lowest overhead in the entire industry.

Total point score for this portfolio is between good and very good. Having a global stock subaccount within the family is a nice touch. Scudder would be wise to add even more investment options to this contract.

# Profile

| | | | |
|---|---|---|---|
| Minimum investment | $2,500 | Telephone exchanges | yes |
| Retirement account minimum | $2,500 | Transfers allowed per year | unlimited |
| Co-annuitant allowed | no | Maximum issuance age | none |
| Co-owner allowed | yes | Maximum annuitization age | none |
| Dollar-cost averaging | yes | Number of subaccounts | 5 |
| Systematic withdrawal plans | yes | Available in all 50 states | no* |

*Not available in the following states: HI, KY, LA, NM, and WY.

---

**Security Benefit Variflex**
**High-Grade Income**
700 Southwest Harrison Street
Topeka, KS 66636
(800) 888-2461

---

| | |
|---|---|
| Performance | ✓✓✓✓ |
| Risk control | ✓✓✓ |
| Expense minimization | ✓✓ |
| Management | ✓✓✓ |
| Investment options | ✓✓✓ |
| Family rating | ✓ |
| Total point score | 16 points |

---

## Performance                                           ✓✓✓✓

During the 3-year and 5-year periods ending December 31, 1994, High-Grade Income had an average annual compound return of 2.8% and 5.8%, respectively. This means that a $10,000 investment made into this subaccount 5 years before that date grew to $13,300 ($10,900, if only the last 3 years of that period are used).

Compared to other corporate bond variable annuity subaccounts, this one ranks in the top third for the 3-year period and in the top half for the 5-year period. The inception month of this subaccount was April 1985. This subaccount is modeled (cloned) after the Security Benefit Life Fund Series E (High-Grade Income) Fund, which also had an inception date of May 1985, and has an asset base of $110 million.

The year-by-year returns for this subaccount are:

| Year | Annual Return | Lehman Bros. Corporate Bond Index |
|---|---|---|
| 1994 | −8.0% | −3.9% |
| 1993 | 11.3% | 12.2% |
| 1992 | 6.2% | 8.7% |
| 1991 | 15.6% | 18.5% |
| 1990 | 5.4% | 7.2% |
| 1989 | 10.5% | 14.0% |
| 1988 | 5.9% | 9.2% |
| 1987 | 1.2% | 2.6% |

## Risk Control                                          ✓✓✓

Over the 3-year period, this fund was a little safer than the average fixed-income subaccount. During the 5-year period, it was slightly riskier.

The typical standard deviation for corporate bond subaccounts was 1.1% during the 3-year period. The standard deviation for Security Benefit Variflex High-Grade Income was 1.3% over this same period, which means that this subaccount was 15% more volatile than its peer group. The average maturity of the bonds in this account is 17 years; the weighted coupon rate averages 7.2%. The typical corporate bond subaccount has an average maturity of just under 11 years and a weighted coupon rate of 7.5%.

The beta (market-related risk) of this subaccount was 1.2 over the 3-year period. Beta for this entire category was 1.1 over this same period. The market index (the Lehman Brothers Aggregate Bond Index for debt subaccounts) always has a beta of 1.0. The *risk-adjusted* return for this variable annuity subaccount can be described as fair.

## Expense Minimization ✓✓

The typical expenses incurred by corporate bond subaccounts are 1.9% per year. The total expenses for Security Benefit Variflex High-Grade Income, 2.1%, are higher than its peer group average. Total expenses include all charges to the investor (except the annual contract charge, which is always expressed as a dollar figure), including management fees, overhead, administration, and mortality expenses. The free annual withdrawals percentage is based on the account value.

| | | | |
|---|---|---|---|
| Maximum surrender charge | 8% | Total expenses | 2.1% |
| Duration of surrender charge | 8 years | Annual contract charge | $30 |
| Declining surrender charge | no | Free annual withdrawals | 10% |

## Management ✓✓✓

Security Benefit Variflex is offered by Security Benefit Life Insurance Company. The company has an A.M. Best rating of A+. The portfolio, and the portfolio it is modeled after, were managed by Jane A. Tedder for the 9 years ending December 31, 1994. The portfolio's size is $110 million. Tedder also manages the Security Income Fund Corporate Bond Series Class A mutual fund.

## Investment Options ✓✓✓

Investors may make additional contributions into this portfolio at any time. This is known as a flexible premium annuity. Investors in this variable annuity can choose from all of the subaccount categories below that have a check mark:

| | | | | | |
|---|---|---|---|---|---|
| ✓ | Aggressive growth | ___ | Government bonds | ✓ | Money market |
| ✓ | Balanced | ✓ | Growth | ___ | Specialty/Sector |
| ✓ | Corporate bonds | ___ | Growth & income | ___ | World bonds |
| ✓ | Global equities (stocks) | ___ | High-yield bonds | | |

## Family Rating ✓

The subaccounts within this variable annuity all have an *increasing* guaranteed death benefit. This means that the beneficiary is guaranteed to receive *the greater of* the contract's value on the date of the annuitant's death or the value of the original investment(s) compounded by 5% each year (less any withdrawals made).

## Summary

Security Benefit Variflex High-Grade Income is a fine choice for anyone interested in a corporate bond portfolio. The average maturity of the subaccount is such that investors will continue to get an attractive current yield but are exposed only to modest interest-rate risk. Jane Tedder has overseen this account since its inception. She is one of the more seasoned variable annuity portfolio managers.

## Profile

| | | | |
|---|---|---|---|
| Minimum investment | $25 | Telephone exchanges | yes |
| Retirement account minimum | $500 | Transfers allowed per year | unlimited |
| Co-annuitant allowed | no | Maximum issuance age | 80 |
| Co-owner allowed | yes | Maximum annuitization age | none |
| Dollar-cost averaging | yes | Number of subaccounts | 7 |
| Systematic withdrawal plans | yes | Available in all 50 states | no* |

*Not available in NY.

---

**Western Reserve Life Freedom Attainer Annuity Bond**
P.O. Box 5068
Clearwater, FL 34618-5068
(800) 443-9975

---

| | |
|---|---|
| Performance | ✓✓✓✓ |
| Risk control | ✓ |
| Expense minimization | ✓✓✓ |
| Management | ✓✓ |
| Investment options | ✓✓✓ |
| Family rating | ✓✓✓ |
| Total point score | 16 points |

## Performance                                              ✓✓✓✓

During the 3-year and 5-year periods ending December 31, 1994, Bond had an average annual compound return of 2.8% and 6.0%, respectively. This means that a $10,000 investment made into this subaccount 5 years before that date grew to $13,400 ($10,900, if only the last 3 years of that period are used).

Compared to other corporate bond variable annuity subaccounts, this one ranks in the top quartile for the 3-year period. The inception month of this subaccount was April 1993. The performance figures (shown below) for periods before the subaccount's inception in April 1993 are hypothetical, based on the underlying clone portfolio's returns. This subaccount is modeled (cloned) after the Western Reserve Life Series Fund Bond Portfolio, which had an inception date of October 1986, and has an asset base of $95 million.

The year-by-year returns for this subaccount and the portfolio it is modeled after are:

| Year | Annual Return | Lehman Bros. Corporate Bond Index |
|---|---|---|
| 1994 | −8.1% | −3.9% |
| 1993 | 12.0% | 12.2% |
| 1992 | 5.4% | 8.7% |
| 1991 | 17.4% | 18.5% |
| 1990 | 5.0% | 7.2% |

## Risk Control                                                    ✓

Over the 3-year period, this fund was somewhat riskier than the average fixed-income subaccount.

The typical standard deviation for corporate bond subaccounts was 1.1% during the 3-year period. The standard deviation for Western Reserve Life Freedom Attainer Annuity Bond was 1.57% over this same period, which means that this subaccount was 44% more volatile than its peer group. The average maturity of the bonds in this account is 22 years; the weighted coupon rate averages 7.0%. The typical corporate bond subaccount has an average maturity of just under 11 years and a weighted coupon rate of 7.5%.

The beta (market-related risk) of this subaccount was 1.5 over the 3-year period. Beta for this entire category was 1.1 over this same period. The market index (the Lehman Brothers Aggregate Bond Index for debt subaccounts) always has a beta of 1.0. The *risk-adjusted* return for this variable annuity subaccount can be described as good.

## Expense Minimization ✓✓✓

The typical expenses incurred by corporate bond subaccounts are 1.9% per year. The total expenses for Western Reserve Life Freedom Attainer Annuity Bond, 2.0%, are higher than its peer group average. Total expenses include all charges to the investor (except the annual contract charge, which is always expressed as a dollar figure), including management fees, overhead, administration, and mortality expenses. The free annual withdrawals percentage is based on the account value.

| | | | |
|---|---|---|---|
| Maximum surrender charge | 6% | Total expenses | 2.0% |
| Duration of surrender charge | 5 years | Annual contract charge | $30 |
| Declining surrender charge | yes | Free annual withdrawals | 10% |

## Management ✓✓

Western Reserve Life Freedom Attainer Annuity is offered by Western Reserve Life Assurance Company of Ohio. The company has a Duff & Phelps rating of AA+ and an A.M. Best rating of A+. The portfolio, and the portfolio it is modeled after, were managed by Ronald V. Speaker for the 5 years ending December 31, 1994. The portfolio's size is $10 million. Speaker also manages the IDEX II Flexible Income mutual fund.

## Investment Options ✓✓✓

Investors may make additional contributions into this portfolio at any time. This is known as a flexible premium annuity. Investors in this variable annuity can choose from all of the subaccount categories below that have a check mark:

| | | |
|---|---|---|
| ✓ Aggressive growth | ✓ Government bonds | ✓ Money market |
| ___ Balanced | ✓ Growth | ___ Specialty/Sector |
| ✓ Corporate bonds | ✓ Growth & income | ___ World bonds |
| ✓ Global equities (stocks) | ___ High-yield bonds | |

## Family Rating ✓✓✓

There are 7 subaccounts within the Western Reserve Life Freedom Attainer Annuity family. Overall, this family of subaccounts can be described as good on a *risk-adjusted* return basis.

The subaccounts within this variable annuity all have an *increasing* guaranteed death benefit. This means that the beneficiary is guaranteed to receive *the greater of* the contract's value on the date of the annuitant's death or the value of the original investment(s) compounded by 5% each year (less any withdrawals made).

## Summary

Western Reserve Life Freedom Attainer Annuity Bond is the right choice for anyone who is willing to take on some extra risk in return for some great returns. Because of the high average maturity of bonds in the portfolio, this investment is best suited for those who believe that interest rates either will stay somewhat level or will decline.

Western Reserve Life Freedom Attainer Annuity offers one of the better variable annuity contracts in the industry. The duration of the surrender charge is low, the potential penalty declines each year, and withdrawals are based on the contract's current value. Having a global stock fund within the family is also a plus.

## Profile

| | | | |
|---|---|---|---|
| Minimum investment | $50 | Telephone exchanges | yes |
| Retirement account minimum | $5,000 | Transfers allowed per year | 12 |
| Co-annuitant allowed | no | Maximum issuance age | 85 |
| Co-owner allowed | no | Maximum annuitization age | 95 |
| Dollar-cost averaging | yes | Number of subaccounts | 7 |
| Systematic withdrawal plans | yes | Available in all 50 states | no* |

*Not available in NJ, OR, or WA.

## Chapter

# 10

# Global Stock Subaccounts

International (also referred to as "foreign") subaccounts invest only in stocks of foreign companies; global subaccounts invest in both foreign and U.S. stocks. For purposes of this book, the universe of global stock subaccounts includes both purely foreign as well as world (global) portfolios.

It is wise to consider investing abroad: Different economies experience prosperity and recession at different times. During the 1980s, foreign stocks were the number-one performing investment, averaging a compound return of over 22% per year, versus 17% for U.S. stocks and 9% for residential real estate.

The table below shows how a number of stock markets performed during the 1993 calendar year. For comparison purposes, price/earnings (p/e) ratios and market capitalization (the value of the country's entire stock market in U.S. dollar terms) figures are included.

The economic outlook of foreign countries is the major factor in management's decision regarding which nations and industries are to be favored. A secondary concern is the future anticipated value of the U.S. dollar relative to foreign currencies. A strong or weak dollar can detract or add to an international subaccount's overall performance. A strong dollar will lower a foreign portfolio's return; a weak dollar will enhance international performance. Trying to gauge the direction of any currency is as difficult as trying to figure out what the U.S. stock market will do tomorrow, next week, or the following year.

Investors who want to avoid being subjected to currency swings may wish to use, for their foreign holdings, a subaccount family that practices currency hedging. With currency hedging, management is buying a type of "insurance policy" that pays off in the event of a strong U.S. dollar. Basically, the foreign or international subaccount that is being hurt by the dollar is making a killing in currency futures contracts. When properly done, the gains in the futures contracts (the insurance policy) offset most or all of the security losses attributed to a strong dollar. Some people may feel that buying currency contracts is risky business for the subaccount; it is not.

| Country | 1993 Return | P/E Ratio* | Market Capitalization* |
|---|---|---|---|
| Australia | 32% | 19.6 | $124 billion |
| Austria | 27% | 73.4 | $19 billion |
| Belgium | 19% | 22.0 | $48 billion |
| Canada | 15% | 78.9 | $170 billion |
| Denmark | 32% | 78.4 | $30 billion |
| Finland | 76% | n/a | $20 billion |
| France | 19% | 29.5 | $278 billion |
| Germany | 34% | 30.6 | $268 billion |
| Hong Kong | 110% | 19.3 | $183 billion |
| Ireland | 39% | 17.8 | $11 billion |
| Italy | 27% | n/a | $96 billion |
| Japan | 25% | 77.8 | $2,005 billion |
| Malaysia | 49% | 35.5 | $112 billion |
| Netherlands | 32% | 20.3 | $142 billion |
| New Zealand | 63% | 21.8 | $17 billion |
| Norway | 36% | 41.9 | $14 billion |
| Singapore | 62% | 24.6 | $58 billion |
| Spain | 26% | 19.9 | $87 billion |
| Sweden | 34% | n/a | $70 billion |
| Switzerland | 44% | 20.3 | $211 billion |
| United Kingdom | 21% | 20.0 | $751 billion |
| United States | 7% | 20.5 | $2,553 billion |
| World Index | 20% | 28.7 | $7,278 billion |
| Europe | 26% | 26.3 | $2,043 billion |
| Pacific Basin | 34% | 52.4 | $2,499 billion |

*All data as of 2/28/94.

Like automobile insurance, currency hedging only pays off if there is an "accident," that is, if the U.S. dollar increases in value against the currencies represented by the portfolio's securities. If the dollar remains level or decreases in value, so much the better; the foreign securities increase in value and the currency contracts become virtually worthless. The price of these contracts becomes a cost of doing business; just like car insurance, the protection is simply renewed. With a currency contract, the contract expires and a new one, covering another period of time, is purchased.

How important is currency hedging on a *risk-adjusted* basis? Consider how a foreign and U.S. stock portfolio fare against each other. Over the 10 years from 1983 to 1993, U.S. stocks had a risk level of 16, versus just over 17 for foreign equities. When currency hedging is added to the foreign portfolio, the international risk level drops to 13; the U.S. level stays at 16.

If we were to construct a grid of the top-performing stock markets around the world, ranked first through fifth and covering a 15-year period ending December 31, 1994, we would have a total of 75 different slots. On this entire grid, the United States would appear only three times. For a broader perspective, use the following table to compare how U.S. securities have fared against their foreign counterparts over the 21 years from 1973 through 1993.

Over the decade from 1983 to 1993, an integrated world economy evolved from the many distinct national economies of the past. At the same time, many investment opportunities once considered uniquely American have gradually shifted to other

## Why Global Stocks and Bonds Deserve a Place
## in Every Investor's Portfolio
### (Total Return by Investment Category: 1973–1994)

| Year | U.S. Stocks | U.S. Bonds | Non-U.S. Stocks | Non-U.S. Bonds |
|---|---|---|---|---|
| 1973 | −14.6 | +2.3 | −14.2 | +6.3 |
| 1974 | −26.5 | +0.2 | −22.1 | +5.3 |
| 1975 | +37.2 | +12.3 | +37.0 | +8.8 |
| 1976 | +24.0 | +15.6 | +3.8 | +10.5 |
| 1977 | −7.2 | +3.0 | +19.4 | +38.9 |
| 1978 | +6.5 | +1.2 | +34.3 | +18.5 |
| 1979 | +18.6 | +2.3 | +6.2 | −5.0 |
| 1980 | +32.3 | +3.1 | +24.4 | +13.7 |
| 1981 | −5.0 | +7.3 | −1.0 | −4.6 |
| 1982 | +21.5 | +31.1 | −0.9 | +11.9 |
| 1983 | +22.6 | +8.0 | +24.6 | +4.3 |
| 1984 | +6.3 | +15.0 | +7.9 | −2.0 |
| 1985 | +31.7 | +21.3 | +56.7 | +37.2 |
| 1986 | +18.6 | +15.6 | +67.9 | +33.9 |
| 1987 | +5.3 | +2.3 | +24.9 | +36.1 |
| 1988 | +16.6 | +7.6 | +28.6 | +3.0 |
| 1989 | +31.6 | +14.2 | +10.8 | −4.5 |
| 1990 | −3.1 | +8.3 | −14.9 | +14.1 |
| 1991 | +30.4 | +16.1 | +12.5 | +17.9 |
| 1992 | +7.7 | +8.1 | −12.2 | +7.1 |
| 1993 | +10.1 | +10.7 | +32.6 | +16.0 |
| 1994 | 1.3 | −3.5 | 7.8 | 6.7 |
| Number of years this category achieved the best results | 6 | 4 | 7 | 5 |

areas around the globe. With over 60% of today's stock market capitalization represented by non-U.S. companies, the case for globally diversifying portfolios has never been stronger. Recent trade agreements, such as NAFTA and GATT, make the case for a global portfolio even stronger. To earn competitive returns, U.S. investors can no longer afford to ignore foreign opportunities.

Increasing your investment returns and reducing your portfolio risk are two compelling reasons for investing worldwide. Global investing allows you to maximize your returns by investing in some of the world's best-managed and most profitable companies. Japan, for example, is the world's leading producer of sophisticated electronics goods; Germany, heavy machinery; the United States, biotechnology; and Southeast Asia, commodity manufactured goods. The most potential for growth today is in countries that are industrializing, have the cheapest labor and the richest natural resources, and yet remain undervalued.

It is commonly known that diversification reduces investment risk. Recent studies have once again proven this most basic investment principle. One study showed that the least volatile investment portfolio would be composed of 60% U.S. equities and 40% foreign equities. These results reflect the importance of balancing a portfolio between U.S. and foreign equities.

The Pacific Basin, which includes Japan, Hong Kong, Korea, Taiwan, Thailand, Singapore, Malaysia, and Australia, has experienced outstanding economic growth and today represents 34% of the world's stock market capital—nearly double what it was 10 years ago.

Japan, the most economically mature country in the Pacific Basin, has become the dominant force behind the development of the newly industrialized countries (NICs) of Hong Kong, Korea, Thailand, Singapore, Malaysia, and Taiwan. As demand for Japanese products has grown and costs in Japan have risen, the search for affordable production of goods has caused Japanese investment to flow into neighboring countries, fostering their development as economically independent and prosperous nations.

The NICs, with some of the world's cheapest labor and richest untapped natural resources, have recently experienced an enormous influx of international investment capital. Today, they represent the world's fastest growing source of low-cost manufacturing.

For the manufacture and assembly of consumer electronics products, the NICs are favored locations. Displaced from high-cost countries such as the United States and Japan, electronics factories in these developing countries significantly benefit from reduced labor costs. Today, in fact, Korea is the world's third largest manufacturer of semiconductors.

The Pacific Basin yields yet another country with the potential for strong economic growth: China. Opportunities to benefit from the industrialization of China will come from firms listed on the Hong Kong Stock Exchange, in such basic areas as electricity, construction materials, public transportation, and fundamental telecommunications. Indeed, these low-technology and essential industries, once growth industries in the United States, are now the foundation of a natural growth progression occurring in the NICs of Southeast Asia.

Companies such as China Light and Power (Hong Kong), Siam Cement (Thailand), and Hyundai (Korea) offer much the same profit potential today as their northern European counterparts did 100 years ago, or their U.S. counterparts 40 years ago, or their Japanese counterparts as recently as 20 years ago.

Investors have long been familiar with the names of many of Europe's major producers—Nestlé, Olivetti, Shell, Bayer, Volkswagen, and Perrier, to name just a few. Europe's impressive manufacturing capacity, its diverse industrial base, its quality labor pools, and its many leading multinational blue-chip corporations can make it an environment for growth, accessible to U.S. investors through variable annuities that have foreign and global subaccounts.

European markets have proven time and again that they represent tremendous investment potential. From 1983 to 1993, European markets have consistently produced greater total returns than the U.S. stock market, which averaged 14.8% over this same period.

### Performance Comparison European Stock Market Returns Ten Years Ended March 31, 1994

| | | | |
|---|---|---|---|
| Austria | 22.5% | Netherlands | 20.2% |
| Belgium | 24.2% | Norway | 12.3% |
| Denmark | 14.3% | Spain | 21.7% |
| France | 20.6% | Sweden | 15.6% |
| Germany | 16.9% | Switzerland | 19.7% |
| Italy | 17.6% | United Kingdom | 16.3% |

**Average Annual Returns: Global Stock Subaccounts vs. Global Stock Mutual Funds**

| Year | Subaccount | Mutual Fund |
|---|---|---|
| 1994 | −1.1% | −2.9% |
| 1993 | 33.0% | 31.3% |
| 1992 | −6.9% | −0.8% |
| 1991 | 10.5% | 18.4% |
| 1990 | −7.7% | −10.8% |
| 1989 | 20.8% | 21.65% |
| 1988 | 8.5% | 14.2% |
| 1987 | −7.0% | 5.0% |
| | | |
| 3-yr. average | 7.2% | 9.1% |
| 5-yr. average | 4.1% | 5.5% |
| 10-yr. average | 1.1% | 15.7% |

With economic deregulation and the elimination of internal trade barriers, many European companies, for the first time in their history, are investing in and competing for exposure to the whole European market. Companies currently restricted to manufacturing and distributing within their national boundaries will soon be able to locate facilities anywhere in Europe, maximizing the efficient employment of labor, capital, and raw materials.

The table above shows year-by-year, as well as 3-, 5-, and 10-year averages for this investment category. The variable annuity subaccount category is compared against the similar mutual fund category. These performance figures are average figures, representing all funds and subaccounts that fall within this investment objective.

As you can see, the variable annuity subaccounts outperformed their mutual fund counterparts for 1994, 1993, and 1990.

Like any other subaccount category, this one should not be looked at in a vacuum. The real beauty of foreign subaccounts shines through when they are combined with other categories of U.S. equities. According to a Stanford University study, one's overall risk level is cut in half when a *global* portfolio of stocks is used instead of one based on U.S. issues alone. And, as already demonstrated, returns are greater when we look for opportunities worldwide instead of just domestically. I recommend a 10% commitment to this category for the conservative investor, 25% for the moderate, and 45% for the aggressive portfolio. As with any category of variable annuities, whenever larger dollar amounts are involved, more than one subaccount per category should be used.

The table on page 108 shows statistics you might find useful when comparing variable annuity subaccounts versus their mutual fund counterparts or "clones." The category averages are based on information available at the beginning of 1995.

Figure 10.1 on page 108 shows the year-by-year returns for this category of variable annuities for the period 1987 through 1994. These are composite figures and therefore include all of the subaccounts that comprise the global stock category.

### Global Stock Category Statistics: Subaccounts vs. Mutual Funds

| Description | Subaccounts | Funds |
| --- | --- | --- |
| **Composition of portfolio** | | |
| U.S. stocks | 0% | 0% |
| Cash | 13% | 9% |
| Foreign stocks | 87% | 89% |
| Bonds | 0% | 2% |
| Other | 0% | 0% |
| **Fees and expenses** | | |
| Underlying fund expense | 1.21% | 1.77% |
| Insurance expense | 1.26% | — |
| Total expenses | 2.47% | 1.77%/3.8%* |
| **Operations** | | |
| Net assets (in millions) | $56 | $313 |
| Manager tenure | 2 years | 4 years |
| **Portfolio statistics** | | |
| Beta | 0.5% | 0.6% |
| Standard deviation | 3.6% | 4.6% |
| Price/earnings ratio | 29 | 27 |
| Turnover ratio (annual) | 56% | 68% |
| Median market capitalization | $5.5 billion | $5.0 billion |
| Number of subaccounts/funds | 110 | 270 |

*Total expenses for this mutual fund category increase to this figure if the average mutual fund commission is added to the 1.77% figure.

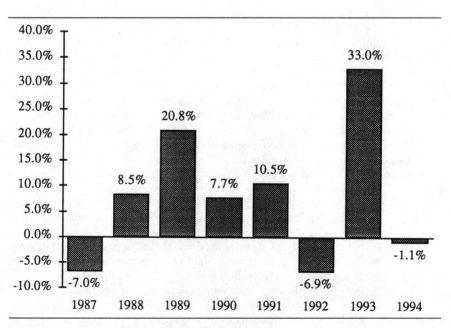

**Figure 10.1** Global Stock Subaccounts

---

**G.T. Global Allocator**
**Europe**
700 Market Street
St. Louis, MO 63101
(800) 237-6580

---

| | |
|---|---|
| Performance | ✓ |
| Risk control | ✓ |
| Expense minimization | ✓✓ |
| Management | ✓ |
| Investment options | ✓✓✓✓ |
| Family rating | ✓✓ |
| Total point score | 11 points |

---

## Performance ✓

During the 3-year and 5-year periods ending December 31, 1994, Europe had an average annual compound return of 2.4% and −1.0%, respectively. This means that a $10,000 investment made into this subaccount 5 years before that date grew to $9,500 ($10,700, if only the last 3 years of that period are used).

The inception month of this subaccount was February 1993. The performance figures (shown below) for periods before the subaccount's inception in February 1993 are hypothetical, based on the underlying clone fund's returns. This subaccount is modeled (cloned) after the G.T. Europe Growth Fund—Class A, which had an inception date of July 1985, and has an asset base of $900 million.

The year-by-year returns for this subaccount and the mutual fund it is modeled after are:

| Year | Annual Return | Morgan Stanley EAFE |
|---|---|---|
| 1994 | −2.0% | 7.8% |
| 1993 | 28.3% | 32.6% |
| 1992 | −11.3% | −12.2% |
| 1991 | 4.3% | 12.1% |
| 1990 | −14.7% | −23.5% |
| 1989 | 40.7% | 10.5% |
| 1988 | 11.1% | 28.3% |
| 1987 | 6.7% | 24.6% |

## Risk Control ✓

The price/earnings (p/e) ratio averages 24 for this portfolio. The typical global stock subaccount has a p/e ratio of 29. In general, the higher the p/e ratio, the riskier the portfolio.

## Expense Minimization ✓✓

The typical expenses incurred by global stock subaccounts are 2.5% per year. The total expenses for G.T. Global Allocator Europe, 2.4%, are lower than its peer group average. Total expenses include all charges to the investor (except the annual contract charge, which is always expressed as a dollar figure), including management fees, overhead, administration, and mortality expenses. The free annual withdrawals percentage is based on the account value.

| | | | |
|---|---|---|---|
| Maximum surrender charge | 6% | Total expenses | 2.4% |
| Duration of surrender charge | 6 years | Annual contract charge | $30 |
| Declining surrender charge | yes | Free annual withdrawals | 10% |

## Management ✓

G.T. Global Allocator is offered by General American Life Insurance Company. The company has a Duff & Phelps rating of AA and an A.M. Best rating of A+. The portfolio and the mutual fund it is modeled after have been managed by a management team since their inceptions. The portfolio's size is $3 million. The typical security in the portfolio has a market capitalization of $3.1 billion.

## Investment Options    ✓✓✓✓

Investors may make additional contributions into this portfolio at any time. This is known as a flexible premium annuity. Investors in this variable annuity can choose from all of the subaccount categories below that have a check mark:

| | | |
|---|---|---|
| ___ Aggressive growth | ✓ Government bonds | ✓ Money market |
| ✓ Balanced | ✓ Growth | ✓ Specialty/Sector |
| ✓ Corporate bonds | ✓ Growth & income | ✓ World bonds |
| ✓ Global equities (stocks) | ___ High-yield bonds | |

## Family Rating    ✓✓

There are 10 subaccounts within the G.T. Global Allocator family. Overall, this family of subaccounts can be described as fair on a *risk-adjusted* return basis.

   The subaccounts within this variable annuity all have an *increasing* guaranteed death benefit. This means that the beneficiary is guaranteed to receive *the greater of* the contract's value on the date of the annuitant's death or the value of the original investment(s) compounded by 5% each year (less any withdrawals made).

## Summary

G.T. Global Allocator Europe is the best choice for the variable annuity investor looking for a pure European play. This region of the world is expected to do quite well during the coming years, but without the tremendous swings found in the Pacific Basin. Often, this subaccount has outperformed the EAFE Index (a way of measuring how foreign stocks perform)—no small feat, considering the fact that the EAFE Index has done better than the S&P 500 over the past quarter-century.

   In money management, G.T. has been around the *global* block. The company has been managing money since 1969. Its central headquarters are in London, but it has several offices and research facilities around the globe. The U.S. offices are in San Francisco.

   The G.T. Global Allocator contract allows investors to switch among a number of interested subaccounts, some of which are quite unique (e.g., a pure Pacific Basin, Latin America, or Europe portfolio).

## Profile

| | | | |
|---|---|---|---|
| Minimum investment | $25 | Telephone exchanges | yes |
| Retirement account minimum | $2,000 | Transfers allowed per year | 12 |
| Co-annuitant allowed | no | Maximum issuance age | none |
| Co-owner allowed | yes | Maximum annuitization age | 85 |
| Dollar-cost averaging | yes | Number of subaccounts | 10 |
| Systematic withdrawal plans | yes | Available in all 50 states | no* |

*Not available in the following states: MD, NJ, OR, PA, TX, VA, and WA.

---

**Lincoln National American Legacy II**
**International**
P.O. Box 2340
Fort Wayne, IN  46801
(800) 421-9900

---

| | |
|---|---|
| Performance | ✓✓✓✓✓ |
| Risk control | ✓✓✓✓✓ |
| Expense minimization | ✓✓✓✓ |
| Management | ✓✓✓✓✓ |
| Investment options | ✓✓✓ |
| Family rating | ✓✓✓✓ |
| Total point score | 26 points |

## Performance ✓✓✓✓✓

During the 3-year and 5-year periods ending December 31, 1994, International had an average annual compound return of 5.5% and 8.5%, respectively. This means that a $10,000 investment made into this subaccount 5 years before that date grew to $15,000 ($11,700, if only the last 3 years of that period are used).

Compared to other global stock variable annuity subaccounts, this one ranks in the top third for the 3-year period. The inception month of this subaccount was May 1990. The performance figures (shown below) for periods before the subaccount's inception in May 1990 are hypothetical, based on the underlying clone fund's returns. This subaccount is modeled (cloned) after the EuroPacific Growth Fund, which had an inception date of April 1984, and has an asset base of $6 billion.

The year-by-year returns for this subaccount and the mutual fund it is modeled after are:

| Year | Annual Return | Morgan Stanley EAFE |
|---|---|---|
| 1994 | −7.8% | 7.8% |
| 1993 | 32.6% | 32.6% |
| 1992 | −2.2% | −12.2% |
| 1991 | 10.7% | 12.1% |
| 1990 | −0.1% | −23.5% |
| 1989 | 24.2% | 10.5% |
| 1988 | 21.0% | 28.3% |
| 1987 | 7.5% | 24.6% |

## Risk Control ✓✓✓✓✓

Over the 3-year period, this fund was somewhat safer than the average equity subaccount.

The typical standard deviation for global stock subaccounts was 3.6% during the 3-year period. The standard deviation for Lincoln National American Legacy II International was 3.0% over this same period, which means that this subaccount was 19% less volatile than its peer group. The price/earnings (p/e) ratio averages 23 for this portfolio. The typical global stock subaccount has a p/e ratio of 29. In general, the higher the p/e ratio, the riskier the portfolio.

The beta (market-related risk) of this subaccount was 0.4 over the 3-year period. Beta for this entire category was 0.5 over this same period. The market index (the S&P 500 Index for equity subaccounts) always has a beta of 1.0. The *risk-adjusted* return for this variable annuity subaccount can be described as fair.

## Expense Minimization   ✓✓✓

The typical expenses incurred by global stock subaccounts are 2.5% per year. The total expenses for Lincoln National American Legacy II International, 2.4%, are lower than its peer group average. Total expenses include all charges to the investor (except the annual contract charge, which is always expressed as a dollar figure), including management fees, overhead, administration, and mortality expenses. The free annual withdrawals percentage is based on the original principal.

| | | | |
|---|---|---|---|
| Maximum surrender charge | 6% | Total expenses | 2.4% |
| Duration of surrender charge | 7 years | Annual contract charge | $35 |
| Declining surrender charge | yes | Free annual withdrawals | 10% |

## Management   ✓✓✓✓✓

Lincoln National American Legacy II is offered by Lincoln National Life Insurance Company. The company has a Duff & Phelps rating of AAA and an A.M. Best rating of A+. The portfolio and its mutual fund "clone" have been managed by Capital Guardian (American Funds) since inception. The portfolio's size is $730 million. The typical security in the portfolio has a market capitalization of $5.6 billion.

## Investment Options   ✓✓✓

Investors may make additional contributions into this portfolio at any time. This is known as a flexible premium annuity. Investors in this variable annuity can choose from all of the subaccount categories below that have a check mark:

| | | |
|---|---|---|
| ___ Aggressive growth | ✓ Government bonds | ✓ Money market |
| ✓ Balanced | ✓ Growth | ___ Specialty/Sector |
| ___ Corporate bonds | ✓ Growth & income | ___ World bonds |
| ✓ Global equities (stocks) | ✓ High-yield bonds | |

## Family Rating   ✓✓✓✓

There are 7 subaccounts within the Lincoln National American Legacy II family. Overall, this family of subaccounts can be described as very good on a *risk-adjusted* return basis.

## Summary

Lincoln National American Legacy II International is the best scoring international or global equity subaccount. The performance of this portfolio is unbelievable. Few foreign equity funds can even match the EAFE Index; this investment smokes it. Not only is the track record something to behold, so is the risk control. I cannot say enough good things about the subaccount. It is truly great.

The Legacy II contract is nothing out of the ordinary except when it comes to the caliber of the investment options. There are so many good subaccounts in this family (almost all of which appear elsewhere in this book), it would be hard for you to go wrong.

## Profile

| | | | |
|---|---|---|---|
| Minimum investment | $300 | Telephone exchanges | yes |
| Retirement account minimum | $1,500 | Transfers allowed per year | 12 |
| Co-annuitant allowed | no | Maximum issuance age | 75 |
| Co-owner allowed | yes | Maximum annuitization age | 85 |
| Dollar-cost averaging | yes | Number of subaccounts | 7 |
| Systematic withdrawal plans | yes | Available in all 50 states | no* |

*Not available in NY.

**Mutual of America Separate Account 2**
**Scudder International**
666 Fifth Avenue
New York, NY 10103
(800) 468-3785

| | |
|---|---|
| Performance | ✓✓✓✓✓ |
| Risk control | ✓✓✓✓ |
| Expense minimization | ✓✓ |
| Management | ✓✓✓✓ |
| Investment options | ✓✓✓ |
| Family rating | ✓✓✓ |
| Total point score | 21 points |

# Performance ✓✓✓✓✓

During the 3-year and 5-year periods ending December 31, 1994, Scudder International had an average annual compound return of 8.4% and 5.1%, respectively. This means that a $10,000 investment made into this subaccount 5 years before that date grew to $12,800 ($12,700 over the last 3 years).

Compared to other global stock variable annuity subaccounts, this one ranks in the top quartile for the 3-year period. The inception month of this subaccount was January 1989. The performance figures (shown below) for periods before the subaccount's inception in January 1989 are hypothetical, based on the underlying clone fund's returns. This subaccount is modeled (cloned) after the Scudder International Fund, which had an inception date of January 1957, and has an asset base of $2.4 billion.

The year-by-year returns for this subaccount and the mutual fund it is modeled after are:

| Year | Annual Return | Morgan Stanley EAFE |
|---|---|---|
| 1994 | −2.4% | 7.8% |
| 1993 | 36.0% | 32.6% |
| 1992 | −4.0% | −12.2% |
| 1991 | 10.4% | 12.1% |
| 1990 | −8.7% | −23.5% |
| 1989 | 27.1% | 10.5% |
| 1988 | 18.8% | 28.3% |
| 1987 | 0.9% | 24.6% |

# Risk Control ✓✓✓✓

Over the 3-year period, this fund was slightly riskier than the average equity subaccount.

The typical standard deviation for global stock subaccounts was 3.6% during the 3-year period. The standard deviation for Mutual of America Separate Account 2 Scudder International was 3.5% over this same period, which means that this subaccount was 2% less volatile than its peer group. The price/earnings (p/e) ratio averages 30 for this portfolio. The typical global stock subaccount has a p/e ratio of 29. In general, the higher the p/e ratio, the riskier the portfolio.

The beta (market-related risk) of this subaccount was 0.4 over the 3-year period. Beta for this entire category was 0.5 over this same period. The market index (the S&P 500 Index for equity subaccounts) always has a beta of 1.0. The *risk-adjusted* return for this variable annuity subaccount can be described as very good.

## Expense Minimization                                      ✓✓

The typical expenses incurred by global stock subaccounts are 2.5% per year. The total expenses for Mutual of America Separate Account 2 Scudder International, 2.8%, are higher than its peer group average. Total expenses include all charges to the investor (except the annual contract charge, which is always expressed as a dollar figure), including management fees, overhead, administration, and mortality expenses. The free annual withdrawals percentage is based on the account value.

| | | | |
|---|---|---|---|
| Maximum surrender charge | 0% | Total expenses | 2.8% |
| Duration of surrender charge | n/a | Annual contract charge | $24 |
| Declining surrender charge | n/a | Free annual withdrawals | 10% |

## Management                                               ✓✓✓✓

Mutual of America Separate Account 2 is offered by Mutual of America Life Insurance Company. The company has a Duff & Phelps rating of AA+ and an A.M. Best rating of A+. The portfolio and the mutual fund it is modeled after were managed by Carol L. Franklin for the 7 years ending December 31, 1994. The portfolio's size is $40 million. The typical security in the portfolio has a market capitalization of $6.8 billion.

## Investment Options                                        ✓✓✓

Investors may make additional contributions into this portfolio at any time. This is known as a flexible premium annuity. Investors in this variable annuity can choose from all of the subaccount categories below that have a check mark:

| | | |
|---|---|---|
| ___ Aggressive growth | ___ Government bonds | ✓ Money market |
| ✓ Balanced | ✓ Growth | ___ Specialty/Sector |
| ✓ Corporate bonds | ✓ Growth & income | ___ World bonds |
| ✓ Global equities (stocks) | ___ High-yield bonds | |

## Family Rating                                             ✓✓✓

There are 12 subaccounts within the Mutual of America Separate Account 2 family. Overall, this family of subaccounts can be described as good on a *risk-adjusted* return basis. The subaccounts within this variable annuity all have a death benefit based on the value at the date of death (what is referred to in the industry as "accumulated value"). Unlike the death benefit found with most variable annuities, the accumulated value death benefit does not protect the beneficiary from possible market loss.

## Summary

Mutual of America Separate Account 2 Scudder International is one of the few global or foreign equity subaccounts to get a perfect rating for its performance and a near-perfect score for its risk minimization. This is a solid choice and is highly recommended. Unfortunately, the contract is available only for qualified accounts (i.e., IRAs, pension plans, Keoghs, and so on).

Several features are worth noting about this Mutual of America variable annuity contract. First, the minimum investment requirement for both nonqualified and qualified accounts is quite low. Second, you can list a co-annuitant—a great boon for individuals or couples who want to postpone triggering a tax event as long as possible. Third, unlimited telephone exchanges are allowed—you can move your money around without paying any type of fee. Fourth, there is no maximum issuance age—no matter how old you are, this investment is open to you. Fifth, you have a dozen portfolios to choose from; Scudder Capital Growth is just one of your options. Finally, there are no penalty charges or surrender schedules to worry about. As an investor, you can leave this contract completely without having to deal with a potential back-end charge.

## Profile

| | | | |
|---|---|---|---|
| Minimum investment | $10 | Telephone exchanges | yes |
| Retirement account minimum | $10 | Transfers allowed per year | unlimited |
| Co-annuitant allowed | yes | Maximum issuance age | none |
| Co-owner allowed | no | Maximum annuitization age | 70.5 |
| Dollar-cost averaging | no | Number of subaccounts | 12 |
| Systematic withdrawal plans | yes | Available in all 50 states | yes |

---

**Pacific Mutual Select Variable Annuity
International**
700 Newport Center Drive
P.O. Box 7500
Newport Beach, CA 92658-7500
(800) 800-7681

| | |
|---|---|
| Performance | ✓✓ |
| Risk control | ✓✓ |
| Expense minimization | ✓✓ |
| Management | ✓✓ |
| Investment options | ✓✓✓✓ |
| Family rating | ✓✓ |
| Total point score | 14 points |

## Performance                                                              ✓✓

During the 3-year and 5-year periods ending December 31, 1994, International had an average annual compound return of 5.2% and 1.7%, respectively. This means that a $10,000 investment made into this subaccount 5 years before that date grew to $11,600 ($10,500 for the last 3 years).

Compared to other global stock variable annuity subaccounts, this one ranks in the bottom quartile for the 3-year and 5-year periods. The inception month of this subaccount was August 1990. The performance figures (shown below) for periods before the subaccount's inception in August 1990 are hypothetical, based on the underlying clone fund's returns. This subaccount is modeled (cloned) after the Pacific Select Fund International Series, which had an inception date of January 1988, and has an asset base of $30 million.

The year-by-year returns for this subaccount and the portfolio it is modeled after are:

| Year | Annual Return | Morgan Stanley EAFE |
|---|---|---|
| 1994 | 1.7% | 7.8% |
| 1993 | 28.5% | 32.6% |
| 1992 | −10.9% | −12.2% |
| 1991 | 9.2% | 12.1% |
| 1990 | −15.4% | −23.5% |
| 1989 | 15.0% | 10.5% |

## Risk Control ✓✓

Over the 3-year and 5-year periods, this fund has been somewhat riskier than the average equity subaccount.

The typical standard deviation for global stock subaccounts was 3.6% during the 3-year period. The standard deviation for Pacific Mutual Select Variable Annuity International was 4.0% over this same period, which means that this subaccount was 10% more volatile than its peer group. The price/earnings (p/e) ratio averages 30 for this portfolio. The typical global stock subaccount has a p/e ratio of 29. In general, the higher the p/e ratio, the riskier the portfolio.

The beta (market-related risk) of this subaccount was 0.5 over the 3-year period. Beta for this entire category was also 0.5 over this same period. The market index (the S&P 500 Index for equity subaccounts) always has a beta of 1.0. The *risk-adjusted* return for this variable annuity subaccount can be described as poor.

## Expense Minimization ✓✓

The typical expenses incurred by global stock subaccounts are 2.5% per year. The total expenses for Pacific Mutual Select Variable Annuity International, 2.8%, are higher than its peer group average. Total expenses include all charges to the investor (except the annual contract charge, which is always expressed as a dollar figure), including management fees, overhead, administration, and mortality expenses. The free annual withdrawals percentage is based on the original principal.

| | | | |
|---|---|---|---|
| Maximum surrender charge | 6% | Total expenses | 2.8% |
| Duration of surrender charge | 6 years | Annual contract charge | $30 |
| Declining surrender charge | yes | Free annual withdrawals | 10% |

## Management ✓✓

Pacific Mutual Select Variable Annuity is offered by Pacific Mutual Life Insurance Company. The company has a Duff & Phelps rating of AA+ and an A.M. Best rating of A+. The portfolio and the mutual fund it is modeled after have been managed by Takeo Nakamura for the past 6 years. The portfolio's size is $11 million. The typical security in the portfolio has a market capitalization of $6.5 billion. Nakamura also manages the Nomura Pacific Basin mutual fund.

## Investment Options ✓✓✓✓

Investors may make additional contributions into this portfolio at any time. This is known as a flexible premium annuity. Investors in this variable annuity can choose from all of the subaccount categories below that have a check mark:

| | | |
|---|---|---|
| ____ Aggressive growth | ✓ Government bonds | ✓ Money market |
| ✓ Balanced | ✓ Growth | ____ Specialty/Sector |
| ✓ Corporate bonds | ✓ Growth & income | ____ World bonds |
| ✓ Global equities (stocks) | ✓ High-yield bonds | |

## Family Rating ✓✓

There are 9 subaccounts within the Pacific Mutual Select Variable Annuity family. Overall, this family of subaccounts can be described as fair on a *risk-adjusted* return basis.

## Summary

Pacific Mutual Select Variable Annuity International is what one could call a defensive foreign or global equity play. This subaccount has done much better than the

EAFE Index during the negative years, but has generally matched or exceeded this same index's returns during the good years.

This is a fine choice for the investor who understands the importance of having a more diversified portfolio. The contract includes some excellent investment options, including a couple of noteworthy bond accounts.

## Profile

| | | | |
|---|---|---|---|
| Minimum investment | $2,000 | Telephone exchanges | yes |
| Retirement account minimum | $5,000 | Transfers allowed per year | unlimited |
| Co-annuitant allowed | yes | Maximum issuance age | 85 |
| Co-owner allowed | yes | Maximum annuitization age | 95 |
| Dollar-cost averaging | yes | Number of subaccounts | 9 |
| Systematic withdrawal plans | yes | Available in all 50 states | no* |

*Not available in NY.

---

**Venture Vision**
**Global Equity**
P.O. Box 818
Boston, MA 02117-0818
(800) 344-1029

| | |
|---|---|
| Performance | ✓✓✓ |
| Risk control | ✓✓✓ |
| Expense minimization | ✓✓ |
| Management | ✓✓ |
| Investment options | ✓✓✓✓ |
| Family rating | ✓✓✓ |
| Total point score | 19 points |

---

## Performance ✓✓✓✓

During the 3-year period ending December 31, 1994, Global Equity had an average annual compound return of 12.3%. This means that a $10,000 investment made into this subaccount 3 years before that date grew to $14,200.

The inception month of this subaccount was April 1993. The performance figures (shown below) for periods before the subaccount's inception in April 1993 are hypothetical, based on the underlying clone fund's returns. This subaccount is modeled (cloned) after the NASL Series Trust Global Equity Trust, which had an inception date of March 1988, and has an asset base of $270 million.

The year-by-year returns for this subaccount and the portfolio it is modeled after are:

| Year | Annual Return | Morgan Stanley EAFE |
|---|---|---|
| 1994 | 0.1% | 7.8% |
| 1993 | 29.6% | 32.6% |
| 1992 | −2.9% | −12.2% |
| 1991 | 11.4% | 12.1% |
| 1990 | 0.0% | −23.5% |

## Risk Control                                                     ✓✓✓

The price/earnings (p/e) ratio averages 31 for this portfolio. The typical global stock subaccount has a p/e ratio of 29. In general, the higher the p/e ratio, the riskier the portfolio.

## Expense Minimization                                             ✓✓

The typical expenses incurred by global stock subaccounts are 2.5% per year. The total expenses for Venture Vision Global Equity, 2.8%, are higher than its peer group average. Total expenses include all charges to the investor (except the annual contract charge, which is always expressed as a dollar figure), including management fees, overhead, administration, and mortality expenses. The free annual withdrawals percentage is based on the original principal.

| | | | |
|---|---|---|---|
| Maximum surrender charge | 3% | Total expenses | 2.8% |
| Duration of surrender charge | 3 years | Annual contract charge | $0 |
| Declining surrender charge | yes | Free annual withdrawals | 10% |

## Management                                                       ✓✓

Venture Vision is offered by North American Security Life Insurance Company. The company has an A.M. Best rating of A. The subaccount and the portfolio it is modeled after were managed by Steven Schaefer for the 6 years ending December 31, 1994. The portfolio's size is $10 million. The typical security in the portfolio has a market capitalization of $6.1 billion.

## Investment Options                                               ✓✓✓✓

Investors may make additional contributions into this portfolio at any time. This is known as a flexible premium annuity. Investors in this variable annuity can choose from all of the subaccount categories below that have a check mark:

| | | |
|---|---|---|
| ___ Aggressive growth | ✓ Government bonds | ✓ Money market |
| ✓ Balanced | ✓ Growth | ___ Specialty/Sector |
| ✓ Corporate bonds | ✓ Growth & income | ✓ World bonds |
| ✓ Global equities (stocks) | ___ High-yield bonds | |

## Family Rating                                                    ✓✓✓

There are 13 subaccounts within the Venture Vision family. Overall, this family of subaccounts can be described as good on a *risk-adjusted* return basis.

   The subaccounts within this variable annuity all have an *increasing* guaranteed death benefit. This means that the beneficiary is guaranteed to receive *the greater of* the contract's value on the date of the annuitant's death or the value of the original investment(s) compounded by 5% each year (less any withdrawals made).

## Summary

Venture Vision Global Equity has been incredibly nimble—completely avoiding the horrendous losses international portfolios incurred in 1990, and missing almost all of the losses these same accounts sustained in 1992. Yet, during the positive times, this subaccount has come very close to matching EAFE Index returns. The wide range of investment options offered by the Venture Vision contract is awesome. This is a highly recommended place to invest your money.

# Profile

| | | | |
|---|---|---|---|
| Minimum investment | $25,000 | Telephone exchanges | yes |
| Retirement account minimum | $25,000 | Transfers allowed per year | 12 |
| Co-annuitant allowed | yes | Maximum issuance age | none |
| Co-owner allowed | yes | Maximum annuitization age | 85 |
| Dollar-cost averaging | yes | Number of subaccounts | 13 |
| Systematic withdrawal plans | yes | Available in all 50 states | no* |

*Not available in the following states: ME, NH, RI, and VT.

# Chapter

# 11

# Government Bond Subaccounts

These subaccounts invest in direct and indirect U.S. government obligations. Government bond subaccounts are comprised of one or more of the following:

Treasury Bills, Notes, and Bonds (T-Bills, T-Notes, T-Bonds), which comprise the entire marketable debt of the U.S. government;

Government National Mortgage Association bonds (GNMAs), which are considered an indirect obligation of the government, but are still backed by the full faith and credit of the United States;

Federal National Mortgage Association bonds (FNMAs), which are not issued by the government, but are considered virtually identical in safety to GNMAs.

The average maturity of securities found in government bond subaccounts ranges quite a bit, depending on the type of subaccount and management's perception of risk and of the future direction of interest rates. (A more thorough discussion of interest rates and the volatility of bond subaccount prices is given in the introductory pages of Chapter 9.)

Over the 15 years ending December 31, 1994, government bonds underperformed long-term corporate bonds only slightly—11.5% versus 11.6% for corporates. A $10,000 investment in U.S. government bonds grew to $51,300 over the 15-year period; a similar initial investment in corporate bonds grew to $51,700.

Within a longer time frame, government bonds have only slightly outperformed inflation. A dollar invested in governments in 1945 grew to $12.42 by the beginning of 1995. This translates into an average compound return of 5.2% per year. Over the 50 years ending December 31, 1994, the worst year for government bonds was 1967, when a loss of 9% was suffered. The best year was 1982, when government bonds posted a gain of 40%. All of these figures are based on total return (current yield plus or minus any appreciation or loss of principal).

Over the 50 years ending December 31, 1994, there were forty-one 10-year periods (1944–1953, 1945–1954, and so on). On a pretax basis, government bonds

**Average Annual Returns: Government Bond
Subaccounts vs. Government Bond Mutual Funds**

| Year | Subaccount | Mutual Fund |
|------|-----------|-------------|
| 1994 | −4.6% | −3.6% |
| 1993 | 8.3% | 8.0% |
| 1992 | 5.5% | 6.0% |
| 1991 | 14.7% | 14.1% |
| 1990 | 6.0% | 8.4% |
| 1989 | 12.8% | 12.0% |
| 1988 | 6.3% | 6.7% |
| 1987 | −0.6% | 1.5% |
| | | |
| 3-yr. average | 3.0% | 3.4% |
| 5-yr. average | 5.9% | 6.4% |
| 10-yr. average | 7.9% | 8.3% |

outperformed inflation during only fifteen of the forty-one 10-year periods. Over the same 50-year period, there have been thirty-one 20-year periods (1944–1963, 1945–1964, and so on). On a pretax basis, government bonds have outperformed inflation during only eight of these thirty-one periods. All eight of those 20-year periods ended between 1986 and 1994.

The table above shows year-by-year, as well as 3-, 5-, and 10-year averages for this investment category. The variable annuity subaccount category is compared against the similar mutual fund category. These performance figures are average figures, representing all funds and subaccounts that fall within this investment objective.

As you can see, the variable annuity subaccounts outperformed their mutual fund counterparts for 1993, 1991, and 1989.

Government bond subaccounts are the perfect choice for the conservative investor who wants to avoid any possibility of defaults. They should probably be avoided by most moderate investors and all aggressive portfolios. Up to 50% of an investor's holdings could be in government bonds.

The prospective investor should always remember that government and corporate bonds are generally not a good investment, once inflation *and* taxes are factored in (money in an annuity compounds tax-deferred, not tax-free; eventually, either you or your heirs will have to pay taxes on the accumulated growth and/or interest). The investor who appreciates the cumulative effects of even low levels of inflation should probably avoid government and corporate bonds except during retirement. I recommend a 20% commitment to this category for the conservative investor and 5% for the moderate portfolio. As is true with any category of variable annuities, whenever larger dollar amounts are involved, more than one subaccount per category should be used.

The table on page 122 shows statistics you might find useful when comparing variable annuity subaccounts versus their mutual fund counterparts or "clones." The category averages are based on information available at the beginning of 1994.

Figure 11.1 shows the year-by-year returns for this category of variable annuities for the period 1987 through 1994. These are composite figures and therefore include all of the subaccounts that comprise the government bond category.

### Government Bond Category Statistics: Subaccounts vs. Mutual Funds

| Description | Subaccounts | Funds |
|---|---|---|
| **Composition of portfolio** | | |
| U.S. stocks | 0% | 0% |
| Cash | 12% | 3% |
| Foreign stocks | 0% | 0% |
| Bonds | 82% | 97% |
| Other | 6% | 0% |
| **Fees and expenses** | | |
| Underlying fund expense | 0.63% | 0.96% |
| Insurance expense | 1.28% | — |
| Total expenses | 1.91% | 0.96%/2.6%* |
| **Operations** | | |
| Net assets (in millions) | $72 | $520 |
| Manager tenure | 4 years | 4 years |
| **Portfolio statistics** | | |
| Average maturity | 11 years | 8 years |
| Standard deviation | 1.3% | 1.0% |
| Average weighted coupon | 6.8% | 7.8% |
| Turnover ratio (annual) | 120% | 161% |
| Number of subaccounts/funds | 75 | 220 |

*Total expenses for this mutual fund category increase to this figure if the average mutual fund commission is added to the 0.96% figure.

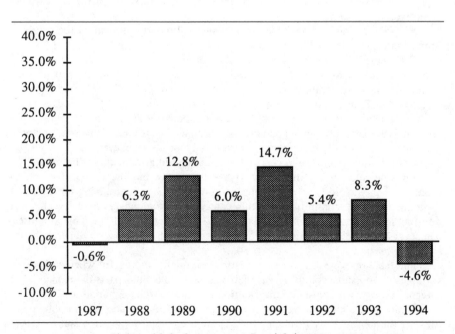

**Figure 11.1** Government Bond Subaccounts

| Best of America IV/Nationwide Government Bond | |
|---|---|
| P.O. Box 16609 | |
| One Nationwide Plaza | |
| Columbus, OH 43216 | |
| (800) 848-6331 | |
| Performance | ✓✓✓ |
| Risk control | ✓✓✓✓ |
| Expense minimization | ✓✓✓✓ |
| Management | ✓✓✓✓ |
| Investment options | ✓✓✓✓✓ |
| Family rating | ✓✓ |
| Total point score | 22 points |

## Performance      ✓✓✓

During the 3-year and 5-year periods ending December 31, 1994, Government Bond had an average annual compound return of 3.2% and 6.5%, respectively (9.6% for 10 years). This means that a $10,000 investment made into this subaccount 5 years before that date grew to $13,700 ($11,000, if only the last 3 years of the period are used).

Compared to other government bond variable annuity subaccounts, this one ranks in the top half for the 3-year period and in the top third for the 5-year period (it ranks in the top 1% for the 10 years ending December 31, 1994). The inception month of this subaccount was November 1982.

The year-by-year returns for this subaccount are:

| Year | Annual Return | Lehman Bros. Government Bond Index |
|---|---|---|
| 1994 | −4.5% | −4.6% |
| 1993 | 8.1% | 10.7% |
| 1992 | 6.5% | 7.2% |
| 1991 | 15.2% | 15.3% |
| 1990 | 8.1% | 8.7% |
| 1989 | 12.5% | 14.2% |
| 1988 | 6.7% | 7.0% |
| 1987 | 0.1% | 2.2% |

## Risk Control      ✓✓✓✓

Over the 3-year period, this fund was as safe as the average fixed-income subaccount. During the 5-year period, it was slightly riskier.

The typical standard deviation for government bond subaccounts was 1.3% during the 3-year period. The standard deviation for Best of America IV/Nationwide Government Bond was 1.2% over this same period, which means that this subaccount was 9% less volatile than its peer group. The average maturity of the bonds in this account is 13 years; the weighted coupon rate averages 8.3%. The typical government bond subaccount has an average maturity of 11 years and a weighted coupon rate of 6.8%.

The beta (market-related risk) of this subaccount was 1.2 over the 3-year period. Beta for this entire category was 1.3 over this same period. The market index (the Lehman Brothers Aggregate Bond Index for debt subaccounts) always has a beta of 1.0. The *risk-adjusted* return for this variable annuity subaccount can be described as fair.

## Expense Minimization    ✓✓✓✓

The typical expenses incurred by government bond subaccounts are 1.9% per year. The total expenses for Best of America IV/Nationwide Government Bond, 1.8%, are lower than its peer group average. Total expenses include all charges to the investor (except the annual contract charge, which is always expressed as a dollar figure), including management fees, overhead, administration, and mortality expenses. The free annual withdrawals percentage is based on the original principal.

| | | | |
|---|---|---|---|
| Maximum surrender charge | 7% | Total expenses | 1.8% |
| Duration of surrender charge | 7 years | Annual contract charge | $30 |
| Declining surrender charge | yes | Free annual withdrawals | 10% |

## Management    ✓✓✓✓

Best of America IV/Nationwide is offered by Nationwide Life Insurance Company. The company has an A.M. Best rating of A+. The portfolio was managed by Wayne T. Frisbee for the 9 years ending December 31, 1994. The portfolio's size is $216 million.

## Investment Options    ✓✓✓✓✓

Investors may make additional contributions into this portfolio at any time. This is known as a flexible premium annuity. Investors in this variable annuity can choose from all of the subaccount categories below that have a check mark:

| | | |
|---|---|---|
| ✓ Aggressive growth | ✓ Government bonds | ✓ Money market |
| ✓ Balanced | ✓ Growth | ✓ Specialty/Sector |
| ✓ Corporate bonds | ✓ Growth & income | ✓ World bonds |
| ✓ Global equities (stocks) | ✓ High-yield bonds | |

## Family Rating    ✓✓

There are 22 subaccounts within the Best of America IV/Nationwide family. Overall, this family of subaccounts can be described as fair on a *risk-adjusted* return basis.

## Summary

Best of America IV/Nationwide Government Bond racks up an impressive score. This bond portfolio has done very well while keeping risk and expense down to a minimum. A big plus for this subaccount is that investors have access to an incredibly large range of investment choices.

The parent company, Nationwide, was a pioneer in hiring portfolio managers from a wide range of mutual fund groups; most of its managers are household names. This type of creativity has made this investment one of the most popular in the industry.

## Profile

| | | | |
|---|---|---|---|
| Minimum investment | none | Telephone exchanges | yes |
| Retirement account minimum | $1,500 | Transfers allowed per year | one per day |
| Co-annuitant allowed | no | Maximum issuance age | none |
| Co-owner allowed | no | Maximum annuitization age | none |
| Dollar-cost averaging | yes | Number of subaccounts | 22 |
| Systematic withdrawal plans | yes | Available in all 50 states | yes |

---

**Franklin Valuemark II**
**U.S. Government Securities**
10 Valley Stream Parkway
Malvern, PA 19355
(800) 342-3863

---

| | |
|---|---|
| Performance | ✓✓ |
| Risk control | ✓✓✓✓✓ |
| Expense minimization | ✓✓✓ |
| Management | ✓✓✓✓ |
| Investment options | ✓✓✓✓✓ |
| Family rating | ✓✓ |
| Total point score | 21 points |

---

## Performance                                                          ✓✓

During the 3-year and 5-year periods ending December 31, 1994, U.S. Government Securities had an average annual compound return of 2.6% and 5.8%, respectively. This means that a $10,000 investment made into this subaccount 5 years before that date grew to $13,300 ($10,800, if only the last 3 years of the period are used).

Compared to other government bond variable annuity subaccounts, this one ranks in the top half for the 3-year period. The inception month of this subaccount was June 1989. The performance figures (shown below) for periods before the subaccount's inception in June 1989 are hypothetical, based on the underlying clone fund's returns. This subaccount is modeled (cloned) after the Franklin U.S. Government Securities Fund, which had an inception date of May 1970, and has an asset base of $14 billion.

The year-by-year returns for this subaccount and the mutual fund it is modeled after are:

| Year | Annual Return | Lehman Bros. Government Bond Index |
|---|---|---|
| 1994 | −5.9% | −3.4% |
| 1993 | 8.2% | 10.7% |
| 1992 | 6.2% | 7.2% |
| 1991 | 14.3% | 15.3% |
| 1990 | 7.4% | 8.7% |
| 1989 | 13.1% | 14.2% |
| 1988 | 7.5% | 7.0% |
| 1987 | 4.3% | 2.2% |

## Risk Control                                                    ✓✓✓✓✓

Over the 3-year period, this fund was a little safer than the average fixed-income subaccount.

The typical standard deviation for government bond subaccounts was 1.3% during the 3-year period. The standard deviation for Franklin Valuemark II U.S. Government Securities was 1.1% over this same period, which means that this subaccount was 15% less volatile than its peer group. The average maturity of the bonds in this account is 17 years; the weighted coupon rate averages 6.9%. The typical government bond subaccount has an average maturity of 11 years and a weighted coupon rate of 6.8%.

The beta (market-related risk) of this subaccount was 1.1 over the 3-year period. Beta for this entire category was 1.3 over this same period. The market index (the Lehman Brothers Aggregate Bond Index for debt subaccounts) always has a beta of 1.0. The *risk-adjusted* return for this variable annuity subaccount can be described as good.

## Expense Minimization    ✓✓✓

The typical expenses incurred by government bond subaccounts are 1.9% per year. The total expenses for Franklin Valuemark II U.S. Government Securities, 2.0%, are higher than its peer group average. Total expenses include all charges to the investor (except the annual contract charge, which is always expressed as a dollar figure), including management fees, overhead, administration, and mortality expenses. The free annual withdrawals percentage is based on the original principal.

| | | | |
|---|---|---|---|
| Maximum surrender charge | 5% | Total expenses | 2.0% |
| Duration of surrender charge | 5 years | Annual contract charge | $30 |
| Declining surrender charge | yes | Free annual withdrawals | 15% |

## Management    ✓✓✓✓

Franklin Valuemark II is offered by Allianz Life Insurance Company of North America. The company has an A.M. Best rating of A+. The portfolio was managed by Jack Lemein for the 5 years ending December 31, 1994. The portfolio's size is $630 million.

## Investment Options    ✓✓✓✓✓

Investors may make additional contributions into this portfolio at any time. This is known as a flexible premium annuity. Investors in this variable annuity can choose from all of the subaccount categories below that have a check mark:

| | | |
|---|---|---|
| ___ Aggressive growth | ✓ Government bonds | ✓ Money market |
| ✓ Balanced | ✓ Growth | ✓ Specialty/Sector |
| ✓ Corporate bonds | ___ Growth & income | ✓ World bonds |
| ✓ Global equities (stocks) | ✓ High-yield bonds | |

## Family Rating    ✓✓

There are 18 subaccounts within the Franklin Valuemark II family. Overall, this family of subaccounts can be described as fair on a *risk-adjusted* return basis.

The subaccounts within this variable annuity all have an *increasing* guaranteed death benefit. This means that the beneficiary is guaranteed to receive *the greater of* the contract's value on the date of the annuitant's death or the value of the original investment(s) compounded by 5% each year (less any withdrawals made).

## Summary

Franklin Valuemark II U.S. Government Securities is a wizard at minimizing risk. Few government or corporate bond subaccounts (or mutual funds) have done as well as this portfolio. Modeled after its government securities fund, the most popular in the country, Franklin has created another winner.

Investors will be pleased not only with this subaccount, but also with several other members of the Franklin Valuemark II group. The company offers one of the most investor-friendly contracts in the entire annuity industry.

## Profile

| | | | |
|---|---|---|---|
| Minimum investment | $2,000 | Telephone exchanges | yes |
| Retirement account minimum | $5,000 | Transfers allowed per year | 12 |
| Co-annuitant allowed | yes | Maximum issuance age | none |
| Co-owner allowed | spouses only | Maximum annuitization age | 80 |
| Dollar-cost averaging | yes | Number of subaccounts | 18 |
| Systematic withdrawal plans | yes | Available in all 50 states | yes |

---

**Franklin Valuemark II
Zero-Coupon 2000**
10 Valley Stream Parkway
Malvern, PA 19355
(800) 342-3863

| | |
|---|---|
| Performance | ✓✓✓ |
| Risk control | ✓ |
| Expense minimization | ✓✓✓✓✓ |
| Management | ✓✓✓ |
| Investment options | ✓✓✓✓ |
| Family rating | ✓✓ |
| Total point score | 20 points |

## Performance                    ✓✓✓✓

During the 3-year and 5-year periods ending December 31, 1994, Zero-Coupon 2000 had an average annual compound return of 4.3% and 7.0%, respectively. This means that a $10,000 investment made into this subaccount 5 years before that date grew to $14,000 ($11,300 over the last 3 years).

Compared to other government bond variable annuity subaccounts, this one ranks in the top 15% for the 3-year period. The inception month of this subaccount was June 1989.

The year-by-year returns for this subaccount are:

| Year | Annual Return | Lehman Bros. Government Bond Index |
|---|---|---|
| 1994 | −8.0% | −3.4% |
| 1993 | 14.0% | 10.7% |
| 1992 | 7.5% | 7.2% |
| 1991 | 18.5% | 15.3% |
| 1990 | 4.5% | 8.7% |

## Risk Control                    ✓

Over the 3-year period, this fund was quite a bit riskier than the average fixed-income subaccount.

The typical standard deviation for government bond subaccounts was 1.3% during the 3-year period. The standard deviation for Franklin Valuemark II Zero-Coupon 2000 was 2.1% over this same period, which means that this subaccount was 62% more volatile than its peer group. The average maturity of the bonds in this account is 7 years. The typical government bond subaccount has an average maturity of 11 years and a weighted coupon rate of 6.8%.

The beta (market-related risk) of this subaccount was 2.1 over the 3-year period. Beta for this entire category was 1.3 over this same period. The market index (the Lehman Brothers Aggregate Bond Index for debt subaccounts) always has a beta of 1.0. The *risk-adjusted* return for this variable annuity subaccount can be described as fair.

## Expense Minimization                                          ✓✓✓✓

The typical expenses incurred by government bond subaccounts are 1.9% per year. The total expenses for Franklin Valuemark II Zero-Coupon 2000, 1.7%, are lower than its peer group average. Total expenses include all charges to the investor (except the annual contract charge, which is always expressed as a dollar figure), including management fees, overhead, administration, and mortality expenses. The free annual withdrawals percentage is based on the original principal.

| | | | |
|---|---|---|---|
| Maximum surrender charge | 5% | Total expenses | 1.7% |
| Duration of surrender charge | 5 years | Annual contract charge | $30 |
| Declining surrender charge | yes | Free annual withdrawals | 15% |

## Management                                                      ✓✓✓

Franklin Valuemark II is offered by Allianz Life Insurance Company of North America. The company has an A.M. Best rating of A+. The portfolio was managed by Jack Lemein for the 5 years ending December 31, 1994. The portfolio's size is $80 million.

## Investment Options                                            ✓✓✓✓

Investors may make additional contributions into this portfolio at any time. This is known as a flexible premium annuity. Investors in this variable annuity can choose from all of the subaccount categories below that have a check mark:

| | | |
|---|---|---|
| ___ Aggressive growth | ✓ Government bonds | ✓ Money market |
| ✓ Balanced | ✓ Growth | ✓ Specialty/Sector |
| ✓ Corporate bonds | ___ Growth & income | ✓ World bonds |
| ✓ Global equities (stocks) | ✓ High-yield bonds | |

## Family Rating                                                    ✓✓

There are 18 subaccounts within the Franklin Valuemark II family. Overall, this family of subaccounts can be described as fair on a *risk-adjusted* return basis.

The subaccounts within this variable annuity all have an *increasing* guaranteed death benefit. This means that the beneficiary is guaranteed to receive *the greater of* the contract's value on the date of the annuitant's death or the value of the original investment(s) compounded by 5% each year (less any withdrawals made).

## Summary

Franklin Valuemark II Zero-Coupon 2000 is one of the few variable annuity subaccount offerings (out of close to 1,500 candidates) that can give investors maximum returns, at a specific date in the future. There are two interesting aspects to this portfolio. First, a continuation of the fine performance this subaccount has enjoyed in the past will be dependent on the future direction of interest rates. Second, this subaccount is one of the few portfolios that has a somewhat finite line; the great majority of the holdings will mature in about 5 years.

Investors will be pleased not only with this subaccount, but also with several other members of the Franklin Valuemark II group. The company offers one of the most investor-friendly contracts in the entire annuity industry. This particular annuity is one of the most popular within the industry.

## Profile

| | | | |
|---|---|---|---|
| Minimum investment | $2,000 | Telephone exchanges | yes |
| Retirement account minimum | $5,000 | Transfers allowed per year | 12 |
| Co-annuitant allowed | yes | Maximum issuance age | none |
| Co-owner allowed | spouses only | Maximum annuitization age | 80 |
| Dollar-cost averaging | yes | Number of subaccounts | 18 |
| Systematic withdrawal plans | yes | Available in all 50 states | yes |

---

**Franklin Valuemark II**
**Zero-Coupon 2010**
10 Valley Stream Parkway
Malvern, PA 19355
(800) 342-3863

| | |
|---|---|
| Performance | ✓✓✓✓ |
| Risk control | |
| Expense minimization | ✓✓✓✓ |
| Management | ✓✓ |
| Investment options | ✓✓✓✓ |
| Family rating | ✓✓ |
| Total point score | 19 points |

---

## Performance                                   ✓✓✓✓

During the 3-year and 5-year periods ending December 31, 1994, Zero-Coupon 2010 had an average annual compound return of 5.7% and 6.8%, respectively. This means that a $10,000 investment made into this subaccount 5 years before that date grew to $13,900 ($11,800 over the past 3 years).

Compared to other government bond variable annuity subaccounts, this one ranks in the top 2% for the 3-year period. The inception month of this subaccount was June 1989.

The year-by-year returns for this subaccount are:

| Year | Annual Return | Lehman Bros. Government Bond Index |
|---|---|---|
| 1994 | −12.2% | −3.4% |
| 1993 | 23.7% | 10.7% |
| 1992 | 8.8% | 7.2% |
| 1991 | 18.4% | 15.3% |
| 1990 | −0.9% | 8.7% |

## Risk Control

Over the 3-year period, this fund was substantially riskier than the average fixed-income subaccount.

The typical standard deviation for government bond subaccounts was 1.3% during the 3-year period. The standard deviation for Franklin Valuemark II Zero-Coupon 2010 was 3.4% over this same period, which means that this subaccount was substantially more volatile than its peer group. The average maturity of the bonds in this account is 16 years. The typical government bond subaccount has an average maturity of 11 years and a weighted coupon rate of 6.8%.

The beta (market-related risk) of this subaccount was 3.0 over the 3-year period. Beta for this entire category was 1.3 over this same period. The market index (the Lehman Brothers Aggregate Bond Index for debt subaccounts) always has a beta of 1.0. The *risk-adjusted* return for this variable annuity subaccount can be described as poor.

## Expense Minimization ✓✓✓✓

The typical expenses incurred by government bond subaccounts are 1.9% per year. The total expenses for Franklin Valuemark II Zero-Coupon 2010, 1.7%, are lower than its peer group average. Total expenses include all charges to the investor (except the annual contract charge, which is always expressed as a dollar figure), including management fees, overhead, administration, and mortality expenses. The free annual withdrawals percentage is based on the original principal.

| | | | |
|---|---|---|---|
| Maximum surrender charge | 5% | Total expenses | 1.7% |
| Duration of surrender charge | 5 years | Annual contract charge | $30 |
| Declining surrender charge | yes | Free annual withdrawals | 15% |

## Management ✓✓

Franklin Valuemark II is offered by Allianz Life Insurance Company of North America. The company has an A.M. Best rating of A+. The portfolio was managed by Jack Lemein for the 5 years ending December 31, 1994. The portfolio's size is $30 million.

## Investment Options ✓✓✓✓

Investors may make additional contributions into this portfolio at any time. This is known as a flexible premium annuity. Investors in this variable annuity can choose from all of the subaccount categories below that have a check mark:

| | | |
|---|---|---|
| ___ Aggressive growth | ✓ Government bonds | ✓ Money market |
| ✓ Balanced | ✓ Growth | ✓ Specialty/Sector |
| ✓ Corporate bonds | ___ Growth & income | ✓ World bonds |
| ✓ Global equities (stocks) | ✓ High-yield bonds | |

## Family Rating ✓✓

There are 18 subaccounts within the Franklin Valuemark II family. Overall, this family of subaccounts can be described as fair on a *risk-adjusted* return basis.

The subaccounts within this variable annuity all have an *increasing* guaranteed death benefit. This means that the beneficiary is guaranteed to receive *the greater of* the contract's value on the date of the annuitant's death or the value of the original investment(s) compounded by 5% each year (less any withdrawals made).

## Summary

Franklin Valuemark II Zero-Coupon 2010 is one of the few variable annuity subaccount offerings (out of close to 1,500 candidates) that can give investors maximum returns, at a specific date in the future. There are two interesting aspects to this portfolio. First, a continuation of the fine performance this subaccount has enjoyed in the past will be dependent on the future direction of interest rates. Second, this subaccount is one of the few portfolios that has a somewhat finite life; the great majority of the holdings will mature in about 15 years.

This length of time for a zero coupon bond means that contract owners will be in for quite a ride. Zero coupon issues are far more volatile than traditional current yielding bonds. Even though performance values will probably swing wildly, there are two things going for the investor. First, no matter what happens, the securities will mature for face value within a somewhat reasonable period of time. Second, you can decide when to get in and out of this portfolio. With a little skill and quite a bit of luck, you may go into this subaccount when the bond market is doing well (i.e., interest rates are either falling or there is a *perception* that they may fall or stabilize) and get out during the bearish times.

Investors will be pleased not only with this subaccount, but also with several other members of the Franklin Valuemark II group. The company offers one of the most investor-friendly contracts in the entire annuity industry.

## Profile

| | | | |
|---|---|---|---|
| Minimum investment | $2,000 | Telephone exchanges | yes |
| Retirement account minimum | $5,000 | Transfers allowed per year | 12 |
| Co-annuitant allowed | yes | Maximum issuance age | none |
| Co-owner allowed | spouses only | Maximum annuitization age | 80 |
| Dollar-cost averaging | yes | Number of subaccounts | 18 |
| Systematic withdrawal plans | yes | Available in all 50 states | yes |

---

### Lincoln National American Legacy II
### U.S. Government/AAA-Rated Securities
P.O. Box 2340
Fort Wayne, IN 46801
(800) 421-9900

---

| | |
|---|---|
| Performance | ✓✓✓ |
| Risk control | ✓✓✓✓ |
| Expense minimization | ✓✓✓ |
| Management | ✓✓✓✓ |
| Investment options | ✓✓✓ |
| Family rating | ✓✓✓✓ |
| Total point score | 21 points |

## Performance                                           ✓✓✓

During the 3-year and 5-year periods ending December 31, 1994, U.S. Government/AAA-Rated Securities had an average annual compound return of 3.2% and 6.1%, respectively. This means that a $10,000 investment made into this subaccount 5 years before that date grew to $13,400 ($11,000, if only the last 3 years of the period are used).

Compared to other government bond variable annuity subaccounts, this one ranks in the top half for the 3-year and 5-year periods. The inception month of this subaccount was December 1985. This subaccount is modeled (cloned) after the U.S. Government Securities Fund (which also has an inception date of October 1985) and has an asset base of $1.7 billion.

The year-by-year returns for this subaccount are:

| Year | Annual Return | Lehman Bros. Government Bond Index |
|------|---------------|-------------------------------------|
| 1994 | −5.6% | −3.4% |
| 1993 | 9.7% | 10.7% |
| 1992 | 6.2% | 7.2% |
| 1991 | 14.4% | 15.3% |
| 1990 | 7.0% | 8.7% |
| 1989 | 9.3% | 14.2% |
| 1988 | 6.6% | 7.0% |
| 1987 | −2.9% | 2.2% |

## Risk Control                                        ✓✓✓✓

Over the 3-year and 5-year periods, this fund was slightly safer than the average fixed-income subaccount.

The typical standard deviation for government bond subaccounts was 1.3% during the 3-year period. The standard deviation for Lincoln National American Legacy II U.S. Government/AAA-Rated Securities was also 1.3% over this same period. This means that this subaccount has been as volatile than its peer group. The average maturity of the bonds in this account is 9 years; the weighted coupon rate averages 9.6%. The typical government bond subaccount has an average maturity of 11 years and a weighted coupon rate of 6.8%.

The beta (market-related risk) of this subaccount was 1.3 over the 3-year period. Beta for this entire category was also 1.3 over this same period. The market index (the Lehman Brothers Aggregate Bond Index for debt subaccounts) always has a beta of 1.0. The *risk-adjusted* return for this variable annuity subaccount can be described as good.

## Expense Minimization                                ✓✓✓

The typical expenses incurred by government bond subaccounts are 1.9% per year. The total expenses for Lincoln National American Legacy II U.S. Government/AAA-Rated Securities, 1.9%, are equivalent to its peer group average. Total expenses include all charges to the investor (except the annual contract charge, which is always expressed as a dollar figure), including management fees, overhead, administration, and mortality expenses. The free annual withdrawals percentage is based on the original principal.

| | | | |
|---|---|---|---|
| Maximum surrender charge | 6% | Total expenses | 1.9% |
| Duration of surrender charge | 7 years | Annual contract charge | $35 |
| Declining surrender charge | yes | Free annual withdrawals | 10% |

## Management ✓✓✓✓

Lincoln National American Legacy II is offered by Lincoln National Life Insurance Company. The company has a Duff & Phelps rating of AAA and an A.M. Best rating of A+. The portfolio has been managed by Capital Guardian since its inception. The portfolio's size is $550 million.

## Investment Options ✓✓✓

Investors may make additional contributions into this portfolio at any time. This is known as a flexible premium annuity. Investors in this variable annuity can choose from all of the subaccount categories below that have a check mark:

| | | |
|---|---|---|
| ___ Aggressive growth | ✓ Government bonds | ✓ Money market |
| ✓ Balanced | ✓ Growth | ___ Specialty/Sector |
| ___ Corporate bonds | ✓ Growth & income | ___ World bonds |
| ✓ Global equities (stocks) | ✓ High-yield bonds | |

## Family Rating ✓✓✓✓

There are 7 subaccounts within the Lincoln National American Legacy II family. Overall, this family of subaccounts can be described as very good on a *risk-adjusted* return basis.

## Summary

Lincoln National American Legacy II U.S. Government/AAA-Rated Securities is managed by the same people who run the American Funds. As mentioned earlier in this book, this is perhaps the best large mutual fund company in the nation. Often, it is difficult to get excited about a government securities bond account, but there are aspects of this subaccount worth pointing out.

First, risk control is very good. By keeping the portfolio loaded up with short- and medium-term securities, Legacy II is making sure its investors do not get badly burned in the event interest rates spike upward. The contract includes some other impressive investment choices: international and high yield. Look for Legacy to add a couple of new subaccounts to its stable during the next year.

## Profile

| | | | |
|---|---|---|---|
| Minimum investment | $300 | Telephone exchanges | yes |
| Retirement account minimum | $1,500 | Transfers allowed per year | 12 |
| Co-annuitant allowed | no | Maximum issuance age | 75 |
| Co-owner allowed | yes | Maximum annuitization age | 85 |
| Dollar-cost averaging | yes | Number of subaccounts | 7 |
| Systematic withdrawal plans | yes | Available in all 50 states | no* |

*Not available in NY.

---

**Pacific Mutual Select Variable Annuity**
**Government Securities**
700 Newport Center Drive
P.O. Box 7500
Newport Beach, CA  92658-7500
(800) 800-7681

| | |
|---|---|
| Performance | ✓✓✓ |
| Risk control | ✓✓✓✓✓ |
| Expense minimization | ✓✓ |
| Management | ✓✓✓✓✓ |
| Investment options | ✓✓✓✓ |
| Family rating | ✓✓ |
| Total point score | 21 points |

---

# Performance                                                   ✓✓✓

During the 3-year and 5-year periods ending December 31, 1994, Government Securities had an average annual compound return of 2.9% and 6.0%, respectively. This means that a $10,000 investment made into this subaccount 5 years before that date grew to $10,900 ($13,400, if only the last 3 years of the period are used).

Compared to other government bond variable annuity subaccounts, this one ranks in the top third for the 3-year period but in the bottom half for the 5-year period. The inception month of this subaccount was August 1990. The performance figures (shown below) for periods before the subaccount's inception in August 1990 are hypothetical, based on the underlying clone fund's returns. This subaccount is modeled (cloned) after the Pacific Select Fund Government Securities Series, which had an inception date of January 1988, and has an asset base of $25 million.

The year-by-year returns for this subaccount and the portfolio it is modeled after are:

| Year | Annual Return | Lehman Bros. Government Bond Index |
|---|---|---|
| 1994 | −6.3% | −3.4% |
| 1993 | 9.4% | 10.7% |
| 1992 | 6.2% | 7.2% |
| 1991 | 15.6% | 15.3% |
| 1990 | 5.8% | 8.7% |
| 1989 | 9.3% | 14.2% |

# Risk Control                                                ✓✓✓✓✓

Over the 3-year period, this fund was slightly safer than the average fixed-income subaccount. During the 5-year period, it was somewhat riskier.

The typical standard deviation for government bond subaccounts was 1.3% during the past 3-year period. The standard deviation for Pacific Mutual Select Variable Annuity Government Securities was 1.2% over this same period. This means that this subaccount has been 9% less volatile than its peer group. The average maturity of the bonds in this account is 16 years; the weighted coupon rate averages 8.1%. The typical government bond subaccount has an average maturity of 11 years and a weighted coupon rate of 6.8%.

The beta (market-related risk) of this subaccount was 1.2 over the 3-year period. Beta for this entire category was 1.3 over this same period. The market index (the Lehman Brothers Aggregate Bond Index for debt subaccounts) always has a beta of

1.0. The *risk-adjusted* return for this variable annuity subaccount can be described as fair.

## Expense Minimization                    ✓✓

The typical expenses incurred by government bond subaccounts are 1.9% per year. The total expenses for Pacific Mutual Select Variable Annuity Government Securities, 2.1%, are higher than its peer group average. Total expenses include all charges to the investor (except the annual contract charge, which is always expressed as a dollar figure), including management fees, overhead, administration, and mortality expenses. The free annual withdrawals percentage is based on the original principal.

| | | | |
|---|---|---|---|
| Maximum surrender charge | 6% | Total expenses | 2.1% |
| Duration of surrender charge | 6 years | Annual contract charge | $30 |
| Declining surrender charge | yes | Free annual withdrawals | 10% |

## Management                    ✓✓✓✓

Pacific Mutual Select Variable Annuity is offered by Pacific Mutual Life Insurance Company. The company has a Duff & Phelps rating of AA+ and an A.M. Best rating of A+. The portfolio and the portfolio it is modeled after were managed by John L. Hague for the 6 years ending December 31, 1994. The portfolio's size is $15 million.

## Investment Options                    ✓✓✓

Investors may make additional contributions into this portfolio at any time. This is known as a flexible premium annuity. Investors in this variable annuity can choose from all of the subaccount categories below that have a check mark:

| | | |
|---|---|---|
| ___ Aggressive growth | ✓ Government bonds | ✓ Money market |
| ✓ Balanced | ✓ Growth | ___ Specialty/Sector |
| ✓ Corporate bonds | ✓ Growth & income | ___ World bonds |
| ✓ Global equities (stocks) | ✓ High-yield bonds | |

## Family Rating                    ✓✓

There are 9 subaccounts within the Pacific Mutual Select Variable Annuity family. Overall, this family of subaccounts can be described as fair on a *risk-adjusted* return basis.

## Summary

Pacific Mutual Select Variable Annuity Government Securities is part of a small universe of subaccounts that is exceptional at reducing investor risk. Management also receives top marks. This is a small subaccount whose nimbleness will be beneficial as interest rates move around.

The Pacific Mutual contract includes a global and high-yield bond subaccount, two important categories often missing from other companies. The structure of the contract is reasonable, but the features offered are great; few variable annuities allow for a co-annuitant and co-owner.

## Profile

| | | | |
|---|---|---|---|
| Minimum investment | $2,000 | Telephone exchanges | yes |
| Retirement account minimum | $5,000 | Transfers allowed per year | unlimited |
| Co-annuitant allowed | yes | Maximum issuance age | 85 |
| Co-owner allowed | yes | Maximum annuitization age | 95 |
| Dollar-cost averaging | yes | Number of subaccounts | 9 |
| Systematic withdrawal plans | yes | Available in all 50 states | no* |

*Not available in NY.

# Chapter

## 12

# Growth Subaccounts

These subaccounts generally seek capital appreciation, with current income as a distant secondary concern. Growth subaccounts typically invest in U.S. common stocks while avoiding speculative issues and aggressive trading techniques. The goal of most of these subaccounts is *long-term* growth. The approaches used to attain this appreciation can vary significantly among growth subaccounts.

Over the 15 years from 1979–1993, growth stocks outperformed government bonds by 74%. Common stocks averaged 15.7% compounded per year, versus 11.5% for government bonds. A $10,000 investment in stocks, as measured by the S&P 500, grew to over $89,300 over the 15-year period; a similar initial investment in government bonds grew to $51,300.

Within a longer time frame, common stocks have also fared quite well. A dollar invested in stocks in 1945 grew to over $330 by the beginning of 1995. This translates into an average compound return of 12.3% per year. Over the 50 years ending December 31, 1994, the worst year for common stocks was 1974, when a loss of 26% was suffered. One year later, these same stocks posted a gain of 37%. The best year was 1954, when growth stocks posted a gain of 53%.

Over the past half-century, growth stocks have outperformed bonds in every single decade. If President George Washington had invested $1 in common stocks with an average return of 12%, his investment would be worth over $68.7 billion today. If he had enough luck to average 14% on his stock portfolio, his portfolio would be large enough to pay our national debt four times over!

The table at the top of page 137 shows year-by-year, as well as 3-, 5-, and 10-year averages for this investment category. The variable annuity subaccount category is compared against the similar mutual fund category. These performance figures are average figures, representing all funds and subaccounts that fall within this investment objective.

As you can see, the variable annuity subaccounts outperformed their mutual fund counterparts for 1991, 1989, and 1987.

Growth subaccounts should be a part of everyone's holdings. They should comprise no more than 25% in a *diversified,* conservative portfolio, 50% for the moderate risk-taker, and 75% for the aggressive investor. I recommend a 10% commitment to this category for the moderate and aggressive portfolio. Notice that other stock categories (international, growth and income, and aggressive growth) are also recommended. As with any category of variable annuities, whenever larger dollar amounts are involved, more than one subaccount per category should be used.

## Average Annual Returns:
## Growth Subaccounts vs. Growth Mutual Funds

| Year | Subaccount | Mutual Fund |
|---|---|---|
| 1994 | −2.9% | −2.1% |
| 1993 | 11.3% | 11.6% |
| 1992 | 6.7% | 8.4% |
| 1991 | 36.9% | 36.7% |
| 1990 | −6.2% | −5.1% |
| 1989 | 27.9% | 26.8% |
| 1988 | 11.2% | 14.9% |
| 1987 | 3.1% | 2.6% |
| | | |
| 3-yr. average | 4.9% | 5.9% |
| 5-yr. average | 8.3% | 8.9% |
| 10-yr. average | 12.0% | 12.8% |

The table below shows statistics you might find useful when comparing variable annuity subaccounts versus their mutual fund counterparts or "clones." These category averages are based on information available at the beginning of 1995.

Figure 12.1 shows the year-by-year returns for this category of variable annuities for the period 1987 through 1994. These are composite figures and therefore include all of the subaccounts that comprise the growth category.

## Growth Category Statistics:
## Subaccounts vs. Mutual Funds

| Description | Subaccounts | Funds |
|---|---|---|
| **Composition of portfolio** | | |
| U.S. stocks | 82% | 82% |
| Cash | 11% | 9% |
| Foreign stocks | 6% | 6% |
| Bonds | 0% | 1% |
| Other | 1% | 2% |
| **Fees and expenses** | | |
| Underlying fund expense | 0.74% | 1.28% |
| Insurance expense | 1.24% | — |
| Total expenses | 1.98% | 1.28%/3.3%* |
| **Operations** | | |
| Net assets (in millions) | $95 | $430 |
| Manager tenure | 5 years | 6 years |
| **Portfolio statistics** | | |
| Beta | 1.1% | 1.0% |
| Standard deviation | 3.9% | 4.4% |
| Price/earnings ratio | 24 | 23 |
| Turnover ratio (annual) | 97% | 81% |
| Median market capitalization | $5.4 billion | $5.2 billion |
| Number of subaccounts/funds | 240 | 450 |

*Total expenses for this mutual fund category increase to this figure if the average mutual fund commission is added to the 1.28% figure.

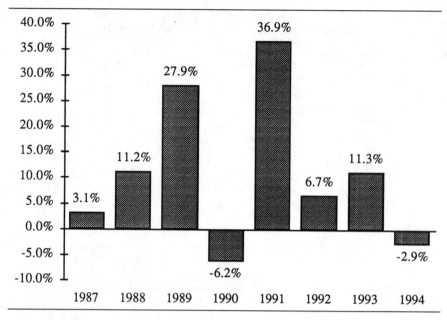

**Figure 12.1** Growth Subaccounts

---

**American Skandia Advisors Plan**
**Neuberger and Berman Growth**
P.O. Box 883
Shelton, CT  06484
(800) 752-6342

| | |
|---|---|
| Performance | ✓ |
| Risk control | ✓✓✓ |
| Expense minimization | ✓✓ |
| Management | ✓ |
| Investment options | ✓✓✓✓ |
| Family rating | ✓ |
| Total point score | 13 points |

## Performance ✓

During the 3-year and 5-year periods ending December 31, 1994, Neuberger and Berman Growth had an average annual compound return of 2.1% and 4.3%, respectively. This means that a $10,000 investment made into this subaccount 5 years before that date grew to $12,300 ($10,600, if only the last 3 years of the period are used).

The inception month of this subaccount was May 1992. The performance figures (shown below) for periods before the subaccount's inception in May 1992 are hypothetical, based on the underlying clone fund's returns. This subaccount is modeled (cloned) after the Neuberger and Berman Advisors Management Trust Growth Portfolio, which had an inception date of September 1984, and has an asset base of $375 million.

The year-by-year returns for this subaccount and the portfolio it is modeled after are:

| Year | Annual Return | S&P 500 |
|---|---|---|
| 1994 | −6.3% | 1.3% |
| 1993 | 5.3% | 10.1% |
| 1992 | 8.0% | 7.6% |
| 1991 | 27.9% | 30.5% |
| 1990 | −9.5% | −3.1% |
| 1989 | 27.6% | 31.7% |
| 1988 | 18.3% | 16.6% |
| 1987 | 0.1% | 5.3% |

## Risk Control ✓✓✓

Over the 3-year and 5-year periods, this fund was slightly riskier than the average equity subaccount.

The typical standard deviation for growth subaccounts was 3.9% during the 3-year period. The standard deviation for American Skandia Advisors Plan Neuberger and Berman Growth was 3.7% over this same period, which means that this subaccount was 4% less volatile than its peer group. The price/earnings (p/e) ratio averages 22 for this portfolio. The typical growth subaccount has a p/e ratio of 24. In general, the higher the p/e ratio, the riskier the portfolio.

The beta (market-related risk) of this subaccount was 1.1 over the 3-year period. Beta for this entire category was 1.1 over this same period. The market index (the S&P 500 Index for equity subaccounts) always has a beta of 1.0. The *risk-adjusted* return for this variable annuity subaccount can be described as fair.

## Expense Minimization ✓✓

The typical expenses incurred by growth subaccounts are 2.0% per year. The total expenses for American Skandia Advisors Plan Neuberger and Berman Growth, 2.2%, are higher than its peer group average. Total expenses include all charges to the investor (except the annual contract charge, which is always expressed as a dollar figure), including management fees, overhead, administration, and mortality expenses. The free annual withdrawals percentage is based on the original principal.

| | | | |
|---|---|---|---|
| Maximum surrender charge | 8% | Total expenses | 2.2% |
| Duration of surrender charge | 7 years | Annual contract charge | $30 |
| Declining surrender charge | no | Free annual withdrawals | 10% |

## Management

American Skandia Advisors Plan is offered by American Skandia Life Assurance Corporation. The company has a Duff & Phelps rating of AA−. The subaccount and the portfolio it is modeled after were managed by Mark R. Goldstein for the 6 years ending December 31, 1994. The portfolio's size is $25 million. The typical security in the portfolio has a market capitalization of $1.8 billion. Goldstein also manages the Neuberger & Berman Manhattan mutual fund.

## Investment Options ✓✓✓✓

Investors may make additional contributions into this portfolio at any time. This is known as a flexible premium annuity. Investors in this variable annuity can choose from all of the subaccount categories below that have a check mark:

| | | |
|---|---|---|
| ✓ Aggressive growth | ___ Government bonds | ✓ Money market |
| ✓ Balanced | ✓ Growth | ✓ Specialty/Sector |
| ✓ Corporate bonds | ✓ Growth & income | ✓ World bonds |
| ✓ Global equities (stocks) | ✓ High-yield bonds | |

## Family Rating ✓

There are 31 subaccounts within the American Skandia Advisors Plan family. Overall, this family of subaccounts can be described as poor on a *risk-adjusted* return basis.

The subaccounts within this variable annuity all have an *increasing* guaranteed death benefit. This means that the beneficiary is guaranteed to receive *the greater of* the contract's value on the date of the annuitant's death or the value of the original investment(s) compounded by 5% each year (less any withdrawals made).

## Summary

American Skandia Advisors Plan Neuberger and Berman Growth is an example of a subaccount that looks fair over any given short term, but great if the investor stays with management's proven techniques. Neuberger and Berman are known as no-nonsense, straight shooters who deliver solid returns over the long haul.

This particular subaccount suffers in the ratings used within this book. Unfortunately, there is no system that can treat each entry equally, once all of the facts are known.

The annuity issuer, American Skandia, continues to add to its already impressive, wide-ranging array of money management companies, including: Alliance, Neuberger & Berman, Janus, INVESCO, Federated, Phoenix, T. Rowe Price, Scudder, J. P. Morgan, Henderson International, and PIMCO. As some of these new portfolios begin to mature, contract owners will see the wisdom in Skandia's selection of investment advisors. Few annuities can boast of the diversity that ASAP (Skandia's acronym for their variable annuity contract) has when it comes to category selection and breadth of management.

A few years ago, American Skandia began to implement a policy wherein only the best specialists would be sought within each investment category. This strategy has been almost completely implemented, and the future looks very promising for this entire group.

## Profile

| | | | |
|---|---|---|---|
| Minimum investment | $1,000 | Telephone exchanges | yes |
| Retirement account minimum | $1,000 | Transfers allowed per year | 12 |
| Co-annuitant allowed | yes | Maximum issuance age | none |
| Co-owner allowed | yes | Maximum annuitization age | none |
| Dollar-cost averaging | yes | Number of subaccounts | 34 |
| Systematic withdrawal plans | yes | Available in all 50 states | no* |

*Not available in NY.

---

**Ameritas Overture III**
**Alger Growth**
One Ameritas Way
P.O. Box 82550
Lincoln, NE  68501
(800) 487-7557

| | |
|---|---|
| Performance | ✓✓✓✓ |
| Risk control | ✓✓ |
| Expense minimization | ✓✓ |
| Management | ✓✓✓ |
| Investment options | ✓✓✓✓ |
| Family rating | ✓✓✓ |
| Total point score | 19 points |

## Performance                    ✓✓✓✓

During the 3-year and 5-year periods ending December 31, 1994, Alger Growth had an average annual compound return of 10.3% and 13.7%, respectively. This means that a $10,000 investment made into this subaccount 5 years before that date grew to $19,000 ($13,400, if only the last 3 years of the period are used).

Compared to other growth variable annuity subaccounts, this one ranks in the top 10% for the 3-year period. The inception month of this subaccount was June 1993. The performance figures (shown below) for periods before the subaccount's inception in June 1993 are based on its predecessor and the underlying clone fund's returns. This subaccount is modeled (cloned) after the Alger Growth Portfolio, which had an inception date of November 1986, and has an asset base of $65 million.

The year-by-year returns for this subaccount and the mutual fund it is modeled after are:

| Year | Annual Return | S&P 500 |
|---|---|---|
| 1994 | 0.2% | 1.3% |
| 1993 | 20.9% | 10.1% |
| 1992 | 11.8% | 7.6% |
| 1991 | 37.9% | 30.5% |
| 1990 | 2.1% | −3.1% |
| 1989 | 35.1% | 31.7% |
| 1988 | 6.4% | 16.6% |
| 1987 | −0.4% | 5.3% |

## Risk Control                    ✓✓

Over the 3-year period, this fund was slightly riskier than the average equity subaccount.

The typical standard deviation for growth subaccounts was 3.9% during the 3-year period. The standard deviation for Ameritas Overture III Alger Growth was 4.2% over this same period. This means that this subaccount was 9% more volatile than its peer group. The price/earnings (p/e) ratio averages 32 for this portfolio. The typical growth subaccount has a p/e ratio of 24. In general, the higher the p/e ratio, the riskier the portfolio.

The beta (market-related risk) of this subaccount was 1.1 over the 3-year period. Beta for this entire category was 1.1 over this same period. The market index

(the S&P 500 Index for equity subaccounts) always has a beta of 1.0. The *risk-adjusted* return for this variable annuity subaccount can be described as very good.

## Expense Minimization    ✓✓

The typical expenses incurred by growth subaccounts are 2.0% per year. The total expenses for Ameritas Overture III Alger Growth, 2.4%, are higher than its peer group average. Total expenses include all charges to the investor (except the annual contract charge, which is always expressed as a dollar figure), including management fees, overhead, administration, and mortality expenses. The free annual withdrawals percentage is based on the account value.

| | | | |
|---|---|---|---|
| Maximum surrender charge | 6% | Total expenses | 2.4% |
| Duration of surrender charge | 7 years | Annual contract charge | $36 |
| Declining surrender charge | no | Free annual withdrawals | 10% |

## Management    ✓✓✓

Ameritas Overture III is offered by Ameritas Variable Life Insurance Company. The company has an A.M. Best rating of A+. The portfolio and the mutual fund it is modeled after were managed by David Alger for the 5 years ending December 31, 1994. The portfolio's size is a mere $1 million. The typical security in the portfolio has a market capitalization of $3.2 billion.

## Investment Options    ✓✓✓✓

Investors may make additional contributions into this portfolio at any time. This is known as a flexible premium annuity. Investors in this variable annuity can choose from all of the subaccount categories below that have a check mark:

| | | |
|---|---|---|
| ✓ Aggressive growth | ___ Government bonds | ✓ Money market |
| ✓ Balanced | ✓ Growth | ___ Specialty/Sector |
| ✓ Corporate bonds | ✓ Growth & income | ___ World bonds |
| ✓ Global equities (stocks) | ✓ High-yield bonds | |

## Family Rating    ✓✓✓

There are 13 subaccounts within the Ameritas Overture III family. Overall, this family of subaccounts can be described as good on a *risk-adjusted* return basis.

## Summary

Ameritas Overture III Alger Growth is an exciting subaccount that is sure to please. The people at Alger are known across the country as being among the best money managers and as possessing quite a bit of creativity and independence (e.g., the firm will not sell its research to other companies). Research has always been the key with this group, and it shows off in the portfolio's return figures.

Ameritas Overture III has a number of excellent subaccounts that were omitted from this book only to avoid duplication (a virtually identical portfolio was offered by another carrier). Some of the penalty provisions are not as liberal as they could be, but this should not be of any concern for the patient investor. After all, variable annuities are supposed to be a medium- to long-term investment, particularly when one is invested in equities.

This is a fine growth portfolio and is highly recommended. Look into other offerings from Ameritas Overture III.

## Profile

| | | | |
|---|---|---|---|
| Minimum investment | $2,000 | Telephone exchanges | yes |
| Retirement account minimum | $2,000 | Transfers allowed per year | 12 |
| Co-annuitant allowed | no | Maximum issuance age | 80 |
| Co-owner allowed | yes | Maximum annuitization age | 95 |
| Dollar-cost averaging | yes | Number of subaccounts | 13 |
| Systematic withdrawal plans | yes | Available in all 50 states | no* |

*Not available in DC, DE, ME, NJ, NY, and VT.

---

**Connecticut Mutual Panorama**
**Growth**
P.O. Box 13217
Kansas City, MO 64199
(800) 234-5606 ext. 5232

---

| | |
|---|---|
| Performance | ✓✓✓✓✓ |
| Risk control | ✓✓✓✓ |
| Expense minimization | ✓✓✓✓ |
| Management | ✓✓ |
| Investment options | ✓ |
| Family rating | ✓✓✓✓✓ |
| Total point score | 21 points |

## Performance ✓✓✓✓✓

During the 3-year and 5-year periods ending December 31, 1994, Growth had an average annual compound return of 9.9% and 10.6%, respectively (14.3% for 10 years). This means that a $10,000 investment made into this subaccount 5 years before that date grew to $16,500 ($13,300, if only the last 3 years of the period are used).

Compared to other growth variable annuity subaccounts, this one ranks in the top 15% for the 3-year period and in the top 10% for the 5-year period. (It ranks in the top 5% for the 10 years ending December 31, 1994.) The inception month of this subaccount was May 1992. The performance figures (shown below) for periods before the subaccount's inception in May 1992 are hypothetical, based on the underlying clone fund's returns. This subaccount is modeled (cloned) after the Connecticut Mutual Growth Account, which had an inception date of September 1985, and has an asset base of $75 million.

The year-by-year returns for this subaccount and the mutual fund it is modeled after are:

| Year | Annual Return | S&P 500 |
|---|---|---|
| 1994 | −1.0% | 1.3% |
| 1993 | 19.9% | 10.1% |
| 1992 | 12.0% | 7.6% |
| 1991 | 36.9% | 30.5% |
| 1990 | −8.0% | −3.1% |
| 1989 | 34.9% | 31.7% |
| 1988 | 14.3% | 16.6% |
| 1987 | −0.3% | 5.3% |

## Risk Control                                    ✓✓✓✓

The price/earnings (p/e) ratio averages 15 for this portfolio. The typical growth subaccount has a p/e ratio of 24. In general, the higher the p/e ratio, the riskier the portfolio.

The beta (market-related risk) of this subaccount was 0.9 over the 3-year period. Beta for this entire category was 1.1 over this same period. The market index (the S&P 500 Index for equity subaccounts) always has a beta of 1.0.

## Expense Minimization                            ✓✓✓✓

The typical expenses incurred by growth subaccounts are 2.0% per year. The total expenses for Connecticut Mutual Panorama Growth, 1.9%, are lower than its peer group average. Total expenses include all charges to the investor (except the annual contract charge, which is always expressed as a dollar figure), including management fees, overhead, administration, and mortality expenses. The free annual withdrawals percentage is based on the account value.

| | | | |
|---|---|---|---|
| Maximum surrender charge | 5% | Total expenses | 1.9% |
| Duration of surrender charge | 5 years | Annual contract charge | $30 |
| Declining surrender charge | no | Free annual withdrawals | 10% |

## Management                                      ✓✓

Connecticut Mutual Panorama is offered by Connecticut Mutual Life Insurance Company. The company has a Duff & Phelps rating of AA and an A.M. Best rating of A+. The portfolio and the mutual fund it is modeled after were managed by Peter M. Antos for the 5 years ending December 31, 1994. The portfolio's size is $18 million. The typical security in the portfolio has a market capitalization of $5.1 billion.

## Investment Options                              ✓

Investors may make additional contributions into this portfolio at any time. This is known as a flexible premium annuity. Investors in this variable annuity can choose from all of the subaccount categories below that have a check mark:

| | | |
|---|---|---|
| ___ Aggressive growth | ___ Government bonds | ✓ Money market |
| ✓ Balanced | ✓ Growth | ___ Specialty/Sector |
| ✓ Corporate bonds | ___ Growth & income | ___ World bonds |
| ___ Global equities (stocks) | ___ High-yield bonds | |

## Family Rating                                   ✓✓✓✓

There are 4 subaccounts within the Connecticut Mutual Panorama family. Overall, this family of subaccounts can be described as excellent on a *risk-adjusted* return basis.

## Summary

Connecticut Mutual Panorama Growth is one of the top-rated growth accounts in this book. Not very often can it be said that a subaccount is regarded as excellent for its performance and the overall caliber of its family, and very good when it comes to risk control.

Connecticut Mutual is good at controlling risk, but falls short when it comes to investment options. Thus, the only real shortcoming of this variable annuity can be corrected by the company's adding more portfolios; a couple of different global securities subaccounts would make this a great choice.

## Profile

| | | | |
|---|---|---|---|
| Minimum investment | $500 | Telephone exchanges | yes |
| Retirement account minimum | $500 | Transfers allowed per year | unlimited |
| Co-annuitant allowed | no | Maximum issuance age | 75 |
| Co-owner allowed | no | Maximum annuitization age | none |
| Dollar-cost averaging | yes | Number of subaccounts | 4 |
| Systematic withdrawal plans | yes | Available in all 50 states | yes |

---

**Dean Witter Variable Annuity II**
**Equity**
Two World Trade Center
74th Floor
New York, NY 10048
(800) 869-3863

---

| | |
|---|---|
| Performance | ✓✓✓✓ |
| Risk control | ✓ |
| Expense minimization | ✓✓✓ |
| Management | ✓✓✓ |
| Investment options | ✓✓✓✓ |
| Family rating | ✓✓✓✓ |
| Total point score | 20 points |

---

## Performance ✓✓✓✓✓

During the 3-year and 5-year periods ending December 31, 1994, Equity had an average annual compound return of 3.1% and 10.3%, respectively. This means that a $10,000 investment made into this subaccount 5 years before that date grew to $16,300 ($11,000, if only the last 3 years of the period are used).

Compared to other growth variable annuity subaccounts, this one ranks in the top quarter for the 3-year period. The inception month of this subaccount was October 1990. The performance figures (shown below) for periods before the subaccount's inception in October 1990 are hypothetical, based on the underlying clone fund's returns. This subaccount is modeled (cloned) after the Dean Witter American Value Fund, which had an inception date of March 1980, and has an asset base of $1.5 billion.

The year-by-year returns for this subaccount and the portfolio it is modeled after are:

| Year | Annual Return | S&P 500 |
|---|---|---|
| 1994 | −6.2% | 1.3% |
| 1993 | 18.1% | 10.1% |
| 1992 | −1.2% | 7.6% |
| 1991 | 56.9% | 30.5% |
| 1990 | −0.9% | −3.1% |
| 1989 | 25.4% | 31.7% |
| 1988 | 10.8% | 16.6% |
| 1987 | 2.8% | 5.3% |

# Risk Control                                                                ✓

Over the 3-year period, this fund was somewhat riskier than the average equity subaccount.

The typical standard deviation for growth subaccounts was 3.8% during the 3-
year period. The standard deviation for Dean Witter Variable Annuity II Equity was
4.6% over this same period, which means that this subaccount was 19% more
volatile than its peer group. The price/earnings (p/e) ratio averages 31 for this portfolio. The typical growth subaccount has a p/e ratio of 24. In general, the higher the
p/e ratio, the riskier the portfolio.

The beta (market-related risk) of this subaccount was 1.2 over the 3-year
period. Beta for this entire category was 1.1 over this same period. The market index
(the S&P 500 Index for equity subaccounts) always has a beta of 1.0. The *risk-
adjusted* return for this variable annuity subaccount can be described as good.

# Expense Minimization                                                      ✓✓✓

The typical expenses incurred by growth subaccounts are 2.0% per year. The total
expenses for Dean Witter Variable Annuity II Equity, 2.0%, is identical to its peer
group average. Total expenses include all charges to the investor (except the annual
contract charge, which is always expressed as a dollar figure), including management
fees, overhead, administration, and mortality expenses. The free annual withdrawals
percentage is based on the original principal.

| | | | |
|---|---|---|---|
| Maximum surrender charge | 6% | Total expenses | 2.0% |
| Duration of surrender charge | 6 years | Annual contract charge | $30 |
| Declining surrender charge | yes | Free annual withdrawals | 15% |

# Management                                                                ✓✓✓

Dean Witter Variable Annuity II is offered by Northbrook Insurance Company. The
company has an A.M. Best rating of A+. The subaccount and the mutual fund it is
modeled after were managed by Anita Kolleeny for the 10 years ending December
31, 1994. The portfolio's size is $90 million. The typical security in the portfolio
has a market capitalization of $3.4 billion.

# Investment Options                                                       ✓✓✓✓

Investors may make additional contributions into this portfolio at any time. This is
known as a flexible premium annuity. Investors in this variable annuity can choose
from all of the subaccount categories below that have a check mark:

| | | |
|---|---|---|
| ___ Aggressive growth | ___ Government bonds | ✓ Money market |
| ✓ Balanced | ✓ Growth | ✓ Specialty/Sector |
| ✓ Corporate bonds | ✓ Growth & income | ___ World bonds |
| ✓ Global equities (stocks) | ✓ High-yield bonds | |

# Family Rating                                                            ✓✓✓✓

There are 11 subaccounts within the Dean Witter Variable Annuity II family. Overall, this family of subaccounts can be described as very good on a *risk-adjusted* return basis.

The subaccounts within this variable annuity all have an *increasing* guaranteed
death benefit. This means that the beneficiary is guaranteed to receive *the greater of*
the contract's value on the date of the annuitant's death or the value of the original
investment(s) compounded by 5% each year (less any withdrawals made).

## Summary

Dean Witter Variable Annuity II Equity is perfect for the growth investor who understands that great returns do not come without accepting a certain amount of risk. Yet, in some ways (e.g., standard deviation and beta), this subaccount is almost tame compared to its peers.

By now, it is no secret that Dean Witter dominates all other brokerage firms offering high-quality variable annuities. Several other Dean Witter subaccounts are included in this book.

The Dean Witter annuity contract includes some very nice features, some of which are not routinely found in the industry. This is a great account. No matter what brokerage firm you deal with, consider opening up a side account with Dean Witter to take advantage of some nice investment opportunities.

## Profile

| | | | |
|---|---|---|---|
| Minimum investment | $1,000 | Telephone exchanges | yes |
| Retirement account minimum | $4,000 | Transfers allowed per year | 12 |
| Co-annuitant allowed | no | Maximum issuance age | 90 |
| Co-owner allowed | yes | Maximum annuitization age | 85 |
| Dollar-cost averaging | yes | Number of subaccounts | 11 |
| Systematic withdrawal plans | yes | Available in all 50 states | yes |

---

**Equitable Momentum
Common Stock Portfolio**
P.O. Box 2919
New York, NY 10116
(800) 528-0204

---

| | |
|---|---|
| Performance | ✓✓✓ |
| Risk control | ✓✓✓ |
| Expense minimization | ✓✓✓ |
| Management | ✓✓✓ |
| Investment options | ✓ |
| Family rating | ✓✓✓ |
| Total point score | 21 points |

## Performance ✓✓✓

During the 3-year and 5-year periods ending December 31, 1994, Common Stock Portfolio had an average annual compound return of 6.5% and 8.3%, respectively (13.9% for 10 years). This means that a $10,000 investment made into this subaccount 5 years before that date grew to $14,900 ($12,100, if only the last 3 years of the period are used).

Compared to other growth variable annuity subaccounts, this one ranks in the top half for the 3-year and 5-year periods. (It ranks in the top quartile for the 10 years ending December 31, 1994.) The inception month of this subaccount was September 1992. The performance figures (shown below) for periods before the subaccount's inception in September 1992 are hypothetical, based on the underlying clone fund's returns. This subaccount is modeled (cloned) after the Hudson River Trust Common Stock Portfolio, which had an inception date of January 1976, and has an asset base of $3.0 billion.

The year-by-year returns for this subaccount and the portfolio it is modeled after are:

| Year | Annual Return | S&P 500 |
|------|------|------|
| 1994 | −3.5% | 1.3% |
| 1993 | 23.1% | 10.1% |
| 1992 | 1.6% | 7.6% |
| 1991 | 36.1% | 30.5% |
| 1990 | −9.3% | −3.1% |
| 1989 | 24.1% | 31.7% |
| 1988 | 21.5% | 16.6% |
| 1987 | 6.1% | 5.3% |

## Risk Control                                          ✓✓✓

Over the 3-year period, this fund was a little safer than the average equity subaccount. During the 5-year period, it was slightly riskier.

The typical standard deviation for growth subaccounts was 3.9% during the 3-year period. The standard deviation for Equitable Momentum Common Stock Portfolio was 3.7% over this same period. This means that this subaccount was 4% less volatile than its peer group. The price/earnings (p/e) ratio averages 19 for this portfolio. The typical growth subaccount has a p/e ratio of 24. In general, the higher the p/e ratio, the riskier the portfolio.

The beta (market-related risk) of this subaccount was 1.1 over the 3-year period. Beta for this entire category was also 1.1 over this same period. The market index (the S&P 500 Index for equity subaccounts) always has a beta of 1.0. The *risk-adjusted* return for this variable annuity subaccount can be described as good.

## Expense Minimization                                  ✓✓✓

The typical expenses incurred by growth subaccounts are 2.0% per year. The total expenses for Equitable Momentum Common Stock Portfolio, 1.8%, are lower than its peer group average. Total expenses include all charges to the investor (except the annual contract charge, which is always expressed as a dollar figure), including management fees, overhead, administration, and mortality expenses. The free annual withdrawals percentage is based on the account value.

| | | | |
|------|------|------|------|
| Maximum surrender charge | 6% | Total expenses | 1.8% |
| Duration of surrender charge | 5 years | Annual contract charge | $30 |
| Declining surrender charge | yes | Free annual withdrawals | 10% |

## Management                                            ✓✓✓

Equitable Momentum is offered by Equitable Life Assurance Society of the United States. The company has a Duff & Phelps rating of A+. The subaccount and portfolio it is modeled after were managed by Tyler J. Smith for the 18 years ending December 31, 1994. The portfolio's size is a mere $1 million. The typical security in the portfolio has a market capitalization of $11.6 billion.

## Investment Options                                    ✓

Investors may make additional contributions into this portfolio at any time. This is known as a flexible premium annuity. Investors in this variable annuity can choose from all of the subaccount categories below that have a check mark:

✓ Aggressive growth      ___ Government bonds      ✓ Money market
✓ Balanced      ✓ Growth      ___ Specialty/Sector
___ Corporate bonds      ___ Growth & income      ___ World bonds
___ Global equities (stocks)      ___ High-yield bonds

## Family Rating ✓✓✓✓

There are 5 subaccounts within the Equitable Momentum family. Overall, this family of subaccounts can be described as very good on a *risk-adjusted* return basis. The subaccounts within this variable annuity all have a death benefit based on the value at the date of death (what is referred to in the industry as "accumulated value"). Unlike the death benefit found with most variable annuities, the accumulated value death benefit does not protect the beneficiary from possible market loss.

## Summary

Equitable Momentum Common Stock Portfolio is, quite simply, very good. This growth portfolio has some great risk-adjusted returns. This is a tiny subaccount that, up to now, either has attracted little attention or has not been properly marketed. Whatever the reason, do not let it slip by you. Unfortunately, the contract is available only for qualified accounts (i.e., IRAs, pension plans, Keoghs, and so on).

    Equitable Momentum offers one of the more attractive contracts within the world of variable annuities, but does not offer nearly enough investment options. This is unfortunate; many of the portfolios it has offered have done well. Equitable needs to add more subaccounts and spread the wealth to new areas.

## Profile

| | | | |
|---|---|---|---|
| Minimum investment | none | Telephone exchanges | yes |
| Retirement account minimum | none | Transfers allowed per year | unlimited |
| Co-annuitant allowed | yes | Maximum issuance age | none |
| Co-owner allowed | no | Maximum annuitization age | none |
| Dollar-cost averaging | yes | Number of subaccounts | 5 |
| Systematic withdrawal plans | yes | Available in all 50 states | no* |

*Not available in CA, PA, or VT.

---

**Fortis Benefits Opportunity Annuity**
**Growth Stock**
P.O. Box 64272
St. Paul, MN 55164
(800) 800-2638

| | |
|---|---|
| Performance | ✓✓✓✓ |
| Risk control | ✓ |
| Expense minimization | ✓✓✓ |
| Management | ✓✓ |
| Investment options | ✓✓✓ |
| Family rating | ✓✓✓ |
| Total point score | 16 points |

## Performance ✓✓✓✓

During the 3-year and 5-year periods ending December 31, 1994, Growth Stock had an average annual compound return of 1.5% and 8.6%, respectively. This means that

a $10,000 investment made into this subaccount 5 years before that date grew to $15,100 ($10,500, if only the last 3 years of the period are used).

Compared to other growth variable annuity subaccounts, this one ranks in the top half for the 3-year period and in the top quintile for the 5-year period. The inception month of this subaccount was June 1988. This subaccount is modeled (cloned) after the Fortis Series Fund Growth Stock Series, which had an inception date of October 1986, and has an asset base of $280 million.

The year-by-year returns for this subaccount are:

| Year | Annual Return | S&P 500 |
|------|--------------|---------|
| 1994 | −4.1% | 1.3% |
| 1993 | 7.3% | 10.1% |
| 1992 | 1.5% | 7.6% |
| 1991 | 51.5% | 30.5% |
| 1990 | −4.4% | −3.1% |
| 1989 | 34.7% | 31.7% |
| 1988 | 3.8% | 16.6% |

## Risk Control ✓

Over the 3-year period, this fund was somewhat riskier than the average equity subaccount. During the 5-year period, it was slightly riskier.

The typical standard deviation for growth subaccounts was 3.9% during the 3-year period. The standard deviation for Fortis Benefits Opportunity Annuity Growth Stock was 4.5% over this same period, which means that this subaccount was 16% more volatile than its peer group. The price/earnings (p/e) ratio averages 36 for this portfolio. The typical growth subaccount has a p/e ratio of 24. In general, the higher the p/e ratio, the riskier the portfolio.

The beta (market-related risk) of this subaccount was 1.1 over the 3-year period. Beta for this entire category was also 1.1 over this same period. The market index (the S&P 500 Index for equity subaccounts) always has a beta of 1.0. The *risk-adjusted* return for this variable annuity subaccount can be described as good.

## Expense Minimization ✓✓✓

The typical expenses incurred by growth subaccounts are 2.0% per year. The total expenses for Fortis Benefits Opportunity Annuity Growth Stock, 2.1%, are higher than its peer group average. Total expenses include all charges to the investor (except the annual contract charge, which is always expressed as a dollar figure), including management fees, overhead, administration, and mortality expenses. The free annual withdrawals percentage is based on the original principal.

| | | | |
|---|---|---|---|
| Maximum surrender charge | 5% | Total expenses | 2.1% |
| Duration of surrender charge | 5 years | Annual contract charge | $35 |
| Declining surrender charge | yes | Free annual withdrawals | 10% |

## Management ✓✓

Fortis Benefits Opportunity Annuity is offered by Fortis Benefits Insurance Company. The company has an A.M. Best rating of A+. The portfolio and mutual fund it is modeled after were managed by Stephen M. Poling for the 8 years ending December 31, 1994. The portfolio's size is $70 million. The typical security in the portfolio has a market capitalization of $2.1 billion. Poling also manages the Fortis Growth mutual fund.

## Investment Options ✓✓✓

Investors may make additional contributions into this portfolio at any time. This is known as a flexible premium annuity. Investors in this variable annuity can choose from all of the subaccount categories below that have a check mark:

| | | |
|---|---|---|
| ___ Aggressive growth | ✓ Government bonds | ✓ Money market |
| ✓ Balanced | ✓ Growth | ___ Specialty/Sector |
| ✓ Corporate bonds | ___ Growth & income | ___ World bonds |
| ✓ Global equities (stocks) | ___ High-yield bonds | |

## Family Rating ✓✓✓

There are 6 subaccounts within the Fortis Benefits Opportunity Annuity family. Overall, this family of subaccounts can be described as good on a *risk-adjusted* return basis.

## Summary

Fortis Benefits Opportunity Annuity Growth Stock has taken greater-than-average risks but has chalked up greater-than-average returns. This investment scores well in all other categories.

The Fortis Benefits variable annuity contract is one of the most appealing in the industry. Investment options include a global equity account, something missing from most other annuities.

## Profile

| | | | |
|---|---|---|---|
| Minimum investment | $50 | Telephone exchanges | yes |
| Retirement account minimum | $50 | Transfers allowed per year | unlimited |
| Co-annuitant allowed | no | Maximum issuance age | 90 |
| Co-owner allowed | yes | Maximum annuitization age | 70.5 |
| Dollar-cost averaging | yes | Number of subaccounts | 6 |
| Systematic withdrawal plans | yes | Available in all 50 states | no* |

*Not available in NJ or NY.

---

**G.T. Global Allocator
America**
700 Market Street
St. Louis, MO  63101
(800) 237-6580

| | |
|---|---|
| Performance | ✓✓✓✓ |
| Risk control | ✓✓ |
| Expense minimization | ✓✓ |
| Management | ✓ |
| Investment options | ✓✓✓✓ |
| Family rating | ✓✓ |
| Total point score | 15 points |

## Performance ✓✓✓✓

During the 3-year and 5-year periods ending December 31, 1994, America had an average annual compound return of 18.2% and 12.8%, respectively. This means that

a $10,000 investment made into this subaccount 5 years before that date grew to $18,300 ($16,500, if only the last 3 years of the period are used).

The inception month of this subaccount was February 1993. The performance figures (shown below) for periods before the subaccount's inception in February 1993 are hypothetical, based on the underlying clone fund's returns. This subaccount is modeled (cloned) after the G.T. America Fund, which had an inception date of June 1987, and has an asset base of $125 million.

The year-by-year returns for this subaccount and the mutual fund it is modeled after are:

| Year | Annual Return | S&P 500 |
|------|------|------|
| 1994 | 17.2% | 1.3% |
| 1993 | 8.3% | 10.1% |
| 1992 | 31.7% | 7.6% |
| 1991 | 19.3% | 30.5% |
| 1990 | −7.4% | −3.1% |
| 1989 | 54.8% | 31.7% |
| 1988 | 11.1% | 16.6% |

## Risk Control                                                          ✓✓

The price/earnings (p/e) ratio averages 15 for this portfolio. The typical growth subaccount has a p/e ratio of 24. In general, the higher the p/e ratio, the riskier the portfolio.

## Expense Minimization                                                  ✓✓

The typical expenses incurred by growth subaccounts are 2.0% per year. The total expenses for G.T. Global Allocator America, 2.2%, are higher than its peer group average. Total expenses include all charges to the investor (except the annual contract charge, which is always expressed as a dollar figure), including management fees, overhead, administration, and mortality expenses. The free annual withdrawals percentage is based on the account value.

| | | | |
|------|------|------|------|
| Maximum surrender charge | 6% | Total expenses | 2.2% |
| Duration of surrender charge | 6 years | Annual contract charge | $30 |
| Declining surrender charge | yes | Free annual withdrawals | 10% |

## Management                                                             ✓

G.T. Global Allocator is offered by General American Life Insurance Company. The company has a Duff & Phelps rating of AA and an A.M. Best rating of A+. The portfolio and mutual fund it is modeled after have been managed by a management team since their inception. The portfolio's size is a mere $1 million. The typical security in the portfolio has a market capitalization of $125 million.

## Investment Options                                                 ✓✓✓✓

Investors may make additional contributions into this portfolio at any time. This is known as a flexible premium annuity. Investors in this variable annuity can choose from all of the subaccount categories below that have a check mark:

| | | |
|------|------|------|
| ___ Aggressive growth | ✓ Government bonds | ✓ Money market |
| ✓ Balanced | ✓ Growth | ✓ Specialty/Sector |
| ✓ Corporate bonds | ✓ Growth & income | ✓ World bonds |
| ✓ Global equities (stocks) | ___ High-yield bonds | |

## Family Rating ✓✓

There are 12 subaccounts within the G.T. Global Allocator family. Overall, this family of subaccounts can be described as fair on a *risk-adjusted* return basis.

The subaccounts within this variable annuity all have an *increasing* guaranteed death benefit. This means that the beneficiary is guaranteed to receive *the greater of* the contract's value on the date of the annuitant's death or the value of the original investment(s) compounded by 5% each year (less any withdrawals made).

## Summary

G.T. Global Allocator America is a relatively new subaccount that has already made a name for itself. Modeled after a mutual fund that has been around for a number of years, this portfolio has been successful at picking small and medium-size stocks. Performance is often quite different (in extremes) from what happens with the S&P 500, making this an excellent choice for someone who already owns growth equities but wants more.

When it comes to money management, G.T. has been around the *global* block. The company has been managing money since 1969. Its central headquarters is in London, but it has several offices and research facilities around the globe. The U.S. offices are in San Francisco.

The G.T. Global Allocator contract allows investors to switch among a number of interested subaccounts, some of which are quite unique (e.g., a pure Pacific Basin, Latin America, or Europe portfolio).

## Profile

| | | | |
|---|---|---|---|
| Minimum investment | $25 | Telephone exchanges | yes |
| Retirement account minimum | $2,000 | Transfers allowed per year | 12 |
| Co-annuitant allowed | no | Maximum issuance age | none |
| Co-owner allowed | yes | Maximum annuitization age | 85 |
| Dollar-cost averaging | yes | Number of subaccounts | 10 |
| Systematic withdrawal plans | yes | Available in all 50 states | no* |

*Not available in the following states: MD, NJ, OR, PA, TX, VA, and WA.

---

**Guardian Investor**
**Guardian Stock**
P.O. Box 26210
Lehigh Valley, PA 18002
(800) 221-3253

| | |
|---|---|
| Performance | ✓✓✓✓ |
| Risk control | ✓✓✓✓ |
| Expense minimization | ✓✓✓✓ |
| Management | ✓✓✓✓ |
| Investment options | ✓✓ |
| Family rating | ✓✓✓ |
| Total point score | 24 points |

## Performance ✓✓✓✓✓

During the 3-year and 5-year periods ending December 31, 1994, Guardian Stock had an average annual compound return of 11.2% and 10.0%, respectively. This means that a $10,000 investment made into this subaccount 5 years before that date grew to $16,100 ($13,800, if only the last 3 years of the period are used).

Compared to other growth variable annuity subaccounts, this one ranked in the top 5% for the 3-year period. The inception month of this subaccount was January 1990. The performance figures (shown below) for periods before the subaccount's inception in January 1990 are hypothetical, based on the underlying clone fund's returns. This subaccount is modeled (cloned) after the Guardian Park Avenue Fund, which had an inception date of June 1972, and has an asset base of $650 million.

The year-by-year returns for this subaccount and the mutual fund it is modeled after are:

| Year | Annual Return | S&P 500 |
|------|------|------|
| 1994 | −2.4% | 1.3% |
| 1993 | 18.5% | 10.1% |
| 1992 | 18.7% | 7.6% |
| 1991 | 34.4% | 30.5% |
| 1990 | −12.3% | −3.1% |
| 1989 | 23.8% | 31.7% |
| 1988 | 20.8% | 16.6% |
| 1987 | 3.0% | 5.3% |

## Risk Control                                         ✓✓✓✓✓

Over the 3-year period, this fund was somewhat safer than the average equity subaccount.

The typical standard deviation for growth subaccounts was 3.9% during the 3-year period. The standard deviation for Guardian Investor Guardian Stock was 3.2% over this same period, which means that this subaccount was 17% less volatile than its peer group. The price/earnings (p/e) ratio averages 16 for this portfolio. The typical growth subaccount has a p/e ratio of 24. In general, the higher the p/e ratio, the riskier the portfolio.

The beta (market-related risk) of this subaccount was 0.8 over the 3-year period. Beta for this entire category was 1.1 over this same period. The market index (the S&P 500 Index for equity subaccounts) always has a beta of 1.0. The *risk-adjusted* return for this variable annuity subaccount can be described as excellent.

## Expense Minimization                                  ✓✓✓✓

The typical expenses incurred by growth subaccounts are 2.0% per year. The total expenses for Guardian Investor Guardian Stock, 1.7%, are lower than its peer group average. Total expenses include all charges to the investor (except the annual contract charge, which is always expressed as a dollar figure), including management fees, overhead, administration, and mortality expenses. The free annual withdrawals percentage is based on the greater of the account value and the original principal.

| | | | |
|---|---|---|---|
| Maximum surrender charge | 6% | Total expenses | 1.7% |
| Duration of surrender charge | 7 years | Annual contract charge | $35 |
| Declining surrender charge | no | Free annual withdrawals | 10% |

## Management   ✓✓✓✓

Guardian Investor is offered by Guardian Insurance & Annuity Company. The company has a Duff & Phelps rating of AAA and an A.M. Best rating of A++. The portfolio and the mutual fund it is modeled after were managed by Charles E. Albers for the 24 years ending December 31, 1994.

## Investment Options   ✓✓

Investors may not add to their initial investment in this portfolio. This is known as a single premium annuity. Investors in this variable annuity can choose from all of the subaccount categories below that have a check mark:

| | | |
|---|---|---|
| ___ Aggressive growth | ___ Government bonds | ✓ Money market |
| ✓ Balanced | ✓ Growth | ✓ Specialty/Sector |
| ✓ Corporate bonds | ___ Growth & income | ___ World bonds |
| ✓ Global equities (stocks) | ___ High-yield bonds | |

## Family Rating   ✓✓✓

There are 7 subaccounts within the Guardian Investor family. Overall, this family of subaccounts can be described as good on a *risk-adjusted* return basis.

## Summary

Guardian Investor Guardian Stock has almost defied common logic. This growth subaccount has demonstrated excellent results while maintaining a risk posture that is about 25% less than other growth portfolios. Conventional wisdom dictates that risk is commensurate with reward, yet this is a glaring example of how wrong such thinking can be, particularly when top-notch management is at the helm. Few subaccounts, in any category, have an overall point score that is equally high.

What makes this portfolio particularly appealing is that a high number of the securities owned are trading at p/e multiples far lower than the market as a whole. This usually translates into smaller losses when stocks are at or near a high and then take a tumble. This type of "p/e insurance," coupled with a low beta, makes this variable annuity account the perfect choice for the nervous investor who is unwilling to give up any return potential.

## Profile

| | | | |
|---|---|---|---|
| Minimum investment | $5,000 | Telephone exchanges | yes |
| Retirement account minimum | $5,000 | Transfers allowed per year | unlimited |
| Co-annuitant allowed | no | Maximum issuance age | 80 |
| Co-owner allowed | spouses only | Maximum annuitization age | 85 |
| Dollar-cost averaging | yes | Number of subaccounts | 7 |
| Systematic withdrawal plans | yes | Available in all 50 states | yes |

---

**John Hancock Independence Annuity
Stock**
John Hancock Place
Boston, MA  02117
(800) 422-0237

---

| | |
|---|---|
| Performance | ✓✓ |
| Risk control | ✓✓✓✓✓ |
| Expense minimization | ✓✓✓✓ |
| Management | ✓✓✓ |
| Investment options | ✓✓ |
| Family rating | ✓✓✓ |
| Total point score | 19 points |

## Performance                                                        ✓✓

During the 3-year and 5-year periods ending December 31, 1994, Stock had an average annual compound return of 5.6% and 8.6%, respectively. This means that a $10,000 investment made into this subaccount 5 years before that date grew to $15,100 ($11,800, if only the last 3 years of the period are used).

Compared to other growth variable annuity subaccounts, this one ranks in the bottom quartile for the 3-year period. The inception month of this subaccount was July 1990. The performance figures (shown below) for periods before the subaccount's inception in July 1990 are hypothetical, based on the underlying clone fund's returns. This subaccount is modeled (cloned) after the John Hancock Variable Series Trust I Stock Portfolio, which had an inception date of April 1972, and has an asset base of $1.0 billion.

The year-by-year returns for this subaccount and the portfolio it is modeled after are:

| Year | Annual Return | S&P 500 |
|---|---|---|
| 1994 | −1.9% | 1.3% |
| 1993 | 11.8% | 10.1% |
| 1992 | 7.4% | 7.6% |
| 1991 | 24.2% | 30.5% |
| 1990 | −9.0% | −3.1% |
| 1989 | 15.6% | 31.7% |
| 1988 | 25.5% | 16.6% |

## Risk Control                                                    ✓✓✓✓✓

Over the 3-year period, this fund was quite a bit safer than the average equity subaccount.

The typical standard deviation for growth subaccounts was 3.9% during the 3-year period. The standard deviation for John Hancock Independence Annuity Stock was 2.8% over this same period, which means that this subaccount was 28% less volatile than its peer group. The price/earnings (p/e) ratio averages 21 for this portfolio. The typical growth subaccount has a p/e ratio of 24. In general, the higher the p/e ratio, the riskier the portfolio.

The beta (market-related risk) of this subaccount was 0.9 over the 3-year period. Beta for this entire category was 1.1 over this same period. The market index (the S&P 500 Index for equity subaccounts) always has a beta of 1.0. The *risk-adjusted* return for this variable annuity subaccount can be described as good.

## Expense Minimization                                         ✓✓✓✓

The typical expenses incurred by growth subaccounts are 2.0% per year. The total expenses for John Hancock Independence Annuity Stock, 1.7%, are lower than its peer group average. Total expenses include all charges to the investor (except the annual contract charge, which is always expressed as a dollar figure), including management fees, overhead, administration, and mortality expenses. The free annual withdrawals percentage is based on the account value.

| | | | |
|---|---|---|---|
| Maximum surrender charge | 8% | Total expenses | 1.7% |
| Duration of surrender charge | 7 years | Annual contract charge | $30 |
| Declining surrender charge | yes | Free annual withdrawals | 10% |

## Management                                                        ✓✓✓

John Hancock Independence Annuity is offered by John Hancock Mutual Life Insurance Company. The company has a Duff & Phelps rating of AAA and an A.M. Best rating of A++. The subaccount and portfolio it is modeled after were managed by Samuel A. Otis for the 22 years ending December 31, 1994. The portfolio's size is $180 million. The typical security in the portfolio has a market capitalization of $11.9 billion.

## Investment Options                                                 ✓✓

Investors may make additional contributions into this portfolio at any time. This is known as a flexible premium annuity. Investors in this variable annuity can choose from all of the subaccount categories below that have a check mark:

| | | |
|---|---|---|
| ✓ Aggressive growth | ___ Government bonds | ✓ Money market |
| ✓ Balanced | ✓ Growth | ✓ Specialty/Sector |
| ✓ Corporate bonds | ___ Growth & income | ___ World bonds |
| ✓ Global equities (stocks) | ___ High-yield bonds | |

## Family Rating                                                     ✓✓✓

There are 7 subaccounts within the John Hancock Independence Annuity family. Overall, this family of subaccounts can be described as good on a *risk-adjusted* return basis.

## Summary

John Hancock Independence Annuity Stock is the right choice for anyone worried about the stock market, for whatever reason. This growth subaccount has returns that are close to those provided by the S&P 500, but with substantially less risk. This is one of the few growth portfolios that gets a perfect score when it comes to risk control.

The John Hancock Independence Annuity has operating expenses that are close to 20% lower than the competition, plus a withdrawal privilege that is based on the value of the account, not the investor's original principal. Investment options include the all-important global stock category. For the more adventuresome, this variable annuity also offers a specialty portfolio.

## Profile

| | | | | |
|---|---|---|---|---|
| Minimum investment | $1,000 | | Telephone exchanges | yes |
| Retirement account minimum | $1,000 | | Transfers allowed per year | 12 |
| Co-annuitant allowed | no | | Maximum issuance age | 84 |
| Co-owner allowed | yes | | Maximum annuitization age | none |
| Dollar-cost averaging | no | | Number of subaccounts | 7 |
| Systematic withdrawal plans | no | | Available in all 50 states | no* |

*Not available in WA.

---

**Kemper Passport
Equity**
120 South LaSalle Street
Chicago, IL 60603
(800) 554-5426

| | |
|---|---|
| Performance | ✓✓✓✓ |
| Risk control | ✓✓✓✓ |
| Expense minimization | ✓✓✓✓ |
| Management | ✓✓ |
| Investment options | ✓✓✓ |
| Family rating | ✓✓✓ |
| Total point score | 21 points |

## Performance                                              ✓✓✓✓✓

During the 3-year and 5-year periods ending December 31, 1994, Equity had an average annual compound return of 3.0% and 11.0%, respectively. This means that a $10,000 investment made into this subaccount 5 years before that date grew to $16,900 ($10,900, if only the last 3 years of the period are used).

The inception month of this subaccount was January 1992. The performance figures (shown below) for periods before the subaccount's inception in January 1992 are hypothetical, based on the underlying clone fund's returns. This subaccount is modeled (cloned) after the Kemper Investors Fund Equity Portfolio, which had an inception date of December 1983, and has an asset base of $290 million.

The year-by-year returns for this subaccount and the portfolio it is modeled after are:

| Year | Annual Return | S&P 500 |
|---|---|---|
| 1994 | −5.2% | 1.3% |
| 1993 | 13.2% | 10.1% |
| 1992 | 1.8% | 7.6% |
| 1991 | 57.0% | 30.5% |
| 1990 | −1.7% | −3.1% |
| 1989 | 31.4% | 31.7% |
| 1988 | 9.6% | 16.6% |
| 1987 | 6.4% | 5.3% |

# Risk Control ✓✓✓

The price/earnings (p/e) ratio averages 30 for this portfolio. The typical growth subaccount has a p/e ratio of 24. In general, the higher the p/e ratio, the riskier the portfolio.

# Expense Minimization ✓✓✓

The typical expenses incurred by growth subaccounts are 2.0% per year. The total expenses for Kemper Passport Equity, 1.9%, are lower than its peer group average. Total expenses include all charges to the investor (except the annual contract charge, which is always expressed as a dollar figure), including management fees, overhead, administration, and mortality expenses. The free annual withdrawals percentage is based on the account value.

| | | | |
|---|---|---|---|
| Maximum surrender charge | 6% | Total expenses | 1.9% |
| Duration of surrender charge | 6 years | Annual contract charge | $30 |
| Declining surrender charge | no | Free annual withdrawals | 10% |

# Management ✓✓

Kemper Passport is offered by Kemper Investors Life Insurance Company. The company has a Duff & Phelps rating of A+ and an A.M. Best rating of A−. The subaccount and portfolio it is modeled after were managed by C. Beth Cotner for the 10 years ending December 31, 1994. The portfolio's size is $45 million. The typical security in the portfolio has a market capitalization of $3.3 billion.

# Investment Options ✓✓✓

Investors may not add to their initial investment in this portfolio. This is known as a single premium annuity. Investors in this variable annuity can choose from all of the subaccount categories below that have a check mark:

| | | |
|---|---|---|
| ___ Aggressive growth | ✓ Government bonds | ✓ Money market |
| ✓ Balanced | ✓ Growth | ___ Specialty/Sector |
| ___ Corporate bonds | ___ Growth & income | ___ World bonds |
| ✓ Global equities (stocks) | ✓ High-yield bonds | |

# Family Rating ✓✓✓

There are 7 subaccounts within the Kemper Passport family. Overall, this family of subaccounts can be described as good on a *risk-adjusted* return basis.

The subaccounts within this variable annuity all have an *increasing* guaranteed death benefit. This means that the beneficiary is guaranteed to receive *the greater of* the contract's value on the date of the annuitant's death or the value of the original investment(s) compounded by 5% each year (less any withdrawals made).

# Summary

Kemper Passport Equity receives top marks for performance, risk control, and expense minimization. This is a great growth portfolio. Manager Cotner oversees enough money to make sure the portfolio is properly diversified, but the subaccount is not big enough to be watered down with a series of second choices.

Kemper has long been a household word when it comes to insurance and mutual funds. By providing some of the best features of both products (i.e., an enhanced death benefit and a good number of investment options), Kemper continues to make a name for itself. Besides this growth subaccount, look into this company's high-yield bond and balanced portfolios.

## Profile

| | | | |
|---|---|---|---|
| Minimum investment | $5,000 | Telephone exchanges | yes |
| Retirement account minimum | $5,000 | Transfers allowed per year | approx. 24 |
| Co-annuitant allowed | yes | Maximum issuance age | 85 |
| Co-owner allowed | yes | Maximum annuitization age | none |
| Dollar-cost averaging | yes | Number of subaccounts | 7 |
| Systematic withdrawal plans | yes | Available in all 50 states | no* |

*Not available in NY.

---

**Keyport Preferred Advisor
SteinRoe Managed Growth**
125 High Street
Boston, MA 02110-2712
(800) 367-3653

| | |
|---|---|
| Performance | ✓✓✓ |
| Risk control | ✓✓✓ |
| Expense minimization | ✓✓ |
| Management | ✓✓✓ |
| Investment options | ✓✓✓ |
| Family rating | ✓✓✓ |
| Total point score | 17 points |

## Performance                                              ✓✓✓

During the 3-year and 5-year periods ending December 31, 1994, SteinRoe Managed Growth had an average annual compound return of 0.2% and 7.3%, respectively. This means that a $10,000 investment made into this subaccount 3 years before that date grew to $14,200 ($10,100 over the last 3 years).

Compared to other growth variable annuity subaccounts, this one ranks in the top half for the 3-year period. The inception month of this subaccount was May 1989. This subaccount is modeled (cloned) after the SteinRoe Variable Investment Trust Managed Growth Stock Portfolio, which had an inception date of May 1987, and has an asset base of $75 million.

The year-by-year returns for this subaccount are:

| Year | Annual Return | S&P 500 |
|---|---|---|
| 1994 | −7.6% | 1.3% |
| 1993 | 3.5% | 10.1% |
| 1992 | 5.2% | 7.6% |
| 1991 | 46.0% | 30.5% |
| 1990 | −3.0% | −3.1% |

# Risk Control ✓✓✓

Over the 3-year period, this fund was as safe as the average equity subaccount.

The typical standard deviation for growth subaccounts was 3.9% during the 3-year period. The standard deviation for Keyport Preferred Advisor SteinRoe Managed Growth was 3.7% over this same period, which means that this subaccount was 5% less volatile than its peer group. The price/earnings (p/e) ratio averages 28 for this portfolio. The typical growth subaccount has a p/e ratio of 24. In general, the higher the p/e ratio, the riskier the portfolio.

The beta (market-related risk) of this subaccount was 1.1 over the 3-year period. Beta for this entire category was also 1.1 over this same period. The market index (the S&P 500 Index for equity subaccounts) always has a beta of 1.0. The *risk-adjusted* return for this variable annuity subaccount can be described as good.

# Expense Minimization ✓✓

The typical expenses incurred by growth subaccounts are 2.0% per year. The total expenses for Keyport Preferred Advisor SteinRoe Managed Growth, 2.4%, are higher than its peer group average. Total expenses include all charges to the investor (except the annual contract charge, which is always expressed as a dollar figure), including management fees, overhead, administration, and mortality expenses. The free annual withdrawals percentage is based on the value of the account at its anniversary amount.

| | | | |
|---|---|---|---|
| Maximum surrender charge | 7% | Total expenses | 2.4% |
| Duration of surrender charge | 7 years | Annual contract charge | $30 |
| Declining surrender charge | yes | Free annual withdrawals | 10% |

# Management ✓✓✓

Keyport Preferred Advisor is offered by Keyport Life Insurance Company. The company has a Duff & Phelps rating of AA− and an A.M. Best rating of A+. The subaccount and portfolio it is modeled after were managed by Michael Carey for the 5 years ending December 31, 1994. The portfolio's size is $75 million. The typical security in the portfolio has a market capitalization of $6.8 billion.

# Investment Options ✓✓✓

Investors may make additional contributions into this portfolio at any time. This is known as a flexible premium annuity. Investors in this variable annuity can choose from all of the subaccount categories below that have a check mark:

- ✓ Aggressive growth
- ✓ Balanced
- ✓ Corporate bonds
- ___ Global equities (stocks)
- ✓ Government bonds
- ✓ Growth
- ✓ Growth & income
- ___ High-yield bonds
- ✓ Money market
- ✓ Specialty/Sector
- ___ World bonds

# Family Rating ✓✓✓

There are 10 subaccounts within the Keyport Preferred Advisor family. Overall, this family of subaccounts can be described as good on a *risk-adjusted* return basis.

The subaccounts within this variable annuity all have an *increasing* guaranteed death benefit. This means that the beneficiary is guaranteed to receive *the greater of* the contract's value on the date of the annuitant's death or the value of the original investment(s) compounded by 5% each year (less any withdrawals made).

## Summary

Keyport Preferred Advisor SteinRoe Managed Growth is a fine example of consistency. This growth account scores well in all of the important categories: performance, risk control, management, investment options, and family rating. This investment has come close to matching the returns of the S&P 500; since its inception, it has actually outperformed the stock market. More than one Keyport subaccount appears in this book.

The Keyport Preferred Advisor is a variable annuity contract that has a declining surrender charge but, more importantly, a free annual withdrawals provision that is based on the current value of the investment, not the original principal. Because it allows co-ownership (a feature not found with most contracts), this variable annuity will be particularly appealing to married couples.

## Profile

| | | | | |
|---|---|---|---|---|
| Minimum investment | $5,000 | | Telephone exchanges | yes |
| Retirement account minimum | $5,000 | | Transfers allowed per year | 12 |
| Co-annuitant allowed | no | | Maximum issuance age | 80 |
| Co-owner allowed | yes | | Maximum annuitization age | 90 |
| Dollar-cost averaging | yes | | Number of subaccounts | 10 |
| Systematic withdrawal plans | yes | | Available in all 50 states | no* |

*Not available in NY.

---

**Lincoln National American Legacy II
Growth**
P.O. Box 2340
Fort Wayne, IN  46801
(800) 421-9900

| | |
|---|---|
| Performance | ✓✓✓ |
| Risk control | ✓✓✓ |
| Expense minimization | ✓✓✓ |
| Management | ✓✓✓ |
| Investment options | ✓✓ |
| Family rating | ✓✓✓ |
| Total point score | 23 points |

## Performance                                          ✓✓✓

During the 3-year and 5-year periods ending December 31, 1994, Growth had an average annual compound return of 7.6% and 9.1%, respectively. This means that a $10,000 investment made into this subaccount 5 years before that date grew to $15,500 ($12,500, if only the last 3 years of the period are used).

Compared to other growth variable annuity subaccounts, this one ranks in the top half for the 3-year and 5-year periods. The inception month of this subaccount was February 1984. This subaccount is modeled (cloned) after the Growth Fund of America, which had an inception date of January 1959, and has an asset base of $5.5 billion.

The year-by-year returns for this subaccount are:

| Year | Annual Return | S&P 500 |
|------|------|------|
| 1994 | −0.9% | 1.3% |
| 1993 | 14.8% | 10.1% |
| 1992 | 9.3% | 7.6% |
| 1991 | 31.5% | 30.5% |
| 1990 | −5.6% | −3.1% |
| 1989 | 29.5% | 31.7% |
| 1988 | 13.0% | 16.6% |
| 1987 | 6.7% | 5.3% |

## Risk Control   ✓✓✓✓

Over the 3-year and 5-year periods, this fund was slightly safer than the average equity subaccount.

The typical standard deviation for growth subaccounts was 3.9% during the 3-year period. The standard deviation for Lincoln National American Legacy II Growth was 3.6% over this same period, which means that this subaccount was 8% less volatile than its peer group. The price/earnings (p/e) ratio averages 26 for this portfolio. The typical growth subaccount has a p/e ratio of 24. In general, the higher the p/e ratio, the riskier the portfolio.

The beta (market-related risk) of this subaccount was 1.0 over the 3-year period. Beta for this entire category was 1.1 over this same period. The market index (the S&P 500 Index for equity subaccounts) always has a beta of 1.0. The *risk-adjusted* return for this variable annuity subaccount can be described as very good.

## Expense Minimization   ✓✓✓✓

The typical expenses incurred by growth subaccounts are 2.0% per year. The total expenses for Lincoln National American Legacy II Growth, 1.9%, are lower than its peer group average. Total expenses include all charges to the investor (except the annual contract charge, which is always expressed as a dollar figure), including management fees, overhead, administration, and mortality expenses. The free annual withdrawals percentage is based on the original principal.

| | | | |
|------|------|------|------|
| Maximum surrender charge | 6% | Total expenses | 1.9% |
| Duration of surrender charge | 7 years | Annual contract charge | $35 |
| Declining surrender charge | yes | Free annual withdrawals | 10% |

## Management   ✓✓✓✓

Lincoln National American Legacy II is offered by Lincoln National Life Insurance Company. The company has a Duff & Phelps rating of AAA and an A.M. Best rating of A+. The portfolio has been managed by Capital Guardian (American Funds) since its inception. The portfolio's size is a whopping $2 billion. The typical security in the portfolio has a market capitalization of $2.6 billion.

## Investment Options                                             ✓✓✓

Investors may make additional contributions into this portfolio at any time. This is known as a flexible premium annuity. Investors in this variable annuity can choose from all of the subaccount categories below that have a check mark:

| | | |
|---|---|---|
| ___ Aggressive growth | ✓ Government bonds | ✓ Money market |
| ✓ Balanced | ✓ Growth | ___ Specialty/Sector |
| ___ Corporate bonds | ✓ Growth & income | ___ World bonds |
| ✓ Global equities (stocks) | ✓ High-yield bonds | |

## Family Rating                                                ✓✓✓✓

There are 7 subaccounts within the Lincoln National American Legacy II family. Overall, this family of subaccounts can be described as very good on a *risk-adjusted* return basis.

## Summary

Lincoln National American Legacy II Growth has been able to beat the market indexes and averages most years. This is quite a statement; only a very small percentage of the variable annuity universe can make such a claim. Besides some of the best return figures around, this growth subaccount is also safer than its peer group average.

Several American Legacy II portfolios are included in this book, and it is easy to understand why. The management company, Capital Guardian Trust, pioneered the highly effective star-team approach to money management. Under this system, a portfolio manager is allowed to pretty much call the shots on a small number of industry groups; success or failure (and bonuses, or lack thereof) can be traced to one person. Each of the portfolio managers shares information with other team members (managers are allowed to invest their own retirement money only in accounts run by other Capital Guardian money managers). Researchers are even given a small slice of the pie. This "win-win" or "lose-lose" way of running a portfolio has been so profitable over the past half-century, other mutual fund companies are beginning to copy this style.

## Profile

| | | | |
|---|---|---|---|
| Minimum investment | $300 | Telephone exchanges | yes |
| Retirement account minimum | $1,500 | Transfers allowed per year | 12 |
| Co-annuitant allowed | no | Maximum issuance age | 75 |
| Co-owner allowed | yes | Maximum annuitization age | 85 |
| Dollar-cost averaging | yes | Number of subaccounts | 7 |
| Systematic withdrawal plans | yes | Available in all 50 states | no* |

*Not available in NY.

---

**MFS/Sun Life (NY) Compass 3**
**Capital Appreciation Series**
67 Broad Street
New York, NY 10004
(800) 447-7569

---

| | |
|---|---|
| Performance | ✓✓ |
| Risk control | ✓✓✓ |
| Expense minimization | ✓✓ |
| Management | ✓ |
| Investment options | ✓✓✓ |
| Family rating | ✓✓✓ |
| Total point score | 14 points |

---

# Performance                                     ✓✓

During the 3-year and 5-year periods ending December 31, 1994, Capital Appreciation Series had an average annual compound return of 6.3% and 7.0%, respectively. This means that a $10,000 investment made into this subaccount 5 years before that date grew to $14,000 ($12,000, if only the last 3 years of the period are used).

The inception month of this subaccount was August 1993. The performance figures (shown below) for periods before the subaccount's inception in August 1993 are hypothetical, based on the underlying clone fund's returns. This subaccount is modeled (cloned) after the MFS Growth Opportunities Fund—Class A, which had an inception date of September 1970, and has an asset base of $710 million.

The year-by-year returns for this subaccount and the mutual fund it is modeled after are:

| Year | Annual Return | S&P 500 |
|---|---|---|
| 1994 | −4.9% | 1.3% |
| 1993 | 16.2% | 10.1% |
| 1992 | 7.7% | 7.6% |
| 1991 | 22.4% | 30.5% |
| 1990 | −4.4% | −3.1% |
| 1989 | 28.5% | 31.7% |
| 1988 | 9.0% | 16.6% |
| 1987 | 3.8% | 5.3% |

# Risk Control                                     ✓✓✓

The price/earnings (p/e) ratio averages 23 for this portfolio. The typical growth subaccount has a p/e ratio of 24. In general, the higher the p/e ratio, the riskier the portfolio.

# Expense Minimization                             ✓✓

The typical expenses incurred by growth subaccounts are 2.0% per year. The total expenses for MFS/Sun Life (NY) Compass 3 Capital Appreciation Series, 2.3%, are higher than its peer group average. Total expenses include all charges to the investor (except the annual contract charge, which is always expressed as a dollar figure), including management fees, overhead, administration, and mortality expenses. The free annual withdrawals percentage is based on the original principal.

| | | | |
|---|---|---|---|
| Maximum surrender charge | 6% | Total expenses | 2.3% |
| Duration of surrender charge | 7 years | Annual contract charge | $30 |
| Declining surrender charge | yes | Free annual withdrawals | 10% |

## Management ✓

MFS/Sun Life (NY) Compass 3 is offered by Sun Life Insurance & Annuity Company of New York. The company has a Duff & Phelps rating of AA and an A.M. Best rating of AAA. The portfolio has been managed by Paul M. McMahon since its inception. The portfolio's size is $420 million. The typical security in the portfolio has a market capitalization of $2.2 billion. McMahon also manages the MFS Growth Opportunities mutual fund.

## Investment Options ✓✓✓

Investors may make additional contributions into this portfolio at any time. This is known as a flexible premium annuity. Investors in this variable annuity can choose from all of the subaccount categories below that have a check mark:

| | | |
|---|---|---|
| ✓ Aggressive growth | ✓ Government bonds | ✓ Money market |
| ✓ Balanced | ✓ Growth | ___ Specialty/Sector |
| ___ Corporate bonds | ___ Growth & income | ✓ World bonds |
| ___ Global equities (stocks) | ✓ High-yield bonds | |

## Family Rating ✓✓✓

There are 7 subaccounts within the MFS/Sun Life (NY) Compass 3 family. Overall, this family of subaccounts can be described as good on a *risk-adjusted* return basis.

The subaccounts within this variable annuity all have an *increasing* guaranteed death benefit. This means that the beneficiary is guaranteed to receive *the greater of* the contract's value on the date of the annuitant's death or the value of the original investment(s) compounded by 5% each year (less any withdrawals made).

## Summary

MFS/Sun Life (NY) Compass 3 Capital Appreciation Series is no stranger to the equities markets. MFS introduced the first mutual fund in the country in the early 1920s (the fund is still around and has an exceptional track record since inception).

MFS/Sun Life Compass 3 Capital Appreciation is the newest variable annuity offering by MFS. Each MFS product represents an improvement or enhancement from previous contracts. For this reason, prospective investors may shy away from an investment vehicle they believe has only a short-term track record. The reality is that a number of the MFS money managers have been around for a long time, managing virtually identical variable annuities no longer offered to new investors.

The Compass 3 contract provides investors with a wide range of investment selections, including an aggressive growth and world bond portfolio, something missing from well over 90% of all other annuities. This variable annuity provides the flexibility needed for a properly diversified investment.

## Profile

| | | | |
|---|---|---|---|
| Minimum investment | $25 | Telephone exchanges | yes |
| Retirement account minimum | $25 | Transfers allowed per year | 12 |
| Co-annuitant allowed | yes | Maximum issuance age | 80 |
| Co-owner allowed | yes | Maximum annuitization age | 85 |
| Dollar-cost averaging | yes | Number of subaccounts | 7 |
| Systematic withdrawal plans | yes | Available in all 50 states | no* |

*Available only in NY.

**MFS/Sun Life (US) Compass 3**
**Capital Appreciation Variable Account**
P.O. Box 1024
Boston, MA 02103
(800) 752-7215

| | |
|---|---|
| Performance | ✓✓✓✓ |
| Risk control | ✓ |
| Expense minimization | ✓✓ |
| Management | ✓✓ |
| Investment options | ✓✓✓ |
| Family rating | ✓✓✓ |
| Total point score | 15 points |

## Performance                                                  ✓✓✓✓

During the 3-year and 5-year periods ending December 31, 1994, Capital Appreciation Variable Account had an average annual compound return of 1.6% and 5.0%, respectively. This means that a $10,000 investment made into this subaccount 5 years before that date grew to $12,800 ($10,500, if only the last 3 years of the period are used).

Compared to other growth variable annuity subaccounts, this one ranks in the top half for the 3-year period and in the top quartile for the 5-year period. The inception month of this subaccount was May 1988. This subaccount's predecessor was the MFS Compass Capital Appreciation Variable Account, which had an inception date of July 1982, and has an asset base of $600 million.

The year-by-year returns for this subaccount are:

| Year | Annual Return | S&P 500 |
|---|---|---|
| 1994 | −15.0% | 1.3% |
| 1993 | 12.3% | 10.1% |
| 1992 | 9.8% | 7.6% |
| 1991 | 33.9% | 30.5% |
| 1990 | −8.9% | −3.1% |
| 1989 | 40.7% | 31.7% |

## Risk Control                                                     ✓

Over the 3-year and 5-year periods, this fund was slightly riskier than the average equity subaccount.

The typical standard deviation for growth subaccounts was 3.9% during the 3-year period. The standard deviation for MFS/Sun Life (US) Compass 3 Capital Appreciation Variable Account was 4.5% over this same period, which means that this subaccount was 15% more volatile than its peer group. The price/earnings (p/e) ratio averages 25 for this portfolio. The typical growth subaccount has a p/e ratio of 24. In general, the higher the p/e ratio, the riskier the portfolio.

The beta (market-related risk) of this subaccount was 1.3 over the 3-year period. Beta for this entire category was 1.1 over this same period. The market index (the S&P 500 Index for equity subaccounts) always has a beta of 1.0. The *risk-adjusted* return for this variable annuity subaccount can be described as very good.

## Expense Minimization                                            ✓✓

The typical expenses incurred by growth subaccounts are 2.0% per year. The total expenses for MFS/Sun Life (US) Compass 3 Capital Appreciation Variable Account,

2.2%, are higher than its peer group average. Total expenses include all charges to the investor (except the annual contract charge, which is always expressed as a dollar figure), including management fees, overhead, administration, and mortality expenses. The free annual withdrawals percentage is based on the original principal.

| | | | |
|---|---|---|---|
| Maximum surrender charge | 6% | Total expenses | 2.2% |
| Duration of surrender charge | 7 years | Annual contract charge | $30 |
| Declining surrender charge | yes | Free annual withdrawals | 10% |

## Management                                              ✓✓

MFS/Sun Life (US) Compass 3 is offered by Sun Life Assurance Company of Canada (US). The company has an A.M. Best rating of A++. The portfolio and its predecessor were managed by William S. Harris for the 6 years ending December 31, 1994. The portfolio's size is $115 million. The typical security in the portfolio has a market capitalization of $4.7 billion.

## Investment Options                                       ✓✓✓

Investors may make additional contributions into this portfolio at any time. This is known as a flexible premium annuity. Investors in this variable annuity can choose from all of the subaccount categories below that have a check mark:

| | | |
|---|---|---|
| ✓ Aggressive growth | ✓ Government bonds | ✓ Money market |
| ✓ Balanced | ✓ Growth | ___ Specialty/Sector |
| ___ Corporate bonds | ___ Growth & income | ✓ World bonds |
| ___ Global equities (stocks) | ✓ High-yield bonds | |

## Family Rating                                            ✓✓✓

There are 7 subaccounts within the MFS/Sun Life (US) Compass 3 family. Overall, this family of subaccounts can be described as good on a *risk-adjusted* return basis.

The subaccounts within this variable annuity all have an *increasing* guaranteed death benefit. This means that the beneficiary is guaranteed to receive *the greater of* the contract's value on the date of the annuitant's death or the value of the original investment(s) compounded by 5% each year (less any withdrawals made).

## Summary

MFS/Sun Life (US) Compass 3 Capital Appreciation Variable Account has higher-than-average risk but also higher-than-average returns. Since its inception, this growth subaccount has outperformed the S&P 500 in every year but one. The contract offers two important investment options: world bonds and high-yield bonds. Both of these categories are misunderstood by a great number of investment advisors.

This growth portfolio is very good on its own. When combined with some of the other subaccounts (e.g., high-yield bonds) within the variable annuity contract, it becomes a real winner.

## Profile

| | | | |
|---|---|---|---|
| Minimum investment | $300 | Telephone exchanges | yes |
| Retirement account minimum | $300 | Transfers allowed per year | 12 |
| Co-annuitant allowed | yes | Maximum issuance age | none |
| Co-owner allowed | yes | Maximum annuitization age | 80 |
| Dollar-cost averaging | yes | Number of subaccounts | 7 |
| Systematic withdrawal plans | yes | Available in all 50 states | no* |

*Not available in NY or VT.

**Minnesota Mutual Multioption A**
**Capital Appreciation**
400 North Robert Street
St. Paul, MN 55101-2098
(800) 328-9343

| | |
|---|---|
| Performance | ✓✓✓ |
| Risk control | ✓ |
| Expense minimization | ✓✓✓ |
| Management | ✓ |
| Investment options | ✓✓✓✓ |
| Family rating | ✓✓✓ |
| Total point score | 15 points |

# Performance ✓✓✓

During the 3-year and 5-year periods ending December 31, 1994, Capital Appreciation had an average annual compound return of 4.5% and 9.1%, respectively. This means that a $10,000 investment made into this subaccount 5 years before that date grew to $15,500 ($11,400, if only the last 3 years of the period are used).

Compared to other growth variable annuity subaccounts, this one ranks in the top half for the 3-year period and in the top third for the 5-year period. The inception month of this subaccount was June 1987. This subaccount is modeled (cloned) after the MIMLIC Series Fund Capital Appreciation Portfolio, which had an inception date of April 1987, and has an asset base of $85 million.

The year-by-year returns for this subaccount are:

| Year | Annual Return | S&P 500 |
|---|---|---|
| 1994 | 1.0% | 1.3% |
| 1993 | 9.1% | 10.1% |
| 1992 | 3.8% | 7.6% |
| 1991 | 40.0% | 30.5% |
| 1990 | −3.2% | −3.1% |
| 1989 | 36.5% | 31.7% |
| 1988 | 6.2% | 16.6% |

# Risk Control ✓

Over the 3-year period, this fund was somewhat riskier than the average equity subaccount. During the 5-year period, it was slightly riskier.

The typical standard deviation for growth subaccounts was 3.9% during the 3-year period. The standard deviation for Minnesota Mutual Multioption A Capital Appreciation was 4.7% over this same period, which means that this subaccount was 21% more volatile than its peer group. The price/earnings (p/e) ratio averages 2 for this portfolio. The typical growth subaccount has a p/e ratio of 24. In general, the higher the p/e ratio, the riskier the portfolio.

The beta (market-related risk) of this subaccount was 1.3 over the 3-year period. Beta for this entire category was 1.1 over this same period. The market index (the S&P 500 Index for equity subaccounts) always has a beta of 1.0. The *risk-adjusted* return for this variable annuity subaccount can be described as good.

# Expense Minimization ✓✓✓

The typical expenses incurred by growth subaccounts are 2.0% per year. The total expenses for Minnesota Mutual Multioption A Capital Appreciation, 2.2%, are higher than its peer group average. Total expenses include all charges to the investor (except the annual contract charge, which is always expressed as a dollar figure), including management fees, overhead, administration, and mortality expenses. The free annual withdrawals percentage is based on the account value after the first year.

| | | | |
|---|---|---|---|
| Maximum surrender charge | 9% | Total expenses | 2.2% |
| Duration of surrender charge | 10 years | Annual contract charge | $0 |
| Declining surrender charge | no | Free annual withdrawals | 10% |

## Management                                           ✓

Minnesota Mutual Multioption A is offered by Minnesota Mutual Life Insurance Company. The company has a Duff & Phelps rating of AAA and an A.M. Best rating of A++. The subaccount and portfolio it is modeled after were managed by James P. Tatera for the 7 years ending December 31, 1994. The portfolio's size is $70 million. The typical security in the portfolio has a market capitalization of $6.9 billion.

## Investment Options                               ✓✓✓

Investors may make additional contributions into this portfolio at any time. This is known as a flexible premium annuity. Investors in this variable annuity can choose from all of the subaccount categories below that have a check mark:

| | | |
|---|---|---|
| ✓ Aggressive growth | ✓ Government bonds | ✓ Money market |
| ✓ Balanced | ✓ Growth | ___ Specialty/Sector |
| ✓ Corporate bonds | ✓ Growth & income | ___ World bonds |
| ✓ Global equities (stocks) | ___ High-yield bonds | |

## Family Rating                                      ✓✓✓

There are 9 subaccounts within the Minnesota Mutual Multioption A family. Overall, this family of subaccounts can be described as good on a *risk-adjusted* return basis.

## Summary

Minnesota Mutual Multioption A Capital Appreciation scores well for performance and expense minimization. The variable annuity contract has an impressive array of investment options, and the family rating is also good.

The duration of the surrender charge, 10 years, and the maximum surrender charge of 9% (which is not declining) are the two major negatives to this investment vehicle. Both of these disadvantages are unimportant for the long-term investor. On a positive note, the maximum issuance and annuitization ages are quite high and unlimited telephone exchanges are allowed.

## Profile

| | | | |
|---|---|---|---|
| Minimum investment | $5,000 | Telephone exchanges | yes |
| Retirement account minimum | $5,000 | Transfers allowed per year | unlimited |
| Co-annuitant allowed | yes | Maximum issuance age | 85 |
| Co-owner allowed | spouses only | Maximum annuitization age | 95 |
| Dollar-cost averaging | yes | Number of subaccounts | 9 |
| Systematic withdrawal plans | yes | Available in all 50 states | no* |

*Not available in NY.

**MONYMaster**
**Equity Portfolio**
1740 Broadway
New York, NY 10019
(800) 800-3219

| | |
|---|---|
| Performance | ✓✓✓ |
| Risk control | ✓✓✓✓✓ |
| Expense minimization | ✓✓✓ |
| Management | ✓✓✓✓ |
| Investment options | ✓ |
| Family rating | ✓✓✓✓✓ |
| Total point score | 21 points |

# Performance                                                    ✓✓✓

During the 3-year and 5-year periods ending December 31, 1994, Equity Portfolio had an average annual compound return of 8.4% and 9.8%, respectively. This means that a $10,000 investment made into this subaccount 5 years before that date grew to $16,000 ($12,700, if only the last 3 years of the period are used).

Compared to other growth variable annuity subaccounts, this one ranks in the top half for the 3-year and 5-year periods. This subaccount is modeled (cloned) after the Quest for Value Fund—Class A, which had an inception date of May 1980, and has an asset base of $250 million.

The year-by-year returns for this subaccount are:

| Year | Annual Return | S&P 500 |
|---|---|---|
| 1994 | 2.5% | 1.3% |
| 1993 | 6.5% | 10.1% |
| 1992 | 16.5% | 7.6% |
| 1991 | 29.7% | 30.5% |
| 1990 | −3.4% | −3.1% |
| 1989 | 21.2% | 31.7% |

# Risk Control                                                   ✓✓✓✓✓

Over the 3-year and 5-year periods, this fund was quite a bit safer than the average equity subaccount.

The typical standard deviation for growth subaccounts was 3.9% during the 3-year period. The standard deviation for MONYMaster Equity Portfolio was 2.8% over this same period, which means that this subaccount was 29% less volatile than its peer group. The price/earnings (p/e) ratio averages 16 for this portfolio. The typical growth subaccount has a p/e ratio of 24. In general, the higher the p/e ratio, the riskier the portfolio.

The beta (market-related risk) of this subaccount was 0.8 over the 3-year period. Beta for this entire category was 1.1 over this same period. The market index (the S&P 500 Index for equity subaccounts) always has a beta of 1.0. The *risk-adjusted* return for this variable annuity subaccount can be described as very good.

# Expense Minimization                                           ✓✓✓

The typical expenses incurred by growth subaccounts are 2.0% per year. The total expenses for MONYMaster Equity Portfolio, 2.0%, are equivalent to its peer group average. Total expenses include all charges to the investor (except the annual contract charge, which is always expressed as a dollar figure), including management fees, overhead, administration, and mortality expenses. The free annual withdrawals percentage is based on the account value.

| | | | |
|---|---|---|---|
| Maximum surrender charge | 7% | Total expenses | 2.0% |
| Duration of surrender charge | 8 years | Annual contract charge | $30 |
| Declining surrender charge | yes | Free annual withdrawals | 10% |

## Management ✓✓✓✓

MONYMaster is offered by MONY Life Insurance Company of America. The portfolio (and/or the mutual fund it is modeled after) was managed by Eileen P. Rominger for the 6 years ending December 31, 1994. The portfolio's size is $60 million. The typical security in the portfolio has a market capitalization of $4.2 billion. Rominger also manages the Quest for Value Fund—Class A.

## Investment Options ✓

Investors may make additional contributions into this portfolio at any time. This is known as a flexible premium annuity. Investors in this variable annuity can choose from all of the subaccount categories below that have a check mark:

| | | |
|---|---|---|
| ✓ Aggressive growth | ___ Government bonds | ✓ Money market |
| ✓ Balanced | ✓ Growth | ___ Specialty/Sector |
| ✓ Corporate bonds | ___ Growth & income | ___ World bonds |
| ___ Global equities (stocks) | ___ High-yield bonds | |

## Family Rating ✓✓✓✓✓

There are 6 subaccounts within the MONYMaster family. Overall, this family of subaccounts can be described as excellent on a *risk-adjusted* return basis.

## Summary

MONYMaster Equity Portfolio demonstrates exceptional risk control while still turning in some impressive results. Few growth portfolios have demonstrated such low volatility. Over the 3-year period, this subaccount was about 35% safer than its peers. Manager Eileen Rominger deserves much of the credit.

MONYMaster deserves kudos for having a "fund" family that is excellent. This is the type of annuity contract that investors can go into and stay with; investment options are superb.

## Profile

| | | | |
|---|---|---|---|
| Minimum investment | $600 | Telephone exchanges | yes |
| Retirement account minimum | $2,000 | Transfers allowed per year | 4 |
| Co-annuitant allowed | no | Maximum issuance age | 85 |
| Co-owner allowed | yes | Maximum annuitization age | 95 |
| Dollar-cost averaging | yes | Number of subaccounts | 6 |
| Systematic withdrawal plans | no | Available in all 50 states | no* |

*Not available in ME, WY, or PR.

---

**Mutual of America Separate Account 2**
**Scudder Capital Growth**
666 Fifth Avenue
New York, NY 10103
(800) 468-3785

| | |
|---|---|
| Performance | ✓✓✓✓ |
| Risk control | ✓✓✓ |
| Expense minimization | ✓✓✓ |
| Management | ✓✓✓ |
| Investment options | ✓✓✓ |
| Family rating | ✓✓✓ |
| Total point score | 19 points |

# Performance ✓✓✓✓

During the 3-year and 5-year periods ending December 31, 1994, Scudder Capital Growth had an average annual compound return of 3.9% and 7.2%, respectively. This means that a $10,000 investment made into this subaccount 5 years before that date grew to $14,200 ($11,200, if only the last 3 years of the period are used).

Compared to other growth variable annuity subaccounts, this one ranks in the top third for the 3-year period. The inception month of this subaccount was January 1989. The performance figures (shown below) for periods before the subaccount's inception in January 1989 are hypothetical, based on the underlying clone fund's returns. This subaccount is modeled (cloned) after the Scudder Capital Growth Fund, which had an inception date of June 1956, and has an asset base of $1.5 billion.

The year-by-year returns for this subaccount and the mutual fund it is modeled after are:

| Year | Annual Return | S&P 500 |
|---|---|---|
| 1994 | -10.9% | 1.3% |
| 1993 | 19.3% | 10.1% |
| 1992 | 5.4% | 7.6% |
| 1991 | 38.0% | 30.5% |
| 1990 | -8.4% | -3.1% |
| 1989 | 33.8% | 31.7% |
| 1988 | 29.7% | 16.6% |
| 1987 | -0.7% | 5.3% |

# Risk Control ✓✓✓

Over the 3-year period, this fund was as safe as the average equity subaccount.

The typical standard deviation for growth subaccounts was 3.9% during the 3-year period. The standard deviation for Mutual of America Separate Account 2 Scudder Capital Growth was 4.2% over this same period, which means that this subaccount was 7% more volatile than its peer group. The price/earnings (p/e) ratio averages 25 for this portfolio. The typical growth subaccount has a p/e ratio of 24. In general, the higher the p/e ratio, the riskier the portfolio.

The beta (market-related risk) of this subaccount was 1.2 over the 3-year period. Beta for this entire category was 1.1 over this same period. The market index (the S&P 500 Index for equity subaccounts) always has a beta of 1.0. The *risk-adjusted* return for this variable annuity subaccount can be described as very good.

## Expense Minimization                                      ✓✓✓

The typical expenses incurred by growth subaccounts are 2.0% per year. The total expenses for Mutual of America Separate Account 2 Scudder Capital Growth, 2.1%, are higher than its peer group average. Total expenses include all charges to the investor (except the annual contract charge, which is always expressed as a dollar figure), including management fees, overhead, administration, and mortality expenses. The free annual withdrawals percentage is based on the account value.

| | | | |
|---|---|---|---|
| Maximum surrender charge | 0% | Total expenses | 2.1% |
| Duration of surrender charge | n/a | Annual contract charge | $24 |
| Declining surrender charge | n/a | Free annual withdrawals | 10% |

## Management                                               ✓✓✓

Mutual of America Separate Account 2 is offered by Mutual of America Life Insurance Company. The company has a Duff & Phelps rating of AA+ and an A.M. Best rating of A+. The portfolio has been managed by Steven Aronoff and William Gadsden since its inception. The portfolio's size is $100 million. The typical security in the portfolio has a market capitalization of $2.6 billion. Aronoff and Gadsden have also managed the Scudder Capital Growth Fund for several years.

## Investment Options                                       ✓✓✓

Investors may make additional contributions into this portfolio at any time. This is known as a flexible premium annuity. Investors in this variable annuity can choose from all of the subaccount categories below that have a check mark:

| | | |
|---|---|---|
| ___ Aggressive growth | ___ Government bonds | ✓ Money market |
| ✓ Balanced | ✓ Growth | ___ Specialty/Sector |
| ✓ Corporate bonds | ✓ Growth & income | ___ World bonds |
| ✓ Global equities (stocks) | ___ High-yield bonds | |

## Family Rating                                            ✓✓✓

There are 12 subaccounts within the Mutual of America Separate Account 2 family. Overall, this family of subaccounts can be described as good on a *risk-adjusted* return basis. The subaccounts within this variable annuity all have a death benefit based on the value at the date of death (what is referred to in the industry as "accumulated value"). Unlike the death benefit found with most variable annuities, the accumulated value death benefit does not protect the beneficiary from possible market loss.

## Summary

Mutual of America Separate Account 2 Scudder Capital Growth has what most investors are looking for: consistency. This subaccount scores well in every category: performance, risk control, expense minimization, management, investment options, and family rating. Unfortunately, the contract is available only for qualified accounts (i.e., IRAs, pension plans, Keoghs, and so on).

Some features are worth noting about this Mutual of America variable annuity contract. First, minimum investment is quite low. Second, a co-annuitant can be listed—a great idea for individuals or couples who want to postpone triggering a tax event as long as possible. Third, unlimited telephone exchanges are allowed—you can move your money around without paying any type of fee. Fourth, there is no maximum issuance age—no matter how old you are, this investment is open to you.

Fifth, you have a dozen portfolios to choose from, Scudder Capital Growth is just one of your options.

## Profile

| | | | |
|---|---|---|---|
| Minimum investment | $10 | Telephone exchanges | yes |
| Retirement account minimum | $10 | Transfers allowed per year | unlimited |
| Co-annuitant allowed | yes | Maximum issuance age | none |
| Co-owner allowed | no | Maximum annuitization age | 70.5 |
| Dollar-cost averaging | no | Number of subaccounts | 12 |
| Systematic withdrawal plans | yes | Available in all 50 states | yes |

---

**Mutual of America Separate Account 2**
**Twentieth Century Investor Growth Fund**
666 Fifth Avenue
New York, NY 10103
(800) 468-3785

---

| | |
|---|---|
| Performance | ✓✓ |
| Risk control | ✓ |
| Expense minimization | ✓✓ |
| Management | ✓ |
| Investment options | ✓✓✓ |
| Family rating | ✓✓✓ |
| Total point score | 12 points |

## Performance                                                          ✓✓

During the 3-year and 5-year periods ending December 31, 1994, Twentieth Century Investor Growth Fund had an average annual compound return of 1.4% and 7.5%, respectively. This means that a $10,000 investment made into this subaccount 5 years before that date grew to $14,400 ($10,400, if only the last 3 years of the period are used).

Compared to other growth variable annuity subaccounts, this one ranked in the bottom for the 3-year and 5-year periods. The inception month of this subaccount was January 1989. The performance figures (shown below) for periods before the subaccount's inception in January 1989 are hypothetical, based on the underlying clone fund's returns. This subaccount is modeled (cloned) after the Twentieth Century Growth Investors, which had an inception date of October 1958, and has an asset base of $4.7 billion.

The year-by-year returns for this subaccount and the mutual fund it is modeled after are:

| Year | Annual Return | S&P 500 |
|---|---|---|
| 1994 | −2.3% | 1.3% |
| 1993 | 9.1% | 10.1% |
| 1992 | −2.2% | 7.6% |
| 1991 | 40.8% | 30.5% |
| 1990 | −2.0% | −3.1% |
| 1989 | 27.8% | 31.7% |
| 1988 | 2.7% | 16.6% |

# Risk Control                                                                  ✓

Over the 3-year period, this fund was quite a bit riskier than the average equity sub-account. During the last 5-year period, it was even riskier.

The typical standard deviation for growth subaccounts was 3.9% during the 3-year period. The standard deviation for Mutual of America Separate Account 2 Twentieth Century Investor Growth Fund was 4.6% over this same period, which means that this subaccount was 19% more volatile than its peer group. The price/earnings (p/e) ratio averages 24 for this portfolio. The typical growth sub-account also has a p/e ratio of 24. In general, the higher the p/e ratio, the riskier the portfolio.

The beta (market-related risk) of this subaccount was 1.3 over the 3-year pe-riod. Beta for this entire category was 1.1 over this same period. The market index (the S&P 500 Index for equity subaccounts) always has a beta of 1.0. The *risk-adjusted* return for this variable annuity subaccount can be described as fair.

# Expense Minimization                                                         ✓✓

The typical expenses incurred by growth subaccounts are 2.0% per year. The total expenses for Mutual of America Separate Account 2 Twentieth Century Investor Growth Fund, 2.3%, are higher than its peer group average. Total expenses include all charges to the investor (except the annual contract charge, which is always ex-pressed as a dollar figure), including management fees, overhead, administration, and mortality expenses. The free annual withdrawals percentage is based on the ac-count value.

| | | | |
|---|---|---|---|
| Maximum surrender charge | 0% | Total expenses | 2.3% |
| Duration of surrender charge | n/a | Annual contract charge | $24 |
| Declining surrender charge | n/a | Free annual withdrawals | 10% |

# Management                                                                    ✓

Mutual of America Separate Account 2 is offered by Mutual of America Life Insur-ance Company. The company has a Duff & Phelps rating of AA+ and an A.M. Best rating of A+. The portfolio and the mutual fund it is modeled after were managed by James Stowers III and Christopher Boyd for the 7 years ending December 31, 1994. The portfolio's size is $60 million. The typical security in the portfolio has a market capitalization of $15.3 billion.

# Investment Options                                                          ✓✓✓

Investors may make additional contributions into this portfolio at any time. This is known as a flexible premium annuity. Investors in this variable annuity can choose from all of the subaccount categories below that have a check mark:

| | | |
|---|---|---|
| ___ Aggressive growth | ___ Government bonds | ✓ Money market |
| ✓ Balanced | ✓ Growth | ___ Specialty/Sector |
| ✓ Corporate bonds | ✓ Growth & income | ___ World bonds |
| ✓ Global equities (stocks) | ___ High-yield bonds | |

# Family Rating                                                               ✓✓✓

There are 12 subaccounts within the Mutual of America Separate Account 2 family. Overall, this family of subaccounts can be described as good on a *risk-adjusted* return basis. The subaccounts within this variable annuity all have a death benefit based on the value at the date of death (what is referred to in the industry as "accumulated value"). Unlike the death benefit found with most variable annuities, the accumulated value death benefit does not protect the beneficiary from possible market loss.

## Summary

Mutual of America Separate Account 2 Twentieth Century Investor Growth Fund is just what you need for a little excitement. Twentieth Century, which oversees this subaccount, is not known for being shy or timid when it comes to investing in equities. This type of growth portfolio can really soar during bull markets. If things get too hot, you can get out of the investment or the entire contract without any penalties or costs. Unfortunately, the contract is available only for qualified accounts (i.e., IRAs, pension plans, Keoghs, and so on).

Some features are worth noting about this Mutual of America variable annuity contract. First, minimum investment is quite low. Second, a co-annuitant can be listed—a great idea for individuals or couples who want to postpone triggering a tax event as long as possible. Third, unlimited telephone exchanges are allowed—you can move your money around without paying any type of fee. Fourth, there is no maximum issuance age—no matter how old you are, this investment is open to you. Fifth, you have a dozen portfolios to choose from; Scudder Capital Growth is just one of your options.

## Profile

| | | | |
|---|---|---|---|
| Minimum investment | $10 | Telephone exchanges | yes |
| Retirement account minimum | $10 | Transfers allowed per year | unlimited |
| Co-annuitant allowed | yes | Maximum issuance age | none |
| Co-owner allowed | no | Maximum annuitization age | 70.5 |
| Dollar-cost averaging | no | Number of subaccounts | 12 |
| Systematic withdrawal plans | yes | Available in all 50 states | yes |

---

### New England Zenith Accumulator
### Capital Growth Series
501 Boylston Street
Boston, MA  02116
(800) 346-0399

---

| | |
|---|---|
| Performance | ✓✓✓ |
| Risk control | ✓✓ |
| Expense minimization | ✓✓✓ |
| Management | ✓✓ |
| Investment options | ✓✓ |
| Family rating | ✓✓✓✓ |
| Total point score | 16 points |

## Performance                                                    ✓✓✓

During the 3-year and 5-year periods ending December 31, 1994, Capital Growth Series had an average annual compound return of −1.2% and 6.8%, respectively (23.6% for 10 years). This means that a $10,000 investment made into this subaccount 5 years before that date grew to $13,900 ($9,600, if only the last 3 years of the period are used).

Compared to other growth variable annuity subaccounts, this one ranked in the top half for the 3-year and 5-year periods (it ranked in the top 2% for the 10 years ending December 31, 1994). The inception month of this subaccount was August 1983.

The year-by-year returns for this subaccount are:

| Year | Annual Return | S&P 500 |
|------|------|------|
| 1994 | −8.3% | 1.3% |
| 1993 | 13.4% | 10.1% |
| 1992 | −7.3% | 7.6% |
| 1991 | 51.9% | 30.5% |
| 1990 | −5.3% | −3.1% |
| 1989 | 29.8% | 31.7% |
| 1988 | −10.0% | 16.6% |
| 1987 | 50.7% | 5.3% |

## Risk Control                                              ✓✓

Over the 3-year period, this fund was slightly riskier than the average equity subaccount. During the 5-year period, it was quite a bit riskier.

The typical standard deviation for growth subaccounts was 3.9% during the 3-year period. The standard deviation for New England Zenith Accumulator Capital Growth Series was 4.3% over this same period, which means that this subaccount was 12% more volatile than its peer group. The price/earnings (p/e) ratio averages 30 for this portfolio. The typical growth subaccount has a p/e ratio of 24. In general, the higher the p/e ratio, the riskier the portfolio.

The beta (market-related risk) of this subaccount was 1.2 over the 3-year period. Beta for this entire category was 1.1 over this same period. The market index (the S&P 500 Index for equity subaccounts) always has a beta of 1.0. The *risk-adjusted* return for this variable annuity subaccount can be described as very good.

## Expense Minimization                                      ✓✓✓

The typical expenses incurred by growth subaccounts are 2.0% per year. The total expenses for New England Zenith Accumulator Capital Growth Series, 2.1%, are higher than its peer group average. Total expenses include all charges to the investor (except the annual contract charge, which is always expressed as a dollar figure), including management fees, overhead, administration, and mortality expenses. The free annual withdrawals percentage is based on the account value.

| | | | |
|------|------|------|------|
| Maximum surrender charge | 7% | Total expenses | 2.1% |
| Duration of surrender charge | 10 years | Annual contract charge | $30 |
| Declining surrender charge | no | Free annual withdrawals | 10% |

## Management                                                ✓✓

New England Zenith Accumulator is offered by New England Mutual Life Insurance Company. The company has a Duff & Phelps rating of AA. The portfolio was managed by G. Kenneth Heebner for the 11 years ending December 31, 1994. The portfolio's size is $350 million. The typical security in the portfolio has a market capitalization of $9.0 billion. Heebner also manages the TNE Growth mutual fund.

## Investment Options                                        ✓✓

Investors may make additional contributions into this portfolio at any time. This is known as a flexible premium annuity. Investors in this variable annuity can choose from all of the subaccount categories below that have a check mark:

| | | |
|---|---|---|
| ___ Aggressive growth | ___ Government bonds | ✓ Money market |
| ✓ Balanced | ✓ Growth | ___ Specialty/Sector |
| ✓ Corporate bonds | ✓ Growth & income | ___ World bonds |
| ___ Global equities (stocks) | ___ High-yield bonds | |

## Family Rating   ✓✓✓

There are 10 subaccounts within the New England Zenith Accumulator family. Overall, this family of subaccounts can be described as very good on a *risk-adjusted return* basis.

## Summary

New England Zenith Accumulator Capital Growth Series is a nice addition to the New England family. This growth portfolio has only stumbled a couple of times, and has always made things right the following year. This is the kind of subaccount you will want to stay with for at least 2 years. Whatever disappointments have occurred have been short-lived.

The New England family of variable annuity subaccounts is one of the few groups whose overall profile is quite positive. The Capital Growth Series represents a fine choice for investors interested in having equities as part of their holdings.

## Profile

| | | | |
|---|---|---|---|
| Minimum investment | $300 | Telephone exchanges | yes |
| Retirement account minimum | $300 | Transfers allowed per year | 4 |
| Co-annuitant allowed | no | Maximum issuance age | 75 |
| Co-owner allowed | no | Maximum annuitization age | 95 |
| Dollar-cost averaging | yes | Number of subaccounts | 10 |
| Systematic withdrawal plans | yes | Available in all 50 states | yes |

---

**Pacific Mutual Select Variable Annuity**
**Growth**
700 Newport Center Drive
P.O. Box 7500
Newport Beach, CA 92658-7500
(800) 800-7681

| | |
|---|---|
| Performance | ✓✓✓✓ |
| Risk control | ✓✓✓ |
| Expense minimization | ✓✓✓ |
| Management | ✓✓✓✓✓ |
| Investment options | ✓✓✓✓ |
| Family rating | ✓✓ |
| Total point score | 23 points |

## Performance   ✓✓✓✓✓

During the 3-year and 5-year periods ending December 31, 1994, Growth had an average annual compound return of 8.2% and 7.3%, respectively. This means that a

$10,000 investment made into this subaccount 5 years before that date grew to $14,200 ($12,700, if only the last 3 years of the period are used).

Compared to other growth variable annuity subaccounts, this one ranked in the top 2% for the 3-year period and in the top third for the 5-year period. The inception month of this subaccount was August 1990. The performance figures (shown below) for periods before the subaccount's inception in August 1990 are hypothetical, based on the underlying clone fund's returns. This subaccount is modeled (cloned) after the Pacific Select Fund Growth Series, which had an inception date of January 1988, and has an asset base of $65 million.

The year-by-year returns for this subaccount and the portfolio it is modeled after are:

| Year | Annual Return | S&P 500 |
|------|---------------|---------|
| 1994 | −11.6% | 1.3% |
| 1993 | 20.4% | 10.1% |
| 1992 | 19.1% | 7.6% |
| 1991 | 39.2% | 30.5% |
| 1990 | −20.3% | −3.1% |
| 1989 | 30.3% | 31.7% |

## Risk Control                                                          ✓✓✓✓

Over the 3-year period, this fund was somewhat safer than the average equity sub-account. During the 5-year period, it was a little riskier.

The typical standard deviation for growth subaccounts was 3.9% during the 3-year period. The standard deviation for Pacific Mutual Select Variable Annuity Growth was 3.8% over this same period, which means that this subaccount was 2% less volatile than its peer group. The price/earnings (p/e) ratio averages 28 for this portfolio. The typical growth subaccount has a p/e ratio of 24. In general, the higher the p/e ratio, the riskier the portfolio.

The beta (market-related risk) of this subaccount was 0.9 over the 3-year period. Beta for this entire category was 1.1 over this same period. The market index (the S&P 500 Index for equity subaccounts) always has a beta of 1.0. The *risk-adjusted* return for this variable annuity subaccount can be described as very good.

## Expense Minimization                                                   ✓✓✓

The typical expenses incurred by growth subaccounts are 2.0% per year. The total expenses for Pacific Mutual Select Variable Annuity Growth, 2.1%, are higher than its peer group average. Total expenses include all charges to the investor (except the annual contract charge, which is always expressed as a dollar figure), including management fees, overhead, administration, and mortality expenses. The free annual withdrawals percentage is based on the original principal.

| | | | |
|---|---|---|---|
| Maximum surrender charge | 6% | Total expenses | 2.1% |
| Duration of surrender charge | 6 years | Annual contract charge | $30 |
| Declining surrender charge | yes | Free annual withdrawals | 10% |

## Management                                            ✓✓✓✓

Pacific Mutual Select Variable Annuity is offered by Pacific Mutual Life Insurance Company. The company has a Duff & Phelps rating of AA+ and an A.M. Best rating of A+. The subaccount and portfolio it is modeled after were managed by Richard Barker, Robert Kirby, and James Rothenberg for the 6 years ending December 31, 1994. The portfolio's size is $30 million. The typical security in the portfolio has a market capitalization of $595 million.

## Investment Options                                    ✓✓✓✓

Investors may make additional contributions into this portfolio at any time. This is known as a flexible premium annuity. Investors in this variable annuity can choose from all of the subaccount categories below that have a check mark:

|          |          |          |
|----------|----------|----------|
| ___ Aggressive growth | ✓ Government bonds | ✓ Money market |
| ✓ Balanced | ✓ Growth | ___ Specialty/Sector |
| ✓ Corporate bonds | ✓ Growth & income | ___ World bonds |
| ✓ Global equities (stocks) | ✓ High-yield bonds | |

## Family Rating                                         ✓✓

There are 9 subaccounts within the Pacific Mutual Select Variable Annuity family. Overall, this family of subaccounts can be described as fair on a *risk-adjusted* return basis.

## Summary

Pacific Mutual Select Variable Annuity Growth is an outstanding example of what great money managers can do. This growth account stands out from the pack; its scores place it in the top 10% of all variable annuity subaccounts. This investment is strongly recommended to all.

The Pacific Mutual contract includes a global stock and high-yield bond subaccount, two important categories often missing from other companies. The structure of the contract is reasonable, but the features offered are great; few variable annuities allow for a co-annuitant and co-owner.

## Profile

| | | | |
|---|---|---|---|
| Minimum investment | $2,000 | Telephone exchanges | yes |
| Retirement account minimum | $5,000 | Transfers allowed per year | unlimited |
| Co-annuitant allowed | yes | Maximum issuance age | 85 |
| Co-owner allowed | yes | Maximum annuitization age | 95 |
| Dollar-cost averaging | yes | Number of subaccounts | 9 |
| Systematic withdrawal plans | yes | Available in all 50 states | no* |

*Not available in NY.

**PaineWebber Advantage Annuity
Growth**
601 Sixth Avenue
Des Moines, IA 50334
(800) 367-6058

| | |
|---|---:|
| Performance | ✓✓✓✓ |
| Risk control | ✓✓✓✓ |
| Expense minimization | ✓✓ |
| Management | ✓✓✓✓ |
| Investment options | ✓✓✓ |
| Family rating | ✓✓ |
| Total point score | 19 points |

## Performance                                                    ✓✓✓✓

During the 3-year and 5-year periods ending December 31, 1994, Growth had an average annual compound return of 2.3% and 6.3%, respectively. This means that a
$10,000 investment made into this subaccount 5 years before that date grew to
$13,600 ($10,700, if only the last 3 years of the period are used).

Compared to other growth variable annuity subaccounts, this one ranked in the
top 40% for the 3-year period and in the top 10% for the 5-year period. The inception month of this subaccount was May 1987. This subaccount is modeled (cloned)
after the PaineWebber Growth Fund—Class A, which had an inception date of
March 1985, and has an asset base of $160 million.

The year-by-year returns for this subaccount are:

| Year | Annual Return | S&P 500 |
|---|---|---|
| 1994 | −12.9% | 1.3% |
| 1993 | 18.0% | 10.1% |
| 1992 | 4.3% | 7.6% |
| 1991 | 40.1% | 30.5% |
| 1990 | −9.5% | −3.1% |
| 1989 | 45.6% | 31.7% |
| 1988 | 16.8% | 16.6% |

## Risk Control                                                    ✓✓✓✓

Over the 3-year and 5-year periods, this fund was slightly safer than the average equity subaccount.

The typical standard deviation for growth subaccounts was 3.9% during the 3-
year period. The standard deviation for PaineWebber Advantage Annuity Growth
was 3.7% over this same period, which means that this subaccount was 5% less
volatile than its peer group. The price/earnings (p/e) ratio averages 29 for this portfolio. The typical growth subaccount has a p/e ratio of 24. In general, the higher the
p/e ratio, the riskier the portfolio.

The beta (market-related risk) of this subaccount was 0.9 over the 3-year period.
Beta for this entire category was 1.1 over this same period. The market index (the S&P
500 Index for equity subaccounts) always has a beta of 1.0. The *risk-adjusted* return
for this variable annuity subaccount can be described as excellent.

# Expense Minimization   ✓✓

The typical expenses incurred by growth subaccounts are 2.0% per year. The total expenses for PaineWebber Advantage Annuity Growth, 2.3%, are higher than its peer group average. Total expenses include all charges to the investor (except the annual contract charge, which is always expressed as a dollar figure), including management fees, overhead, administration, and mortality expenses. The free annual withdrawals percentage is based on the account value.

| | | | |
|---|---|---|---|
| Maximum surrender charge | 5% | Total expenses | 2.3% |
| Duration of surrender charge | 5 years | Annual contract charge | $30 |
| Declining surrender charge | yes | Free annual withdrawals | 10% |

# Management   ✓✓✓✓

PaineWebber Advantage Annuity is offered by American Republic Insurance Company. The portfolio and the mutual fund it is modeled after were managed by Ellen R. Harris for the 10 years ending December 31, 1994. The portfolio's size is $50 million. The typical security in the portfolio has a market capitalization of $1.2 billion.

# Investment Options   ✓✓✓

Investors may make additional contributions into this portfolio at any time. This is known as a flexible premium annuity. Investors in this variable annuity can choose from all of the subaccount categories below that have a check mark:

| | | | | | |
|---|---|---|---|---|---|
| ___ | Aggressive growth | ✓ | Government bonds | ✓ | Money market |
| ✓ | Balanced | ✓ | Growth | ___ | Specialty/Sector |
| ___ | Corporate bonds | ✓ | Growth & income | ✓ | World bonds |
| ✓ | Global equities (stocks) | ___ | High-yield bonds | | |

# Family Rating   ✓✓

There are 7 subaccounts within the PaineWebber Advantage Annuity family. Overall, this family of subaccounts can be described as fair on a *risk-adjusted* return basis.

The subaccounts within this variable annuity all have an *increasing* guaranteed death benefit. This means that the beneficiary is guaranteed to receive *the greater of* the contract's value on the date of the annuitant's death or the value of the original investment(s) compounded by 5% each year (less any withdrawals made).

# Summary

PaineWebber Advantage Annuity Growth is one of just a small handful of great, well-known brokerage firm annuities. This particular stock account has not only done very well, it has also shown less risk than its category average. "Thank you PaineWebber" for this portfolio and for having a fairly structured contract that is investor-friendly.

# Profile

| | | | |
|---|---|---|---|
| Minimum investment | $1,000 | Telephone exchanges | yes |
| Retirement account minimum | $5,000 | Transfers allowed per year | unlimited |
| Co-annuitant allowed | no | Maximum issuance age | 85 |
| Co-owner allowed | no | Maximum annuitization age | 85 |
| Dollar-cost averaging | no | Number of subaccounts | 7 |
| Systematic withdrawal plans | no | Available in all 50 states | yes |

---

**Security Benefit Variflex**
**Growth**
700 Southwest Harrison Street
Topeka, KS 66636
(800) 888-2461

---

| | |
|---|---|
| Performance | ✓✓✓✓ |
| Risk control | ✓✓✓✓ |
| Expense minimization | ✓✓✓ |
| Management | ✓✓✓✓ |
| Investment options | ✓✓✓ |
| Family rating | ✓ |
| Total point score | 19 points |

## Performance                                                   ✓✓✓✓

During the 3-year and 5-year periods ending December 31, 1994, Growth had an average annual compound return of 6.2% and 7.5%, respectively (10.1% for 10 years). This means that a $10,000 investment made into this subaccount 5 years before that date grew to $14,400 ($12,000, if only the last 3 years of the period are used).

Compared to other growth variable annuity subaccounts, this one ranked in the top half for the 3-year and 5-year periods. The inception month of this subaccount was June 1984. This subaccount is modeled (cloned) after the Security Equity Fund, which had an inception date of September 1962, and has an asset base of $400 million.

The year-by-year returns for this subaccount are:

| Year | Annual Return | S&P 500 |
|---|---|---|
| 1994 | −2.8% | 1.3% |
| 1993 | 12.4% | 10.1% |
| 1992 | 9.8% | 7.6% |
| 1991 | 34.5% | 30.5% |
| 1990 | −10.9% | −3.1% |
| 1989 | 33.3% | 31.7% |
| 1988 | 8.8% | 16.6% |
| 1987 | 5.0% | 5.3% |

## Risk Control                                                  ✓✓✓✓

Over the 3-year and 5-year periods, this fund was slightly safer than the average equity subaccount.

The typical standard deviation for growth subaccounts was 3.9% during the 3-year period. The standard deviation for Security Benefit Variflex Growth was 3.8% over this same period, which means that this subaccount was 3% less volatile than its peer group. The price/earnings (p/e) ratio averages 22 for this portfolio. The typical growth subaccount has a p/e ratio of 24. In general, the higher the p/e ratio, the riskier the portfolio.

The beta (market-related risk) of this subaccount was 1.1 over the 3-year period. Beta for this entire category was also 1.1 over this same period. The market index (the S&P 500 Index for equity subaccounts) always has a beta of 1.0. The *risk-adjusted* return for this variable annuity subaccount can be described as good.

## Expense Minimization ✓✓✓

The typical expenses incurred by growth subaccounts are 2.0% per year. The total expenses for Security Benefit Variflex Growth, 2.1%, are higher than its peer group average. Total expenses include all charges to the investor (except the annual contract charge, which is always expressed as a dollar figure), including management fees, overhead, administration, and mortality expenses. The free annual withdrawals percentage is based on the account value.

| | | | |
|---|---|---|---|
| Maximum surrender charge | 8% | Total expenses | 2.1% |
| Duration of surrender charge | 8 years | Annual contract charge | $30 |
| Declining surrender charge | no | Free annual withdrawals | 10% |

## Management ✓✓✓✓

Security Benefit Variflex is offered by Security Benefit Life Insurance Company. The company has an A.M. Best rating of A+. The portfolio and the mutual fund it is modeled after have been managed by Terry Milberger for over 33 years. The portfolio's size is $250 million. The typical security in the portfolio has a market capitalization of $5.1 billion.

## Investment Options ✓✓✓

Investors may make additional contributions into this portfolio at any time. This is known as a flexible premium annuity. Investors in this variable annuity can choose from all of the subaccount categories below that have a check mark:

| | | |
|---|---|---|
| ✓ Aggressive growth | ___ Government bonds | ✓ Money market |
| ✓ Balanced | ✓ Growth | ___ Specialty/Sector |
| ✓ Corporate bonds | ___ Growth & income | ___ World bonds |
| ✓ Global equities (stocks) | ___ High-yield bonds | |

## Family Rating ✓

There are 7 subaccounts within the Security Benefit Variflex family.

The subaccounts within this variable annuity all have an *increasing* guaranteed death benefit. This means that the beneficiary is guaranteed to receive *the greater of* the contract's value on the date of the annuitant's death or the value of the original investment(s) compounded by 5% each year (less any withdrawals made).

## Summary

Security Benefit Variflex Growth is very good when it comes to returns and low risk. Management is to be commended for doing such a good job. It is hoped that the contract will offer more diverse options in the future. Once this shortcoming is corrected, this will become a complete investment vehicle to be reckoned with; for now, stay with the growth account.

## Profile

| | | | |
|---|---|---|---|
| Minimum investment | $25 | Telephone exchanges | yes |
| Retirement account minimum | $500 | Transfers allowed per year | unlimited |
| Co-annuitant allowed | no | Maximum issuance age | 80 |
| Co-owner allowed | yes | Maximum annuitization age | none |
| Dollar-cost averaging | yes | Number of subaccounts | 7 |
| Systematic withdrawal plans | yes | Available in all 50 states | no* |

*Not available in NY.

---

**Seligman/Canada Life Trillium
Capital**
Vantage Computer Systems
P.O. Box 13326
Kansas City, MO 64199
(800) 221-2783

---

| | |
|---|---|
| Performance | ✓✓✓✓✓ |
| Risk control | ✓✓ |
| Expense minimization | ✓ |
| Management | ✓✓✓ |
| Investment options | ✓✓✓ |
| Family rating | ✓✓ |
| Total point score | 16 points |

---

# Performance                                        ✓✓✓✓✓

During the 3-year and 5-year periods ending December 31, 1994, Capital had an average annual compound return of 2.4% and 9.9%, respectively. This means that a
$10,000 investment made into this subaccount 5 years before that date grew to
$16,000 ($10,700, if only the last 3 years of the period are used).

Compared to other growth variable annuity subaccounts, this one ranked in the
top 15% for the 3-year period and in the top half for the 5-year period. The inception
month of this subaccount was May 1993. The performance figures (shown below)
for periods before the subaccount's inception in May 1993 are hypothetical, based
on the underlying clone fund's returns. This subaccount is modeled (cloned) after
the Seligman Mutual Benefit Portfolios Capital Portfolio, which had an inception
date of July 1988, and has an asset base of $8 million.

The year-by-year returns for this subaccount and the portfolio it is modeled
after are:

| Year | Annual Return | S&P 500 |
|---|---|---|
| 1994 | −6.8% | 1.3% |
| 1993 | 9.4% | 10.1% |
| 1992 | 5.1% | 7.6% |
| 1991 | 61.2% | 30.5% |
| 1990 | −7.4% | −3.1% |
| 1989 | 14.6% | 31.7% |

# Risk Control                                             ✓✓

Over the 3-year and 5-year periods, this fund was somewhat riskier than the average
equity subaccount.

The typical standard deviation for growth subaccounts was 3.9% during the
3-year period. The standard deviation for Seligman/Canada Life Trillium Capital
was 4.8% over this same period, which means that this subaccount was 23% more
volatile than its peer group. The price/earnings (p/e) ratio averages 26 for this
portfolio. The typical growth subaccount has a p/e ratio of 24. In general, the
higher the p/e ratio, the riskier the portfolio.

The beta (market-related risk) of this subaccount was 1.3 over the 3-year
period. Beta for this entire category was 1.1 over this same period. The market
index (the S&P 500 Index for equity subaccounts) always has a beta of 1.0. The
*risk-adjusted* return for this variable annuity subaccount can be described as good.

## Expense Minimization ✓

The typical expenses incurred by growth subaccounts are 2.0% per year. The total expenses for Seligman/Canada Life Trillium Capital, 2.5%, are higher than its peer group average. Total expenses include all charges to the investor (except the annual contract charge, which is always expressed as a dollar figure), including management fees, overhead, administration, and mortality expenses. The free annual withdrawals percentage is based on the original principal.

| | | | |
|---|---|---|---|
| Maximum surrender charge | 6% | Total expenses | 2.5% |
| Duration of surrender charge | 7 years | Annual contract charge | $36 |
| Declining surrender charge | yes | Free annual withdrawals | 10% |

## Management ✓✓✓

Seligman/Canada Life Trillium is offered by Canada Life Insurance Company of America. The company has a Duff & Phelps rating of AAA and an A.M. Best rating of A++. The subaccount and portfolio it is modeled after were managed by Loris D. Muzzatti for the 6 years ending December 31, 1994. The portfolio's size is less than $1 million. The typical security in the portfolio has a market capitalization of $2.6 billion. Muzzatti also manages the Seligman Capital Fund—Class A mutual fund.

## Investment Options ✓✓✓

Investors may make additional contributions into this portfolio at any time. This is known as a flexible premium annuity. Investors in this variable annuity can choose from all of the subaccount categories below that have a check mark:

| | | | | | |
|---|---|---|---|---|---|
| ____ | Aggressive growth | ____ | Government bonds | ✓ | Money market |
| ✓ | Balanced | ✓ | Growth | ____ | Specialty/Sector |
| ✓ | Corporate bonds | ✓ | Growth & income | ____ | World bonds |
| ✓ | Global equities (stocks) | ____ | High-yield bonds | | |

## Family Rating ✓✓

There are 6 subaccounts within the Seligman/Canada Life Trillium family. Overall, this family of subaccounts can be described as fair on a *risk-adjusted* return basis.

   The subaccounts within this variable annuity all have an *increasing* guaranteed death benefit. This means that the beneficiary is guaranteed to receive *the greater of* the contract's value on the date of the annuitant's death or the value of the original investment(s) compounded by 5% each year (less any withdrawals made).

## Summary

Seligman/Canada Life Trillium Capital is not for the conservative investor, but is the right choice if you are looking for excellent returns. Expenses on this contract have been on the high side so far, but investment returns easily overshadow such a minor concern. The contract includes the all-important global equity subaccount—something sorely missing from the majority of variable annuities.

## Profile

| | | | |
|---|---|---|---|
| Minimum investment | $2,000 | Telephone exchanges | yes |
| Retirement account minimum | $5,000 | Transfers allowed per year | 15 |
| Co-annuitant allowed | no | Maximum issuance age | 80 |
| Co-owner allowed | yes | Maximum annuitization age | 85 |
| Dollar-cost averaging | yes | Number of subaccounts | 6 |
| Systematic withdrawal plans | yes | Available in all 50 states | no* |

*Not available in the following states: CA, ME, MN, ND, NH, NJ, NY, OR, VT, and WA.

Western Reserve Life Freedom Attainer Annuity
Growth
P.O. Box 5068
Clearwater, FL 34618-5068
(800) 443-9975

| | |
|---|---|
| Performance | ✓✓✓✓ |
| Risk control | ✓✓ |
| Expense minimization | ✓✓✓ |
| Management | ✓✓✓ |
| Investment options | ✓✓✓ |
| Family rating | ✓✓✓ |
| Total point score | 18 points |

## Performance                                                        ✓✓✓✓

During the 3-year and 5-year periods ending December 31, 1994, Growth had an average annual compound return of −2.0% and 7.9%, respectively. This means that a $10,000 investment made into this subaccount 5 years before that date grew to $14,600 ($9,400, if only the last 3 years of the period are used).

Compared to other growth variable annuity subaccounts, this one ranked in the top half for the 3-year period. The inception month of this subaccount was January 1993. The performance figures (shown below) for periods before the subaccount's inception in January 1993 are hypothetical, based on the underlying clone fund's returns. This subaccount is modeled (cloned) after the Western Reserve Life Series Fund Growth Portfolio, which had an inception date of October 1986, and has an asset base of $950 million.

The year-by-year returns for this subaccount and the portfolio it is modeled after are:

| Year | Annual Return | S&P 500 |
|---|---|---|
| 1994 | −9.5% | 1.3% |
| 1993 | 2.7% | 10.1% |
| 1992 | 1.1% | 7.6% |
| 1991 | 57.8% | 30.5% |
| 1990 | −1.4% | −3.1% |
| 1989 | 44.6% | 31.7% |

## Risk Control                                                            ✓✓

Over the 3-year period, this fund was slightly riskier than the average equity subaccount.

The typical standard deviation for growth subaccounts was 3.9% during the 3-year period. The standard deviation for Western Reserve Life Freedom Attainer Annuity Growth was 4.2% over this same period, which means that this subaccount was 9% more volatile than its peer group. The price/earnings (p/e) ratio averages 21 for this portfolio. The typical growth subaccount has a p/e ratio of 24. In general, the higher the p/e ratio, the riskier the portfolio.

The beta (market-related risk) of this subaccount was 1.2 over the 3-year period. Beta for this entire category was 1.1 over this same period. The market index (the S&P 500 Index for equity subaccounts) always has a beta of 1.0. The *risk-adjusted* return for this variable annuity subaccount can be described as good.

## Expense Minimization   ✓✓✓

The typical expenses incurred by growth subaccounts are 2.0% per year. The total expenses for Western Reserve Life Freedom Attainer Annuity Growth, 2.1%, are higher than its peer group average. Total expenses include all charges to the investor (except the annual contract charge, which is always expressed as a dollar figure), including management fees, overhead, administration, and mortality expenses. The free annual withdrawals percentage is based on the account value.

| | | | |
|---|---|---|---|
| Maximum surrender charge | 6% | Total expenses | 2.1% |
| Duration of surrender charge | 5 years | Annual contract charge | $30 |
| Declining surrender charge | yes | Free annual withdrawals | 10% |

## Management   ✓✓✓

Western Reserve Life Freedom Attainer Annuity is offered by Western Reserve Life Assurance Company of Ohio. The company has a Duff & Phelps rating of AA+ and an A.M. Best rating of A+. The subaccount and the portfolio it is modeled after were managed by Thomas F. Marsico for the 5 years ending December 31, 1994. The portfolio's size is $60 million. The typical security in the portfolio has a market capitalization of $9.0 billion. Marsico has also managed the IDEX Fund II Growth Portfolio—Class A mutual fund for the past 9 years.

## Investment Options   ✓✓✓

Investors may make additional contributions into this portfolio at any time. This is known as a flexible premium annuity. Investors in this variable annuity can choose from all of the subaccount categories below that have a check mark:

| | | |
|---|---|---|
| ✓ Aggressive growth | ✓ Government bonds | ✓ Money market |
| ___ Balanced | ✓ Growth | ___ Specialty/Sector |
| ✓ Corporate bonds | ✓ Growth & income | ___ World bonds |
| ✓ Global equities (stocks) | ___ High-yield bonds | |

## Family Rating   ✓✓✓

There are 7 subaccounts within the Western Reserve Life Freedom Attainer Annuity family. Overall, this family of subaccounts can be described as good on a *risk-adjusted* return basis.

The subaccounts within this variable annuity all have an *increasing* guaranteed death benefit. This means that the beneficiary is guaranteed to receive *the greater of* the contract's value on the date of the annuitant's death or the value of the original investment(s) compounded by 5% each year (less any withdrawals made).

## Summary

Western Reserve Life Freedom Attainer Annuity Growth is a very good performer, based on its risk-adjusted returns. In most categories, this equity subaccount rates well; its total returns are its strong suit.

Western Reserve Life Freedom Attainer Annuity offers one of the better variable annuity contracts in the industry. The duration of the surrender charge is low, the potential penalty declines each year, and withdrawals are based on the contract's current value. Having a global stock fund within the family is also a plus.

## Profile

| | | | |
|---|---|---|---|
| Minimum investment | $50 | Telephone exchanges | yes |
| Retirement account minimum | $5,000 | Transfers allowed per year | 12 |
| Co-annuitant allowed | no | Maximum issuance age | 85 |
| Co-owner allowed | no | Maximum annuitization age | 95 |
| Dollar-cost averaging | yes | Number of subaccounts | 7 |
| Systematic withdrawal plans | yes | Available in all 50 states | no* |

*Not available in NJ, OR, or WA.

# Chapter

## 13

# Growth and Income Subaccounts

These subaccounts attempt to produce both capital appreciation and current income, with priority given to appreciation potential in the stocks purchased. Growth and income subaccount portfolios include seasoned, well-established firms that pay relatively high cash dividends. The goal of these subaccounts is to provide long-term growth without excessive volatility in share price.

Portfolio composition is almost exclusively comprised of U.S. stocks; emphasis is on utility, computer, energy, retail, and financial common stocks. By selecting securities that have comparatively high yields, overall risk is reduced; dividends will help prop up the overall return of growth and income subaccounts during negative market conditions.

Over the 50 years ending December 31, 1994, common stocks outperformed inflation, on average: 70% of the time over 1-year periods; over 82% of the time over 5-year intervals; 83% of the time over 10-year periods; and 100% of the time over any given 20-year period of time. Over the same 50-year period, high-quality, long-term corporate bonds outperformed inflation, on average: 60% of the time over 1 year periods; 50% of the time over 5-year intervals; 46% of the time over 10-year periods; and 48% over any given 20-year period.

The table at the top of page 192 shows year-by-year, as well as 3-, 5-, and 10-year averages for this investment category. The variable annuity subaccount category is compared against the similar mutual fund category. These performance figures are average figures, representing all funds and subaccounts that fall within this investment objective.

As you can see, the variable annuity subaccounts outperformed their mutual fund counterparts only in 1994, 1988 and for the 3-year period.

I recommend a 10% commitment to this category for the conservative investor, 15% for the moderate, and 10% for the aggressive portfolio. This is one of the few categories of subaccounts that is recommended for all types of portfolios. As with any category of variable annuities, whenever larger dollar amounts are involved, more than one subaccount per category should be used.

The table at the bottom of page 192 shows statistics you might find useful when comparing variable annuity subaccounts versus their mutual fund counterparts or

**Average Annual Returns: Growth & Income
Subaccounts vs. Growth & Income Mutual Funds**

| Year | Subaccount | Mutual Fund |
|------|------------|-------------|
| 1994 | −0.3% | −1.5% |
| 1993 | 10.6% | 10.8% |
| 1992 | 7.7% | 8.3% |
| 1991 | 26.7% | 28.8% |
| 1990 | −6.3% | −4.7% |
| 1989 | 21.3% | 23.3% |
| 1988 | 16.9% | 14.8% |
| 1987 | 0.1% | 2.1% |
| | | |
| 3-yr. average | 6.6% | 5.8% |
| 5-yr. average | 7.6% | 7.8% |
| 10-yr. average | 12.2% | 13.3% |

clones. These category averages are based on information available at the beginning of 1995.

Figure 13.1 shows the year-by-year returns for this category of variable annuities for the period 1987 through 1994. These are composite figures and therefore include all of the subaccounts that comprise the growth and income category.

**Growth and Income Category Statistics:
Subaccounts vs. Mutual Funds**

| Description | Subaccounts | Funds |
|------------|-------------|-------|
| **Composition of portfolio** | | |
| U.S. stocks | 82% | 81% |
| Cash | 8% | 7% |
| Foreign stocks | 8% | 5% |
| Bonds | 2% | 3% |
| Other | 0% | 4% |
| **Fees and expenses** | | |
| Underlying fund expense | 0.65% | 1.19% |
| Insurance expense | 1.28% | — |
| Total expenses | 1.93% | 1.19%/3.2%* |
| **Operations** | | |
| Net assets (in millions) | $542 | $635 |
| Manager tenure | 4 years | 6 years |
| **Portfolio statistics** | | |
| Beta | 0.9% | 0.9% |
| Standard deviation | 2.9% | 3.5% |
| Price/earnings ratio | 21 | 21 |
| Turnover ratio (annual) | 51% | 62% |
| Median market capitalization | $9.6 billion | $8.0 billion |
| Number of subaccounts/funds | 140 | 450 |

*Total expenses for this mutual fund category increase to this figure if the average mutual fund commission is added to the 1.19% figure.

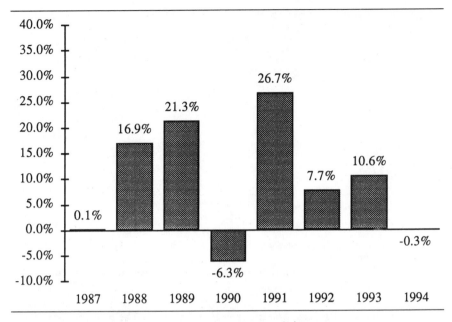

**Figure 13.1** Growth & Income Subaccounts

---

**Aetna Variable Annuity Account D MAP IV
Variable Fund**
151 Farmington Avenue
Hartford, CT 06156
(203) 273-9794

| | |
|---|---|
| Performance | ✓ |
| Risk control | ✓✓✓ |
| Expense minimization | ✓✓✓✓✓ |
| Management | ✓✓✓ |
| Investment options | ✓✓ |
| Family rating | ✓✓✓✓ |
| Total point score | 20 points |

## Performance ✓

During the 3-year and 5-year periods ending December 31, 1994, Variable Fund had an average annual compound return of 2.8% and 6.7%, respectively (13.2% for 10 years). This means that a $10,000 investment made into this subaccount 5 years before that date grew to $13,800 ($10,900, if only the last 3 years of the period are used).

Compared to other growth and income variable annuity subaccounts, this one ranked in the bottom quartile for the 3-year period but in the top quartile for the 5-year period (it ranked in the top 15% for the 10 years ending December 31, 1994). The inception month of this subaccount was April 1990. The performance figures (shown below) for periods before the subaccount's inception in April 1990 are hypothetical, based on the underlying clone fund's returns. This subaccount is modeled (cloned) after the Aetna Variable Fund, which had an inception date of September 1954, and has an asset base of $5 billion.

The year-by-year returns for this subaccount and the portfolio it is modeled after are:

| Year | Annual Return | S&P 500 |
|------|--------|---------|
| 1994 | −2.2% | 1.3% |
| 1993 | 5.4% | 10.1% |
| 1992 | 5.4% | 7.6% |
| 1991 | 24.8% | 30.5% |
| 1990 | 2.0% | −3.1% |
| 1989 | 27.5% | 31.7% |
| 1988 | 13.2% | 16.6% |
| 1987 | 4.2% | 5.3% |

## Risk Control                                           ✓✓✓✓

Over the 3-year and 5-year periods, this fund was quite a bit safer than the average equity subaccount.

The typical standard deviation for growth and income subaccounts was 2.9% during the 3-year period. The standard deviation for Aetna Variable Annuity Account D MAP IV Variable Fund was 2.6% over this same period, which means that this subaccount was 10% less volatile than its peer group. The price/earnings (p/e) ratio averages 20 for this portfolio. The typical growth and income subaccount has a p/e ratio of 21. In general, the higher the p/e ratio, the riskier the portfolio.

The beta (market-related risk) of this subaccount was 0.8 over the 3-year period. Beta for this entire category was 0.9 over this same period. The market index (the S&P 500 Index for equity subaccounts) always has a beta of 1.0. The *risk-adjusted* return for this variable annuity subaccount can be described as very good.

## Expense Minimization                                    ✓✓✓✓✓

The typical expenses incurred by growth and income subaccounts are 1.9% per year. The total expenses for Aetna Variable Annuity Account D MAP IV Variable Fund, 1.6%, are lower than its peer group average. Total expenses include all charges to the investor (except the annual contract charge, which is always expressed as a dollar figure), including management fees, overhead, administration, and mortality expenses.

| | | | |
|---|---|---|---|
| Maximum surrender charge | 0% | Total expenses | 1.6% |
| Duration of surrender charge | n/a | Annual contract charge | $15 |
| Declining surrender charge | n/a | Free annual withdrawals | 100% |

## Management                                              ✓✓✓

Aetna Variable Annuity Account D MAP IV is offered by Aetna Investment Services, Inc. The company has a Duff & Phelps rating of AAA and an A.M. Best rating of A++. The subaccount and the portfolio it is modeled after were managed by Richard DiChillo, Martin Duffy, and Neil Yarhouse for the 18 years ending December 31, 1994. The portfolio's size is $440 million. The typical security in the portfolio has a market capitalization of $12 billion.

## Investment Options                                      ✓✓

Investors may make additional contributions into this portfolio at any time. This is known as a flexible premium annuity. Investors in this variable annuity can choose from all of the subaccount categories below that have a check mark:

| | | |
|---|---|---|
| ___ Aggressive growth | ___ Government bonds | ✓ Money market |
| ✓ Balanced | ✓ Growth | ___ Specialty/Sector |
| ✓ Corporate bonds | ✓ Growth & income | ___ World bonds |
| ___ Global equities (stocks) | ___ High-yield bonds | |

## Family Rating                                          ✓✓✓✓

There are 10 subaccounts within the Aetna Variable Annuity Account D MAP IV family. Overall, this family of subaccounts can be described as excellent on a *risk-adjusted* return basis. The subaccounts within this variable annuity all have a death benefit based on the value at the date of death (what is referred to in the industry as "accumulated value"). Unlike the death benefit found with most variable annuities, the accumulated value death benefit does not protect the beneficiary from possible market loss.

## Summary

Aetna Variable Annuity Account D MAP IV Variable Fund is the perfect choice for anyone willing to give up some return potential in exchange for "sleep-at-night" safety. There is only one growth and income subaccount that scores better when it comes to risk reduction; however, no other contract scores higher when it comes to reducing investor costs, and no other contract includes more top-notch investment choices. This variable annuity is a strongly recommended investment vehicle. The contract is available only for qualified accounts (i.e., IRAs, pension plans, Keoghs, and so on).

## Profile

| | | | |
|---|---|---|---|
| Minimum investment | n/a | Telephone exchanges | yes |
| Retirement account minimum | $1,000,000 | Transfers allowed per year | 24 |
| Co-annuitant allowed | yes | Maximum issuance age | none |
| Co-owner allowed | yes | Maximum annuitization age | none |
| Dollar-cost averaging | yes | Number of subaccounts | 10 |
| Systematic withdrawal plans | yes | Available in all 50 states | no* |

*Not available in the following states: MD, NJ, OR, SC, and WV.

---

### American Skandia Advisors Plan
### Alger Income & Growth
P.O. Box 883
Shelton, CT 06484
(800) 752-6342

| | |
|---|---|
| Performance | ✓ |
| Risk control | ✓ |
| Expense minimization | ✓ |
| Management | ✓ |
| Investment options | ✓✓✓✓ |
| Family rating | ✓ |
| Total point score | 10 points |

## Performance                                                    ✓

During the 3-year and 5-year periods ending December 31, 1994, Alger Income & Growth had an average annual compound return of 1.8% and 4.9%, respectively.

This means that a $10,000 investment made into this subaccount 5 years before that date grew to $12,700 ($10,500, if only the last 3 years of the period are used).

Compared to other growth and income variable annuity subaccounts, this one ranked in the bottom quartile for the 3-year and 5-year periods. The inception month of this subaccount was May 1992. The performance figures (shown below) for periods before the subaccount's inception in May 1992 are hypothetical, based on the underlying clone fund's returns. This subaccount is modeled (cloned) after the Alger Income & Growth Portfolio, which had an inception date of November 1988, and has an asset base of $35 million.

The year-by-year returns for this subaccount and the portfolio it is modeled after are:

| Year | Annual Return | S&P 500 |
|------|------|------|
| 1994 | −9.6% | 1.3% |
| 1993 | 8.8% | 10.1% |
| 1992 | 7.1% | 7.6% |
| 1991 | 21.8% | 30.5% |
| 1990 | −1.1% | −3.1% |
| 1989 | 5.9% | 31.7% |
| 1988 | 16.0% | 16.6% |

## Risk Control                                               ✓

Over the 3-year period, this fund was as safe as the average equity subaccount. During the 5-year period, it was somewhat safer.

The typical standard deviation for growth and income subaccounts was 2.9% during the 3-year period. The standard deviation for American Skandia Advisors Plan Alger Income & Growth was 3.2% over this same period, which means that this subaccount was 11% more volatile than its peer group. The price/earnings (p/e) ratio averages 20 for this portfolio. The typical growth and income subaccount has a p/e ratio of 21. In general, the higher the p/e ratio, the risker the portfolio.

The beta (market-related risk) of this subaccount was 0.9 over the 3-year period. Beta for this entire category was also 0.9 over this same period. The market index (the S&P 500 Index for equity subaccounts) always has a beta of 1.0. The *risk-adjusted* return for this variable annuity subaccount can be described as fair.

## Expense Minimization                                        ✓

The typical expenses incurred by growth and income subaccounts are 1.9% per year. The total expenses for American Skandia Advisors Plan Alger Income & Growth, 2.7%, are higher than its peer group average. Total expenses include all charges to the investor (except the annual contract charge, which is always expressed as a dollar figure), including management fees, overhead, administration, and mortality expenses. The free annual withdrawals percentage is based on the original principal.

| | | | |
|---|---|---|---|
| Maximum surrender charge | 8% | Total expenses | 2.7% |
| Duration of surrender charge | 7 years | Annual contract charge | $30 |
| Declining surrender charge | no | Free annual withdrawals | 10% |

## Management ✓

American Skandia Advisors Plan is offered by American Skandia Life Assurance Corporation. The company has a Duff & Phelps rating of AA−. The subaccount and the portfolio it is modeled after were managed by David Alger for the 6 years ending December 31, 1994. David Alger also manages the Alger Income & Growth mutual fund. The portfolio's size is $35 million. The typical security in the portfolio has a market capitalization of $3.6 billion.

## Investment Options ✓✓✓✓

Investors may make additional contributions into this portfolio at any time. This is known as a flexible premium annuity. Investors in this variable annuity can choose from all of the subaccount categories below that have a check mark:

| | | |
|---|---|---|
| ✓ Aggressive growth | ___ Government bonds | ✓ Money market |
| ✓ Balanced | ✓ Growth | ✓ Specialty/Sector |
| ✓ Corporate bonds | ✓ Growth & income | ✓ World bonds |
| ✓ Global equities (stocks) | ___ High-yield bonds | |

## Family Rating ✓

There are 31 subaccounts within the American Skandia Advisors Plan family. The subaccounts within this variable annuity all have an *increasing* guaranteed death benefit. This means that the beneficiary is guaranteed to receive *the greater of* the contract's value on the date of the annuitant's death or the value of the original investment(s) compounded by 5% each year (less any withdrawals made).

## Summary

American Skandia Advisors Plan Alger Income & Growth is the type of subaccount that is often overlooked by the hasty investor. At first, there appears to be little that is appealing about this portfolio, but keep in mind that it has beaten out well over 90% of all the competition. The total score is low *for this book,* but this portfolio is still one of the 100 best.

   The management style at Alger is such that the addition or subtraction of 1 or 2 years from a performance grid can make this investment look very good during some periods and substandard during others. What cannot be denied is that, over the long term, this is a winner.

   A few years ago, American Skandia began to implement a policy wherein only the best specialists within each investment category would be sought. This strategy has been almost completely implemented, and the future looks very promising for this entire group.

## Profile

| | | | |
|---|---|---|---|
| Minimum investment | $1,000 | Telephone exchanges | yes |
| Retirement account minimum | $1,000 | Transfers allowed per year | 12 |
| Co-annuitant allowed | yes | Maximum issuance age | none |
| Co-owner allowed | yes | Maximum annuitization age | none |
| Dollar-cost averaging | yes | Number of subaccounts | 34 |
| Systematic withdrawal plans | yes | Available in all 50 states | no* |

*Not available in NY.

---

**Best of America IV/Nationwide**
**Total Return**
P.O. Box 16609
One Nationwide Plaza
Columbus, OH  43216
(800) 848-6331

---

| | |
|---|---|
| Performance | ✓✓✓✓ |
| Risk control | ✓✓✓✓ |
| Expense minimization | ✓✓✓✓ |
| Management | ✓✓✓✓ |
| Investment options | ✓✓✓✓✓ |
| Family rating | ✓✓ |

---

| | |
|---|---|
| Total point score | 23 points |

## Performance                                                    ✓✓✓✓

During the 3-year and 5-year periods ending December 31, 1994, Total Return had an average annual compound return of 5.3% and 7.7%, respectively (12.9% for 10 years). This means that a $10,000 investment made into this subaccount 5 years before that date grew to $14,500 ($11,700, if only the last 3 years of the period are used).

Compared to other growth and income variable annuity subaccounts, this one ranked in the top third for the 3-year period but in the bottom quartile for the 5-year period. (It ranked in the top half for the 10 years ending December 31, 1994.) The inception month of this subaccount was November 1982.

The year-by-year returns for this subaccount are:

| Year | Annual Return | S&P 500 |
|---|---|---|
| 1994 | −0.2% | 1.3% |
| 1993 | 9.5% | 10.1% |
| 1992 | 6.8% | 7.6% |
| 1991 | 36.7% | 30.5% |
| 1990 | −9.2% | −3.1% |
| 1989 | 11.8% | 31.7% |
| 1988 | 18.5% | 16.6% |
| 1987 | −2.0% | 5.3% |

## Risk Control                                                    ✓✓✓✓

Over the 3-year period, this fund was quite a bit safer than the average equity subaccount. During the 5-year period, it was a little safer.

The typical standard deviation for growth and income subaccounts was 2.9% during the 3-year period. The standard deviation for Best of America IV/Nationwide Total Return was 3.0% over this same period, which means that this subaccount was 5% more volatile than its peer group. The price/earnings (p/e) ratio averages 20 for this portfolio. The typical growth and income subaccount has a p/e ratio of 21. In general, the higher the p/e ratio, the riskier the portfolio.

The beta (market-related risk) of this subaccount was 0.9 over the 3-year period. Beta for this entire category was also 0.9 over this same period. The market index (the S&P 500 Index for equity subaccounts) always has a beta of 1.0. The *risk-adjusted* return for this variable annuity subaccount can be described as good.

## Expense Minimization ✓✓✓✓

The typical expenses incurred by growth and income subaccounts are 1.9% per year. The total expenses for Best of America IV/Nationwide Total Return, 1.8%, are lower than its peer group average. Total expenses include all charges to the investor (except the annual contract charge, which is always expressed as a dollar figure), including management fees, overhead, administration, and mortality expenses. The free annual withdrawals percentage is based on the original principal.

| | | | |
|---|---|---|---|
| Maximum surrender charge | 7% | Total expenses | 1.8% |
| Duration of surrender charge | 7 years | Annual contract charge | $30 |
| Declining surrender charge | yes | Free annual withdrawals | 10% |

## Management ✓✓✓✓

Best of America IV/Nationwide is offered by Nationwide Life Insurance Company. The company has an A.M. Best rating of A+. The portfolio was managed by John Schaffner for the 12 years ending December 31, 1994. The portfolio's size is $170 million. The typical security in the portfolio has a market capitalization of $12.8 billion. Schaffner also managed the Nationwide Growth mutual fund for the 13 years ending December 31, 1994.

## Investment Options ✓✓✓✓✓

Investors may make additional contributions into this portfolio at any time. This is known as a flexible premium annuity. Investors in this variable annuity can choose from all of the subaccount categories below that have a check mark:

| | | |
|---|---|---|
| ✓ Aggressive growth | ✓ Government bonds | ✓ Money market |
| ✓ Balanced | ✓ Growth | ✓ Specialty/Sector |
| ✓ Corporate bonds | ✓ Growth & income | ✓ World bonds |
| ✓ Global equities (stocks) | ✓ High-yield bonds | |

## Family Rating ✓✓

There are 22 subaccounts within the Best of America IV/Nationwide family. Overall, this family of subaccounts can be described as fair on a *risk-adjusted* return basis.

## Summary

Best of America IV/Nationwide Total Return is a great addition to any portfolio; it ranks very highly in every category. The only somewhat weak spot with this investment vehicle originates with some of the other members of the annuity family. Thus, by carefully choosing just a few of the Nationwide choices, you will be selecting some real winners.

The parent company, Nationwide, was a pioneer in hiring portfolio managers from a wide range of mutual fund groups, most of which are household names. This type of creativity has made this investment one of the most popular in the industry. More than one Nationwide subaccount appears in this book.

## Profile

| | | | |
|---|---|---|---|
| Minimum investment | none | Telephone exchanges | yes |
| Retirement account minimum | $1,500 | Transfers allowed per year | 1 per day |
| Co-annuitant allowed | no | Maximum issuance age | none |
| Co-owner allowed | no | Maximum annuitization age | none |
| Dollar-cost averaging | yes | Number of subaccounts | 22 |
| Systematic withdrawal plans | yes | Available in all 50 states | yes |

---

**First Variable Vista II**
**Equity-Income**
600 Atlantic Avenue
28th Floor
Boston, MA 02210
(800) 228-1035

---

| | |
|---|---|
| Performance | ✓✓ |
| Risk control | ✓✓ |
| Expense minimization | ✓ |
| Management | ✓✓ |
| Investment options | ✓✓✓ |
| Family rating | ✓✓ |
| Total point score | 12 points |

## Performance                                                  ✓✓

During the 3-year and 5-year periods ending December 31, 1994, Equity-Income had an average annual compound return of 4.2% and 6.8%, respectively. This means that a $10,000 investment made into this subaccount 5 years before that date grew to $13,900 ($11,300, if only the last 3 years of the period are used).

Compared to other growth and income variable annuity subaccounts, this one ranked in the top half for the 3-year period and in the top third for the 5-year period. The inception month of this subaccount was August 1990. The performance figures (shown below) for periods before the subaccount's inception in August 1990 are hypothetical, based on the underlying clone fund's returns. This subaccount is modeled (cloned) after the Variable Investors Series Equity-Income Portfolio, which had an inception date of May 1988, and has an asset base of $18 million.

The year-by-year returns for this subaccount and the portfolio it is modeled after are:

| Year | Annual Return | S&P 500 |
|---|---|---|
| 1994 | −1.0% | 1.3% |
| 1993 | 16.2% | 10.1% |
| 1992 | −0.3% | 7.6% |
| 1991 | 28.0% | 30.5% |
| 1990 | −4.0% | −3.1% |
| 1989 | 25.0% | 31.7% |

## Risk Control                                                  ✓✓

Over the 3-year and 5-year periods, this fund was somewhat safer than the average equity subaccount.

The typical standard deviation for growth and income subaccounts was 2.9% during the 3-year period. The standard deviation for First Variable Vista II Equity-Income was 3.2% over this same period, which means that this subaccount was 10% more volatile than its peer group. The price/earnings (p/e) ratio averages 21 for this portfolio. The typical growth and income subaccount also has a p/e ratio of 21. In general, the higher the p/e ratio, the riskier the portfolio.

The beta (market-related risk) of this subaccount was 0.9 over the 3-year period. Beta for this entire category was also 0.9 over this same period. The market index (the S&P 500 Index for equity subaccounts) always has a beta of 1.0. The *risk-adjusted* return for this variable annuity subaccount can be described as very good.

## Expense Minimization ✓

The typical expenses incurred by growth and income subaccounts are 1.9% per year. The total expenses for First Variable Vista II Equity-Income, 2.6%, are higher than its peer group average. Total expenses include all charges to the investor (except the annual contract charge, which is always expressed as a dollar figure), including management fees, overhead, administration, and mortality expenses. The free annual withdrawals percentage is based on the account value.

| | | | |
|---|---|---|---|
| Maximum surrender charge | 5% | Total expenses | 2.6% |
| Duration of surrender charge | 5 years | Annual contract charge | $30 |
| Declining surrender charge | yes | Free annual withdrawals | 10% |

## Management ✓✓

First Variable Vista II is offered by First Variable Life Insurance Company. The subaccount and the portfolio it is modeled after were managed by John Kaweske, Ronald Lout, and Charles Mayer for the 6 years ending December 31, 1994. The portfolio's size is less than $1 million. The typical security in the portfolio has a market capitalization of $6.7 billion.

## Investment Options ✓✓✓

Investors may make additional contributions into this portfolio at any time. This is known as a flexible premium annuity. Investors in this variable annuity can choose from all of the subaccount categories below that have a check mark:

| | | |
|---|---|---|
| ___ Aggressive growth | ✓ Government bonds | ✓ Money market |
| ✓ Balanced | ✓ Growth | ___ Specialty/Sector |
| ___ Corporate bonds | ✓ Growth & income | ___ World bonds |
| ✓ Global equities (stocks) | ✓ High-yield bonds | |

## Family Rating ✓✓

There are 7 subaccounts within the First Variable Vista II family. Overall, this family of subaccounts can be described as fair on a *risk-adjusted* return basis.

The subaccounts within this variable annuity all have an *increasing* guaranteed death benefit. This means that the beneficiary is guaranteed to receive *the greater of* the contract's value on the date of the annuitant's death or the value of the original investment(s) compounded by 5% each year (less any withdrawals made).

## Summary

First Variable Vista II Equity-Income has demonstrated some pretty good returns while being about 20% safer than other growth and income subaccounts. The portfolio is now called the Tilt Utility. The contract includes both a global stock and high-yield bond portfolio, two types of investment choices not commonly found within a variable annuity contract.

The First Variable contract is one of the best. The duration of the surrender charge is low, the surrender penalty is on a declining scale, and free withdrawals are based on the contract's value, not the original principal. Co-ownership and co-annuitants are two other options not commonly found. Finally, there is an increasing death benefit.

## Profile

| | | | |
|---|---|---|---|
| Minimum investment | $250 | Telephone exchanges | yes |
| Retirement account minimum | $1,000 | Transfers allowed per year | 12 |
| Co-annuitant allowed | spouses only | Maximum issuance age | none |
| Co-owner allowed | yes | Maximum annuitization age | 85 |
| Dollar-cost averaging | yes | Number of subaccounts | 7 |
| Systematic withdrawal plans | yes | Available in all 50 states | no* |

*Not available in NY or PR.

---

**General American Separate Account 2**
**Equity Index**
700 Market Street
St. Louis, MO  63101
(800) 233-6699

| | |
|---|---|
| Performance | ✓✓ |
| Risk control | ✓✓✓ |
| Expense minimization | ✓✓✓✓✓ |
| Management | ✓✓✓ |
| Investment options | ✓ |
| Family rating | ✓✓✓ |
| Total point score | 17 points |

## Performance                                          ✓✓

During the 3-year and 5-year periods ending December 31, 1994, Equity Index had an average annual compound return of 5.0% and 7.3%, respectively. This means that a $10,000 investment made into this subaccount 5 years before that date grew to $14,200 ($11,600, if only the last 3 years of the period are used).

Compared to other growth and income variable annuity subaccounts, this one ranked in the top half for the 3-year period and in the top 15% for the 5-year period. The inception month of this subaccount was May 1988.

The year-by-year returns for this subaccount are:

| Year | Annual Return | S&P 500 |
|---|---|---|
| 1994 | 0.2% | 1.3% |
| 1993 | 8.7% | 10.1% |
| 1992 | 6.4% | 7.6% |
| 1991 | 28.9% | 30.5% |
| 1990 | −4.8% | −3.1% |
| 1989 | 28.5% | 31.7% |

## Risk Control                                          ✓✓✓

Over the 3-year period, this fund was 25% safer than the average equity subaccount. During the 5-year period, it was somewhat safer.

The typical standard deviation for growth and income subaccounts was 2.9% during the 3-year period. The standard deviation for General American Separate Account 2 Equity Index was 3.0% over this same period, which means that this subaccount was 4% more volatile than its peer group. The price/earnings (p/e) ratio averages 22 for this portfolio. The typical growth and income subaccount has a p/e ratio of 21. In general, the higher the p/e ratio, the riskier the portfolio.

The beta (market-related risk) of this subaccount was 1.0 over the 3-year period. Beta for this entire category was 0.9 over this same period. The market index (the S&P 500 Index for equity subaccounts) always has a beta of 1.0. The *risk-adjusted* return for this variable annuity subaccount can be described as good.

## Expense Minimization    ✓✓✓✓

The typical expenses incurred by growth and income subaccounts are 1.9% per year. The total expenses for General American Separate Account 2 Equity Index, 1.3%, are lower than its peer group average. Total expenses include all charges to the investor (except the annual contract charge, which is always expressed as a dollar figure), including management fees, overhead, administration, and mortality expenses. The free annual withdrawals percentage is based on the account value.

| | | | |
|---|---|---|---|
| Maximum surrender charge | 9% | Total expenses | 1.3% |
| Duration of surrender charge | 9 years | Annual contract charge | $0 |
| Declining surrender charge | no | Free annual withdrawals | 10% |

## Management    ✓✓✓

General American Separate Account 2 is offered by General American Life Insurance Company. The company has a Duff & Phelps rating of AA and an A.M. Best rating of A+. The portfolio was managed by Doug Koester for the 6 years ending December 31, 1994. The portfolio's size is $16 million. The typical security in the portfolio has a market capitalization of $13.2 billion.

## Investment Options    ✓

Investors may make additional contributions into this portfolio at any time. This is known as a flexible premium annuity. Investors in this variable annuity can choose from all of the subaccount categories below that have a check mark:

| | | |
|---|---|---|
| ___ Aggressive growth | ___ Government bonds | ✓ Money market |
| ✓ Balanced | ✓ Growth | ___ Specialty/Sector |
| ✓ Corporate bonds | ✓ Growth & income | ___ World bonds |
| ___ Global equities (stocks) | ___ High-yield bonds | |

## Family Rating    ✓✓✓

There are 7 subaccounts within the General American Separate Account 2 family. Overall, this family of subaccounts can be described as good on a *risk-adjusted* return basis. The subaccounts within this variable annuity all have a death benefit based on the value at the date of death (what is referred to in the industry as "accumulated value"). Unlike the death benefit found with most variable annuities, the accumulated value death benefit does not protect the beneficiary from possible market loss.

## Summary

General American Separate Account 2 Equity Index has shown some very respectable returns while subjecting its investors to 25% less risk than the typical growth and income subaccount. The contract has some of the lowest expenses in the industry.

## Profile

| | | | |
|---|---|---|---|
| Minimum investment | $25 | Telephone exchanges | yes |
| Retirement account minimum | $25 | Transfers allowed per year | unlimited |
| Co-annuitant allowed | no | Maximum issuance age | none |
| Co-owner allowed | no | Maximum annuitization age | none |
| Dollar-cost averaging | no | Number of subaccounts | 7 |
| Systematic withdrawal plans | yes | Available in all 50 states | no* |

*Not available in NY.

---

**Hartford Director**
**Index Fund**
P.O. Box 2999
Hartford, CT 06104-2999
(800) 862-6668

| | |
|---|---|
| Performance | ✓✓ |
| Risk control | ✓✓✓ |
| Expense minimization | ✓✓✓✓ |
| Management | ✓✓✓ |
| Investment options | ✓✓✓✓ |
| Family rating | ✓✓✓ |
| Total point score | 19 points |

## Performance                                                    ✓✓

During the 3-year and 5-year periods ending December 31, 1994, Index Fund had an average annual compound return of 4.3% and 6.6%, respectively. This means that a $10,000 investment made into this subaccount 5 years before that date grew to $13,800 ($11,300, if only the last 3 years of the period are used).

Compared to other growth and income variable annuity subaccounts, this one ranked in the bottom half for the 3-year period but in the top 40% for the 5-year period. The inception month of this subaccount was May 1987. This subaccount is modeled (cloned) after the Hartford Index Fund, which also had an inception date of May 1987, and has an asset base of $130 million.

The year-by-year returns for this subaccount are:

| Year | Annual Return | S&P 500 |
|---|---|---|
| 1994 | −0.3% | 1.3% |
| 1993 | 7.8% | 10.1% |
| 1992 | 5.5% | 7.6% |
| 1991 | 27.9% | 30.5% |
| 1990 | −5.2% | −3.1% |
| 1989 | 28.7% | 31.7% |
| 1988 | 14.8% | 16.6% |

## Risk Control                                                    ✓✓✓

Over the 3-year period, this fund was 20% safer than the average equity subaccount. During the 5-year period, it was slightly safer.

The typical standard deviation for growth and income subaccounts was 2.9% during the 3-year period. The standard deviation for Hartford Director Index Fund was 3.1% over this same period, which means that this subaccount was 6% more volatile than its peer group. The price/earnings (p/e) ratio averages 22 for this portfolio. The typical growth and income subaccount has a p/e ratio of 21. In general, the higher the p/e ratio, the riskier the portfolio.

The beta (market-related risk) of this subaccount was 1.0 over the 3-year period. Beta for this entire category was 0.9 over this same period. The market index (the S&P 500 Index for equity subaccounts) always has a beta of 1.0. The *risk-adjusted* return for this variable annuity subaccount can be described as good.

## Expense Minimization ✓✓✓

The typical expenses incurred by growth and income subaccounts are 1.9% per year. The total expenses for Hartford Director Index Fund, 1.9%, are identical to its peer group average. Total expenses include all charges to the investor (except the annual contract charge, which is always expressed as a dollar figure), including management fees, overhead, administration, and mortality expenses. The free annual withdrawals percentage is based on the original principal.

| | | | |
|---|---|---|---|
| Maximum surrender charge | 7% | Total expenses | 1.9% |
| Duration of surrender charge | 7 years | Annual contract charge | $25 |
| Declining surrender charge | yes | Free annual withdrawals | 10% |

## Management ✓✓✓

Hartford Director is offered by Hartford Life Insurance Company. The company has a Duff & Phelps rating of AAA and an A.M. Best rating of A++. The portfolio was managed by Rodger Metzger for the 6 years ending December 31, 1994. The portfolio's size is $95 million. The typical security in the portfolio has a market capitalization of $13.2 billion.

## Investment Options ✓✓✓

Investors may make additional contributions into this portfolio at any time. This is known as a flexible premium annuity. Investors in this variable annuity can choose from all of the subaccount categories below that have a check mark:

| | | |
|---|---|---|
| ✓ Aggressive growth | ✓ Government bonds | ✓ Money market |
| ✓ Balanced | ✓ Growth | ___ Specialty/Sector |
| ✓ Corporate bonds | ✓ Growth & income | ___ World bonds |
| ✓ Global equities (stocks) | ___ High-yield bonds | |

## Family Rating ✓✓✓

There are 9 subaccounts within the Hartford Director family. Overall, this family of subaccounts can be described as good on a *risk-adjusted* return basis.

The subaccounts within this variable annuity all have an *increasing* guaranteed death benefit. This means that the beneficiary is guaranteed to receive *the greater of* the contract's value on the date of the annuitant's death or the value of the original investment(s) compounded by 5% each year (less any withdrawals made).

## Summary

Hartford Director Index Fund is a growth and income subaccount that lives up to its name. Since its inception, this equity-oriented portfolio has come close to matching the returns offered by the S&P 500. The title of this account does not reveal its safety factor. On a risk-adjusted return basis, this portfolio has done better than the indexes. In fact, it has been about 25% safer than the average equity subaccount.

The two strong suits of the Hartford Director variable annuity contract are its expense minimization policy and the fine choice of investment options contract owners have to choose from.

## Profile

| | | | |
|---|---|---|---|
| Minimum investment | $50 | Telephone exchanges | yes |
| Retirement account minimum | $1,000 | Transfers allowed per year | unlimited |
| Co-annuitant allowed | yes | Maximum issuance age | 85 |
| Co-owner allowed | yes | Maximum annuitization age | 90 |
| Dollar-cost averaging | yes | Number of subaccounts | 9 |
| Systematic withdrawal plans | yes | Available in all 50 states | yes |

---

**Life of Virginia Commonwealth**
**Life of Virginia Common Stock Index**
6610 West Broad Street
Richmond, VA  23230
(800) 521-8884

| | |
|---|---|
| Performance | ✓✓✓✓ |
| Risk control | ✓✓✓ |
| Expense minimization | ✓✓ |
| Management | ✓✓✓✓ |
| Investment options | ✓✓✓✓ |
| Family rating | ✓✓✓ |
| Total point score | 20 points |

## Performance                                          ✓✓✓✓

During the 3-year and 5-year periods ending December 31, 1994, Life of Virginia Common Stock Index had an average annual compound return of 6.3% and 7.2%, respectively. This means that a $10,000 investment made into this subaccount 5 years before that date grew to $14,200 ($12,000, if only the last 3 years of the period are used).

Compared to other growth and income variable annuity subaccounts, this one ranked in the top third for the 3-year period and in the top 40% for the 5-year period. The inception month of this subaccount was May 1988.

The year-by-year returns for this subaccount are:

| Year | Annual Return | S&P 500 |
|---|---|---|
| 1994 | −1.2% | 1.3% |
| 1993 | 13.3% | 10.1% |
| 1992 | 7.2% | 7.6% |
| 1991 | 32.9% | 30.5% |
| 1990 | −11.2% | −3.1% |
| 1989 | 24.1% | 31.7% |

## Risk Control                                          ✓✓✓

Over the 3-year period, this fund was 30% safer than the average equity subaccount. During the 5-year period, it was slightly safer.

The typical standard deviation for growth and income subaccounts was 2.9% during the 3-year period. The standard deviation for Life of Virginia Commonwealth Common Stock Index was 3.1% over this same period, which means that this subaccount was 8% more volatile than its peer group. The price/earnings (p/e) ratio averages 22 for this portfolio. The typical growth and income subaccount return has a p/e ratio of 21. In general, the higher the p/e ratio, the riskier the portfolio.

The beta (market-related risk) of this subaccount was 1.0 over the 3-year period. Beta for this entire category was 0.9 over this same period. The market index (the S&P 500 Index for equity subaccounts) always has a beta of 1.0. The *risk-adjusted* return for this variable annuity subaccount can be described as good.

## Expense Minimization ✓✓

The typical expenses incurred by growth and income subaccounts are 1.9% per year. The total expenses for Life of Virginia Commonwealth Life of Virginia Common Stock Index, 2.2%, are higher than its peer group average. Total expenses include all charges to the investor (except the annual contract charge, which is always expressed as a dollar figure), including management fees, overhead, administration, and mortality expenses. The free annual withdrawals percentage is based on the account value.

| | | | |
|---|---|---|---|
| Maximum surrender charge | 6% | Total expenses | 2.2% |
| Duration of surrender charge | 6 years | Annual contract charge | $30 |
| Declining surrender charge | yes | Free annual withdrawals | 10% |

## Management ✓✓✓✓

Life of Virginia Commonwealth is offered by Life Insurance Company of Virginia. The company has a Duff & Phelps rating of AA+ and an A.M. Best rating of A+. The portfolio was managed by Mark Burka for the 7 years ending December 31, 1994. The portfolio's size is $3 million. The typical security in the portfolio has a market capitalization of $13.6 billion.

## Investment Options ✓✓✓✓

Investors may make additional contributions into this portfolio at any time. This is known as a flexible premium annuity. Investors in this variable annuity can choose from all of the subaccount categories below that have a check mark:

| | | |
|---|---|---|
| ✓ Aggressive growth | ✓ Government bonds | ✓ Money market |
| ✓ Balanced | ✓ Growth | ___ Specialty/Sector |
| ✓ Corporate bonds | ✓ Growth & income | ___ World bonds |
| ✓ Global equities (stocks) | ✓ High-yield bonds | |

## Family Rating ✓✓✓

There are 22 subaccounts within the Life of Virginia Commonwealth family. Overall, this family of subaccounts can be described as good on a *risk-adjusted* return basis.

The subaccounts within this variable annuity all have an *increasing* guaranteed death benefit. This means that the beneficiary is guaranteed to receive *the greater of* the contract's value on the date of the annuitant's death or the value of the original investment(s) compounded by 5% each year (less any withdrawals made).

## Summary

Great performance and management—these are the words that best describe the Life of Virginia Commonwealth Common Stock Index portfolio. The track record of this subaccount is quite good; once you factor in the risk level, the rating changes from very good to excellent.

Burka has done a fine job in running this growth and income investment. Besides the stock index subaccount, a number of other great choices are offered by the Life of Virginia variable annuity.

## Profile

| | | | |
|---|---|---|---|
| Minimum investment | $5,000 | Telephone exchanges | yes |
| Retirement account minimum | $5,000 | Transfers allowed per year | 12 |
| Co-annuitant allowed | no | Maximum issuance age | 75 |
| Co-owner allowed | yes | Maximum annuitization age | none |
| Dollar-cost averaging | yes | Number of subaccounts | 22 |
| Systematic withdrawal plans | yes | Available in all 50 states | no* |

*Not available in ME, NY, or WA.

---

**Lincoln National American Legacy II**
**Growth-Income**
P.O. Box 2340
Fort Wayne, IN  46801
(800) 421-9900

| | |
|---|---|
| Performance | ✓✓ |
| Risk control | ✓✓✓✓ |
| Expense minimization | ✓✓✓✓ |
| Management | ✓✓✓✓ |
| Investment options | ✓✓✓ |
| Family rating | ✓✓✓✓ |
| Total point score | 21 points |

## Performance                                              ✓✓

During the 3-year and 5-year periods ending December 31, 1994, Growth-Income had an average annual compound return of 5.9% and 6.9%, respectively. This means that a $10,000 investment made into this subaccount 5 years before that date grew to $14,000 ($11,900, if only the last 3 years of the period are used).

Compared to other growth and income variable annuity subaccounts, this one ranked in the bottom half for the 3-year period but in the top half for the 5-year period. The inception month of this subaccount was February 1984. This subaccount is modeled (cloned) after the Investment Company of America, which had an inception date of January 1934, and has an asset base of $19 billion.

The year-by-year returns for this subaccount are:

| Year | Annual Return | S&P 500 |
|---|---|---|
| 1994 | 0.7% | 1.3% |
| 1993 | 10.8% | 10.1% |
| 1992 | 6.5% | 7.6% |
| 1991 | 22.5% | 30.5% |
| 1990 | −3.9% | −3.1% |
| 1989 | 23.8% | 31.7% |
| 1988 | 12.9% | 16.6% |
| 1987 | −0.7% | 5.3% |

# Risk Control ✓✓✓✓

Over the 3-year period, this fund was 40% safer than the average equity subaccount. During the 5-year period, it was a third safer.

The typical standard deviation for growth and income subaccounts was 2.9% during the 3-year period. The standard deviation for Lincoln National American Legacy II Growth-Income was 2.5% over this same period, which means that this subaccount was 15% less volatile than its peer group. The price/earnings (p/e) ratio averages 22 for this portfolio. The typical growth and income subaccount has a p/e ratio of 21. In general, the higher the p/e ratio, the riskier the portfolio.

The beta (market-related risk) of this subaccount was 0.8 over the 3-year period. Beta for this entire category was 0.9 over this same period. The market index (the S&P 500 Index for equity subaccounts) always has a beta of 1.0. The *risk-adjusted* return for this variable annuity subaccount can be described as very good.

# Expense Minimization ✓✓✓✓

The typical expenses incurred by growth and income subaccounts are 1.9% per year. The total expenses for Lincoln National American Legacy II Growth-Income, 1.9%, are lower than its peer group average. Total expenses include all charges to the investor (except the annual contract charge, which is always expressed as a dollar figure), including management fees, overhead, administration, and mortality expenses. The free annual withdrawals percentage is based on the original principal.

| | | | |
|---|---|---|---|
| Maximum surrender charge | 6% | Total expenses | 1.9% |
| Duration of surrender charge | 7 years | Annual contract charge | $35 |
| Declining surrender charge | yes | Free annual withdrawals | 10% |

# Management ✓✓✓✓

Lincoln National American Legacy II is offered by Lincoln National Life Insurance Company. The company has a Duff & Phelps rating of AAA and an A.M. Best rating of A+. The portfolio has been managed by Capital Guardian (American Funds) since its inception. The portfolio's size is $2.7 billion. The typical security in the portfolio has a market capitalization of $11 billion.

# Investment Options ✓✓✓

Investors may make additional contributions into this portfolio at any time. This is known as a flexible premium annuity. Investors in this variable annuity can choose from all of the subaccount categories below that have a check mark:

| | | |
|---|---|---|
| ___ Aggressive growth | ✓ Government bonds | ✓ Money market |
| ✓ Balanced | ✓ Growth | ___ Specialty/Sector |
| ___ Corporate bonds | ✓ Growth & income | ___ World bonds |
| ✓ Global equities (stocks) | ✓ High-yield bonds | |

# Family Rating ✓✓✓✓

There are 7 subaccounts within the Lincoln National American Legacy II family. Overall, this family of subaccounts can be described as very good on a *risk-adjusted* return basis.

## Summary

Lincoln National American Legacy II Growth-Income is yet another investment managed by Capital Guardian and Trust Company and included in this book. So many good things can be said about this entire variable annuity family (and the large mutual fund family this company also oversees), I may be beginning to sound as though they have sent me some kind of bonus.

This variable annuity is run by some very frugal men and women who do not like to advertise. For a company that has shunned publicity for many years (and continues to do so), one may wonder how Legacy II and the American Funds have attracted so much money. The answer lies in consistency—a steady track record that looks better the longer it is studied. This is one of the few companies run by a board of directors that is more concerned with existing investors than with offering some type of gimmicky new product or promotional piece as a hook for new investors.

The Lincoln National American Legacy II Growth-Income subaccount is highly recommended. It is one of my favorites. Enough said.

## Profile

| | | | |
|---|---|---|---|
| Minimum investment | $300 | Telephone exchanges | yes |
| Retirement account minimum | $1,500 | Transfers allowed per year | 12 |
| Co-annuitant allowed | no | Maximum issuance age | 75 |
| Co-owner allowed | yes | Maximum annuitization age | 85 |
| Dollar-cost averaging | yes | Number of subaccounts | 7 |
| Systematic withdrawal plans | yes | Available in all 50 states | no* |

*Not available in NY.

---

**Mass Mutual Separate Account 2 Flex V Annuity**
**Equity Fund**
1295 State Street
Springfield, MA  01111
(800) 272-2216

| | |
|---|---|
| Performance | ✓✓ |
| Risk control | ✓✓✓✓ |
| Expense minimization | ✓✓✓✓ |
| Management | ✓✓✓✓ |
| Investment options | ✓ |
| Family rating | ✓✓✓ |
| Total point score | 18 points |

## Performance    ✓✓

During the 3-year and 5-year periods ending December 31, 1994, Equity Fund had an average annual compound return of 6.6% and 8.1%, respectively (12.2% for 10 years). This means that a $10,000 investment made into this subaccount 5 years before that date grew to $14,800 ($12,100, if only the last 3 years of the period are used).

Compared to other growth and income variable annuity subaccounts, this one ranked in the bottom half for the 3-year period but in the top half for the 5-year period. The inception month of this subaccount was April 1987.

The year-by-year returns for this subaccount are:

| Year | Annual Return | S&P 500 |
|---|---|---|
| 1994 | 2.8% | 1.3% |
| 1993 | 8.1% | 10.1% |
| 1992 | 9.1% | 7.6% |
| 1991 | 24.0% | 30.5% |
| 1990 | −1.7% | −3.1% |
| 1989 | 21.6% | 31.7% |
| 1988 | 15.0% | 16.6% |
| 1987 | 0.8% | 5.3% |

## Risk Control ✓✓✓

Over the 3-year period, this fund was 40% safer than the average equity subaccount. During the 5-year period, it was 25% safer.

The typical standard deviation for growth and income subaccounts was 2.9% during the 3-year period. The standard deviation for Mass Mutual Separate Account 2 Flex V Annuity Equity Fund was 2.5% over this same period, which means that this subaccount was 13% less volatile than its peer group. The price/earnings (p/e) ratio averages 21 for this portfolio. The typical growth and income subaccount also has a p/e ratio of 21. In general, the higher the p/e ratio, the riskier the portfolio.

The beta (market-related risk) of this subaccount was 0.8 over the 3-year period. Beta for the entire category was 0.9 over this same period. The market index (the S&P 500 Index for equity subaccounts) always has a beta of 1.0. The *risk-adjusted* return for this variable annuity subaccount can be described as good.

## Expense Minimization ✓✓✓

The typical expenses incurred by growth and income subaccounts are 1.9% per year. The total expenses for Mass Mutual Separate Account 2 Flex V Annuity Equity Fund, 1.8%, are lower than its peer group average. Total expenses include all charges to the investor (except the annual contract charge, which is always expressed as a dollar figure), including management fees, overhead, administration, and mortality expenses. The free annual withdrawals percentage is based on the account value.

| | | | |
|---|---|---|---|
| Maximum surrender charge | 8% | Total expenses | 1.8% |
| Duration of surrender charge | 9 years | Annual contract charge | $35 |
| Declining surrender charge | no | Free annual withdrawals | 10% |

## Management ✓✓✓

Mass Mutual Separate Account 2 Flex V Annuity is offered by Massachusetts Mutual Life Insurance Company. The company has a Duff & Phelps rating of AAA. The portfolio has been managed by David B. Salerno since its inception. The portfolio's size is $525 million. The typical security in the portfolio has a market capitalization of $6.6 billion.

## Investment Options ✓

Investors may make additional contributions into this portfolio at any time. This is known as a flexible premium annuity. Investors in this variable annuity can choose from all of the subaccount categories below that have a check mark:

| | | |
|---|---|---|
| ___ Aggressive growth | ___ Government bonds | ✓ Money market |
| ✓ Balanced | ___ Growth | ___ Specialty/Sector |
| ✓ Corporate bonds | ✓ Growth & income | ___ World bonds |
| ___ Global equities (stocks) | ___ High-yield bonds | |

## Family Rating ✓✓✓

There are 5 subaccounts within the Mass Mutual Separate Account 2 Flex V Annuity family. Overall, this family of subaccounts can be described as good on a *risk-adjusted* return basis.

## Summary

Mass Mutual Separate Account 2 Flex V Annuity Equity Fund is a fine example of what can happen when some great money managers are in charge. By providing its contract owners with decent returns and one-third less risk than with comparable accounts elsewhere, this growth and income subaccount continues to attract a large number of investors.

Mass Mutual Separate Account 2 Flex V Annuity can boast of an expense minimization record that is about 20% less than its competitors'. This type of control is particularly important for a conservative portfolio that contains a moderate weighting in bonds and cash. The actual contract is also pleasing: the low surrender charge and schedule make it a delight to uncertain investors. Finally, withdrawal privileges (based on account value, not original principal) during the penalty period are some of the most liberal in the industry. It is hoped that Mass Mutual will add more investment options to the present fine stable of offerings.

## Profile

| | | | |
|---|---|---|---|
| Minimum investment | $50 | Telephone exchanges | yes |
| Retirement account minimum | $50 | Transfers allowed per year | 4 |
| Co-annuitant allowed | no | Maximum issuance age | 75 |
| Co-owner allowed | yes | Maximum annuitization age | none |
| Dollar-cost averaging | yes | Number of subaccounts | 5 |
| Systematic withdrawal plans | yes | Available in all 50 states | yes |

---

**Minnesota Mutual Multioption A**
**Index 500**
400 North Robert Street
St. Paul, MN  55101-2098
(800) 328-9343

---

| | |
|---|---|
| Performance | ✓✓ |
| Risk control | ✓✓✓ |
| Expense minimization | ✓✓✓✓ |
| Management | ✓✓✓ |
| Investment options | ✓✓✓✓ |
| Family rating | ✓✓✓ |
| Total point score | 19 points |

# Performance   ✓✓

During the 3-year and 5-year periods ending December 31, 1994, Index 500 had an average annual compound return of 4.7% and 6.9%, respectively. This means that a $10,000 investment made into this subaccount 5 years before that date grew to $14,000 ($11,500, if only the last 3 years of the period are used).

Compared to other growth and income variable annuity subaccounts, this one ranked in the bottom half of the 3-year period but in the top quartile for the 5-year period. The inception month of this subaccount was June 1987. This subaccount is modeled (cloned) after the MIMLIC Series Fund Index 500 Portfolio, which had an inception date of April 1987, and has an asset base of $60 million.

The year-by-year returns for this subaccount are:

| Year | Annual Return | S&P 500 |
|------|------|------|
| 1994 | −0.1% | 1.3% |
| 1993 | 8.4% | 10.1% |
| 1992 | 6.0% | 7.6% |
| 1991 | 28.1% | 30.5% |
| 1990 | −5.1% | −3.1% |
| 1989 | 29.0% | 31.7% |
| 1988 | 16.1% | 16.6% |

# Risk Control   ✓✓✓

Over the 3-year period, this fund was 25% safer than the average equity subaccount. During the 5-year period, it was slightly safer.

The typical standard deviation for growth and income subaccounts was 2.9% during the 3-year period. The standard deviation for Minnesota Mutual Multioption A Index 500 was 3.1% over this same period, which means that this subaccount was 6% more volatile than its peer group. The price/earnings (p/e) ratio averages 22 for this portfolio. The typical growth and income subaccount was a p/e ratio of 21. In general, the higher the p/e ratio, the riskier the portfolio.

The beta (market-related risk) of this subaccount was 1.0 over the 3-year period. Beta for this entire category was 0.9 over this same period. The market index (the S&P Index for equity subaccounts) always has a beta of 1.0. The *risk-adjusted* return for this variable annuity subaccount can be described as good.

# Expense Minimization   ✓✓✓✓

The typical expenses incurred by growth and income subaccounts are 1.9% per year. The total expenses for Minnesota Mutual Multioption A Index 500, 1.8%, are lower than its peer group average. Total expenses include all charges to the investor (except the annual contract charge, which is always expressed as a dollar figure), including management fees, overhead, administration, and mortality expenses. The free annual withdrawals percentage is based on the account value after the first year.

| | | | |
|---|---|---|---|
| Maximum surrender charge | 9% | Total expenses | 1.8% |
| Duration of surrender charge | 10 years | Annual contract charge | $0 |
| Declining surrender charge | no | Free annual withdrawals | 10% |

## Management    ✓✓✓

Minnesota Mutual Multioption A is offered by Minnesota Mutual Life Insurance Company. The company has a Duff & Phelps rating of AAA and an A.M. Best rating of A++. The portfolio was managed by James P. Tatera for the 7 years ending December 31, 1994. The portfolio's size is $45 million. The typical security in the portfolio has a market capitalization of $13.1 billion.

## Investment Options    ✓✓✓✓

Investors may make additional contributions into this portfolio at any time. This is known as a flexible premium annuity. Investors in this variable annuity can choose from all of the subaccount categories below that have a check mark:

| | | |
|---|---|---|
| ✓ Aggressive growth | ✓ Government bonds | ✓ Money market |
| ✓ Balanced | ✓ Growth | ___ Specialty/Sector |
| ✓ Corporate bonds | ✓ Growth & income | ___ World bonds |
| ✓ Global equities (stocks) | ___ High-yield bonds | |

## Family Rating    ✓✓✓

There are 9 subaccounts within the Minnesota Mutual Multioption A family. Overall, this family of subaccounts can be described as good on a *risk-adjusted* return basis.

## Summary

Minnesota Mutual Multioption A Index 500 is a nice choice, particularly for the risk-conscious growth and income investor. In the early 1990s, this subaccount was close to 25% safer than the typical equity portfolio.

The duration of the surrender charge, 10 years, and the maximum surrender charge of 9% (which is not declining) are the two major negatives to this investment vehicle, although both of these disadvantages are unimportant for long-term investors. On a positive note, the maximum issuance and annuitization ages are quite high, and unlimited telephone exchanges are allowed. The contract's expense minimization and overall family rating represent this investment vehicle's real strong suits.

## Profile

| | | | |
|---|---|---|---|
| Minimum investment | $5,000 | Telephone exchanges | yes |
| Retirement account minimum | $5,000 | Transfers allowed per year | unlimited |
| Co-annuitant allowed | yes | Maximum issuance age | 85 |
| Co-owner allowed | spouses only | Maximum annuitization age | 95 |
| Dollar-cost averaging | yes | Number of subaccounts | 9 |
| Systematic withdrawal plans | yes | Available in all 50 states | no* |

*Not available in NY.

---

**Mutual of America Separate Account 2**
**All America**
666 Fifth Avenue
New York, NY 10103
(800) 468-3785

---

| | |
|---|---|
| Performance | ✓ |
| Risk control | ✓✓ |
| Expense minimization | ✓✓✓ |
| Management | ✓ |
| Investment options | ✓✓✓ |
| Family rating | ✓✓✓ |
| Total point score | 13 points |

---

# Performance   ✓

During the 3-year and 5-year periods ending December 31, 1994, All America had an average annual compound return of 4.1% and 6.3%, respectively. This means that a $10,000 investment made into this subaccount 5 years before that date grew to $13,600 ($11,300, if only the last 3 years of the period are used).

Compared to other growth and income variable annuity subaccounts, this one ranked in the bottom half for the 3-year and 5-year periods. The inception month of this subaccount was January 1985.

The year-by-year returns for this subaccount are:

| Year | Annual Return | S&P 500 |
|---|---|---|
| 1994 | −0.1% | 1.3% |
| 1993 | 10.7% | 10.1% |
| 1992 | 2.2% | 7.6% |
| 1991 | 23.2% | 30.5% |
| 1990 | −2.5% | −3.1% |
| 1989 | 24.7% | 31.7% |
| 1988 | 9.2% | 16.6% |
| 1987 | 8.9% | 5.3% |

# Risk Control   ✓✓

Over the 3-year and 5-year periods, this fund was a little safer than the average equity subaccount.

The typical standard deviation for growth and income subaccounts was 2.9% during the 3-year period. The standard deviation for Mutual of America Separate Account 2 All America was 3.0% over this same period, which means that this subaccount was 4% more volatile than its peer group. The price/earnings (p/e) ratio averages 22 for this portfolio. The typical growth and income subaccount has a p/e ratio of 21. In general, the higher the p/e ratio, the riskier the portfolio.

The beta (market-related risk) of this subaccount was 0.9 over the 3-year period. Beta for this entire category was also 0.9 over this same period. The market index (the S&P 500 Index for equity subaccounts) always has a beta of 1.0. The *risk-adjusted* return for this variable annuity subaccount can be described as good.

## Expense Minimization                                        ✓✓✓

The typical expenses incurred by growth and income subaccounts are 1.9% per year. The total expenses for Mutual of America Separate Account 2 All America, 2.0%, are higher than its peer group average. Total expenses include all charges to the investor (except the annual contract charge, which is always expressed as a dollar figure), including management fees, overhead, administration, and mortality expenses. The free annual withdrawals percentage is based on the account value.

| | | | |
|---|---|---|---|
| Maximum surrender charge | 0% | Total expenses | 2.0% |
| Duration of surrender charge | n/a | Annual contract charge | $24 |
| Declining surrender charge | n/a | Free annual withdrawals | 10% |

## Management                                                      ✓

Mutual of America Separate Account 2 is offered by Mutual of America Life Insurance Company. The company has a Duff & Phelps rating of AA+ and an A.M. Best rating of A+. The portfolio was managed by Thomas Verage for the 5 years ending December 31, 1994. The portfolio's size is $125 million. The typical security in the portfolio has a market capitalization of $9.1 billion.

## Investment Options                                          ✓✓✓

Investors may make additional contributions into this portfolio at any time. This is known as a flexible premium annuity. Investors in this variable annuity can choose from all of the subaccount categories below that have a check mark:

| | | |
|---|---|---|
| ___ Aggressive growth | ___ Government bonds | ✓ Money market |
| ✓ Balanced | ✓ Growth | ___ Specialty/Sector |
| ✓ Corporate bonds | ✓ Growth & income | ___ World bonds |
| ✓ Global equities (stocks) | ___ High-yield bonds | |

## Family Rating                                               ✓✓✓

There are 12 subaccounts within the Mutual of America Separate Account 2 family. Overall, this family of subaccounts can be described as good on a *risk-adjusted* return basis. The subaccounts within this variable annuity all have a death benefit based on the value at the date of death (what is referred to in the industry as "accumulated value"). Unlike the death benefit found with most variable annuities, the accumulated value death benefit does not protect the beneficiary from possible market loss.

## Summary

Mutual of America Separate Account 2 All America is a much better investment than the numbers might suggest. As an example, even though it has outperformed the S&P 500 only a few times, it has come close in a number of other years—a quite impressive achievement when you consider this is a growth *and* income subaccount. It has also been conservative regarding risk control.

Some features are worth noting about this Mutual of America variable annuity contract. First, minimum investment for both nonqualified and qualified accounts is quite low. Second, a co-annuitant can be listed—a great boon for individuals or couples who want to postpone triggering a tax event as long as possible. Third, unlimited telephone exchanges are allowed—you can move your money around without paying any type of fee. Fourth, there is no maximum issuance age—no matter how old you are, this investment is open to you. Fifth, there are a dozen portfolios to choose from; All America is just one of the options.

## Profile

| | | | |
|---|---|---|---|
| Minimum investment | $10 | Telephone exchanges | yes |
| Retirement account minimum | $10 | Transfers allowed per year | unlimited |
| Co-annuitant allowed | yes | Maximum issuance age | none |
| Co-owner allowed | no | Maximum annuitization age | 70.5 |
| Dollar-cost averaging | no | Number of subaccounts | 12 |
| Systematic withdrawal plans | yes | Available in all 50 states | yes |

---

**Pacific Mutual Select Variable Annuity
Equity-Income**
700 Newport Center Drive
P.O. Box 7500
Newport Beach, CA 92658-7500
(800) 800-7681

---

| | |
|---|---|
| Performance | ✓✓ |
| Risk control | ✓✓ |
| Expense minimization | ✓✓ |
| Management | ✓✓ |
| Investment options | ✓✓✓✓ |
| Family rating | ✓✓ |
| Total point score | 14 points |

## Performance                                                    ✓✓

During the 3-year and 5-year periods ending December 31, 1994, Equity-Income had an average annual compound return of 3.1% and 5.4%, respectively. This means that a $10,000 investment made into this subaccount 5 years before that date grew to $13,000 ($11,000, if only the last 3 years of the period are used).

Compared to other growth and income variable annuity subaccounts, this one ranked in the bottom half for the 3-year and 5-year periods. The inception month of this subaccount was August 1990. The performance figures (shown below) for periods before the subaccount's inception in August 1990 are hypothetical, based on the underlying clone fund's returns. This subaccount is modeled (cloned) after the Pacific Select Fund Equity-Income Series, which had an inception date of January 1988, and has an asset base of $30 million.

The year-by-year returns for this subaccount and the portfolio it is modeled after are:

| Year | Annual Return | S&P 500 |
|---|---|---|
| 1994 | −1.5% | 1.3% |
| 1993 | 7.0% | 10.1% |
| 1992 | 4.1% | 7.6% |
| 1991 | 30.1% | 30.5% |
| 1990 | −8.9% | −3.1% |
| 1989 | 26.5% | 31.7% |

## Risk Control                                                   ✓✓

Over the 3-year and 5-year periods, this fund was as safe as the average equity subaccount.

The typical standard deviation for growth and income subaccounts was 2.9% during the 3-year period. The standard deviation for Pacific Mutual Select Variable Annuity Equity-Income was 3.4% over this same period, which means that this subaccount was 19% more volatile than its peer group. The price/earnings (p/e) ratio averages 21 for this portfolio. The typical growth and income subaccount also has a p/e ratio of 21. In general, the higher the p/e ratio, the riskier the portfolio.

The beta (market-related risk) of this subaccount was 1.0 over the 3-year period. Beta for this entire category was 0.9 over this same period. The market index (the S&P 500 Index for equity subaccounts) always has a beta of 1.0. The *risk-adjusted* return for this variable annuity subaccount can be described as fair.

## Expense Minimization                                    ✓✓

The typical expenses incurred by growth and income subaccounts are 1.9% per year. The total expenses for Pacific Mutual Select Variable Annuity Equity-Income, 2.2%, are higher than its peer group average. Total expenses include all charges to the investor (except the annual contract charge, which is always expressed as a dollar figure), including management fees, overhead, administration, and mortality expenses. The free annual withdrawals percentage is based on the original principal.

| | | | |
|---|---|---|---|
| Maximum surrender charge | 6% | Total expenses | 2.2% |
| Duration of surrender charge | 6 years | Annual contract charge | $30 |
| Declining surrender charge | yes | Free annual withdrawals | 10% |

## Management                                               ✓✓

Pacific Mutual Select Variable Annuity is offered by Pacific Mutual Life Insurance Company. The company has a Duff & Phelps rating of AA+ and an A.M. Best rating of A+. The subaccount and the portfolio it is modeled after were managed by Robert Kirby, James Rothenberg, and Douglas Urban for the 6 years ending December 31, 1994. The portfolio's size is $18 million. The typical security in the portfolio has a market capitalization of $7.2 billion.

## Investment Options                                       ✓✓✓✓

Investors may make additional contributions into this portfolio at any time. This is known as a flexible premium annuity. Investors in this variable annuity can choose from all of the subaccount categories below that have a check mark:

| | | |
|---|---|---|
| ___ Aggressive growth | ✓ Government bonds | ✓ Money market |
| ✓ Balanced | ✓ Growth | ___ Specialty/Sector |
| ✓ Corporate bonds | ✓ Growth & income | ___ World bonds |
| ✓ Global equities (stocks) | ✓ High-yield bonds | |

## Family Rating                                            ✓✓

There are 9 subaccounts within the Pacific Mutual Select Variable Annuity family. Overall, this family of subaccounts can be described as fair on a *risk-adjusted* return basis.

## Summary

Pacific Mutual Select Variable Annuity Equity-Income is a fine choice for the growth and income investor. This subaccount has had respectable returns without incurring any added risk.

The expenses for this contract are a little on the high side, but this will change once the portfolios become bigger. This is a fine investment that offers contract owners the ability to move into a global stock or high-yield bond portfolio. The contract includes some very nice features. This variable annuity is recommended.

## Profile

| | | | |
|---|---|---|---|
| Minimum investment | $2,000 | Telephone exchanges | yes |
| Retirement account minimum | $5,000 | Transfers allowed per year | unlimited |
| Co-annuitant allowed | yes | Maximum issuance age | 85 |
| Co-owner allowed | yes | Maximum annuitization age | 95 |
| Dollar-cost averaging | yes | Number of subaccounts | 9 |
| Systematic withdrawal plans | yes | Available in all 50 states | no* |

*Not available in NY.

---

**Prudential Discovery Plus**
**High Dividend Stock**
Prudential Plaza
Newark, NJ 07102-3777
(201) 802-6000

| | |
|---|---|
| Performance | ✓✓✓✓✓ |
| Risk control | ✓✓✓✓✓ |
| Expense minimization | ✓✓✓✓ |
| Management | ✓✓✓✓✓ |
| Investment options | ✓✓✓ |
| Family rating | ✓✓✓ |
| Total point score | 25 points |

## Performance ✓✓✓✓✓

During the 3-year and 5-year periods ending December 31, 1994, High Dividend Stock had an average annual compound return of 9.6% and 9.6%, respectively. This means that a $10,000 investment made into this subaccount 5 years before that date grew to $13,200 ($15,800, if only the last 3 years of the period are used).

Compared to other growth and income variable annuity subaccounts, this one ranked in the top quartile for the 3-year period and in the top 5% for the 5-year period. The inception month of this subaccount was February 1989. This subaccount is modeled (cloned) after the Prudential Series Fund High Dividend Stock Portfolio, which had an inception date of February 1988, and has an asset base of $500 million.

The year-by-year returns for this subaccount are:

| Year | Annual Return | S&P 500 |
|---|---|---|
| 1994 | 0.2% | 1.3% |
| 1993 | 20.8% | 10.1% |
| 1992 | 8.8% | 7.6% |
| 1991 | 26.0% | 30.5% |
| 1990 | −4.9% | −3.1% |
| 1989 | 21.2% | 31.7% |

## Risk Control

Over the 3-year period, this fund was 60% safer than the average equity subaccount. During the 5-year period, it was 40% safer.

The typical standard deviation for growth and income subaccounts was 2.9% during the 3-year period. The standard deviation for Prudential Discovery Plus High Dividend Stock was 2.2% over this same period, which means that this subaccount was 22% less volatile than its peer group. The price/earnings (p/e) ratio averages 19 for this portfolio. The typical growth and income subaccount has a p/e ratio of 21. In general, the higher the p/e ratio, the riskier the portfolio.

The beta (market-related risk) of this subaccount was 0.6 over the 3-year period. Beta for this entire category was 0.9 over this same period. The market index (the S&P 500 Index for equity subaccounts) always has a beta of 1.0. The *risk-adjusted* return for this variable annuity subaccount can be described as excellent.

## Expense Minimization    ✓✓✓

The typical expenses incurred by growth and income subaccounts are 1.9% per year. The total expenses for Prudential Discovery Plus High Dividend Stock, 1.8%, are lower than its peer group average. Total expenses include all charges to the investor (except the annual contract charge, which is always expressed as a dollar figure), including management fees, overhead, administration, and mortality expenses. The free annual withdrawals percentage is based on the account value.

| | | | |
|---|---|---|---|
| Maximum surrender charge | 7% | Total expenses | 1.8% |
| Duration of surrender charge | 6 years | Annual contract charge | $0 |
| Declining surrender charge | yes | Free annual withdrawals | 10% |

## Management    ✓✓✓✓✓

Prudential Discovery Plus is offered by Prudential Insurance Company of America. The company has a Duff & Phelps rating of AA+. The subaccount and the portfolio it is modeled after were managed by Warren E. Spitz for the 6 years ending December 31, 1994. The portfolio's size is $340 million. The typical security in the portfolio has a market capitalization of $3.5 billion. Spitz has also managed the Prudential Equity-Income Fund—Class B mutual fund since 1987.

## Investment Options    ✓✓✓

Investors may make additional contributions into this portfolio at any time. This is known as a flexible premium annuity. Investors in this variable annuity can choose from all of the subaccount categories below that have a check mark:

| | | |
|---|---|---|
| ___ Aggressive growth | ✓ Government bonds | ✓ Money market |
| ✓ Balanced | ✓ Growth | ✓ Specialty/Sector |
| ✓ Corporate bonds | ✓ Growth & income | ___ World bonds |
| ✓ Global equities (stocks) | ✓ High-yield bonds | |

## Family Rating    ✓✓✓

There are 12 subaccounts within the Prudential Discovery Plus family. Overall, this family of subaccounts can be described as good on a *risk-adjusted* return basis.

## Summary

Prudential Discovery Plus High Dividend Stock is the powerhouse of the growth and income variable annuity universe. This subaccount is nothing short of great. Returns have been unbelievable for a portfolio that only has about half the risk of other equity accounts. Management is to be commended for doing a superb job. The "rock" has done it again. This investment is highly recommended.

## Profile

| | | | |
|---|---|---|---|
| Minimum investment | $10,000 | Telephone exchanges | yes |
| Retirement account minimum | $10,000 | Transfers allowed per year | 4 |
| Co-annuitant allowed | yes | Maximum issuance age | 85 |
| Co-owner allowed | yes | Maximum annuitization age | 90 |
| Dollar-cost averaging | yes | Number of subaccounts | 12 |
| Systematic withdrawal plans | no | Available in all 50 states | yes |

---

**SAFECO Life Resource Account**
**Equity**
P.O. Box 34690
Seattle, WA 98124-3882
(800) 426-7649

| | |
|---|---|
| Performance | ✓✓✓✓✓ |
| Risk control | ✓ |
| Expense minimization | ✓✓✓ |
| Management | ✓✓✓ |
| Investment options | ✓✓ |
| Family rating | ✓✓✓ |
| Total point score | 17 points |

## Performance                                              ✓✓✓✓✓

During the 3-year and 5-year periods ending December 31, 1994, Equity had an average annual compound return of 13.2% and 11.2%, respectively. This means that a $10,000 investment made into this subaccount 5 years before that date grew to $17,000 ($14,500, if only the last 3 years of the period are used).

Compared to other growth and income variable annuity subaccounts, this one ranked in the top quartile for the 3-year period and in the top 1% for the 5-year period. The inception month of this subaccount was July 1987.

The year-by-year returns for this subaccount are:

| Year | Annual Return | S&P 500 |
|---|---|---|
| 1994 | 7.6% | 1.3% |
| 1993 | 26.3% | 10.1% |
| 1992 | 6.8% | 7.6% |
| 1991 | 25.3% | 30.5% |
| 1990 | −6.4% | −3.1% |
| 1989 | 25.5% | 31.7% |
| 1988 | 24.5% | 16.6% |

## Risk Control                                                    ✓

Over the 3-year and 5-year periods, this fund was as safe as the average equity subaccount.

The typical standard deviation for growth and income subaccounts was 2.9% during the 3-year period. The standard deviation for SAFECO Life Resource Account Equity was 3.9% over this same period, which means that this subaccount was

33% more volatile than its peer group. The price/earnings (p/e) ratio averages 22 for this portfolio. The typical growth and income subaccount has a p/e ratio of 21. In general, the higher the p/e ratio, the riskier the portfolio.

The beta (market-related risk) of this subaccount was 1.0 over the 3-year period. Beta for this entire category was 0.9 over this same period. The market index (the S&P 500 Index for equity subaccounts) always has a beta of 1.0. The *risk-adjusted* return for this variable annuity subaccount can be described as very good.

## Expense Minimization                                    ✓✓✓

The typical expenses incurred by growth and income subaccounts are 1.9% per year. The total expenses for SAFECO Life Resource Account Equity, 2.0%, are higher than its peer group average. Total expenses include all charges to the investor (except the annual contract charge, which is always expressed as a dollar figure), including management fees, overhead, administration, and mortality expenses. The free annual withdrawals percentage is based on the account value.

| | | | |
|---|---|---|---|
| Maximum surrender charge | 9% | Total expenses | 2.0% |
| Duration of surrender charge | 8 years | Annual contract charge | $30 |
| Declining surrender charge | no | Free annual withdrawals | 10% |

## Management                                              ✓✓✓

SAFECO Life Resource Account is offered by SAFECO Life Insurance Company. The company has an A.M. Best rating of A+. The portfolio was managed by Douglas Johnson for the 7 years ending December 31, 1994. The portfolio's size is $65 million. The typical security in the portfolio has a market capitalization of $1.6 billion. Johnson also manages the SAFECO Equity mutual fund.

## Investment Options                                      ✓✓

Investors may make additional contributions into this portfolio at any time. This is known as a flexible premium annuity. Investors in this variable annuity can choose from all of the subaccount categories below that have a check mark:

| | | |
|---|---|---|
| ___ Aggressive growth | ___ Government bonds | ✓ Money market |
| ✓ Balanced | ✓ Growth | ___ Specialty/Sector |
| ✓ Corporate bonds | ✓ Growth & income | ___ World bonds |
| ✓ Global equities (stocks) | ___ High-yield bonds | |

## Family Rating                                           ✓✓✓

There are 7 subaccounts within the SAFECO Life Resource Account family. Overall, this family of subaccounts can be described as good on a *risk-adjusted* return basis. The contract has a "standard" death benefit (beneficiary gets the greater of the original investment or value at death).

## Summary

SAFECO Life Resource Account Equity has performed spectacularly. This growth and income account has only been slightly risker than other equity portfolios, but it has been worth it. This is the flagship investment of the SAFECO variable annuity, and management certainly deserves the spotlight. Unfortunately, the contract is available only for qualified accounts (i.e., IRAs, pension plans, Keoghs, and so on).

# Profile

| | | | | |
|---|---|---|---|---|
| Minimum investment | $30 | Telephone exchanges | yes |
| Retirement account minimum | $30 | Transfers allowed per year | 4 |
| Co-annuitant allowed | no | Maximum issuance age | 75 |
| Co-owner allowed | no | Maximum annuitization age | none |
| Dollar-cost averaging | yes | Number of subaccounts | 7 |
| Systematic withdrawal plans | yes | Available in all 50 states | no* |

*Not available in ME or NY.

---

**Security First Life Separate Account A**
**Security First Growth & Income**
Holden Group
P.O. Box 92193
Los Angeles, CA 90009
(800) 284-4536

| | |
|---|---|
| Performance | ✓✓✓ |
| Risk control | ✓✓✓✓ |
| Expense minimization | ✓✓ |
| Management | ✓✓✓✓ |
| Investment options | ✓✓✓ |
| Family rating | ✓✓✓ |
| Total point score | 19 points |

# Performance ✓✓✓

During the 3-year and 5-year periods ending December 31, 1994, Security First Growth & Income had an average annual compound return of 7.3% and 6.4%, respectively. This means that a $10,000 investment made into this subaccount 5 years before that date grew to $13,600 ($12,400, if only the last 3 years of the period are used).

Compared to other growth and income variable annuity subaccounts, this one ranked in the top 40% for the 3-year period but in the bottom quartile for the 5-year period. The inception month of this subaccount was March 1987. This subaccount is modeled (cloned) after the Security First Trust Growth and Income Series, which had an inception date of October 1985, and has an asset base of $60 million.

The year-by-year returns for this subaccount are:

| Year | Annual Return | S&P 500 |
|---|---|---|
| 1994 | 1.7% | 1.3% |
| 1993 | 12.7% | 10.1% |
| 1992 | 7.8% | 7.6% |
| 1991 | 25.3% | 30.5% |
| 1990 | −12.2% | −3.1% |
| 1989 | 21.4% | 31.7% |
| 1988 | 20.3% | 16.6% |

## Risk Control ✓✓✓✓

Over the 3-year period, this fund was 40% safer than the average equity subaccount. During the 5-year period, it was a little safer.

The typical standard deviation for growth and income subaccounts was 2.9% during the 3-year period. The standard deviation for Security First Life Separate Account A Security First Growth & Income was 2.6% over this same period, which means that this subaccount was 10% less volatile than its peer group. The price/earnings (p/e) ratio averages 21 for this portfolio. The typical growth and income subaccount also has a p/e ratio of 21. In general, the higher the p/e ratio, the riskier the portfolio.

The beta (market-related risk) of this subaccount was 0.7 over the 3-year period. Beta for this entire category was 0.9 over this same period. The market index (the S&P 500 Index for equity subaccounts) always has a beta of 1.0. The *risk-adjusted* return for this variable annuity subaccount can be described as good.

## Expense Minimization ✓✓

The typical expenses incurred by growth and income subaccounts are 1.9% per year. The total expenses for Security First Life Separate Account A Security First Growth & Income are higher than its peer group average. Total expenses include all charges to the investor (except the annual contract charge, which is always expressed as a dollar figure), including management fees, overhead, administration, and mortality expenses. The free annual withdrawals percentage is based on the account value.

| | | | |
|---|---|---|---|
| Maximum surrender charge | 7% | Total expenses | 2.3% |
| Duration of surrender charge | 7 years | Annual contract charge | $0 |
| Declining surrender charge | yes | Free annual withdrawals | 10% |

## Management ✓✓✓✓

Security First Life Separate Account A is offered by Security First Life Insurance Company. The company has an A.M. Best rating of A. The portfolio was managed by Brian C. Rogers for the 5 years ending December 31, 1994. The portfolio's size is a mere $15 million. The typical security in the portfolio has a market capitalization of $8.7 billion. Rogers also manages the T. Rowe Price Equity-Income mutual fund.

## Investment Options ✓✓✓

Investors may make additional contributions into this portfolio at any time. This is known as a flexible premium annuity. Investors in this variable annuity can choose from all of the subaccount categories below that have a check mark:

| | | |
|---|---|---|
| ___ Aggressive growth | ___ Government bonds | ✓ Money market |
| ✓ Balanced | ✓ Growth | ___ Specialty/Sector |
| ✓ Corporate bonds | ✓ Growth & income | ___ World bonds |
| ✓ Global equities (stocks) | ___ High-yield bonds | |

## Family Rating ✓✓✓

There are 8 subaccounts within the Security First Life Separate Account A family. Overall, this family of subaccounts can be described as good on a *risk-adjusted* return basis. The subaccounts within this variable annuity all have a death benefit based on the value at the date of death (what is referred to in the industry as "accumulated value"). Unlike the death benefit found with most variable annuities, the accumulated value death benefit does not protect the beneficiary from possible market loss.

## Summary

Security First Trust Growth & Income Series has done a good job of getting its investors good returns with very little risk. It is one of the better growth and income subaccounts available. The variable annuity contract includes some other good choices, including a global stock portfolio.

## Profile

| | | | |
|---|---|---|---|
| Minimum investment | $1,000 | Telephone exchanges | yes |
| Retirement account minimum | $1,000 | Transfers allowed per year | unlimited |
| Co-annuitant allowed | no | Maximum issuance age | none |
| Co-owner allowed | yes | Maximum annuitization age | none |
| Dollar-cost averaging | yes | Number of subaccounts | 8 |
| Systematic withdrawal plans | no | Available in all 50 states | no* |

*Not available in NY.

---

**Xerox Account ForPerformance**
**Lord Abbett Growth & Income**
10 Valley Stream Parkway
Malvern, PA 19355
(800) 343-8496

| | |
|---|---|
| Performance | ✓✓✓ |
| Risk control | ✓✓✓ |
| Expense minimization | ✓✓✓ |
| Management | ✓✓✓✓ |
| Investment options | ✓✓ |
| Family rating | ✓✓✓ |
| Total point score | 23 points |

## Performance ✓✓✓

During the 3-year and 5-year periods ending December 31, 1994, Lord Abbett Growth & Income had an average annual compound return of 9.4% and 10.6%, respectively. This means that a $10,000 investment made into this subaccount 5 years before that date grew to $16,500 ($13,100, if only the last 3 years of the period are used).

Compared to other growth and income variable annuity subaccounts, this one ranked in the top third for the 3-year period. The inception month of this subaccount was January 1993. The performance figures (shown below) for periods before the subaccount's inception in January 1993 are hypothetical, based on the underlying clone fund's returns. This subaccount is modeled (cloned) after the Lord Abbett Series Fund Growth and Income Portfolio, which had an inception date of December 1989, and has an asset base of $75 million.

The year-by-year returns for this subaccount and the mutual fund it is modeled after are:

| Year | Annual Return | S&P 500 |
|------|------|------|
| 1994 | 1.3% | 1.3% |
| 1993 | 13.2% | 10.1% |
| 1992 | 14.0% | 7.6% |
| 1991 | 25.4% | 30.5% |
| 1990 | 0.8% | −3.1% |
| 1989 | 29.0% | 31.7% |

## Risk Control                                    ✓✓✓

Over the 3-year period, this fund was 40% safer than the average equity subaccount.

The typical standard deviation for growth and income subaccounts was 2.9% during the 3-year period. The standard deviation for Xerox Account ForPerformance Lord Abbett Growth & Income was 2.6% over this same period, which means that this subaccount was 9% less volatile than its peer group. The price/earnings (p/e) ratio averages 20 for this portfolio. The typical growth and income subaccount has a p/e ratio of 21. In general, the higher the p/e ratio, the riskier the portfolio.

The beta (market-related risk) of this subaccount was 0.8 over the 3-year period. Beta for this entire category was 0.9 over this same period. The market index (the S&P Index for equity subaccounts) always has a beta of 1.0. The *risk-adjusted* return for this variable annuity subaccount can be described as very good.

## Expense Minimization                             ✓✓✓

The typical expenses incurred by growth and income subaccounts are 1.9% per year. The total expenses for Xerox Account ForPerformance Lord Abbett Growth & Income, 1.9%, are identical to its peer group average. Total expenses include all charges to the investor (except the annual contract charge, which is always expressed as a dollar figure), including management fees, overhead, administration, and mortality expenses. The free annual withdrawals percentage is based on the original principal.

| | | | |
|------|------|------|------|
| Maximum surrender charge | 5% | Total expenses | 1.9% |
| Duration of surrender charge | 5 years | Annual contract charge | $30 |
| Declining surrender charge | yes | Free annual withdrawals | 10% |

## Management                                       ✓✓✓✓

Xerox Account ForPerformance is offered by Xerox Financial Services Life Insurance. The portfolio and the mutual fund it is modeled after were managed by W. Thomas Hudson, Jr. for the 5 years ending December 31, 1994. The portfolio's size is $75 million. The typical security in the portfolio has a market capitalization of $4.9 billion. Hudson also manages the Lord Abbett Fundamental Value mutual fund.

## Investment Options                               ✓✓

Investors may make additional contributions into this portfolio at any time. This is known as a flexible premium annuity. Investors in this variable annuity can choose from all of the subaccount categories below that have a check mark:

| | | |
|---|---|---|
| ___ Aggressive growth | ___ Government bonds | ✓ Money market |
| ___ Balanced | ___ Growth | ___ Specialty/Sector |
| ✓ Corporate bonds | ✓ Growth & income | ___ World bonds |
| ✓ Global equities (stocks) | ✓ High-yield bonds | |

## Family Rating                                    ✓✓✓✓

There are 8 subaccounts within the Xerox Account ForPerformance family. Overall, this family of subaccounts can be described as very good on a *risk-adjusted* return basis.

## Summary

Xerox Account ForPerformance Lord Abbett Growth & Income represents one of the very best equity portfolios you can get: it rates either very good or excellent in every category. Its only shortcoming is that there are too few subaccount selections. As Xerox becomes an even bigger player in the financial services industry, this shortcoming should be corrected. This is a highly recommended choice. Its total point score makes it one of the three most desired growth and income subaccounts.

## Profile

| | | | |
|---|---|---|---|
| Minimum investment | $2,000 | Telephone exchanges | yes |
| Retirement account minimum | $5,000 | Transfers allowed per year | 12 |
| Co-annuitant allowed | no | Maximum issuance age | 81 |
| Co-owner allowed | yes | Maximum annuitization age | 81 |
| Dollar-cost averaging | yes | Number of subaccounts | 8 |
| Systematic withdrawal plans | yes | Available in all 50 states | no* |

*Not available in the following states: CA, DE, ME, NH, NJ, NY, and VT.

# Chapter

**14**

# High-Yield Bond Subaccounts

Sometimes referred to as junk bond subaccounts, these portfolios invest in corporate bonds rated lower than BBB or BAA. The world of bonds is divided into two general categories: (1) investment grade and (2) high-yield. Investment grade, sometimes referred to as bank quality, means that the bond issue has been rated AAA, AA, A, or BAA. Certain institutions and fiduciaries are forbidden to invest their clients' monies in anything less than investment grade. Everything less than bank quality is considered junk.

The world of bonds is not black and white. There are several categories of high-yield bonds. Junk bond subaccounts contain issues that range from BBB to C; a rating less than single-C means that the bond is in default, and payment of interest and/or principal is in arrears. High-yield bond subaccounts perform best during good economic times. Such issues should be avoided by traditional investors during recessionary periods because the underlying corporations may have difficulty making interest and principal payments when business slows down. However, these bonds, like common stocks, can perform very well during the second half of a recession.

Although junk bonds may exhibit greater volatility than their investment grade peers, they are safer when it comes to *interest rate* risk. Because junk issues have high-yielding coupons and shorter maturities than quality corporate bond subaccounts, they fluctuate less in value when interest rates change. Thus, during expansionary periods in the economy, when interest rates are rising, high-yield subaccounts will generally drop less in value than high-quality corporate or government bond subaccounts. Conversely, when interest rates are falling, government or corporate bonds will often appreciate more in value than junk subaccounts.

High-yield bonds resemble equities at least as much as they do traditional bonds, in terms of economic cycles and important technical factors. Studies show that only 19% of the average junk subaccount's total return is explained by the up- or down-movement of the Lehman Brothers Gov't/Corp. Bond Index. To give an idea of how low this number is: 94% of a typical *high-quality* corporate bond subaccount's

## Lower Quality = Higher Volatility

| Rating | 1985 | 1986 | 1987 | 1988 | 1989 | 1990 | 1991 | 1992 | 1993 |
|--------|------|------|------|------|------|------|------|------|------|
| BB | 37.3% | 19.4% | 16.4% | 14.4% | 12.1% | 5.9% | 23.2% | 14.8% | 15.9% |
| B | 26.3 | 17.3 | 3.2 | 16.5 | 1.3 | −9.2 | 46.1 | 20.0 | 18.2 |
| CCC | 5.0 | −14.0 | 19.1 | 10.0 | −25.6 | −36.5 | 72.4 | 16.2 | 29.9 |

performance is explainable by movement in the same index. Indeed, even international bond subaccounts have a higher correlation coefficient than junk: 25% of their performance can be explained by the index.

The high end of the junk bond market, those debentures rated BBB and BB, have been able to withstand the general beating the junk bond market incurred during the late 1980s and early 1990s. Moderate and conservative investors who want high-yield bonds as part of their portfolio should focus on subaccounts that have a high percentage of their assets in higher-rated bonds—BB or better.

The table above shows the average annual returns of different high-yield bonds for the 9 years from 1985 through 1994. The ratings, from Standard & Poor's, represent the three highest categories of junk bonds: BB, B, and CCC. Above BB is BBB, the lowest rating for a *high-quality* bond.

Well over 90% of the junk bonds in existence at the end of 1989 had been issued since 1982. Not surprisingly, the mutual fund and variable annuity industries helped finance this growth. According to Salomon Brothers (the firm responsible for the Lehman Brothers corporate and government bond indexes used in this book), junk bond defaults averaged only 0.84% from 1980 to 1984. This rate almost tripled from 1985 to 1989, when defaults averaged 2.2% per year. In 1990, defaults surged to 4.6%. Analysis based on historical data did not predict this huge increase in defaults. The default rate dropped to 1% in 1994. Junk bonds rated BB are going to perform closer to high-quality bonds than will lower-rated junk. For example, during 1990, BB-rated bonds declined only slightly in price and actually delivered positive total returns. Bonds rated CCC declined over 36% in price.

The table below shows year-by-year, as well as 3-, 5-, and 10-year averages for this investment category. The variable annuity subaccount category is compared

## Average Annual Returns: High-Yield Bond Subaccounts vs. High-Yield Bond Mutual Funds

| Year | Subaccount | Mutual Fund |
|------|-----------|-------------|
| 1994 | −4.0% | −3.9% |
| 1993 | 18.1% | 18.9% |
| 1992 | 16.6% | 17.5% |
| 1991 | 35.7% | 37.3% |
| 1990 | −7.7% | −10.3% |
| 1989 | −1.4% | −0.2% |
| 1988 | 11.7% | 13.0% |
| 1987 | 0.5% | 1.6% |
| 3-yr. average | 9.9% | 10.6% |
| 5-yr. average | 10.6% | 10.5% |
| 10-yr. average | 9.0% | 9.9% |

against the similar mutual fund category. These performance figures are average figures, representing all funds and subaccounts that fall within this investment objective.

As you can see, the variable annuity subaccounts outperformed their mutual fund counterparts for 1990 and for the last 5-year period. The difference between these two investment vehicles was very close for all other periods.

I recommend that only moderate investors consider making a 10%–20% commitment to this category. Aggressive investors should probably avoid high-yield subaccounts, although conservative investors would be wise to review the junk bond subaccounts in this chapter. As with any category of variable annuities, whenever larger dollar amounts are involved, more than one subaccount per category should be used.

The table below shows statistics you might find useful when comparing variable annuity subaccounts versus their mutual fund counterparts or "clones." These are category averages based on available information at the beginning of 1995.

Figure 14.1 below shows the year-by-year returns for this category of variable annuities, for the period 1987 through 1994. These are composite figures and therefore include all of the subaccounts that comprise the high-yield category.

### High-Yield Bond Category Statistics: Subaccounts vs. Mutual Funds

| Description | Subaccounts | Funds |
|---|---|---|
| **Composition of portfolio** | | |
| Stocks | 3% | 2% |
| Cash | 7% | 6% |
| Foreign stocks | 0% | 0% |
| Bonds | 87% | 89% |
| Other | 3% | 3% |
| **Fees and expenses** | | |
| Underlying fund expense | 0.79% | 1.25% |
| Insurance expense | 1.29% | — |
| Total expenses | 2.08% | 1.25%/3.8%* |
| **Operations** | | |
| Net assets (in millions) | $49 | $555 |
| Manager tenure | 6 years | 6 years |
| **Portfolio statistics** | | |
| Average maturity | 9 years | 8 years |
| Standard deviation | 1.6% | 2.5% |
| Average weighted coupon | 10.0% | 10.6% |
| Turnover ratio (annual) | 107% | 92% |
| Number of subaccounts/funds | 60 | 80 |

*Total expenses for this mutual fund category increase to this figure if the average mutual fund commission is added to the 1.25% figure.

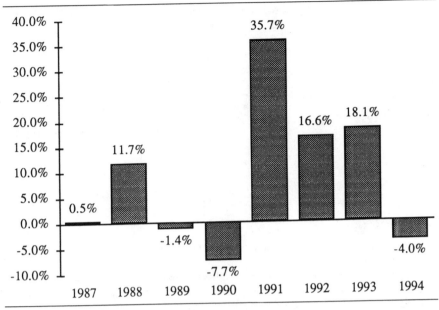

**Figure 14.1** High-Yield Bond Subaccounts

**First Investors Variable Annuity C**
**High-Yield**
95 Wall Street
New York, NY 10005
(800) 832-7783

| | |
|---|---|
| Performance | ✓✓ |
| Risk control | ✓✓✓ |
| Expense minimization | ✓✓✓✓ |
| Management | ✓✓✓ |
| Investment options | ✓✓✓ |
| Family rating | ✓✓✓ |
| Total point score | 18 points |

## Performance                                    ✓✓

During the 3-year and 5-year periods ending December 31, 1994, High-Yield had an average annual compound return of 8.5% and 9.3%, respectively. This means that a $10,000 investment made into this subaccount 5 years before that date grew to $15,600 ($12,800 over the past 3 years).

Compared to other high-yield bond variable annuity subaccounts, this one ranked in the bottom half for the 3-year and 5-year periods. The inception month of this subaccount was October 1990. The performance figures (shown below) for periods before the subaccount's inception in October 1990 are hypothetical, based on the underlying clone fund's returns. This subaccount is modeled (cloned) after the First Investors Life Series High-Yield Series, which had an inception date of November 1987, and has an asset base of $30 million.

The year-by-year returns for this subaccount and the portfolio it is modeled after are:

| Year | Annual Return | First Boston High-Yield Bond Index |
|------|---------------|-------------------------------------|
| 1994 | −2.6% | −1.0% |
| 1993 | 16.9% | 18.9% |
| 1992 | 12.2% | 16.7% |
| 1991 | 32.5% | 43.8% |
| 1990 | −16.5% | −6.4% |
| 1989 | −8.3% | 0.4% |
| 1988 | 13.1% | 11.4% |
| 1989 | −2.5% | 6.5% |

## Risk Control                                    ✓✓✓

Over the 3-year period, this fund was substantially safer than the average hybrid subaccount.

The typical standard deviation for high-yield bond subaccounts was 1.6% during the 3-year period. The standard deviation for First Investors Variable Annuity C High-Yield was 1.2% over this same period, which means that this subaccount was 25% less volatile than its peer group. The average maturity of the bonds in this account is 9 years; the weighted coupon rate averages 10.6%. The typical high-yield bond subaccount also has an average maturity of 9 years and a weighted coupon rate of 10.0%.

The beta (market-related risk) of this subaccount was 0.1 over the 3-year period. Beta for this entire category was 0.6 over this same period. The market index (the S&P 500 Index for "hybrid" subaccounts or the Lehman Brothers Aggregate Bond Index for debt subaccounts) always has a beta of 1.0. The *risk-adjusted* return for this variable annuity subaccount can be described as excellent.

## Expense Minimization                              ✓✓✓✓

The typical expenses incurred by high-yield bond subaccounts are 2.1% per year. The total expenses for First Investors Variable Annuity C High-Yield, 1.9%, are lower than its peer group average. Total expenses include all charges to the investor (except the annual contract charge, which is always expressed as a dollar figure), including management fees, overhead, administration, and mortality expenses.

| | | | |
|---|---|---|---|
| Maximum surrender charge | 0% | Total expenses | 1.9% |
| Duration of surrender charge | n/a | Annual contract charge | $0 |
| Declining surrender charge | n/a | Free annual withdrawals | 100% |

## Management                                        ✓✓✓

First Investors Variable Annuity C is offered by First Investors Life Insurance Company. The company has an A.M. Best rating of B+. The subaccount and the portfolio it is modeled after were managed by George V. Ganter for the 7 years ending December 31, 1994. The portfolio's size is $7 million. Ganter also manages the First Investors High-Yield mutual fund.

## Investment Options                                ✓✓✓

Investors may make additional contributions into this portfolio at any time. This is known as a flexible premium annuity. Investors in this variable annuity can choose from all of the subaccount categories below that have a check mark:

| | | |
|---|---|---|
| ✓ Aggressive growth | ✓ Government bonds | ✓ Money market |
| ___ Balanced | ✓ Growth | ___ Specialty/Sector |
| ✓ Corporate bonds | ✓ Growth & income | ___ World bonds |
| ✓ Global equities (stocks) | ✓ High-yield bonds | |

## Family Rating                                    ✓✓✓

There are 9 subaccounts within the First Investors Variable Annuity C family. Overall, this family of subaccounts can be described as good on a *risk-adjusted* return basis.

## Summary

First Investors Variable Annuity C High-Yield is a fine candidate for anyone interested in reducing the overall risk level of a portfolio. Contrary to popular belief, high-yield bonds have a surprisingly good record for total return. Out of all of the domestic debt categories, this one is the best. First Investors, through the stewardship of portfolio manager George Ganter, has been able to build a portfolio that is substantially safer than most other types of investment vehicles.

It is surprising that this First Investors' portfolio has not attracted more money. However, the general public's loss can work to your advantage. First Investors includes the all-important global category among the choices offered by the variable annuity. Overseas securities are a critical step toward proper diversification, adding enhanced returns and lowering overall risk.

## Profile

| | | | |
|---|---|---|---|
| Minimum investment | $2,000 | Telephone exchanges | no |
| Retirement account minimum | $2,000 | Transfers allowed per year | unlimited |
| Co-annuitant allowed | no | Maximum issuance age | 80 |
| Co-owner allowed | yes | Maximum annuitization age | 85 |
| Dollar-cost averaging | yes | Number of subaccounts | 9 |
| Systematic withdrawal plans | yes | Available in all 50 states | no* |

*Not available in the following states: AK, AR, DE, HI, ID, KS, ME, MT, ND, NH, NM, NV, SC, SD, and VT.

---

**Franklin Valuemark II**
**High Income**
10 Valley Stream Parkway
Malvern, PA 19355
(800) 342-3863

| | |
|---|---|
| Performance | ✓ |
| Risk control | ✓✓✓ |
| Expense minimization | ✓✓✓ |
| Management | ✓✓ |
| Investment options | ✓✓✓✓✓ |
| Family rating | ✓✓ |
| Total point score | 16 points |

## Performance                                        ✓

During the 3-year and 5-year periods ending December 31, 1994, High Income had an average annual compound return of 8.1% and 7.8%, respectively. This means that a $10,000 investment made into this subaccount 5 years before that date grew to $14,600 ($12,600 over the last 3 years).

Compared to other high-yield bond variable subaccounts, this one ranked in the bottom half for the 3-year period. The inception month of this subaccount was June 1989. The performance figures (shown below) for periods before the subaccount's inception in June 1989 are hypothetical, based on the underlying clone fund's returns. This subaccount is modeled (cloned) after the Franklin AGE High-Income Fund, which had an inception date of December 1969, and has an asset base of $2.2 billion.

The year-by-year returns for this subaccount and the mutual fund it is modeled after are:

| Year | Annual Return | First Boston High-Yield Bond Index |
|---|---|---|
| 1994 | −3.6% | −1.0% |
| 1993 | 14.1% | 18.9% |
| 1992 | 14.7% | 16.7% |
| 1991 | 28.2% | 43.8% |
| 1990 | −9.9% | −6.4% |
| 1989 | 4.6% | 0.4% |
| 1988 | 14.1% | 11.4% |

## Risk Control ✓✓✓

Over the 3-year period, this fund was dramatically safer than the average hybrid subaccount.

The typical standard deviation for high-yield bond subaccounts was 1.6% during the 3-year period. The standard deviation for Franklin Valuemark II High Income was 1.2% over this same period, which means that this subaccount was 22% less volatile than its peer group. The average maturity of the bonds in this account is 11 years; the weighted coupon rate averages 9.4%. The typical high-yield bond subaccount has an average maturity of 9 years and a weighted coupon rate of 10.0%.

The beta (market-related risk) of this subaccount was 0.1 over the 3-year period. Beta for this entire category was 0.6 over this same period. The market index (the S&P 500 Index for "hybrid" subaccounts or the Lehman Brothers Aggregate Bond Index for debt subaccounts) always has a beta of 1.0. The *risk-adjusted* return for this variable annuity subaccount can be described as excellent.

## Expense Minimization ✓✓✓

The typical expenses incurred by high-yield bond subaccounts are 2.1% per year. The total expenses for Franklin Valuemark II High Income, 2.1%, are equivalent to its peer group average. Total expenses include all charges to the investor (except the annual contract charge, which is always expressed as a dollar figure), including management fees, overhead, administration, and mortality expenses. The free annual withdrawals percentage is based on the original principal.

| | | | |
|---|---|---|---|
| Maximum surrender charge | 5% | Total expenses | 2.1% |
| Duration of surrender charge | 5 years | Annual contract charge | $30 |
| Declining surrender charge | yes | Free annual withdrawals | 15% |

## Management ✓✓

Franklin Valuemark II is offered by Allianz Life Insurance Company of North America. The company has an A.M. Best rating of A+. The portfolio has been managed by Martin Wiskemann and Betsy Hofman-Schwab since its inception. The portfolio's size is $150 million. Wiskemann and Hofman-Schwab also manage the Franklin Tax-Advantaged High-Yield Securities mutual fund.

## Investment Options ✓✓✓✓

Investors may make additional contributions into this portfolio at any time. This is known as a flexible premium annuity. Investors in this variable annuity can choose from all of the subaccount categories below that have a check mark:

| | | |
|---|---|---|
| ___ Aggressive growth | ✓ Government bonds | ✓ Money market |
| ✓ Balanced | ✓ Growth | ✓ Specialty/Sector |
| ✓ Corporate bonds | ___ Growth & income | ✓ World bonds |
| ✓ Global equities (stocks) | ✓ High-yield bonds | |

## Family Rating ✓✓

There are 18 subaccounts within the Franklin Valuemark II family. Overall, this family of subaccounts can be described as fair on a *risk-adjusted* return basis.

The subaccounts within this variable annuity all have an *increasing* guaranteed death benefit. This means that the beneficiary is guaranteed to receive *the greater of* the contract's value on the date of the annuitant's death or the value of the original investment(s) compounded by 5% each year (less any withdrawals made).

## Summary

Franklin Valuemark II High Income is the right choice for investors who have mixed feelings about getting involved with junk bonds. The differentiating factor here is that Franklin buys the better-rated bonds, making sure not to tarnish the reputation built up for almost half a century. It is difficult to appreciate how conservatively managed this subaccount is.

The Franklin Valuemark II is one of the best annuity contracts in the industry. Valuemark II has some of the very best contract provisions: 15% free withdrawals per year (vs. an industry average of 10%), a 5-year penalty schedule (vs. a 7-year average), allowing co-annuitants and co-ownership between spouses, and availability in all 50 states. It is no surprise that this variable annuity is has become the industry's number-one seller. The number of investment choices is immense; several other members of this family appear elsewhere in this book.

## Profile

| | | | |
|---|---|---|---|
| Minimum investment | $2,000 | Telephone exchanges | yes |
| Retirement account minimum | $5,000 | Transfers allowed per year | 12 |
| Co-annuitant allowed | yes | Maximum issuance age | none |
| Co-owner allowed | spouses only | Maximum annuitization age | 80 |
| Dollar-cost averaging | yes | Number of subaccounts | 18 |
| Systematic withdrawal plans | yes | Available in all 50 states | yes |

---

**Life of Virginia Commonwealth
Oppenheimer High Income**
6610 West Broad Street
Richmond, VA  23230
(800) 521-8884

---

| | |
|---|---|
| Performance | ✓✓✓✓ |
| Risk control | ✓✓✓ |
| Expense minimization | ✓✓✓✓ |
| Management | ✓✓✓✓✓ |
| Investment options | ✓✓✓✓ |
| Family rating | ✓✓✓ |
| Total point score | 23 points |

---

## Performance                                                   ✓✓✓✓

During the 3-year and 5-year periods ending December 31, 1994, Oppenheimer High Income had an average annual compound return of 11.7% and 13.8%, respectively. This means that a $10,000 investment made into this subaccount 5 years before that date grew to $19,100 ($13,900, if only the last 3 years of the period are used).

Compared to other high-yield bond variable annuity subaccounts, this one ranked in the top half for the 3-year period and in the top 3% for the 5-year period. The inception month of this subaccount was May 1988. This subaccount is modeled (cloned) after the Oppenheimer Variable Account High Income Fund, which had an inception date of April 1986, and has an asset base of $100 million.

The year-by-year returns for this subaccount are:

| Year | Annual Return | First Boston High-Yield Bond Index |
|---|---|---|
| 1994 | −4.3% | −1.0% |
| 1993 | 24.9% | 18.9% |
| 1992 | 16.5% | 16.7% |
| 1991 | 32.5% | 43.8% |
| 1990 | 3.4% | −6.4% |
| 1989 | 3.6% | 0.4% |

## Risk Control                                                   ✓✓✓

Over the 3-year and 5-year periods, this fund was substantially safer than the average hybrid subaccount.

The typical standard deviation for high-yield bond subaccounts was 1.6% during the 3-year period. The standard deviation for Life of Virginia Commonwealth Oppenheimer High Income was 1.3% over this same period, which means that this subaccount was 16% less volatile than its peer group. The average maturity of the bonds in this account is 8 years; the weighted coupon rate averages 9.4%. The typical high-yield bond subaccount has an average maturity of 9 years and a weighted coupon rate of 10.0%.

The beta (market-related risk) of this subaccount was 0.1 over the 3-year period. Beta for this entire category was 0.6 over this same period. The market index (the S&P 500 Index for "hybrid" subaccounts or the Lehman Brothers Aggregate

Bond Index for debt subaccounts) always has a beta of 1.0. The *risk-adjusted* return for this variable annuity subaccount can be described as excellent.

## Expense Minimization ✓✓✓

The typical expenses incurred by high-yield bond subaccounts are 2.1% per year. The total expenses for Life of Virginia Commonwealth Oppenheimer High Income, 1.9%, are lower than its peer group average. Total expenses include all charges to the investor (except the annual contract charge, which is always expressed as a dollar figure), including management fees, overhead, administration, and mortality expenses. The free annual withdrawals percentage is based on the account value.

| | | | |
|---|---|---|---|
| Maximum surrender charge | 6% | Total expenses | 1.9% |
| Duration of surrender charge | 6 years | Annual contract charge | $30 |
| Declining surrender charge | yes | Free annual withdrawals | 10% |

## Management ✓✓✓✓

Life of Virginia Commonwealth is offered by Life Insurance Company of Virginia. The company has a Duff & Phelps rating of AA+ and an A.M. Best rating of A+. The portfolio was managed by David P. Negri for the 5 years ending December 31, 1994. The portfolio's size is $10 million.

## Investment Options ✓✓✓

Investors may make additional contributions into this portfolio at any time. This is known as a flexible premium annuity. Investors in this variable annuity can choose from all of the subaccount categories below that have a check mark:

| | | |
|---|---|---|
| ✓ Aggressive growth | ✓ Government bonds | ✓ Money market |
| ✓ Balanced | ✓ Growth | ___ Specialty/Sector |
| ✓ Corporate bonds | ✓ Growth & income | ___ World bonds |
| ✓ Global equities (stocks) | ✓ High-yield bonds | |

## Family Rating ✓✓✓

There are 22 subaccounts within the Life of Virginia Commonwealth family. Overall, this family of subaccounts can be described as good on a *risk-adjusted* return basis.

The subaccounts within this variable annuity all have an *increasing* guaranteed death benefit. This means that the beneficiary is guaranteed to receive *the greater of* the contract's value on the date of the annuitant's death or the value of the original investment(s) compounded by 5% each year (less any withdrawals made).

## Summary

Life of Virginia Commonwealth Oppenheimer High Income has never had a negative year. This high-yield bond portfolio's performance has been very good, particularly over the 3-year period ending December 31, 1994. Expense minimization, an important consideration in any bond account, is quite low.

Life of Virginia has a variable annuity that offers more investment choices than almost any other company. With close to two dozen choices, contract owners can switch among a number of investment styles and philosophies. A stepped-up death benefit and declining surrender charge are icing-on-the-cake features.

## Profile

| | | | | |
|---|---|---|---|---|
| Minimum investment | $5,000 | | Telephone exchanges | yes |
| Retirement account minimum | $5,000 | | Transfers allowed per year | 12 |
| Co-annuitant allowed | no | | Maximum issuance age | 75 |
| Co-owner allowed | yes | | Maximum annuitization age | none |
| Dollar-cost averaging | yes | | Number of subaccounts | 22 |
| Systematic withdrawal plans | yes | | Available in all 50 states | no* |

*Not available in ME, NY, or WA.

---

**Lincoln National American Legacy II
High-Yield Bond**
P.O. Box 2340
Fort Wayne, IN 46801
(800) 421-9900

| | |
|---|---|
| Performance | ✓ |
| Risk control | ✓✓✓ |
| Expense minimization | ✓✓✓✓ |
| Management | ✓✓ |
| Investment options | ✓✓✓ |
| Family rating | ✓✓✓✓ |
| Total point score | 17 points |

## Performance                                                        ✓

During the 3-year and 5-year periods ending December 31, 1994, High-Yield Bond had an average annual compound return of 5.5% and 8.5%, respectively. This means that a $10,000 investment made into this subaccount 5 years before that date grew to $15,000 ($11,700, if only the last 3 years of the period are used).

Compared to other high-yield bond variable annuity subaccounts, this one ranked in the bottom quartile for the 3-year period but in the top quartile for the 5-year period. The inception month of this subaccount was February 1984. This subaccount is modeled (cloned) after the American High Income Trust, which also has an inception date of February 1984, and has an asset base of $820 million.

The year-by-year returns for this subaccount are:

| Year | Annual Return | First Boston High-Yield Bond Index |
|---|---|---|
| 1994 | −7.8% | −1.0% |
| 1993 | 14.9% | 18.9% |
| 1992 | 11.0% | 16.7% |
| 1991 | 24.9% | 43.8% |
| 1990 | 2.5% | −6.4% |
| 1989 | 9.1% | 0.4% |
| 1988 | 13.1% | 11.4% |
| 1987 | 3.5% | 6.5% |

## Risk Control                                              ✓✓✓

Over the 3-year and 5-year periods, this fund was dramatically safer than the average hybrid subaccount.

The typical standard deviation for high-yield bond subaccounts was 1.6% during the 3-year period. The standard deviation for Lincoln National American Legacy II High-Yield Bond was 1.1% over this same period. This means that this subaccount was 33% less volatile than its peer group. The average maturity of the bonds in this account is 7 years; the weighted coupon rate averages 9.0%. The typical high-yield bond subaccount has an average maturity of 9 years and a weighted coupon rate of 10.0%.

The beta (market-related risk) of this subaccount was 0.6 over the 3-year period. Beta for this entire category was also 0.6 over this same period. The market index (the S&P 500 Index for "hybrid" subaccounts or the Lehman Brothers Aggregate Bond Index for debt subaccounts) always has a beta of 1.0. The *risk-adjusted* return for this variable annuity subaccount can be described as excellent.

## Expense Minimization                                      ✓✓✓✓

The typical expenses incurred by high-yield bond subaccounts are 2.1% per year. The total expenses for Lincoln National American Legacy II High-Yield Bond, 1.9%, are lower than its peer group average. Total expenses include all charges to the investor (except the annual contract charge, which is always expressed as a dollar figure), including management fees, overhead, administration, and mortality expenses. The free annual withdrawals percentage is based on the original principal.

| | | | |
|---|---|---|---|
| Maximum surrender charge | 6% | Total expenses | 1.9% |
| Duration of surrender charge | 7 years | Annual contract charge | $35 |
| Declining surrender charge | yes | Free annual withdrawals | 10% |

## Management

Lincoln National American Legacy II is offered by Lincoln National Life Insurance Company. The company has a Duff & Phelps rating of AAA and an A.M. Best rating of A+. The portfolio and mutual fund it has been modeled after have been managed by Capital Guardian (American Funds) since its inception. The portfolio's size is $425 million.

## Investment Options                                        ✓✓✓

Investors may make additional contributions into this portfolio at any time. This is known as a flexible premium annuity. Investors in this variable annuity can choose from all of the subaccount categories below that have a check mark:

| | | |
|---|---|---|
| ___ Aggressive growth | ✓ Government bonds | ✓ Money market |
| ✓ Balanced | ✓ Growth | ___ Specialty/Sector |
| ___ Corporate bonds | ✓ Growth & income | ___ World bonds |
| ✓ Global equities (stocks) | ✓ High-yield bonds | |

## Family Rating                                             ✓✓✓✓

There are 7 subaccounts within the Lincoln National American Legacy II family. Overall, this family of subaccounts can be described as very good on a *risk-adjusted* return basis.

## Summary

Lincoln National American Legacy II High-Yield Bond has a track record few other portfolios can equal. This subaccount, and its predecessor under the former Legacy I contract, has only had one negative year. Risk control is very impressive, beating out close to 90% of the competition. Performance over the 5-year period ending December 31, 1994, puts this subaccount in the top quartile. Because of the management style at Capital Guardian, the group that directs all of the Legacy II subaccounts, this high-yield bond portfolio is highly recommended.

## Profile

| | | | |
|---|---|---|---|
| Minimum investment | $300 | Telephone exchanges | yes |
| Retirement account minimum | $1,500 | Transfers allowed per year | 12 |
| Co-annuitant allowed | no | Maximum issuance age | 75 |
| Co-owner allowed | yes | Maximum annuitization age | 85 |
| Dollar-cost averaging | yes | Number of subaccounts | 7 |
| Systematic withdrawal plans | yes | Available in all 50 states | no* |

*Not available in NY.

---

**MFS/Sun Life (US) Compass 3**
**High-Yield Variable Account**
P.O. Box 1024
Boston, MA  02103
(800) 752-7215

---

| | |
|---|---|
| Performance | ✓✓✓✓✓ |
| Risk control | ✓✓ |
| Expense minimization | ✓✓ |
| Management | ✓✓✓✓ |
| Investment options | ✓✓✓ |
| Family rating | ✓✓✓ |
| Total point score | 19 points |

## Performance                    ✓✓✓✓✓

During the 3-year and 5-year periods ending December 31, 1994, High-Yield Variable Account had an average annual compound return of 9.3% and 10.4%, respectively. This means that a $10,000 investment made into this subaccount 5 years before that date grew to $16,400 ($13,100 over the last 3 years).

Compared to other high-yield bond variable annuity subaccounts, this one ranked in the top 15% for the 3-year period but in the bottom half for the 5-year period. The inception month of this subaccount was April 1988. This subaccount is modeled (cloned) after the MFS High-Income Fund—Class A, which had an inception date of February 1978, and has an asset base of $650 million.

The year-by-year returns for this subaccount are:

| Year | Annual Return | First Boston High-Yield Bond Index |
|------|---------------|------------------------------------|
| 1994 | −3.1% | −1.0% |
| 1993 | 18.5% | 18.9% |
| 1992 | 13.7% | 16.7% |
| 1991 | 46.5% | 43.8% |
| 1990 | −14.3% | −6.4% |
| 1989 | −2.4% | 0.4% |

## Risk Control                                                    ✓✓

Over the 3-year period, this fund has been substantially safer than the average hybrid subaccount. During the 5-year period, it has been somewhat safer.

The typical standard deviation for high-yield bond subaccounts was 1.6% during the 3-year period. The standard deviation for MFS/Sun Life (US) Compass 3 High-Yield Variable Account was 2.0% over this same period, which means that this subaccount was 26% more volatile than its peer group. The average maturity of the bonds in this account is 9 years; the weighted coupon rate averages 10.3%. The typical high-yield bond subaccount also has an average maturity of 9 years and a weighted coupon rate of 10.0%.

The *risk-adjusted* return for this variable annuity subaccount can be described as very good.

## Expense Minimization                                            ✓✓

The typical expenses incurred by high-yield bond subaccounts are 2.1% per year. The total expenses for MFS/Sun Life (US) Compass 3 High-Yield Variable Account, 2.3%, are higher than its peer group average. Total expenses include all charges to the investor (except the annual contract charge, which is always expressed as a dollar figure), including management fees, overhead, administration, and mortality expenses. The free annual withdrawals percentage is based on the original principal.

| | | | |
|---|---|---|---|
| Maximum surrender charge | 6% | Total expenses | 2.3% |
| Duration of surrender charge | 7 years | Annual contract charge | $30 |
| Declining surrender charge | yes | Free annual withdrawals | 10% |

## Management                                                      ✓✓✓✓

MFS/Sun Life (US) Compass 3 is offered by Sun Life Assurance Company of Canada (US). The company has an A.M. Best rating of A++. The portfolio and the mutual fund it is modeled after have been managed by Joan S. Batchelder since inception. The portfolio's size is $45 million. Batchelder also manages the MFS High-Income mutual fund.

## Investment Options                                              ✓✓✓

Investors may make additional contributions into this portfolio at any time. This is known as a flexible premium annuity. Investors in this variable annuity can choose from all of the subaccount categories below that have a check mark:

| | | |
|---|---|---|
| ✓ Aggressive growth | ✓ Government bonds | ✓ Money market |
| ✓ Balanced | ✓ Growth | ___ Specialty/Sector |
| ___ Corporate bonds | ___ Growth & income | ✓ World bonds |
| ___ Global equities (stocks) | ✓ High-yield bonds | |

## Family Rating                                                   ✓✓✓

There are 7 subaccounts within the MFS/Sun Life (US) Compass 3 family. Overall, this family of subaccounts can be described as good on a *risk-adjusted* return basis.

The subaccounts within this variable annuity all have an *increasing* guaranteed death benefit. This means that the beneficiary is guaranteed to receive *the greater of* the contract's value on the date of the annuitant's death or the value of the original investment(s) compounded by 5% each year (less any withdrawals made).

## Summary

For performance, MFS/Sun Life (US) Compass 3 High-Yield Variable Account is simply the best. Portfolio manager Batchelder has done a magnificent job overseeing this and similar portfolios for close to a decade. No other high-yield bond subaccount in this book has done as well as this one.

## Profile

| | | | |
|---|---|---|---|
| Minimum investment | $300 | Telephone exchanges | yes |
| Retirement account minimum | $300 | Transfers allowed per year | 12 |
| Co-annuitant allowed | yes | Maximum issuance age | none |
| Co-owner allowed | yes | Maximum annuitization age | 80 |
| Dollar-cost averaging | yes | Number of subaccounts | 7 |
| Systematic withdrawal plans | yes | Available in all 50 states | no* |

*Not available in NY or VT.

---

**Pacific Mutual Select Variable Annuity**
**High-Yield Bond**
700 Newport Center Drive
P.O. Box 7500
Newport Beach, CA 92658-7500
(800) 800-7681

| | |
|---|---|
| Performance | ✓ |
| Risk control | ✓✓✓✓✓ |
| Expense minimization | ✓✓✓ |
| Management | ✓✓✓✓ |
| Investment options | ✓✓✓✓ |
| Family rating | ✓✓ |
| Total point score | 19 points |

## Performance                                                   ✓

During the 3-year and 5-year periods ending December 31, 1994, High-Yield Bond had an average annual compound return of 10.7% and 10.6%, respectively. This means that a $10,000 investment made into this subaccount 5 years before that date grew to $16,500 ($13,600 over the last 3 years).

Compared to other high-yield bond variable annuity subaccounts, this one ranked in the bottom quartile for the 3-year period but in the top half for the 5-year period. The inception month of this subaccount was August 1990. The performance figures (shown below) for periods before the subaccount's inception in August 1990 are hypothetical, based on the underlying clone fund's returns. This subaccount is modeled (cloned) after the Pacific Select Fund High-Yield Bond Series, which had an inception date of January 1988, and has an asset base of $20 million.

The year-by-year returns for this subaccount and the portfolio it is modeled after are:

| Year | Annual Return | First Boston High-Yield Bond Index |
|------|---------------|-------------------------------------|
| 1994 | −0.9% | −1.0% |
| 1993 | 16.6% | 18.9% |
| 1992 | 17.3% | 16.7% |
| 1991 | 23.4% | 43.8% |
| 1990 | −1.0% | −6.4% |
| 1989 | 0.1% | 0.4% |

## Risk Control                                    ✓✓✓✓✓

Over the 3-year and 5-year periods, this fund was substantially safer than the average hybrid subaccount.

The typical standard deviation for high-yield bond subaccounts was 1.6% during the 3-year period. The standard deviation for Pacific Mutual Select Variable Annuity High-Yield Bond was 0.8% over this same period, which means that this subaccount was 50% less volatile than its peer group. The average maturity of the bonds in this account is 9 years; the weighted coupon rate averages 9.3%. The typical high-yield bond subaccount also has an average maturity of 9 years and a weighted coupon rate of 10.0%.

The *risk-adjusted* return for this variable annuity subaccount can be described as very good.

## Expense Minimization                             ✓✓✓

The typical expenses incurred by high-yield bond subaccounts are 2.1% per year. The total expenses for Pacific Mutual Select Variable Annuity High-Yield Bond, 2.1%, are equivalent to its peer group average. Total expenses include all charges to the investor (except the annual contract charge, which is always expressed as a dollar figure), including management fees, overhead, administration, and mortality expenses. The free annual withdrawals percentage is based on the original principal.

| | | | |
|---|---|---|---|
| Maximum surrender charge | 6% | Total expenses | 2.1% |
| Duration of surrender charge | 6 years | Annual contract charge | $30 |
| Declining surrender charge | yes | Free annual withdrawals | 10% |

## Management                                            ✓✓✓

Pacific Mutual Select Variable Annuity is offered by Pacific Mutual Life Insurance Company. The company has a Duff & Phelps rating of AA+ and an A.M. Best rating of A+. The subaccount and the portfolio it is modeled after were managed by Larry Card for the 6 years ending December 31, 1994. The portfolio's size is $6 million.

## Investment Options                                    ✓✓✓

Investors may make additional contributions into this portfolio at any time. This is known as a flexible premium annuity. Investors in this variable annuity can choose from all of the subaccount categories below that have a check mark:

| | | |
|---|---|---|
| ___ Aggressive growth | ✓ Government bonds | ✓ Money market |
| ✓ Balanced | ✓ Growth | ___ Specialty/Sector |
| ✓ Corporate bonds | ✓ Growth & income | ___ World bonds |
| ✓ Global equities (stocks) | ✓ High-yield bonds | |

## Family Rating                                         ✓✓

There are 9 subaccounts within the Pacific Mutual Select Variable Annuity family. Overall, this family of subaccounts can be described as fair on a *risk-adjusted* return basis.

## Summary

Mutual Select Variable Annuity High-Yield Bond is the only portfolio of its kind to get a rating of excellent for its risk reduction. This high-yield bond subaccount has been about 90% safer than other investments that fit in the same category. The volatility of this investment has shown about half the level of the competition's. This may well be the best choice for any investor who has doubts about getting into the high-yield marketplace.

The Mutual Select contract is also recommended. There are some fine alternative choices within this investment family. Among a relatively small group of variable annuities, this entire family is considered to be quite good on a risk-adjusted return basis.

## Profile

| | | | |
|---|---|---|---|
| Minimum investment | $2,000 | Telephone exchanges | yes |
| Retirement account minimum | $5,000 | Transfers allowed per year | unlimited |
| Co-annuitant allowed | yes | Maximum issuance age | 85 |
| Co-owner allowed | yes | Maximum annuitization age | 95 |
| Dollar-cost averaging | yes | Number of subaccounts | 9 |
| Systematic withdrawal plans | yes | Available in all 50 states | no* |

*Not available in NY.

---

**Penn Mutual Diversifier II**
**High-Yield Bond**
Independence Square
Philadelphia, PA 19172
(800) 548-1119

---

| | |
|---|---|
| Performance | ✓✓✓ |
| Risk control | ✓✓✓ |
| Expense minimization | ✓✓✓ |
| Management | ✓✓✓ |
| Investment options | ✓✓✓✓ |
| Family rating | ✓✓✓ |
| Total point score | 19 points |

## Performance                                                      ✓✓✓

During the 3-year and 5-year periods ending December 31, 1994, High-Yield Bond had an average annual compound return of 7.4% and 8.5%, respectively. This means that a $10,000 investment made into this subaccount 5 years before that date grew to $15,000 ($12,400 over the last 3 years).

Compared to other high-yield bond variable annuity subaccounts, this one ranked in the top half for the 3-year period but in the bottom quartile for the 5-year period. The inception month of this subaccount was August 1984.

The year-by-year returns for this subaccount are:

| Year | Annual Return | First Boston High-Yield Bond Index |
|---|---|---|
| 1994 | −8.5% | −1.0% |
| 1993 | 18.3% | 18.9% |
| 1992 | 14.4% | 16.7% |
| 1991 | 34.5% | 43.8% |
| 1990 | −9.6% | −6.4% |
| 1989 | −1.9% | 0.4% |
| 1988 | 16.2% | 11.4% |
| 1987 | −2.0% | 6.5% |

## Risk Control                                                      ✓✓✓

Over the 3-year period, this fund was dramatically safer than the average hybrid subaccount. During the 5-year period, it was quite a bit safer.

The typical standard deviation for high-yield bond subaccounts was 1.6% during the 3-year period. The standard deviation for Penn Mutual Diversifier II High-Yield Bond was 1.5% over this same period, which means that this subaccount was 3% less volatile than its peer group. The average maturity of the bonds in this account is 8 years; the weighted coupon rate averages 11.6%. The typical high-yield bond subaccount has an average maturity of 9 years and a weighted coupon rate of 10.0%.

The *risk-adjusted* return for this variable annuity subaccount can be described as very good.

## Expense Minimization                                              ✓✓✓

The typical expenses incurred by high-yield bond subaccounts are 2.1% per year. The total expenses for Penn Mutual Diversifier II High-Yield Bond, 2.1%, are equivalent to its peer group average. Total expenses include all charges to the investor (except the annual contract charge, which is always expressed as a dollar figure), including management fees, overhead, administration, and mortality expenses. The free annual withdrawals percentage is based on the account value.

| | | | |
|---|---|---|---|
| Maximum surrender charge | 7% | Total expenses | 2.1% |
| Duration of surrender charge | 10 years | Annual contract charge | $30 |
| Declining surrender charge | no | Free annual withdrawals | 10% |

## Management                                     ✓✓✓

Penn Mutual Diversifier II is offered by Penn Mutual Life Insurance Company. The company has a Duff & Phelps rating of AA− and an A.M. Best rating of A+. The portfolio was managed by Catherine H. Bray for the 7 years ending December 31, 1994. The portfolio's size is $30 million.

## Investment Options                              ✓✓✓✓

Investors may make additional contributions into this portfolio at any time. This is known as a flexible premium annuity. Investors in this variable annuity can choose from all of the subaccount categories below that have a check mark:

| | | |
|---|---|---|
| ___ Aggressive growth | ___ Government bonds | ✓ Money market |
| ✓ Balanced | ✓ Growth | ___ Specialty/Sector |
| ✓ Corporate bonds | ✓ Growth & income | ___ World bonds |
| ✓ Global equities (stocks) | ✓ High-yield bonds | |

## Family Rating                                   ✓✓✓

There are 10 subaccounts within the Penn Mutual Diversifier II family. Overall, this family of subaccounts can be described as good on a *risk-adjusted* return basis.

   The subaccounts within this variable annuity all have an *increasing* guaranteed death benefit. This means that the beneficiary is guaranteed to receive *the greater of* the contract's value on the date of the annuitant's death or the value of the original investment(s) compounded by 5% each year (less any withdrawals made).

## Summary

Penn Mutual Diversifier II High-Yield Bond is consistent for its returns and risk minimization. This is a fine choice to fill the bond portion of your portfolio. The contract's strong suit is the number of investment choices to select from.

   The 10-year penalty schedule is one of the most onerous in the industry, but the contract is able to counter this concern by providing a healthy number of investment options that can be easily moved into as conditions or personal outlooks change. Fortunately, free annual withdrawals are based on the account value.

## Profile

| | | | |
|---|---|---|---|
| Minimum investment | $250 | Telephone exchanges | yes |
| Retirement account minimum | $2,500 | Transfers allowed per year | 12 |
| Co-annuitant allowed | yes | Maximum issuance age | 80 |
| Co-owner allowed | yes | Maximum annuitization age | 85 |
| Dollar-cost averaging | yes | Number of subaccounts | 10 |
| Systematic withdrawal plans | yes | Available in all 50 states | yes |

---

**Prudential Discovery Plus
High-Yield Bond**
Prudential Plaza
Newark, NJ 07102-3777
(201) 802-6000

---

| | |
|---|---|
| Performance | ✓✓✓✓ |
| Risk control | ✓✓✓ |
| Expense minimization | ✓✓✓✓ |
| Management | ✓✓✓✓ |
| Investment options | ✓✓✓ |
| Family rating | ✓✓✓ |
| Total point score | 21 points |

---

# Performance                                              ✓✓✓✓

During the 3-year and 5-year periods ending December 31, 1994, High-Yield Bond had an average annual compound return of 9.6% and 9.5%, respectively. This means that a $10,000 investment made into this subaccount 5 years before that date grew to $15,700 ($13,200 over the last 3 years).

Compared to other high-yield bond variable annuity subaccounts, this one ranked in the top half for the 3-year period but in the bottom quartile for the 5-year period. The inception month of this subaccount was February 1989. The performance figures (shown below) for periods before the subaccount's inception in February 1989 are hypothetical, based on the underlying clone fund's returns. This subaccount is modeled (cloned) after the Prudential High-Yield Fund—Class B, which had an inception date of March 1979, and has an asset base of $3.9 billion.

The year-by-year returns for this subaccount and the mutual fund it is modeled after are:

| Year | Annual Return | First Boston High-Yield Bond Index |
|---|---|---|
| 1994 | −3.9% | −1.0% |
| 1993 | 18.6% | 18.9% |
| 1992 | 16.1% | 16.7% |
| 1991 | 37.5% | 43.8% |
| 1990 | −12.9% | −6.4% |
| 1989 | −3.2% | 0.4% |
| 1988 | 12.1% | 11.4% |

# Risk Control                                              ✓✓✓

Over the 3-year period, this fund has been dramatically safer than the average hybrid subaccount. During the 5-year period, it has been somewhat safer.

The typical standard deviation for high-yield bond subaccounts was 1.6% during the 3-year period. The standard deviation for Prudential Discovery Plus High-Yield Bond was also 1.6% over this same period. The average maturity of the bonds in this account is 8 years; the weighted coupon rate averages 10.2%. The typical high-yield bond subaccount has an average maturity of 9 years and a weighted coupon rate of 10.0%.

The *risk-adjusted* return for this variable annuity subaccount can be described as very good.

## Expense Minimization    ✓✓✓✓

The typical expenses incurred by high-yield bond subaccounts are 2.1% per year. The total expenses for Prudential Discovery Plus High-Yield Bond, 1.9%, are lower than its peer group average. Total expenses include all charges to the investor (except the annual contract charge, which is always expressed as a dollar figure), including management fees, overhead, administration, and mortality expenses. The free annual withdrawals percentage is based on the account value.

| | | | |
|---|---|---|---|
| Maximum surrender charge | 7% | Total expenses | 1.9% |
| Duration of surrender charge | 6 years | Annual contract charge | $0 |
| Declining surrender charge | yes | Free annual withdrawals | 10% |

## Management    ✓✓✓✓

Prudential Discovery Plus is offered by Prudential Insurance Company of America. The company has a Duff & Phelps rating of AA+. The portfolio was managed by George Edwards for the 5 years ending December 31, 1994. The portfolio's size is $117 million.

## Investment Options    ✓✓✓

Investors may make additional contributions into this portfolio at any time. This is known as a flexible premium annuity. Investors in this variable annuity can choose from all of the subaccount categories below that have a check mark:

| | | |
|---|---|---|
| ___ Aggressive growth | ✓ Government bonds | ✓ Money market |
| ✓ Balanced | ✓ Growth | ✓ Specialty/Sector |
| ✓ Corporate bonds | ✓ Growth & income | ___ World bonds |
| ✓ Global equities (stocks) | ✓ High-yield bonds | |

## Family Rating    ✓✓✓

There are 12 subaccounts within the Prudential Discovery Plus family. Overall, this family of subaccounts can be described as good on a *risk-adjusted* return basis.

## Summary

Prudential Discovery Plus High-Yield Bond boasts one of the top-performing scores within its category. This subaccount does well or very well for every characteristic; performance, management, and risk control are particular strong points. With an average maturity of less than 10 years and a typical yield of over 10%, this subaccount is subject to little interest rate risk. Thus, this would be a particularly attractive choice for the total return investor who has some concerns about the future direction of interest rates.

## Profile

| | | | |
|---|---|---|---|
| Minimum investment | $10,000 | Telephone exchanges | yes |
| Retirement account minimum | $10,000 | Transfers allowed per year | 4 |
| Co-annuitant allowed | yes | Maximum issuance age | 85 |
| Co-owner allowed | yes | Maximum annuitization age | 90 |
| Dollar-cost averaging | yes | Number of subaccounts | 12 |
| Systematic withdrawal plans | no | Available in all 50 states | yes |

Travelers Universal Annuity
Fidelity High Income
One Tower Square
Hartford, CT 06183
(800) 842-0125

| | |
|---|---|
| Performance | ✓✓✓✓ |
| Risk control | ✓✓✓ |
| Expense minimization | ✓✓✓✓ |
| Management | ✓✓✓✓✓ |
| Investment options | ✓✓✓✓✓ |
| Family rating | ✓✓✓ |
| Total point score | 24 points |

## Performance                                                         ✓✓✓✓

During the 3-year and 5-year periods ending December 31, 1994, Fidelity High Income had an average annual compound return of 12.0% and 12.6%, respectively. This means that a $10,000 investment made into this subaccount 5 years before that date grew to $18,100 ($14,000 over the last 3 years).

Compared to other high-yield bond variable annuity subaccounts, this one ranked in the top third for the 3-year and 5-year periods. The inception month of this subaccount was February 1992. The performance figures (shown below) for periods before the subaccount's inception in February 1992 are hypothetical, based on the underlying clone fund's returns. This subaccount is modeled (cloned) after the Fidelity VIP Fund High Income Portfolio, which had an inception date of October 1985, and has an asset base of $375 million.

The year-by-year returns for this subaccount and the portfolio it is modeled after are:

| Year | Annual Return | First Boston High-Yield Bond Index |
|---|---|---|
| 1994 | −2.8% | −1.0% |
| 1993 | 19.0% | 18.9% |
| 1992 | 21.8% | 16.7% |
| 1991 | 33.4% | 43.8% |
| 1990 | −3.5% | −6.4% |
| 1989 | −5.4% | 0.4% |
| 1988 | 10.3% | 11.4% |
| 1987 | −0.1% | 6.5% |

## Risk Control                                                          ✓✓✓

Over the 3-year period, this fund was dramatically safer than the average hybrid subaccount. During the 5-year period, it was quite a bit safer.

The typical standard deviation for high-yield bond subaccounts was 1.6% during the 3-year period. The standard deviation for Travelers Universal Annuity Fidelity High Income was 1.4% over this same period, which means that this subaccount was 11% less volatile than its peer group. The average maturity of the bonds in this account is 9 years; the weighted coupon rate averages 9.7%. The typical high-yield bond subaccount also has an average maturity of 9 years and a weighted coupon rate of 10.0%.

The beta (market-related risk) of this subaccount was zero over the 3-year period. Beta for this entire category was 0.6 over this same period. The market index (the S&P 500 Index for "hybrid" subaccounts or the Lehman Brothers Aggregate Bond Index for debt subaccounts) always has a beta of 1.0. The *risk-adjusted* return for this variable annuity subaccount can be described as very good.

## Expense Minimization                    ✓✓✓

The typical expenses incurred by high-yield bond subaccounts are 2.1% per year. The total expenses for Travelers Universal Annuity Fidelity High Income, 1.9%, are lower than its peer group average. Total expenses include all charges to the investor (except the annual contract charge, which is always expressed as a dollar figure), including management fees, overhead, administration, and mortality expenses. The free annual withdrawals percentage is based on the account value.

| | | | |
|---|---|---|---|
| Maximum surrender charge | 5% | Total expenses | 1.9% |
| Duration of surrender charge | 5 years | Annual contract charge | $30 |
| Declining surrender charge | yes | Free annual withdrawals | 10% |

## Management                    ✓✓✓✓✓

Travelers Universal Annuity is offered by Travelers Insurance Company. The company has a Duff & Phelps rating of A+ and an A.M. Best rating of A−. The subaccount and the portfolio it is modeled after were managed by Barry J. Coffman for the 9 years ending December 31, 1994. The portfolio's size is $25 million.

## Investment Options                    ✓✓✓✓✓

Investors may make additional contributions into this portfolio at any time. This is known as a flexible premium annuity. Investors in this variable annuity can choose from all of the subaccount categories below that have a check mark:

| | | |
|---|---|---|
| ✓ Aggressive growth | ✓ Government bonds | ✓ Money market |
| ✓ Balanced | ✓ Growth | ___ Specialty/Sector |
| ✓ Corporate bonds | ✓ Growth & income | ✓ World bonds |
| ✓ Global equities (stocks) | ✓ High-yield bonds | |

## Family Rating                    ✓✓✓

There are 23 subaccounts within the Travelers Universal Annuity family. Overall, this family of subaccounts can be described as good on a *risk-adjusted* return basis.

The subaccounts within this variable annuity all have an *increasing* guaranteed death benefit. This means that the beneficiary is guaranteed to receive *the greater of* the contract's value on the date of the annuitant's death or the value of the original investment(s) compounded by 5% each year (less any withdrawals made).

## Summary

Travelers Universal Annuity Fidelity High Income is the highest point scorer in its category. It is also one of the few subaccounts where the management can be characterized as excellent. Coffman has done a superb job of running this subaccount, which has turned out some of the best risk-adjusted returns in the financial community.

The Travelers Universal Annuity is also to be applauded. The number of investment options is awesome. Dollar-cost averaging, systematic withdrawal plans, and unlimited telephone exchanges help round out this advantageous investment vehicle. This is one of the few contracts available in all 50 states.

## Profile

| | | | |
|---|---|---|---|
| Minimum investment | $20 | Telephone exchanges | yes |
| Retirement account minimum | $1,000 | Transfers allowed per year | unlimited |
| Co-annuitant allowed | no | Maximum issuance age | 85 |
| Co-owner allowed | no | Maximum annuitization age | varies |
| Dollar-cost averaging | yes | Number of subaccounts | 23 |
| Systematic withdrawal plans | yes | Available in all 50 states | yes |

---

**Xerox Account ForPerformance**
**Van Kampen Merritt High-Yield**
10 Valley Stream Parkway
Malvern, PA 19355
(800) 343-8496

---

| | |
|---|---|
| Performance | ✓✓✓ |
| Risk control | ✓✓✓ |
| Expense minimization | ✓✓ |
| Management | ✓✓✓ |
| Investment options | ✓✓ |
| Family rating | ✓✓✓✓ |
| Total point score | 17 points |

## Performance                                          ✓✓✓

During the 3-year and 5-year periods ending December 31, 1994, Van Kampen Merritt High-Yield had an average annual compound return of 10.0% and 11.1%, respectively. This means that a $10,000 investment made into this subaccount 5 years before that date grew to $16,900 ($13,300 over the last 3 years).

Compared to other high-yield bond variable annuity subaccounts, this one ranks in the top half for the 3-year period. The inception month of this subaccount was December 1989. The performance figures (shown below) for periods before the subaccount's inception in December 1989 are hypothetical, based on the underlying clone fund's returns. This subaccount is modeled (cloned) after the Van Kampen Merritt High-Yield Fund—Class, which had an inception date of June 1986, and has an asset base of $275 million.

The year-by-year returns for this subaccount and the mutual fund it is modeled after are:

| Year | Annual Return | First Boston High-Yield Bond Index |
|---|---|---|
| 1994 | −5.8% | −1.0% |
| 1993 | 20.2% | 18.9% |
| 1992 | 17.5% | 16.7% |
| 1991 | 26.7% | 43.8% |
| 1990 | 0.4% | −6.4% |
| 1989 | −8.5% | 0.4% |

## Risk Control                                                    ✓✓✓

Over the 3-year period, this fund was dramatically safer than the average hybrid subaccount.

The typical standard deviation for high-yield bond subaccounts was 1.6% during the 3-year period. The standard deviation for Xerox Account ForPerformance Van Kampen Merritt High-Yield was 1.4% over this same period, which means that this subaccount was 10% less volatile than its peer group. The average maturity of the bonds in this account is 7 years; the weighted coupon rate averages 8.9%. The typical high-yield bond subaccount has an average maturity of 9 years and a weighted coupon rate of 10.0%.

The *risk-adjusted* return for this variable annuity subaccount can be described as excellent.

## Expense Minimization                                            ✓✓

The typical expenses incurred by high-yield bond subaccounts are 2.1% per year. The total expenses for Xerox Account ForPerformance Van Kampen Merritt High-Yield, 2.3%, are higher than its peer group average. Total expenses include all charges to the investor (except the annual contract charge, which is always expressed as a dollar figure), including management fees, overhead, administration, and mortality expenses. The free annual withdrawals percentage is based on the original principal.

| | | | |
|---|---|---|---|
| Maximum surrender charge | 5% | Total expenses | 2.3% |
| Duration of surrender charge | 5 years | Annual contract charge | $30 |
| Declining surrender charge | yes | Free annual withdrawals | 10% |

## Management                                                      ✓✓✓

Xerox Account ForPerformance is offered by Xerox Financial Services Life Insurance. The portfolio and the mutual fund it is modeled after were managed by Kevin Mathews and Daniel H. Smith for the 5 years ending December 31, 1994. The portfolio's size is $13 million.

## Investment Options                                              ✓✓

Investors may make additional contributions into this portfolio at any time. This is known as a flexible premium annuity. Investors in this variable annuity can choose from all of the subaccount categories below that have a check mark:

| | | |
|---|---|---|
| ___ Aggressive growth | ___ Government bonds | ✓ Money market |
| ___ Balanced | ___ Growth | ___ Specialty/Sector |
| ✓ Corporate bonds | ✓ Growth & income | ___ World bonds |
| ✓ Global equities (stocks) | ✓ High-yield bonds | |

## Family Rating                                                   ✓✓✓✓

There are 8 subaccounts within the Xerox Account ForPerformance family. Overall, this family of subaccounts can be described as very good on a *risk-adjusted* return basis.

## Summary

Xerox Account ForPerformance Van Kampen Merritt High-Yield is a fine example of a portfolio that is able to balance returns and risk. Returns have been commendable; *risk-adjusted* returns deserve even greater praise.

The two pluses of this variable annuity are (1) the companies backing the product—Xerox and Van Kampen Merritt—and (2) the quality of the overall fund family. This investment is a smart choice for all.

## Profile

| | | | |
|---|---|---|---|
| Minimum investment | $2,000 | Telephone exchanges | yes |
| Retirement account minimum | $5,000 | Transfers allowed per year | 12 |
| Co-annuitant allowed | no | Maximum issuance age | 81 |
| Co-owner allowed | yes | Maximum annuitization age | 81 |
| Dollar-cost averaging | yes | Number of subaccounts | 8 |
| Systematic withdrawal plans | yes | Available in all 50 states | no* |

*Not available in the following states: CA, DE, ME, NH, NJ, NY, and VT.

Chapter

# 15

# Metals Subaccounts

No metals subaccounts made it into this book because the *risk-adjusted* returns for this category over the 3-year and 5-year periods ending December 31, 1994, have not been good. However, there have been periods in the past when the returns were good, and there will be similar times in the future. More importantly, metals can be a *small* part of your holdings now. Because a category has not performed well over the past few years does not mean that it will not have incredible returns over the next 6 months, year, or 2 years. In fact, a strong case can be made for investing in an area, or sector, that has been recently beaten down (presumably, most of the risk has already been eliminated).

Metals subaccounts make their purchases in one or more of the following ways: bullion, South African gold stocks, and non-South African mining stocks. The United States, Canada, and Australia are the three major *stock-issuing* producers of metals outside of South Africa. Metals, also referred to as gold subaccounts, often own minor positions in other precious metals stocks, such as silver and platinum.

The proportion and type of metal held by a subaccount can have a great impact on its performance and volatility. Outright ownership of gold bullion is almost always less volatile than ownership of stock of a gold mining company. Thus, compared to subaccounts that hold high levels of bullion, greater gains or losses occur in metals subaccounts purchasing only gold stocks. Silver has nearly twice the volatility of gold, yet has not had any greater return over the long term.

Gold, or metals, subaccounts do particularly well during periods of political uncertainty and inflationary concern. Over the past several hundred years, gold and silver have been a hedge against inflation. Most readers will be surprised to learn that, historically, both metals have outperformed inflation by less than 1% annually.

Metals subaccounts are the riskiest category of variable annuities described in this book. This is true regardless of the composition of the gold subaccount. Although this is a high-risk investment when viewed alone, ownership of a metals

### Average Annual Returns: Metals (Gold) Subaccounts vs. Metals Mutual Funds

| Year | Subaccount | Mutual Fund |
|---|---|---|
| 1994 | −4.7% | −11.7% |
| 1993 | 60.6% | 83.8% |
| 1992 | −6.4% | −15.0% |
| 1991 | −3.0% | −4.4% |
| 1990 | −17.2% | −23.9% |
| 1989 | 18.2% | 25.6% |
| 1988 | −21.9% | −17.8% |
| 1987 | 33.2% | 36.8% |
| | | |
| 3-yr. average | 11.4% | 10.5% |
| 5-yr. average | 3.0% | −0.5% |
| 10-yr. average | n/a | 5.5% |

subaccount can actually reduce a portfolio's overall risk level and often enhance its total return because gold usually has a negative correlation to other investments; that is, when one investment goes down in value, gold will often go up. Thus, a portfolio comprised strictly of government bonds will actually exhibit more risk *and* less return than one comprised of 90% governments and 10% in a metals subaccount.

The following table shows year-by-year, as well as 3-, 5-, and 10-year averages for this investment category. The variable annuity subaccount category is compared against the similar mutual fund category. These performance figures are averages, representing all funds and subaccounts that fall within this investment objective.

As you can see, the variable annuity subaccounts outperformed their mutual fund counterparts for 1994, 1992, 1991, 1990, and the 3-year and 5-year periods.

Metals subaccounts should be avoided by anyone who cannot tolerate wide price swings in any *single* part of a portfolio. These subaccounts are designed as an integral part of a diversified portfolio for the investor who looks at the *overall* return of his or her holdings. I recommend a 5% commitment to this category for the aggressive portfolio. As with any category of variable annuities, whenever larger dollar amounts are involved, more than one subaccount per category should be used.

The table on page 256 shows statistics you might find useful when comparing variable annuity subaccounts versus their mutual fund counterparts or clones. These category averages are based on information available at the beginning of 1995.

Figure 15.1 on page 256 shows the year-by-year returns for this category of variable annuities for the period 1987 through 1994. These are composite figures and therefore include all of the subaccounts that comprise the metals category.

## Metals Category Statistics:
## Subaccounts vs. Mutual Funds

| Description | Subaccounts | Funds |
|---|---|---|
| **Composition of portfolio** | | |
| U.S. stocks | 11% | 11% |
| Cash | 12% | 8% |
| Foreign stocks | 70% | 76% |
| Bonds | 7% | 0% |
| Other | 0% | 5% |
| **Fees and expenses** | | |
| Underlying fund expense | 1.1% | 1.9% |
| Insurance expense | 1.02% | — |
| Total expenses | 2.12% | 1.9%/4.1%* |
| **Operations** | | |
| Net assets (in millions) | $13 | $159 |
| Manager tenure | 5 years | 6 years |
| **Portfolio statistics** | | |
| Beta | n/a | −0.3 |
| Standard deviation | 6.4% | 7.2% |
| Price/earnings ratio | 44 | 43 |
| Turnover ratio (annual) | 3% | 82% |
| Median market capitalization | $1.7 billion | $1.6 billion |
| Number of subaccounts/funds | 5 | 31 |

*Total expenses for this mutual fund category increase to this figure
if the average mutual fund commission is added to the 1.9% figure.

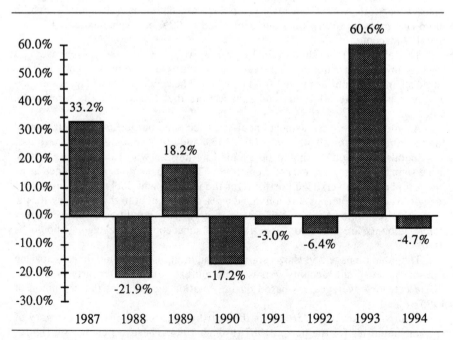

**Figure 15.1** Metals Subaccounts

## Chapter

# 16

# Specialty Subaccounts

These subaccounts primarily invest in the common stocks of a single industry, or sector, such as natural resources (e.g., timber, mining, and so on) or real estate. Traditionally, most if not all of the companies represented in these subaccounts are domestic. Some other sources (but not this book) include metals and utilities under the heading of specialty.

Specialty subaccounts are the most volatile group you can invest in, particularly when the definition of specialty includes metals funds. (Utilities are the most conservative industry within this broad category.) Despite its often high levels of volatility, this category can actually reduce the overall level of risk of one's portfolio because specialty subaccounts can have a random or negative correlation (they may go up when other parts of the portfolio are moving sideways or going down).

Whether you should include one or more specialty subaccounts (or mutual funds) in your portfolio will depend, first, on your time horizon. The longer the expected holding period, the greater the likelihood that a sector or specialty subaccount will turn out to be rewarding. Occasionally, a specialty account can increase 40% to 100% during the very first year of ownership, but these types of accounts can also drop by 25% to 50% the following year. In short, this category often has no consistency or predictability.

How you view your investments is the second consideration. If you are someone who looks at how individual parts of the whole are doing (i.e., the growth subaccount, the world bonds subaccount, and so on), then the ups and downs of most specialty subaccounts are probably not for you. If, instead, you look at the whole, realizing the overall risk reduction is an important component of properly managing your money, then this category has merit.

The table at the top of page 258 shows year-by-year, as well as 3-, 5-, and 10-year averages for this investment category. The variable annuity subaccount category is compared against the similar mutual fund category. These performance figures are averages, representing all funds and subaccounts that fall within this investment objective.

As you can see, the variable annuity subaccounts outperformed their mutual fund counterparts for 1990 and 1988.

I recommend a 5% commitment to this category for the aggressive portfolio. As with any category of variable annuities, whenever larger dollar amounts are involved, more than one subaccount per category should be used.

## Average Annual Returns: Specialty Subaccounts vs. Mutual Funds

| Year | Subaccount | Mutual Fund |
|------|-----------|-------------|
| 1994 | −3.7% | −2.3% |
| 1993 | 17.9% | 29.4% |
| 1992 | 2.9% | 4.6% |
| 1991 | 15.2% | 25.0% |
| 1990 | −8.7% | −9.2% |
| 1989 | 16.1% | 26.8% |
| 1988 | 10.6% | 7.1% |
| 1987 | 6.6% | 6.6% |
| | | |
| 3-yr. average | 5.6% | 8.0% |
| 5-yr. average | 4.1% | 8.5% |
| 10-yr. average | n/a | 11.5% |

The table below shows statistics you might find useful when comparing variable annuity subaccounts versus their mutual fund counterparts or clones. These category averages are based on information available at the beginning of 1995.

Figure 16.1 shows the year-by-year returns for this category of variable annuities for the period 1987 through 1994. These are composite figures and therefore include all of the subaccounts that comprise the specialty category.

## Specialty Stock Category Statistics: Subaccounts vs. Mutual Funds

| Description | Subaccounts | Funds |
|-------------|-------------|-------|
| **Composition of portfolio** | | |
| U.S. stocks | 54% | 62% |
| Cash | 10% | 9% |
| Foreign stocks | 14% | 24% |
| Bonds | 5% | 3% |
| Other | 17% | 2% |
| **Fees and expenses** | | |
| Underlying fund expense | 1.3% | 1.6% |
| Insurance expense | 1.2% | — |
| Total expenses | 2.5% | 1.6%/4.2%* |
| **Operations** | | |
| Net assets (in millions) | $130 | $270 |
| Manager tenure | 4 years | 5 years |
| **Portfolio statistics** | | |
| Beta | 0.6% | 0.6% |
| Standard deviation | 3.5% | 4.4% |
| Price/earnings ratio | 28 | 27 |
| Turnover ratio (annual) | 19% | 89% |
| Median market capitalization | $1.7 billion | $3.2 billion |
| Number of subaccounts/funds | 28 | 180 |

*Total expenses for this mutual fund category increase to this figure if the average mutual fund commission is added to the 1.6% figure.

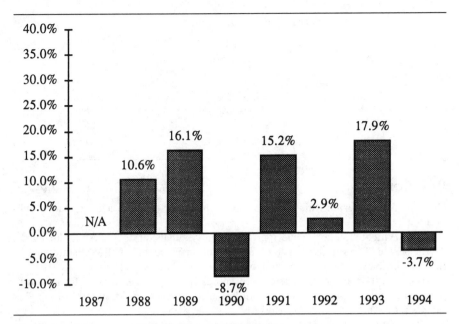

**Figure 16.1** Specialty Subaccounts

---

**Franklin Valuemark II**
**Real Estate Securities**
10 Valley Stream Parkway
Malvern, PA 19355
(800) 342-3863

| | |
|---|---|
| Performance | ✓✓✓✓ |
| Risk control | ✓✓✓✓ |
| Expense minimization | ✓✓✓ |
| Management | ✓✓✓✓ |
| Investment options | ✓✓✓✓ |
| Family rating | ✓✓ |
| Total point score  / | 26 points |

## Performance  ✓✓✓✓

During the 3-year and 5-year periods ending December 31, 1994, Real Estate Securities had an average annual compound return of 9.6% and 2.7%, respectively. This means that a $10,000 investment made into this subaccount 5 years before that date grew to $13,200 ($11,400, if only the last 3 years of the period are used).

Compared to other specialty variable annuity subaccounts, this one ranked in the top quartile for the 3-year period. The inception month of this subaccount was June 1989.

The year-by-year returns for this subaccount are:

| Year | Annual Return | S&P 500 |
|------|------|------|
| 1994 | 1.5% | 1.3% |
| 1993 | 17.3% | 10.1% |
| 1992 | 10.6% | 7.6% |
| 1991 | 31.7% | 30.5% |
| 1990 | −13.2% | −3.1% |

## Risk Control                                    ✓✓✓✓✓

Over the 3-year period, this fund was somewhat safer than the average equity subaccount.

The typical standard deviation for specialty subaccounts was 3.5% during the 3-year period. The standard deviation for Franklin Valuemark II Real Estate Securities was 3.6% over this same period, which means that this subaccount was 1% more volatile than its peer group. The price/earnings (p/e) ratio averages 32 for this portfolio. The typical specialty subaccount has a p/e ratio of 28. In general, the higher the p/e ratio, the riskier the portfolio.

The beta (market-related risk) of this subaccount was 0.6 over the 3-year period. Beta for this entire category was also 0.6 over this same period. The market index (the S&P 500 Index for equity and hybrid subaccounts) always has a beta of 1.0. The *risk-adjusted* return for this variable annuity subaccount can be described as very good.

## Expense Minimization                             ✓✓✓✓

The typical expenses incurred by specialty subaccounts are 2.5% per year. The total expenses for Franklin Valuemark II Real Estate Securities, 2.1%, are lower than its peer group average. Total expenses include all charges to the investor (except the annual contract charge, which is always expressed as a dollar figure), including management fees, overhead, administration, and mortality expenses. The free annual withdrawals percentage is based on the original principal.

| | | | |
|---|---|---|---|
| Maximum surrender charge | 5% | Total expenses | 2.1% |
| Duration of surrender charge | 5 years | Annual contract charge | $30 |
| Declining surrender charge | yes | Free annual withdrawals | 15% |

## Management                                       ✓✓✓✓✓

Franklin Valuemark II is offered by Allianz Life Insurance Company of North America. The company has an A.M. Best rating of A+. The portfolio was managed by Matthew Avery and Edward Jamieson for the 5 years ending December 31, 1994. The portfolio's size is $67 million. The typical security in the portfolio has a market capitalization of $592 million.

## Investment Options                               ✓✓✓✓✓

Investors may make additional contributions into this portfolio at any time. This is known as a flexible premium annuity. Investors in this variable annuity can choose from all of the subaccount categories below that have a check mark:

| | | |
|---|---|---|
| ___ Aggressive growth | ✓ Government bonds | ✓ Money market |
| ✓ Balanced | ✓ Growth | ✓ Specialty/Sector |
| ✓ Corporate bonds | ___ Growth & income | ✓ World bonds |
| ✓ Global equities (stocks) | ✓ High-yield bonds | |

## Family Rating                                                        ✓✓

There are 18 subaccounts within the Franklin Valuemark II family. Overall, this family of subaccounts can be described as fair on a *risk-adjusted* return basis.

The subaccounts within this variable annuity all have an *increasing* guaranteed death benefit. This means that the beneficiary is guaranteed to receive *the greater of* the contract's value on the date of the annuitant's death or the value of the original investment(s) compounded by 5% each year (less any withdrawals made).

## Summary

Franklin Valuemark II Real Estate Securities is the highest scoring real estate and specialty subaccount to appear in this book. Performance and risk control have been nothing short of excellent. Management is also superb. The range of other investment categories offered by the Valuemark II contract is also equally impressive. Few investments in any category can match the risk-adjusted returns offered by this great Franklin portfolio.

## Profile

| | | | |
|---|---|---|---|
| Minimum investment | $2,000 | Telephone exchanges | yes |
| Retirement account minimum | $5,000 | Transfers allowed per year | 12 |
| Co-annuitant allowed | yes | Maximum issuance age | none |
| Co-owner allowed | spouses only | Maximum annuitization age | 80 |
| Dollar-cost averaging | yes | Number of subaccounts | 18 |
| Systematic withdrawal plans | yes | Available in all 50 states | yes |

---

### Golden American GoldenSelect
### Natural Resources
1001 Jefferson Street
Suite 400
Wilmington, DE  19801
(800) 243-3706

---

| | |
|---|---|
| Performance | ✓✓ |
| Risk control | ✓✓ |
| Expense minimization | ✓✓✓ |
| Management | ✓✓ |
| Investment options | ✓✓✓ |
| Family rating | ✓ |
| Total point score | 13 points |

## Performance                                                          ✓✓

During the 3-year and 5-year periods ending December 31, 1994, Natural Resources had an average annual compound return of 10.4% and 3.5%, respectively. This means that a $10,000 investment made into this subaccount 5 years before that date grew to $11,900 ($13,500 over the last 3 years).

Compared to other specialty variable annuity subaccounts, this one ranks in the bottom half for the 3-year period. The inception month of this subaccount was January 1989.

The year-by-year returns for this subaccount are:

| Year | Annual Return | S&P 500 |
|------|------|------|
| 1994 | 1.5% | 1.3% |
| 1993 | 48.4% | 10.1% |
| 1992 | −10.7% | 7.6% |
| 1991 | 3.7% | 30.5% |
| 1990 | −14.7% | −3.1% |

## Risk Control                                                    ✓✓

Over the 3-year period, this fund was somewhat riskier than the average equity subaccount.

The typical standard deviation for specialty subaccounts was 3.5% during the 3-year period. The standard deviation for Golden American GoldenSelect Natural Resources was 5.0% over this same period, which means that this subaccount was 42% more volatile than its peer group. The price/earnings (p/e) ratio averages 37 for this portfolio. The typical specialty subaccount has a p/e ratio of 28. In general, the higher the p/e ratio, the riskier the portfolio.

The *risk-adjusted* return for this variable annuity subaccount can be described as poor.

## Expense Minimization                                          ✓✓✓

The typical expenses incurred by specialty subaccounts are 2.5% per year. The total expenses for Golden American GoldenSelect Natural Resources, 2.5%, are equivalent to its peer group average. Total expenses include all charges to the investor (except the annual contract charge, which is always expressed as a dollar figure), including management fees, overhead, administration, and mortality expenses. The free annual withdrawals percentage is based on the account value.

| | | | | |
|---|---|---|---|---|
| Maximum surrender charge | 6% | Total expenses | 2.5% |
| Duration of surrender charge | 6 years | Annual contract charge | $40 |
| Declining surrender charge | no | Free annual withdrawals | 15% |

## Management                                                      ✓✓

Golden American GoldenSelect is offered by Golden American Life Insurance Company. The portfolio was managed by Henry Bingham and John Van Eck for the 5 years ending December 31, 1994. The portfolio's size is $15 million. The typical security in the portfolio has a market capitalization of $3.0 billion. Bingham and Van Eck also manage the Van Eck International Investors mutual fund.

## Investment Options                                            ✓✓✓

Investors may make additional contributions into this portfolio at any time. This is known as a flexible premium annuity. Investors in this variable annuity can choose from all of the subaccount categories below that have a check mark:

| | | |
|---|---|---|
| ✓ Aggressive growth | ___ Government bonds | ✓ Money market |
| ✓ Balanced | ✓ Growth | ✓ Specialty/Sector |
| ✓ Corporate bonds | ✓ Growth & income | ___ World bonds |
| ✓ Global equities (stocks) | ___ High-yield bonds | |

## Family Rating ✓

There are 11 subaccounts within the Golden American GoldenSelect family.

The subaccounts within this variable annuity all have an *increasing* guaranteed death benefit. This means that the beneficiary is guaranteed to receive *the greater of* the contract's value on the date of the annuitant's death or the value of the original investment(s) compounded by 5% each year (less any withdrawals made).

## Summary

Golden American GoldenSelect Natural Resources represents the only natural resources portfolio that made it into this book. Returns for a portfolio of this type can be quite extreme and, at times, quite rewarding. The diversification it brings to most portfolios makes this a good choice for the overwhelming majority of investors. It is rare to find a subaccount of this type that has not only done well, but also can reduce one's overall level of risk.

## Profile

| | | | |
|---|---|---|---|
| Minimum investment | $1,500 | Telephone exchanges | yes |
| Retirement account minimum | $10,000 | Transfers allowed per year | unlimited |
| Co-annuitant allowed | yes | Maximum issuance age | 85 |
| Co-owner allowed | yes | Maximum annuitization age | 90 |
| Dollar-cost averaging | yes | Number of subaccounts | 11 |
| Systematic withdrawal plans | yes | Available in all 50 states | no* |

*Not available in CT, ME, or NY.

---

**Manulife Financial Variable Annuity Separate Account 2**
**Real Estate Securities**
200 Bloor Street East
Toronto, Ontario Canada M4W-IE5
(800) 387-2728

| | |
|---|---|
| Performance | ✓✓✓✓✓ |
| Risk control | ✓✓✓✓ |
| Expense minimization | ✓✓✓✓✓ |
| Management | ✓✓✓✓✓ |
| Investment options | ✓ |
| Family rating | ✓✓✓✓✓ |
| Total point score | 25 points |

## Performance ✓✓✓✓✓

During the 3-year and 5-year periods ending December 31, 1994, Real Estate Securities had an average annual compound return of 12.0% and 13.1%, respectively. This means that a $10,000 investment made into this subaccount 5 years before that date grew to $18,500 ($14,000, if only the last 3 years of the period are used).

Compared to other specialty variable annuity subaccounts, this one ranked in the top 3% for the 3-year period and in the top 7% for the 5-year period. The inception month of this subaccount was November 1987.

The year-by-year returns for this subaccount are:

| Year | Annual Return | S&P 500 |
|------|---------------|---------|
| 1994 | −3.7% | 1.3% |
| 1993 | 21.4% | 10.1% |
| 1992 | 20.1% | 7.6% |
| 1991 | 39.7% | 30.5% |
| 1990 | −5.5% | −3.1% |
| 1989 | 8.2% | 31.7% |
| 1988 | 10.6% | 16.6% |

## Risk Control                                                    ✓✓✓✓

Over the 3-year period, this fund was as safe as the average equity subaccount. During the 5-year period, it was slightly safer.

The typical standard deviation for specialty subaccounts was 3.5% during the 3-year period. The standard deviation for Manulife Financial Variable Annuity Separate Account 2 Real Estate Securities was 4.6% over this same period, which means that this subaccount was 29% more volatile than its peer group. The price/earnings (p/e) ratio averages 26 for this portfolio. The typical specialty subaccount has a p/e ratio of 28. In general, the higher the p/e ratio, the riskier the portfolio.

The beta (market-related risk) of this subaccount was 0.9 over the 3-year period. Beta for this entire category was 0.6 over this same period. The market index (the S&P 500 Index for equity and hybrid subaccounts) always has a beta of 1.0. The *risk-adjusted* return for this variable annuity subaccount can be described as excellent.

## Expense Minimization                                            ✓✓✓✓✓

The typical expenses incurred by specialty subaccounts are 2.5% per year. The total expenses for Manulife Financial Variable Annuity Separate Account 2 Real Estate Securities, 1.5%, are lower than its peer group average. Total expenses include all charges to the investor (except the annual contract charge, which is always expressed as a dollar figure), including management fees, overhead, administration, and mortality expenses. The free annual withdrawals percentage is based on the account value.

| | | | |
|------|------|------|------|
| Maximum surrender charge | 8% | Total expenses | 1.5% |
| Duration of surrender charge | 8 years | Annual contract charge | $30 |
| Declining surrender charge | yes | Free annual withdrawals | 10% |

## Management                                                      ✓✓✓✓✓

Manulife Financial Variable Annuity Separate Account 2 is offered by Manufacturers Life Insurance Company of America. The company has a Duff & Phelps rating of AAA and an A.M. Best rating of A++. The portfolio was managed by Stephen Kahn for the 7 years ending December 31, 1994. The portfolio's size is $13 million. The typical security in the portfolio has a market capitalization of $475 million.

## Investment Options                                              ✓

Investors may make additional contributions into this portfolio at any time. This is known as a flexible premium annuity. Investors in this variable annuity can choose from all of the subaccount categories below that have a check mark:

| | | |
|---|---|---|
| ✓ Aggressive growth | ___ Government bonds | ✓ Money market |
| ✓ Balanced | ✓ Growth | ✓ Specialty/Sector |
| ✓ Corporate bonds | ___ Growth & income | ___ World bonds |
| ___ Global equities (stocks) | ___ High-yield bonds | |

## Family Rating                                     ✓✓✓✓

There are 6 subaccounts within the Manulife Financial Variable Annuity Separate Account 2 family. Overall, this family of subaccounts can be described as excellent on a *risk-adjusted* return basis. The subaccounts within this variable annuity all have a death benefit based on the value at the date of death (what is referred to in the industry as "accumulated value"). Unlike the death benefit found with most variable annuities, the accumulated value death benefit does not protect the beneficiary from possible market loss.

## Summary

Manulife Financial Variable Annuity Separate Account 2 Real Estate Securities is one of only two real estate portfolios recommended—and this one has the better track record. The low level of risk incurred by this subaccount is also very impressive.

The only negative thing that can be said about this investment is that the parent company, Manulife Financial, does not offer a wide range of other choices. The contract is currently limited to a total of 6 different subaccounts. The overall rating of these different investments is excellent, however, and less than 10% of the competition can make that claim.

It would be a mistake not to seriously consider this real estate subaccount. Manulife Financial is a wise place to invest your money. This type of account should also reduce the overall risk level of your portfolio.

## Profile

| | | | |
|---|---|---|---|
| Minimum investment | $1,000 | Telephone exchanges | yes |
| Retirement account minimum | $1,000 | Transfers allowed per year | 6 |
| Co-annuitant allowed | yes | Maximum issuance age | 70 |
| Co-owner allowed | yes | Maximum annuitization age | none |
| Dollar-cost averaging | yes | Number of subaccounts | 6 |
| Systematic withdrawal plans | no | Available in all 50 states | no* |

*Not available in ME, NJ, NY, and PR.

Chapter

# 17

# Utility Stock Subaccounts

No utilities subaccounts made it into this book because the *risk-adjusted* returns for this category over the 3-year and 5-year periods ending December 31, 1994, were not good. Like metals subaccounts, the picture for this category can change in a matter of months, and it should not be omitted from serious consideration. Particularly regarding utilities, a strong case can be made for purchasing this industry group at a depressed price.

These subaccounts look for both growth and income, and they invest in common stocks of utility companies across the country. Somewhere between one-third and one-half of these subaccounts' total return comes from common stock dividends. Utility subaccounts normally stay away from speculative issues; instead, they focus on well-established companies that have a solid history of paying good dividends. Surprisingly, the goal of most of these subaccounts is *long-term* growth (their average dividend of 5% has represented less than one-half to one-third the total return these subaccounts have enjoyed over the past 5, 10, and 15 years).

Utility and metal subaccounts are the only two sector, or specialty, subaccount categories mentioned in this book. Subaccounts that invest in only one industry, or sector, should be avoided by most investors, for two reasons. First, the subaccount manager's ability to find attractive stocks or bonds is limited if he or she is only able to choose securities from one particular geographic area or industry. Second, the track record of sector subaccounts as a whole is pretty bad. In fact, *as a general category,* these specialty subaccounts represent the worst of both worlds: above-average risk and substandard returns. If the term *aggressive growth* has little appeal to you, then the words *sector subaccount* should frighten you.

Utility subaccounts are the one exception to the aforementioned description. Utility subaccounts sound safe and are safe. Any category of stocks that relies fairly heavily on a high level of reinvested dividends has a built-in safety cushion. A comparatively high dividend income means that you have to count on, or worry less about, the appreciation of the underlying issues.

Four things generally determine the profitability of a utility company: (1) how much it pays for energy, (2) the general level of interest rates, (3) the company's expected use of nuclear power, and (4) the political climate.

The price of oil and gas is directly passed on to the consumer, but the utility companies are sensitive to this issue. Higher fuel prices mean that the utility industry has less latitude to increase its profit margins. Thus, higher fuel prices can mean smaller profits and/or dividends to investors.

Next to energy costs, interest is the industry's greatest expense. Utility companies are heavily debt-laden. Their interest costs directly affect their profitability. When rates go down and companies are able to refinance their debt, the savings can be enormous. Paying 8% interest on a couple of hundred million dollars' worth of bonds each year is much more appealing than having to shell out 10% on the same amount of debt. A lower interest rate environment translates into more money left over for shareholders.

Depending on your viewpoint, nuclear power has been an issue, or a problem, for the United States for a few decades. Other countries seem to have come to grips with the matter, but we still remain quite divided. Although new power plants have not been successfully proposed in this country for several years, no one knows what the future may hold. Venturing into nuclear power always seems to be much more expensive than ever anticipated by the utility companies and the independent experts they rely on for advice. Because of these uncertainties, subaccount managers try to seek out utility companies that have no foreseeable plans to develop any, or more, nuclear power facilities. Whether this is good long-term planning for the country remains to be seen, but such avoidance keeps share prices more stable and predictable.

Finally, the political climate is an important concern when calculating whether utility subaccounts should be part of your portfolio. The Public Utilities Commission (PUC) is a political animal and can directly reflect the views of a state's government. Most of us are concerned about our utility bills; the powers that be are more likely to be reelected if they are able to keep rate increases to a minimum. Modest or minimum increases can be healthy for the utility companies; freezing rates for a couple of years is a bad sign.

The table below shows year-by-year, as well as 3-, 5-, and 10-year averages for this investment category. The variable annuity subaccount category is compared against the similar mutual fund category. These performance figures are averages, representing all funds and subaccounts that fall within this investment objective.

As you can see, the variable annuity subaccounts outperformed their mutual fund counterparts for 1990 and 1987.

Utility stock prices closely follow the long-term bond market. If the economy surges and long-term interest rates go up, utility stock prices are likely to go down. Utility stocks are also vulnerable to a general stock market decline, although they

### Average Annual Returns: Utility Subaccounts vs. Utility Mutual Funds

| Year | Subaccount | Mutual Fund |
|---|---|---|
| 1994 | −9.9% | −8.3% |
| 1993 | 9.4% | 14.7% |
| 1992 | 7.2% | 9.4% |
| 1991 | 15.9% | 20.2% |
| 1990 | 4.0% | −2.4% |
| 1989 | 8.5% | 29.5% |
| 1988 | 6.7% | 13.3% |
| 1987 | 6.0% | −4.2% |
| 3-yr. average | 2.5% | 5.2% |
| 5-yr. average | 4.7% | 6.8% |
| 10-yr. average | n/a | 11.0% |

are considered less risky than other types of common stock because of their dividends and the monopoly position of most utilities. Typically, utilities have fallen about two-thirds as much as other common stocks during market downturns.

Worldwide, there is a tremendous opportunity for growth in this industry. The average per-capita production of electricity in many developing countries (2,500 kilowatt hours) is only *one-fifth* of the level in the United States (12,100 kilowatt hours). All over the world, previously underdeveloped countries are making economic strides as they move toward free market systems. When emerging countries become developed economically, their citizens demand higher standards of living. As a result, their requirements for electricity, water, and telephones should rise dramatically. Also, many countries are selling their utility companies to public owners, opening a new arena for investors.

The net result of all of this for investors is that variable annuities are beginning to offer *global* utilities subaccounts. Increased diversification (allowing a subaccount to invest in utility companies all over the world instead of just in the United States), coupled with tremendous long-term growth potential, should make this a dynamic industry group for the next few decades.

I recommend a 10% commitment to this category for the conservative portfolio and up to 5% for the moderate investor. As with any category of variable annuities, whenever larger dollar amounts are involved, more than one subaccount per category should be used.

The table below shows statistics you might find useful when comparing variable annuity subaccounts versus their mutual fund counterparts or clones. These category averages are based on information available at the beginning of 1995.

### Utility Stock Category Statistics: Subaccounts vs. Mutual Funds

| Description | Subaccounts | Funds |
|---|---|---|
| **Composition of portfolio** | | |
| U.S. stocks | 58% | 69% |
| Cash | 23% | 8% |
| Foreign stocks | 4% | 11% |
| Bonds | 12% | 10% |
| Other | 3% | 2% |
| **Fees and expenses** | | |
| Underlying fund expense | 0.6% | 1.1% |
| Insurance expense | 1.09% | — |
| Total expenses | 1.69% | 1.10%/3.7%* |
| **Operations** | | |
| Net assets (in millions) | $418 | $613 |
| Manager tenure | 3 years | 4 years |
| **Portfolio statistics** | | |
| Beta | 0.3% | 0.4% |
| Standard deviation | 1.7% | 2.6% |
| Price/earnings ratio | 16 | 17 |
| Turnover ratio (annual) | 10% | 48% |
| Median market capitalization | $3.7 billion | $6.5 billion |
| Number of subaccounts/funds | 7 | 45 |

*Total expenses for this mutual fund category increase to this figure if the average mutual fund commission is added to the 1.10% figure.

Figure 17.1 shows the year-by-year returns for this category of variable annuities for the period 1987 through 1994. These are composite figures and therefore include all of the subaccounts that comprise the utilities category.

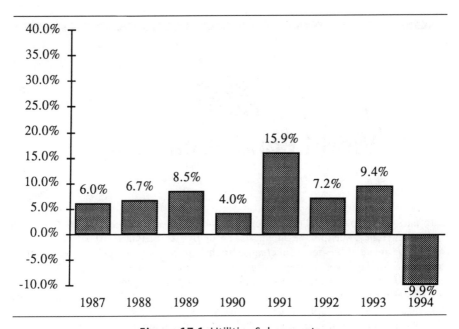

**Figure 17.1** Utilities Subaccounts

# Chapter

# 18

# World Bond Subaccounts

International, also referred to as foreign, subaccounts purchase securities issued in a foreign currency, such as the Japanese yen or British pound. Prospective investors need to be aware of the potential changes in the value of the foreign currency relative to the U.S. dollar. As an example, if you were to invest in U.K. bonds that had a current yield of 15% and the British pound appreciated 12% against the U.S. dollar, your total return for the year would be 27%. Conversely, if the pound declined by 20% against the U.S. dollar, your total return would be − 5%.

World bond, also known as global bond, subaccounts invest in securities issued all over the world, including the United States. A world bond subaccount usually invests in bonds issued by stable governments in a handful of countries. These subaccounts try to avoid purchasing foreign government debt instruments from politically or economically unstable nations.

World bond subaccounts seek higher interest rates, no matter where the search may take them. Inclusion into the portfolio is dependent on management's perception of interest rates, the country's projected currency strength against the U.S. dollar, and the predicted political and economic stability.

Because foreign markets do not necessarily move in tandem with U.S. markets, each country represents varying investment opportunities at different times. The current value of the world bond market is estimated to be close to $12 trillion. Half of this marketplace is comprised of U.S. bonds; Japan ranks second with 20% of the market.

Over the 25 years ending December 31, 1994, international bonds outperformed U.S. bonds and inflation. They have come close to matching the return of U.S. common stocks. From 1964 through 1994, there were twenty-one 10-year periods (e.g., 1964–1973, 1965–1974, and so on). The Non-U.S. Bond Index *outperformed* the U.S. Bond Index in eighteen of the past twenty-one 10-year periods from 1964 to 1994.

Assessing the economic environment to evaluate its effects on interest rates and bond values requires an understanding of two important factors: (1) inflation and (2) supply. During inflationary periods, when there is too much money chasing too few goods, government tightening of the money supply helps create a balance between an economy's cash resources and its available goods. Money supply refers to the amount of cash made available for spending, borrowing, or investing. Controlled by the central banks of each nation, money supply is a primary tool for managing inflation, interest rates, and economic growth. A prudent tightening of the money supply can help bring on disinflation—decelerated loan demand, reduced durable goods orders, and falling prices. During disinflationary times, interest rates also fall, strengthening the underlying value of existing bonds. Although such factors ultimately contribute to a healthier economy, they also mean lower yields for government bond investors. A trend toward disinflation currently exists in markets around the world. The worldwide growth in money supply is at its lowest level in 20 years.

When governments implement policies designed to reduce inflation, interest rates drop. This disinflation can be disquieting to individuals who specifically invest for high monthly income. In reality, falling interest rates mean higher bond values, and investors seeking long-term growth or high total return can therefore benefit from declining rates. Inflation, which drives interest rates higher, is the true enemy of bond investors. It diminishes bond values and erodes the buying power of the interest income that investors receive. Income-seeking investors need to find economies where inflation is coming under control, yet interest rates are still high enough to provide favorable bond yields.

Not all bond markets will peak at the same level, but they do tend to follow patterns. Targeting those countries where interest rates are at peak levels and inflation is falling not only results in higher income but also creates significant potential for capital appreciation when rates ultimately decline.

Each year, from 1984 through 1994, at least three government bond markets have provided yields higher than those available in the United States (Salomon Brothers, Inc.). With almost 50% of the world's bonds found outside the United States, investors must look beyond U.S. borders to find bonds offering yields and total returns that meet their investment objectives.

Even with high income as the primary goal, investors must consider credit and market risk. By investing primarily in variable annuity subaccounts that purchase government-guaranteed bonds from the world's most creditworthy nations, you can get an extra measure of credit safety for payment of interest and repayment of principal. By diversifying across multiple markets, subaccount managers can significantly reduce market risk as well. Diversification is a proven technique for controlling market risk.

Figure 18.1 shows how volatility can be decreased by increasing one's exposure to foreign (non-U.S.) bonds. The figures used for this study, conducted by G.T. Capital Management, cover the 10-year period ending December 31, 1994.

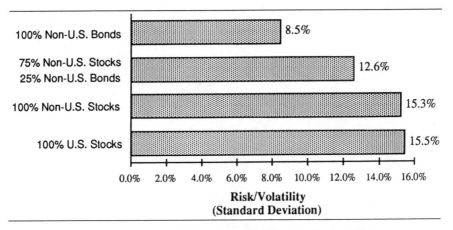

**Figure 18.1** How Global Diversification Can Reduce Risk

Most investors understand the concept of investing in global bonds for the income, or yield, they provide. However, many investors do not realize that global bonds may offer more than just yield. Successful management of global bond portfolios has three components: (1) capital appreciation, (2) yield, and (3) currency management. Investors searching strictly for high yields may lose out on capital appreciation opportunities. By the same token, those looking solely for capital appreciation often give up current income. Finally, individuals who invest in global bonds without applying the principles of currency management can see their investment erode when exchanges rates change adversely.

Investing in global bonds provides the potential for capital appreciation during periods of declining interest rates. An inverse relationship exists between bond values and interest rates. When interest rates fall, as is the case in most bond markets in the world today, existing bond values climb. Conversely, as interest rates rise, the value of existing bonds declines. For example, if an investor holds a bond paying 9% and interest rates for newly issued bonds climb to 10%, the value of the 9% bond declines. However, if interest rates for newly issued bonds decline to 8%, the bond paying 9% appreciates in value, reflecting the desirability of the higher-yielding bond.

If you are limiting your bond portfolio to U.S. investments, you are missing out on over half of the world's bond market opportunities. Currently, over half of the world's government bonds are issued in countries other than the United States. Investing in global bonds can help position U.S. investors' portfolios to benefit from capital growth opportunities in world bond markets, while capturing income from those bonds. Each year, from 1985 through 1994, at least three government bond markets have provided yields higher than those available in the United States.

Inflation has historically been the key factor in driving worldwide interest rates higher. Inflation diminishes bond returns and erodes the buying power of the interest income that investors receive. In the 1990s, a worldwide trend toward disinflation is developing. Our own Federal Reserve has been actively battling inflation, and as a result has been able to keep rates relatively low in an effort to strengthen the U.S. economy. This trend should spread to other nations such as Germany and Japan over the next few years. Targeting those countries where interest rates are at peak

### Average Annual Returns: World Bond Subaccounts vs. World Bond Mutual Funds

| Year | Subaccount | Mutual Fund |
|---|---|---|
| 1994 | −6.5% | −5.8% |
| 1993 | 11.7% | 16.0% |
| 1992 | 0.1% | 2.5% |
| 1991 | 10.1% | 13.5% |
| 1990 | 11.9% | 12.7% |
| 1989 | 6.2% | 6.2% |
| 1988 | 3.0% | 4.5% |
| 1987 | 23.1% | 18.0% |
| 3-yr. average | 1.4% | 3.8% |
| 5-yr. average | 6.0% | 7.5% |
| 10-yr. average | 12.0% | 9.5% |

levels and inflation is falling not only results in higher income but also creates significant potential for capital appreciation.

The table on page 272 shows year-by-year, as well as 3-, 5-, and 10-year averages for this investment category. The variable annuity subaccount category is compared against the similar mutual fund category. These performance figures are averages, representing all funds and subaccounts that fall within this investment objective.

As you can see, the variable annuity subaccounts outperformed their mutual fund counterparts for 1987 and for the 10-year period.

World bond subaccounts, particularly those that have a high concentration in foreign issues, are an excellent risk-reduction tool that should be utilized by the vast majority of investors. Conservative portfolios should have no more than 50% of their diversified holdings in world bonds, moderates should have no more than 30%, and aggressive investors should have no more than 20%. I recommend that conservative, moderate, and aggressive investors all have 10% to 20% of their overall holdings in world bond subaccounts. As with any category of variable annuities, whenever larger dollar amounts are involved, more than one subaccount per category should be used.

The table below shows statistics you might find useful when comparing variable annuity subaccounts versus their mutual fund counterparts or clones. These category averages are based on information available at the beginning of 1995.

Figure 18.2 shows the year-by-year returns for this category of variable annuities for the period 1987 through 1994. These are composite figures and therefore include all of the subaccounts that comprise the world bond category.

## World Bond Category Statistics: Subaccounts vs. Mutual Funds

| Description | Subaccounts | Funds |
|---|---|---|
| **Composition of portfolio** | | |
| Stocks | 1% | 1% |
| Cash | 24% | 17% |
| Foreign stocks | 0% | 0% |
| Bonds | 75% | 80% |
| Other | 1% | 2% |
| **Fees and expenses** | | |
| Underlying fund expense | 1.1% | 1.5% |
| Insurance expense | 1.3% | — |
| Total expenses | 2.4% | 1.5%/3.4%* |
| **Operations** | | |
| Net assets (in millions) | $25 | $262 |
| Manager tenure | 5 years | 3 years |
| **Portfolio statistics** | | |
| Average maturity | 7 years | 8 years |
| Standard deviation | 1.5% | 2.0% |
| Average weighted coupon | 7.9% | 8.1% |
| Turnover ratio (annual) | 133% | 206% |
| Number of subaccounts/funds | 35 | 75 |

*Total expenses for this mutual fund category increase to this figure if the average mutual fund commission is added to the 1.5% figure.

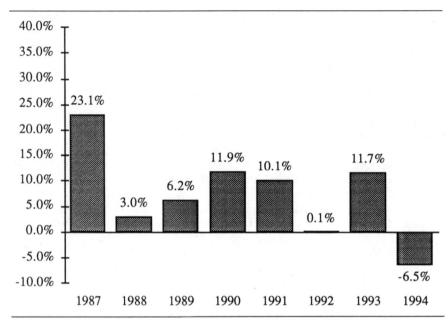

**Figure 18.2** World Bond Subaccounts

---

**Best of America IV/Nationwide**
**Van Eck Global Bond**
P.O. Box 16609
One Nationwide Plaza
Columbus, OH 43216
(800) 848-6331

| | |
|---|---|
| Performance | ✓✓ |
| Risk control | ✓ |
| Expense minimization | ✓✓✓✓ |
| Management | ✓✓ |
| Investment options | ✓✓✓✓ |
| Family rating | ✓✓ |
| Total point score | 17 points |

## Performance                                                   ✓✓

During the 3-year and 5-year periods ending December 31, 1994, Van Eck Global Bond had an average annual compound return of −1.1% and 4.5%, respectively. This means that a $10,000 investment made into this subaccount 5 years before that date grew to $12,500 ($9,700, if only the last 3 years of the period are used).

Compared to other world bond variable annuity subaccounts, this one ranked in the top half for the 3-year period. The inception month of this subaccount was September 1989. The performance figures (shown below) for periods before the subaccount's inception in September 1989 are hypothetical, based on the underlying clone fund's returns. This subaccount is modeled (cloned) after the Van Eck World Income Fund, which had an inception date of April 1987, and has an asset base of $275 million.

The year-by-year returns for this subaccount and the mutual fund it is modeled after are:

| Year | Annual Return | Salomon Bros. Non-US$ World Gov't Bond Index |
|------|------|------|
| 1994 | −2.6% | 6.7% |
| 1993 | 6.4% | 15.1% |
| 1992 | −6.5% | 4.8% |
| 1991 | 16.9% | 16.2% |
| 1990 | 9.8% | 15.3% |
| 1989 | 11.4% | −3.4% |
| 1988 | 11.2% | 2.4% |

## Risk Control                                                        ✓

Over the 3-year period, this fund was quite a bit riskier than the average fixed-income subaccount.

The typical standard deviation for world bond subaccounts was 1.5% during the 3-year period. The standard deviation for Best of America IV/Nationwide Van Eck Global Bond was 2.5% over this same period, which means that this subaccount was 70% more volatile than its peer group. The average maturity of the bonds in this account is 10 years; the weighted coupon rate averages 9.6%. The typical world bond subaccount has an average maturity of 7 years and a weighted coupon rate of 7.9%.

The beta (market-related risk) of this subaccount was 1.8 over the 3-year period. Beta for this entire category was 0.9 over this same period. The market index (the Lehman Brothers Aggregate Bond Index for debt subaccounts) always has a beta of 1.0. The *risk-adjusted* return for this variable annuity subaccount can be described as poor.

## Expense Minimization                                          ✓✓✓✓

The typical expenses incurred by world bond subaccounts are 2.4% per year. The total expenses for Best of America IV/Nationwide Van Eck Global Bond, 2.4%, are equivalent to its peer group average. Total expenses include all charges to the investor (except the annual contract charge, which is always expressed as a dollar figure), including management fees, overhead, administration, and mortality expenses. The free annual withdrawals percentage is based on the original principal.

| | | | |
|---|---|---|---|
| Maximum surrender charge | 7% | Total expenses | 2.4% |
| Duration of surrender charge | 7 years | Annual contract charge | $30 |
| Declining surrender charge | yes | Free annual withdrawals | 10% |

## Management                                                        ✓✓

Best of America IV/Nationwide is offered by Nationwide Life Insurance Company. The company has an A.M. Best rating of A+. The portfolio and the mutual fund it is modeled after were managed by David R. Kenerson, Jr. for the 5 years ending December 31, 1994. The portfolio's size is $84 million.

## Investment Options                                            ✓✓✓✓

Investors may make additional contributions into this portfolio at any time. This is known as a flexible premium annuity. Investors in this variable annuity can choose from all of the subaccount categories below that have a check mark:

| | | |
|---|---|---|
| ✓ Aggressive growth | ✓ Government bonds | ✓ Money market |
| ✓ Balanced | ✓ Growth | ✓ Specialty/Sector |
| ✓ Corporate bonds | ✓ Growth & income | ✓ World bonds |
| ✓ Global equities (stocks) | ✓ High-yield bonds | |

## Family Rating                                                              ✓✓

There are 22 subaccounts within the Best of America IV/Nationwide family. Overall, this family of subaccounts can be described as fair on a *risk-adjusted* return basis.

## Summary

Best of America IV/Nationwide Van Eck Global Bond is a fine selection for investors who need to add foreign bonds to their holdings. Globally diversified investors can often end up with better returns and far less risk than those who invest solely in U.S. government securities.

Often, the deciding factor between the performance of one bond subaccount versus that of another is how well overhead is controlled. This Van Eck portfolio has one of the best expense minimization policies in the industry. However, the contract's real attraction is the number of options investors can choose from.

## Profile

| | | | |
|---|---|---|---|
| Minimum investment | none | Telephone exchanges | yes |
| Retirement account minimum | $1,500 | Transfers allowed per year | one per day |
| Co-annuitant allowed | no | Maximum issuance age | none |
| Co-owner allowed | no | Maximum annuitization age | none |
| Dollar-cost averaging | yes | Number of subaccounts | 22 |
| Systematic withdrawal plans | yes | Available in all 50 states | yes |

---

### Franklin Valuemark II
### Global Income
10 Valley Stream Parkway
Malvern, PA 19355
(800) 342-3863

| | |
|---|---|
| Performance | ✓✓✓✓ |
| Risk control | ✓✓ |
| Expense minimization | ✓✓✓✓✓ |
| Management | ✓✓✓✓ |
| Investment options | ✓✓✓✓✓ |
| Family rating | ✓✓ |
| Total point score | 22 points |

## Performance                                                              ✓✓✓✓

During the 3-year and 5-year periods ending December 31, 1994, Global Income had an average annual compound return of 1.9% and 4.9%, respectively. This means that a $10,000 investment made into this subaccount 5 years before that date grew to $12,700 ($10,600, if only the last 3 years of the period are used).

Compared to other world bond variable annuity subaccounts, this one ranked in the top half for the 3-year period. The inception month of this subaccount was June 1989.

The year-by-year returns for this subaccount are:

| Year | Annual Return | Salomon Bros. Non-US$ World Gov't Bond Index |
|------|--------------|---------------------------------------------|
| 1994 | −6.3% | 6.7% |
| 1993 | 15.1% | 15.1% |
| 1992 | −1.8% | 4.8% |
| 1991 | 10.7% | 16.2% |
| 1990 | 8.3% | 15.3% |
| 1989 | 5.6% | −3.4% |

## Risk Control ✓✓

Over the 3-year period, this fund was quite a bit riskier than the average fixed-income subaccount.

The typical standard deviation for world bond subaccounts was 1.5% during the 3-year period. The standard deviation for Franklin Valuemark II Global Income was 1.7% over this same period, which means that this subaccount was 17% more volatile than its peer group. The average maturity of the bonds in this account is 7 years; the weighted coupon rate averages 8.8%. The typical world bond subaccount also has an average maturity of 7 years and a weighted coupon rate of 7.9%.

The beta (market-related risk) of this subaccount was 0.4 over the 3-year period. Beta for this entire category was 0.9 over this same period. The market index (the Lehman Brothers Aggregate Bond Index for debt subaccounts) always has a beta of 1.0. The *risk-adjusted* return for this variable annuity subaccount can be described as poor.

## Expense Minimization ✓✓✓✓

The typical expenses incurred by world bond subaccounts are 2.4% per year. The total expenses for Franklin Valuemark II Global Income, 2.1%, are lower than its peer group average. Total expenses include all charges to the investor (except the annual contract charge, which is always expressed as a dollar figure), including management fees, overhead, administration, and mortality expenses. The free annual withdrawals percentage is based on the original principal.

| | | | |
|---|---|---|---|
| Maximum surrender charge | 5% | Total expenses | 2.1% |
| Duration of surrender charge | 5 years | Annual contract charge | $30 |
| Declining surrender charge | yes | Free annual withdrawals | 15% |

## Management ✓✓✓

Franklin Valuemark II is offered by Allianz Life Insurance Company of North America. The company has an A.M. Best rating of A+. The portfolio was managed by Edward Jamieson and William Kohli for the 5 years ending December 31, 1994. The portfolio's size is $160 million. Kohli also manages the Franklin Global Government Income mutual fund.

## Investment Options ✓✓✓✓

Investors may make additional contributions into this portfolio at any time. This is known as a flexible premium annuity. Investors in this variable annuity can choose from all of the subaccount categories below that have a check mark:

| | | |
|---|---|---|
| ___ Aggressive growth | ✓ Government bonds | ✓ Money market |
| ✓ Balanced | ✓ Growth | ✓ Specialty/Sector |
| ✓ Corporate bonds | ___ Growth & income | ✓ World bonds |
| ✓ Global equities (stocks) | ✓ High-yield bonds | |

## Family Rating                                                    ✓✓

There are 18 subaccounts within the Franklin Valuemark II family. Overall, this family of subaccounts can be described as fair on a *risk-adjusted* return basis.

The subaccounts within this variable annuity all have an *increasing* guaranteed death benefit. This means that the beneficiary is guaranteed to receive *the greater of* the contract's value on the date of the annuitant's death or the value of the original investment(s) compounded by 5% each year (less any withdrawals made).

## Summary

Franklin Valuemark Funds Global Income Fund ties for first place as the top-scoring global bond subaccount. This portfolio has turned in some very good numbers, not only for sheer performance, but also for expense minimization.

The Valuemark II annuity is one of the most generous in the industry. Withdrawal privileges and investment options are extremely liberal. This is a highly recommended choice.

## Profile

| | | | |
|---|---|---|---|
| Minimum investment | $2,000 | Telephone exchanges | yes |
| Retirement account minimum | $5,000 | Transfers allowed per year | 12 |
| Co-annuitant allowed | yes | Maximum issuance age | none |
| Co-owner allowed | spouses only | Maximum annuitization age | 80 |
| Dollar-cost averaging | yes | Number of subaccounts | 18 |
| Systematic withdrawal plans | yes | Available in all 50 states | yes |

---

**MFS/Sun Life (US) Compass 3**
**World Government Variable Account**
P.O. Box 1024
Boston, MA 02103
(800) 752-7215

---

| | |
|---|---|
| Performance | ✓✓✓✓ |
| Risk control | ✓✓ |
| Expense minimization | ✓✓✓ |
| Management | ✓✓✓✓ |
| Investment options | ✓✓✓ |
| Family rating | ✓✓✓ |
| Total point score | 20 points |

## Performance                                                    ✓✓✓✓

During the 3-year and 5-year periods ending December 31, 1994, World Government Variable Account had an average annual compound return of 2.6% and 6.7%, respectively. This means that a $10,000 investment made into this subaccount 5 years before that date grew to $13,800 ($10,800, if only the last 3 years of the period are used).

Compared to other world bond variable annuity subaccounts, this one ranked in the top third for the 3-year period and in the top half for the 5-year period. The inception month of this subaccount was May 1988.

The year-by-year returns for this subaccount are:

| Year | Annual Return | Salomon Bros. Non-US$ World Gov't Bond Index |
|------|------|------|
| 1994 | −6.5% | 6.7% |
| 1993 | 16.9% | 15.1% |
| 1992 | −1.1% | 4.8% |
| 1991 | 12.2% | 16.2% |
| 1990 | 14.1% | 15.3% |
| 1989 | 6.8% | −3.4% |

## Risk Control                    ✓✓

Over the 3-year and 5-year periods, this fund was quite a bit riskier than the average fixed-income subaccount.

The typical standard deviation for world bond subaccounts was 1.5% during the 3-year period. The standard deviation for MFS/Sun Life (US) Compass 3 World Government Variable Account was 2.2% over this same period, which means that this subaccount was 50% more volatile than its peer group. The average maturity of the bonds in this account is 5 years; the weighted coupon rate averages 7.9%. The typical world bond subaccount has an average maturity of 7 years and a weighted coupon rate of 7.9%.

The beta (market-related risk) of this subaccount was 1.5 over the 3-year period. Beta for this entire category was 0.9 over this same period. The market index (the Lehman Brothers Aggregate Bond Index for debt subaccounts) always has a beta of 1.0. The *risk-adjusted* return for this variable annuity subaccount can be described as poor.

## Expense Minimization                    ✓✓✓

The typical expenses incurred by world bond subaccounts are 2.4% per year. The total expenses for MFS/Sun Life (US) Compass 3 World Government Variable Account, 2.6%, are higher than its peer group average. Total expenses include all charges to the investor (except the annual contract charge, which is always expressed as a dollar figure), including management fees, overhead, administration, and mortality expenses. The free annual withdrawals percentage is based on the original principal.

| | | | |
|------|------|------|------|
| Maximum surrender charge | 6% | Total expenses | 2.6% |
| Duration of surrender charge | 7 years | Annual contract charge | $30 |
| Declining surrender charge | yes | Free annual withdrawals | 10% |

## Management                    ✓✓✓✓

MFS/Sun Life (US) Compass 3 is offered by Sun Life Assurance Company of Canada (US). The company has an A.M. Best rating of A++. The portfolio was managed by Leslie J. Nanberg for the 6 years ending December 31, 1994. The portfolio's size is $25 million. Nanberg has also managed the MFS World Governments Fund—Class A mutual fund since 1984.

## Investment Options                                            ✓✓✓

Investors may make additional contributions into this portfolio at any time. This is known as a flexible premium annuity. Investors in this variable annuity can choose from all of the subaccount categories below that have a check mark:

| | | | | | |
|---|---|---|---|---|---|
| ✓ | Aggressive growth | ✓ | Government bonds | ✓ | Money market |
| ✓ | Balanced | ✓ | Growth | ___ | Specialty/Sector |
| ___ | Corporate bonds | ___ | Growth & income | ✓ | World bonds |
| ___ | Global equities (stocks) | ✓ | High-yield bonds | | |

## Family Rating                                                ✓✓✓

There are 7 subaccounts within the MFS/Sun Life (US) Compass 3 family. Overall, this family of subaccounts can be described as good on a *risk-adjusted* return basis.

The subaccounts within this variable annuity all have an *increasing* guaranteed death benefit. This means that the beneficiary is guaranteed to receive *the greater of* the contract's value on the date of the annuitant's death or the value of the original investment(s) compounded by 5% each year (less any withdrawals made).

## Summary

MFS/Sun Life (US) Compass 3 World Government Variable Account is modeled after the oldest global bond mutual fund in the country, and it shows. Performance has been exceptional. This subaccount is not disappointing on any level.

## Profile

| | | | |
|---|---|---|---|
| Minimum investment | $300 | Telephone exchanges | yes |
| Retirement account minimum | $300 | Transfers allowed per year | 12 |
| Co-annuitant allowed | yes | Maximum issuance age | none |
| Co-owner allowed | yes | Maximum annuitization age | 80 |
| Dollar-cost averaging | yes | Number of subaccounts | 7 |
| Systematic withdrawal plans | yes | Available in all 50 states | no* |

*Not available in NY or VT.

---

**PaineWebber Advantage Annuity**
**Global Income**
601 Sixth Avenue
Des Moines, IA  50334
(800) 367-6058

---

| | |
|---|---|
| Performance | ✓✓✓✓ |
| Risk control | ✓✓✓✓✓ |
| Expense minimization | ✓✓✓ |
| Management | ✓✓✓✓✓ |
| Investment options | ✓✓✓ |
| Family rating | ✓✓ |
| Total point score | 22 points |

## Performance                                                  ✓✓✓✓

During the 3-year and 5-year periods ending December 31, 1994, Global Income had an average annual compound return of 3.0% and 3.7%, respectively. This means that

a $10,000 investment made into this subaccount 5 years before that date grew to $12,000 ($11,000, if only the last 3 years of the period are used).

Compared to other world bond variable annuity subaccounts, this one ranked in the top half for the 3-year period but in the bottom half for the 5-year period. The inception month of this subaccount was May 1988. This subaccount is modeled (cloned) after the PaineWebber Global Income Fund—Class B, which had an inception date of March 1987, and has an asset base of $1.3 billion.

The year-by-year returns for this subaccount are:

| Year | Annual Return | Salomon Bros. Non-US$ World Gov't Bond Index |
|------|---------------|-----------------------------------------------|
| 1994 | −13.3% | 6.7% |
| 1993 | 15.0% | 15.1% |
| 1992 | −0.1% | 4.8% |
| 1991 | 8.7% | 16.2% |
| 1990 | 13.3% | 15.3% |
| 1989 | 5.5% | −3.4% |

## Risk Control ✓✓✓✓

Over the 3-year period, this fund has been somewhat riskier than the average fixed-income subaccount. During the 5-year period, it has been slightly riskier.

The typical standard deviation for world bond subaccounts was 1.5% during the 3-year period. The standard deviation for PaineWebber Advantage Annuity Global Income was 1.3% over this same period, which means that this subaccount was 14% less volatile than its peer group. The average maturity of the bonds in this account is 14 years; the weighted coupon rate averages 8.5%. The typical world bond subaccount has an average maturity of 7 years and a weighted coupon rate of 7.9%.

The beta (market-related risk) of this subaccount was 0.9 over the 3-year period. Beta for this entire category was also 0.9 over this same period. The market index (the Lehman Brothers Aggregate Bond Index for debt subaccounts) always has a beta of 1.0. The *risk-adjusted* return for this variable annuity subaccount can be described as fair.

## Expense Minimization ✓✓✓

The typical expenses incurred by world bond subaccounts are 2.4% per year. The total expenses for PaineWebber Advantage Annuity Global Income, 2.5%, are higher than its peer group average. Total expenses include all charges to the investor (except the annual contract charge, which is always expressed as a dollar figure), including management fees, overhead, administration, and mortality expenses. The free annual withdrawals percentage is based on the account value.

| | | | |
|---|---|---|---|
| Maximum surrender charge | 5% | Total expenses | 2.5% |
| Duration of surrender charge | 5 years | Annual contract charge | $30 |
| Declining surrender charge | yes | Free annual withdrawals | 10% |

## Management ✓✓✓✓

PaineWebber Advantage Annuity is offered by American Republic Insurance Company. The portfolio and the mutual fund it is modeled after were managed by Nimrod Fachler and Stuart Waugh for the 7 years ending December 31, 1994. The portfolio's size is $75 million.

## Investment Options                                          ✓✓✓

Investors may make additional contributions into this portfolio at any time. This is known as a flexible premium annuity. Investors in this variable annuity can choose from all of the subaccount categories below that have a check mark:

| | | |
|---|---|---|
| ___ Aggressive growth | ✓ Government bonds | ✓ Money market |
| ✓ Balanced | ✓ Growth | ___ Specialty/Sector |
| ___ Corporate bonds | ✓ Growth & income | ✓ World bonds |
| ✓ Global equities (stocks) | ___ High-yield bonds | |

## Family Rating                                               ✓✓

There are 7 subaccounts within the PaineWebber Advantage Annuity family. Overall, this family of subaccounts can be described as fair on a *risk-adjusted* return basis.

The subaccounts within this variable annuity all have an *increasing* guaranteed death benefit. This means that the beneficiary is guaranteed to receive *the greater of* the contract's value on the date of the annuitant's death or the value of the original investment(s) compounded by 5% each year (less any withdrawals made).

## Summary

PaineWebber Advantage Annuity Global Income ties for first place as the top point scorer in its category. Total return figures have been very good; risk control is exceptional. This subaccount is the perfect choice for anyone who is fearful about going abroad to look for bonds. This investment will allow you to sleep well at night.

## Profile

| | | | |
|---|---|---|---|
| Minimum investment | $1,000 | Telephone exchanges | yes |
| Retirement account minimum | $5,000 | Transfers allowed per year | unlimited |
| Co-annuitant allowed | no | Maximum issuance age | 85 |
| Co-owner allowed | no | Maximum annuitization age | 85 |
| Dollar-cost averaging | no | Number of subaccounts | 7 |
| Systematic withdrawal plans | no | Available in all 50 states | yes |

---

**Venture Variable Annuity**
**Global Government Bond**
P.O. Box 818
Boston, MA 02117-0818
(800) 334-1029

---

| | |
|---|---|
| Performance | ✓✓✓✓ |
| Risk control | ✓✓ |
| Expense minimization | ✓✓✓✓ |
| Management | ✓✓✓✓ |
| Investment options | ✓✓✓✓ |
| Family rating | ✓ |
| Total point score | 21 points |

## Performance                                                 ✓✓✓✓

During the 3-year and 5-year periods ending December 31, 1994, Global Government Bond had an average annual compound return of 3.2% and 7.1%, respectively.

This means that a $10,000 investment made into this subaccount 5 years before that date grew to $14,100 ($11,000, if only the last 3 years of the period are used).

Compared to other world bond variable annuity subaccounts, this one ranked in the top 1% for the 3-year period and in the top half for the 5-year performance. The inception month of this subaccount was March 1988.

The year-by-year returns for this subaccount are:

| Year | Annual Return | Salomon Bros. Non-US$ World Gov't Bond Index |
|---|---|---|
| 1994 | −7.1% | 6.7% |
| 1993 | 17.3% | 15.1% |
| 1992 | 0.9% | 4.8% |
| 1991 | 14.3% | 16.2% |
| 1990 | 11.9% | 15.3% |
| 1989 | 3.0% | −3.4% |

## Risk Control ✓✓

Over the 3-year period, this fund was substantially riskier than the average fixed-income subaccount. During the 5-year period, it was quite a bit riskier.

The typical standard deviation for world bond subaccounts was 1.5% during the 3-year period. The standard deviation for Venture Variable Annuity Global Government Bond was 2.0% over this same period, which means that this subaccount was 33% more volatile than its peer group. The average maturity of the bonds in this account is 10 years; the weighted coupon rate averages 7.4%. The typical world bond subaccount has an average maturity of 7 years and a weighted coupon rate of 7.9%.

The beta (market-related risk) of this subaccount was 1.6 over the 3-year period. Beta for this entire category was 0.9 over this same period. The market index (the Lehman Brothers Aggregate Bond Index for debt subaccounts) always has a beta of 1.0. The *risk-adjusted* return for this variable annuity subaccount can be described as poor.

## Expense Minimization ✓✓✓✓

The typical expenses incurred by world bond subaccounts are 2.4% per year. The total expenses for Venture Variable Annuity Global Government Bond, 2.5%, are higher than its peer group average. Total expenses include all charges to the investor (except the annual contract charge, which is always expressed as a dollar figure), including management fees, overhead, administration, and mortality expenses. The free annual withdrawals percentage is based on the original principal.

| | | | |
|---|---|---|---|
| Maximum surrender charge | 6% | Total expenses | 2.5% |
| Duration of surrender charge | 6 years | Annual contract charge | $30 |
| Declining surrender charge | yes | Free annual withdrawals | 10% |

## Management ✓✓✓

Venture Variable Annuity is offered by North American Security Life Insurance Company. The company has an A.M. Best rating of A. The portfolio was managed by Astrid Vogler for the 6 years ending December 31, 1994. The portfolio's size is $150 million.

## Investment Options                                      ✓✓✓✓

Investors may make additional contributions into this portfolio at any time. This is known as a flexible premium annuity. Investors in this variable annuity can choose from all of the subaccount categories below that have a check mark:

| | | |
|---|---|---|
| ___ Aggressive growth | ✓ Government bonds | ✓ Money market |
| ✓ Balanced | ✓ Growth | ___ Specialty/Sector |
| ✓ Corporate bonds | ✓ Growth & income | ✓ World bonds |
| ✓ Global equities (stocks) | ___ High-yield bonds | |

## Family Rating                                            ✓

There are 13 subaccounts within the Venture Variable Annuity family. Overall, this family of subaccounts can be described as poor on a *risk-adjusted* return basis.

The subaccounts within this variable annuity all have an *increasing* guaranteed death benefit. This means that the beneficiary is guaranteed to receive *the greater of* the contract's value on the date of the annuitant's death or the value of the original investment(s) compounded by 5% each year (less any withdrawals made).

## Summary

Venture Variable Annuity Global Government Bond is the number-two point scorer within its category. Volatility has been a little on the high side, but the subaccount's returns make everything else worthwhile.

The Venture Variable Annuity has some of most diverse investment options available. The company's global government bond portfolio represents the flagship of the family. For the return-conscious, this represents a top choice.

## Profile

| | | | |
|---|---|---|---|
| Minimum investment | $30 | Telephone exchanges | yes |
| Retirement account minimum | $30 | Transfers allowed per year | 12 |
| Co-annuitant allowed | yes | Maximum issuance age | 80 |
| Co-owner allowed | yes | Maximum annuitization age | 85 |
| Dollar-cost averaging | yes | Number of subaccounts | 13 |
| Systematic withdrawal plans | yes | Available in all 50 states | no* |

*Not available in the following states: ME, NH, NV, NY, RI, and VT.

# GLOSSARY OF ANNUITY TERMS

**advisor**    The organization or individual employed by a variable annuity company to give professional advice on the subaccount's investments and asset management practices (also called the investment advisor).

**annuitant**    One of four parties named in the annuity contract. Unlike the contract owner or beneficiary, the person (or persons) named as the annuitant (or co-annuitant) must be a living person (not an entity such as a living trust, partnership, corporation, and so on). The person named as the "measuring life" does not have to be related to the beneficiary or owner. An annuity contract (investment) continues until terminated or liquidated by the contract owner(s) or by the death of the annuitant, whichever happens first. See also *contract owner*.

**annuitization**    The orderly process of liquidating part or all of one's annuity contract. The contract owner decides whether distributions are to be made on a monthly, quarterly, semiannual, or annual basis. The duration of the distributions depends on the value of the contract at the time of annuitization, the period selected, and the amount of each distribution. The period selected, which is chosen by the contract owner, may be for 3 years or longer or may be based on the lifetime of one or more persons (e.g., "Payments to continue as long as either I or my spouse is alive"). Some insurance companies allow the investor (contract owner) to have a specific dollar amount sent out each period (e.g., each month, quarter, or other choice) until the contract is completely paid out.

**beneficiary**    One of four parties named in the annuity contract. The beneficiary can be an individual, a couple, a series of people (e.g., children, relatives, friends, charities), or an entity such as a living trust. The beneficiary, who has no rights or voice in any annuity matter, receives the value of the annuity (or death benefit) upon the annuitant's death. See also *contract owner*.

**beta**    Measures the stock market-related risk of a security or portfolio. The S&P 500 always has a beta of 1.00, whether the market is going up, down, or sideways. The security or portfolio being measured against the market (the S&P 500) may end up having a beta of 1.00, or a beta that is below or above 1.00. If the portfolio has a beta that is greater than 1.00, its market-related risk is higher than the S&P 500; a beta of less than 1.00 means that the market-related risk is less than that of the S&P 500. A higher-than-average (1.00) beta means that the portfolio or security is likely to outperform the market during good periods and underperform it (drop more than the S&P 500) during bad times. A lower-than-average beta means that the portfolio or security will have a tendency to underperform the market during good periods (e.g., not go up as much), but perform better (not drop as much) during stock market declines.

**bottom up**   A type of security analysis. Management that follows the bottom-up approach is more concerned with the company than with the economy in general. (For a contrasting style, see *top down.*)

**broker/dealer**   A firm that buys and sells variable annuities and other securities to the public.

**CFS**   Certified Fund Specialist; the designation awarded only to brokers, financial planners, CPAs, insurance agents, and other investment advisors who either recommend or sell variable annuities or mutual funds. Fewer than 1,500 people across the country have passed this certification program. For additional information about the CFS program or to get the name of a CFS in your area, call (800) 848-2029.

**co-annuitant**   An option included in some annuity contracts. Where there are two "measuring lives" (the annuitant and co-annuitant), a forced annuitization or contract liquidation is much less likely.

**contract owner**   One of four parties named in the annuity contract. (The others are the annuitant, the beneficiary, and the insurance company.) The contract owner can be an individual or entity. Some contracts allow co-ownership, which means that spouses could equally own or control the investment. The contract owner is the party who decides how the money is to be invested, when changes are to be made, and, until the annuitant's death, how long the contract (investment) should last.

**CPI**   Consumer Price Index; the mostly commonly used yardstick to measure the rate of inflation in the United States.

**diversification**   A policy, followed in all variable annuities, of spreading investments among a number of different securities to reduce the risk inherent in investing.

**dollar-cost averaging**   The practice of investing equal amounts of money at regular intervals, regardless of whether securities markets are moving up or down. This procedure may reduce average unit (share) costs to the investor, who acquires more units in periods of lower securities prices but fewer units in periods of higher prices.

**EAFE Index**   A way to compare stock market returns from foreign countries. The Europe, Australia, Far East Index is market weighted; Japan represents about 40% of the index.

**exchange privilege**   An option enabling contract owners (investors) to transfer their investment from one subaccount to another within the same subaccount family as their needs or objectives change. Typically, subaccounts allow investors to use the exchange privilege several times a year without a charge or fee.

**fixed-rate**   Either a specific type of variable annuity subaccount or a type of annuity contract. A fixed-rate annuity is different from a variable annuity in that the fixed-rate contract offers the investor a locked-in rate of return (similar to a bank CD rate); the investor's only investment choice is whether to lock-in a rate for 1, 3, 5, 7, or 10 years (or whatever periods of time are offered by the annuity contract). With a fixed-rate annuity, the contract owner (investor) cannot choose a stock, bond, or money market option. If a *variable annuity investor* chooses a fixed rate, he or she has decided to lock-in a specific rate of return for part or all of the money being invested (the balance may be divided by the investor in one or more of the other subaccounts offered by the insurer).

**fund**   A mutual fund portfolio whose investment objective is often indicated by its title (e.g., The XYZ *Growth* Fund). There are over 6,500 different mutual funds, all of which are dedicated to one of approximately a dozen different investment objectives (e.g., growth, specialty, money market, and so on).

**insurer**    The insurance company that offers or packages the annuity. The term is also applicable when describing different forms of life insurance.

**investment company**    A corporation, trust, or partnership that invests the contract owners' money in securities appropriate to the subaccount's objective. Among the benefits of investment companies, compared to direct investments, are professional management and diversification. Mutual funds (also known as open-end investment companies) are the most popular type of investment company.

**investment objective**    The goal that the investor and subaccount pursue together: long-term capital growth, current income, and so on.

**large cap stocks**    Equities issued by companies that have a net worth of at least several billion dollars.

**management fee**    The amount paid by a mutual subaccount to the investment advisor for its services. The average annual fee, industrywide, is about one-half of 1% (0.50%) of subaccount assets.

**portfolio**    A collection of securities owned by an individual or an institution (such as a variable annuity subaccount). A subaccount's portfolio may include a combination of stocks, bonds, and money market securities.

**prospectus**    The official booklet, describing a variable annuity, that must be furnished to all investors. It contains information required by the U.S. Securities and Exchange Commission on such subjects as the subaccounts' investment objectives, services, and fees.

**sales charge**    An amount charged to purchase units of a variable annuity. Over 95% of all variable annuities have no sales charge and impose no up-front commission.

**small cap stocks**    Equities (stocks) issued by corporations in amounts that the marketplace considers small. Some financial writers consider a company that has a capitalization of $500 million or less to be small cap, other writers have a cut-off point of $1 billion or less.

**standard deviation**    A means of measuring how volatile an investment is, compared with its norm. A high standard deviation indicates a large swing in price or movement; a low standard deviation means that the investment's return is more predictable. When comparing one variable annuity subaccount or mutual fund against another, it is helpful to know the category's average in order to better determine whether the particular portfolio being studied is more or less volatile than its peer group. For example, XYZ Government Bond Portfolio has a standard deviation of 2.2%. The category average for government bond subaccounts is 2.0%, indicating that XYZ is approximately 10% more volatile, in good and bad markets, than the typical government bond subaccount.

**subaccount**    Where part or all of a variable annuity investor's money goes; how the money is invested depends on the number of subaccounts offered by the insurance company (e.g., world bonds, utilities, growth, and so on) and how the investor decides to divide up his or her money (e.g., 25% in growth and income, 30% in international stocks, 40% in government bonds, and 5% in a balanced portfolio).

**top down**    A type of security analysis. Management that follows the top-down approach is very concerned with the general level of the economy and any fiscal policy being followed by the government.

**variable**    An indication that the investor (contract owner) can choose from one or more subaccounts that have similar or different investment objectives (e.g., growth, growth and income, international stocks, corporate bonds, and so on). The word *variable* is used to describe the type of annuity (either fixed-rate or variable) or insurance policy (e.g., traditional whole life versus variable life insurance).

**withdrawal plan**    A program in which shareholders receive payments from their subaccount(s) at regular intervals. The frequency of payments is determined by the investor and may be monthly, quarterly, semiannually, or annually. There are two methods to choose from: (1) a systematic withdrawal plan or (2) annuitization.

**1035 exchange**    A reference to the Internal Revenue Code (IRC) section that allows contract owners to switch their existing annuity, fixed or variable, for another contract offered by another company, without triggering a taxable event. The key to a 1035 exchange (also known as a tax-free exchange) is to make sure that the money or account is not touched by the investor (contract owner).

## Pertinent Federal Legislation

**Investment Advisors Act of 1940**    A body of law that regulates certain activities of the investment advisors to variable annuities.

**Investment Company Act of 1940**    A highly detailed regulatory statute applying to the subaccount itself. Contains numerous provisions designed to prevent self-dealing and other conflicts of interest, to provide for the safekeeping of subaccount assets, and to prohibit the payment of excessive fees and charges by the subaccount and its contract owners.

**Securities Act of 1933**    A law requiring the subaccount's units to be registered with the SEC prior to their sale; in essence, this Act ensures that the subaccount provides potential investors with a current prospectus. The types of advertisements that may be used by a variable annuity are limited under this law.

**Securities Exchange Act of 1934**    The law that regulates the purchase and sale of all types of securities, including variable annuity subaccount units.

# ABOUT THE AUTHOR

**Gordon K. Williamson, JD, MBA, MS, CFP, CLU, ChFC, RP** is one of the most highly trained investment counselors in the United States. Williamson, a former tax attorney, is a Certified Financial Planner and branch manager of a national brokerage firm. He has been admitted to The Registry of Financial Planning Practitioners, the highest honor one can attain as a financial planner. He holds the two highest designations in the life insurance industry, Chartered Life Underwriter and Chartered Financial Consultant. He is also a real estate broker with an MBA in real estate.

Gordon is the founder and Executive Director of the Institute of Certified Fund Specialists, a professional educational program that leads to the designation "CFS" (800/848-2029).

Mr. Williamson is the author of 20 books, including: *The 100 Best Mutual Funds You Can Buy* (1995 edition), *All About Annuities, The 401(k) Book, How You Can Survive and Prosper in the Clinton Years, Sooner Than You Think,* and *Low Risk Investing.* He has been the financial editor of various magazines and newspapers and a stock market consultant for a television station.

Gordon K. Williamson is an investment advisory firm located in La Jolla, California. The firm specializes in financial planning for individuals and institutions ($100,000 minimum account size). Additional information can be obtained by phoning (800) 748-5552 or (619) 454-3938.